The Ecology of Language

The Ecology of Language

Essays by Einar Haugen

Selected and Introduced
by Anwar S. Dil

Stanford University Press, Stanford, California   1972

Language Science and National Development

A Series Sponsored by the
Linguistic Research Group of Pakistan

General Editor: Anwar S. Dil

Stanford University Press
Stanford, California
© 1972 by Einar Haugen
Printed in the United States of America
ISBN 0-8047-0802-9
LC 73-183888

Contents

Acknowledgments

The Linguistic Research Group of Pakistan and the Editor of the Language Science and National Development Series are deeply grateful to Professor Einar Haugen, Associate Member of the Group, for giving us the privilege of presenting his selected writings as the fourth volume in our series established in 1970 to commemorate the International Education Year.

We are indebted to the editors and publishers of the following publications. The ready permission on the part of the holders of the copyrights, acknowledged in each case, is a proof of the existing international cooperation and goodwill that gives hope for better collaboration among scholars of all nations for international exchange of knowledge.

Language and Immigration. Norwegian-American Studies and Records, Vol. 10, 1938.1-43, with permission of the Norwegian-American Historical Association.

Problems of Linguistic Research Among Scandinavian Immigrants in America. American Council of Learned Societies Bulletin 34, March 1942, 35-57, with permission of the Council.

Problems of Bilingualism. Lingua 2.271-90 (1950), with permission of the Editor.

The Analysis of Linguistic Borrowing. Language 26.210-31 (1950), with permission of the Linguistic Society of America.

The Confusion of Tongues. The Norwegian Language in America: A Study in Bilingual Behavior, Vols. I and II, by Einar Haugen (Philadelphia: University of Pennsylvania Press, 1953), Chapter 4, pp. 53-73 and 298-300.

Language Planning in Modern Norway. Scandinavian Studies 33. 68-81 (1961), with permission of the Society for the Advancement of Scandinavian Study.

Schizoglossia and the Linguistic Norm. Georgetown University Monograph Series on Languages and Linguistics: Monograph No. 15, Report of the Thirteenth Annual Round Table Meeting (Washington, D. C. : Georgetown University Press, 1962), pp. 63-73, with permission of the publisher.

Construction and Reconstruction in Language Planning: Ivar Aafen's grammar. Word 21. 188-207 (1965).

Linguistics and Language Planning. Sociolinguistics, ed. by William Bright (The Hague: Mouton & Company, 1966), pp. 50-71, with permission of the publisher.

Semicommunication: The Language Gap in Scandinavia. Sociological Inquiry 36. 280-97 (1966), with permission of the Editor.

Dialect, Language, Nation. American Anthropologist 68, No. 6. 922-35 (1966), with permission of the American Anthropological Association.

National and International Languages. Voice of America Forum Series, 10 (1966).

The Scandinavian Languages as Cultural Artifacts. Language Problems of Developing Nations, ed. by J. A. Fishman, C. A. Ferguson, J. Das Gupta (New York: John Wiley & Sons, 1968), pp. 267-84, with permission of the publisher.

Language Planning, Theory, and Practice. Actes du Xe Congrès International des Linguistes, Bucarest, 1967, ed. by

A. Graur (Bucharest: Éditions de L'Académie de la Republique
Socialiste de Roumanie, 1969), pp. 701-11.

Linguistics and Dialinguistics. Georgetown University
Monograph Series on Languages and Linguistics: Monograph No. 23,
Report of the Twenty-First Annual Round Table Meeting (Washington,
D. C. : Georgetown University Press, 1970), pp. 1-12, with permis-
sion of the publisher.

The Ecology of Language. The Linguistic Reporter, Supplement 25, Winter 1971, pp. 19-26, with permission of the Center for
Applied Linguistics, Washington, D. C.

The Editor completed work on this volume during 1970-72
while he was in residence as Visiting Scholar in Linguistics at Stanford University. The financial assistance from Harvard University
for a grant from the Clark-Harvard Graduate Society funds to cover
typing expenses of the manuscript is gratefully acknowledged.

The Editor wishes to record his thanks to Wallace E.
Lambert of McGill University, Joshua A. Fishman of Yeshiva Uni-
versity, Susan Ervin-Tripp of the University of California, Heinz
Kloss of the Forschungsstelle für Nationalitaten und Sprachenfragen,
Marburg, Germany, and other language scholars who have sent us
materials for our forthcoming volumes.

I am personally grateful to Fernando Valderrama and
William J. Platts of the Department of Education, Unesco, Paris,
for their encouragement while I was a Consultant in Language Science
to Unesco during the summer of 1971. I am also indebted for several
valuable suggestions regarding the Language Science and National
Development Series to Ayọ Bamgboṣe of the University of Ibadan,
Nigeria, Maria Borodulina of the Institute of Foreign Languages,
Moscow, Miklós Hutterer of the University of Budapest, Hungary,
Dennis Craig of the University of West Indies, Jamaica, and other
colleagues in the Unesco meetings of advisory experts in linguistics,
sociolinguistics, and anthropology in educational development held
during that period at the Unesco headquarters. Thanks are due to
Evelyn S. Firchow, Kaaren Grimstad, Nils Hasselmo, and Wayne

O'Neil for their help in the compilation of the bibliography of Professor Haugen's published works. Acknowledgments are also due to Elizabeth Spurr and Dorothy Riedel of Stanford University Press for assistance in many ways. The typing of the camera-ready manuscript was done by my daughter, Shaheen Dil, a student at the School of Advanced International Studies, Johns Hopkins University, Washington, D. C. She certainly deserves a word of appreciation.

This book is affectionately dedicated to EVA L. HAUGEN on the happy occasion of her husband's 65th birthday and their 40th wedding anniversary.

EDITOR'S NOTE

These essays have been reprinted from the originals with only minor changes made in the interest of uniformity of style and appearance. A few changes in wording have been made in consultation with the author. In some cases notes and bibliographical entries have been corrected and updated. Footnotes marked by asterisks have been added by the Editor. Chapters have been arranged chronologically (publication of chapter 16 was delayed).

Introduction

Einar Haugen was born in 1906 in Sioux City, Iowa, to which his parents had migrated from Norway seven years earlier. After graduating from St. Olaf College in Northfield, Minnesota, in 1928, he did graduate work in English and Scandinavian at the University of Illinois, Urbana, receiving a Ph.D. degree in 1931. The same year he accepted an appointment as assistant professor at the University of Wisconsin, where he was subsequently named Torger Thompson Professor of Scandinavian in 1938 and Vilas Research Professor in Scandinavian and Linguistics in 1962. In 1964, after thirty-three years as chairman of Scandinavian Studies at Wisconsin, during which time the program developed from an idea to a full-fledged department offering a variety of language, literature, and area courses leading to the doctoral degree, Haugen joined Harvard University as Victor S. Thomas Professor of Scandinavian and Linguistics.

Haugen has served as director of the Linguistic Institutes at the University of Wisconsin, and has taught courses in bilingualism at the Linguistic Institutes at the University of Michigan (1948), Georgetown University (1954), and Indiana University (1964). He was President of the Linguistic Society of America in 1950 and President of the Ninth International Congress of Linguists held at Cambridge, Massachusetts, in 1962. In 1966, he was elected President of the Permanent International Committee of Linguists (CIPL). One of the most international-minded of American linguists, he has concerned himself with establishing points of continuing interaction among scholars in other countries. He has been a visiting professor at Oslo University (1938) and the University of Iceland (1955-56), and has served as consultant to the English language Educational Council of Japan for their teacher-training programs. He is a member of

the American Academy of Arts and Sciences, the Norwegian, Icelandic, Swedish, and Danish academies of science, and the Linguistic Research Group of Pakistan. He has been decorated by the kings
of Norway and Sweden, and awarded honorary degrees by the University of Michigan (1953), St. Olaf College (1958), the University of
Oslo (1961), and the University of Iceland (1971).

Haugen's bilingual boyhood as the child of recent immigrants
gave him an early sensitivity to language problems. He likes to say
that people often choose their careers in order to explore and solve
a personal problem. In his case it was a language problem that
turned his interests to linguistics and especially to the social aspects
of linguistics. He learned English from his playmates, but spoke
Norwegian at home: two varieties of Norwegian, as it happened,
since his mother, a schoolteacher, spoke the standard dialect and
his father the rural dialect of his native community. At the age of
eight, Haugen went to Norway with his parents for a stay of over two
years, and there he learned to use his father's dialect in its old-
country setting. Compared to the Norwegian standard, this was a
conservative and highly divergent dialect, almost a different language.
Here he also had his first experiences with the national controversy
over the two standards of Norwegian, the Riksmål and Landsmål
varieties. On his return to the United States, he had to relearn
English to the tune of his classmates' ridicule. These experiences,
combined with his parents' enthusiasm for Norwegian language and
culture, pointed the way to his lifelong commitment to the study and
promotion of Scandinavian languages.

An important part of Haugen's work in the field of Scandinavian has been his textbook writing. He has published three well-
known textbooks, Beginning Norwegian (1937), Reading Norwegian
(1939), and Spoken Norwegian (1945), the last written on the invitation of the U.S. Armed Forces Institute during World War II, and
revised in collaboration with K. G. Chapman (1964) with a complete
set of tapes and recordings. His Norwegian-English Dictionary was
published jointly in 1965 by the University of Wisconsin Press and
Oslo University Press. In the early thirties he directed a project
that resulted in the largest word count of any Scandinavian language,
published as Norwegian Word Studies (1942). He has also been active
as editor and translator of Scandinavian classics, among them

Voyages to Vinland (1941), a collection of Icelandic sagas dealing
with the Norse discovery of America in the tenth century; The First
Grammatical Treatise (1951), a twelfth-century Icelandic work;
three Icelandic plays under the title Fire and Ice (1967); and Halvdan
Koht's Life of Ibsen (1971).

He has always regarded Otto Jespersen as his first linguistic mentor, whom he met through his books. At the University of
Wisconsin Haugen entered a stimulating linguistic milieu, where he
learned of the Prague School, Bloomfield and Sapir, and joined the
still recent Linguistic Society of America. He interested himself in
the general linguistic problems that concerned his generation, and
contributed to their solution through articles and reviews in Language,
including especially his presidential address to the Linguistic Society
of America in 1950. It was and is characteristic of him that he is
suspicious of excessive abstraction and formalism in linguistics, and
prefers to see language in its relation to people and society rather
than as an autonomous structure.

The book that first brought Haugen international renown as
a scholar was The Norwegian Language in America: A Study in Bilingual Behavior (1953), which has been widely hailed as the best
work so far on the linguistic problems of immigrants. A monumental study based on twenty years of fieldwork among Norwegian immigrants in the Midwest, it is remarkable for its application of linguistic insights to language behavior in a broad sociocultural setting.
Along with Uriel Weinreich's Languages in Contact, which was published in the same year, Haugen's book marked the beginning of a
new era of sociolinguistic research. Weinreich himself acknowledged
his debt to Haugen's earlier writings and called the book "a goldmine
of well analyzed examples of interlingual influence" and a model for
the future study of language contact. Haugen's ability to express his
technical research findings in simple and pleasant style makes his
book within easy reach of social scientists as well as general readers.

In 1956, Haugen published Bilingualism in the Americas:
A Bibliography and Research Guide, a general survey and classification of bilingualism that he rightly hoped would stimulate further
research in the field. (He has recently completed a supplementary

review of the literature since 1956, which will appear as a chapter
in Thomas A. Sebeok's Current Trends in Linguistics, Volume X.)
Next came his well-known Language Conflict and Language Planning:
The Case of Modern Norwegian (1966), the first comprehensive case
study of a subject that is becoming increasingly important, especially
in nation-states seeking national identity through a language of their
own. Though Haugen's work shows that language planning is only to
a small degree a technical linguistic problem, which partly explains
why linguists have tended to keep aloof from such work, he shows at
the same time that objective accounts of language planning experiments can be of great help to linguists in their effort to understand
the history and function of language in society.

Perhaps the most impressive element in Haugen's work as
a linguist is his concern with what he calls the ecology of language,
which he defines as "the study of interactions between any given
language and its environment." Since his student days, when he
became interested in investigating the problems of bilingualism and
language planning with particular interest in the social groups he
knew best, he has been attracted by language problems of the type
brushed aside by some linguists. For Haugen general linguistics
and sociolinguistics complement each other to mutual benefit as is
shown, for example, by the priority questions he poses for the ecological study of a language: its classification in relation to other
languages, its present status in the typology of ecological classification and where it is going in comparison with other languages of the
world, its users in relation to their locale, social class, religion,
and other relevant sociocultural groupings. In his effort to show
that such linguistic research is possible through an integrated approach, Haugen is currently working on his book on the history and
structure of the Scandinavian languages. To the extent that he has
pioneered some bold and interesting directions in contemporary
sociolinguistic thought, his work deserves the attention of social
scientists internationally. It is our hope that the essays selected for
this volume will serve as a stimulating introduction to an increasingly
important area.

Anwar S. Dil

Committee on Linguistics,
Stanford University
January 1972

The Ecology of Language

1 | Language and Immigration

America's profusion of tongues has made her a modern Babel, but a Babel in reverse. City and countryside have teemed with all the accents of Europe and the rest of the world, yet America has never swerved from the Anglo-Saxon course set by her founding fathers. In the course of a century and a half the United States has absorbed her millions and taught them her language more perfectly than Rome taught the Gauls and the Iberians in centuries of dominion. Oriental and African, Spaniard and Frenchman, Jew and Gentile have all been domesticated, and this without leaving any serious impression on American English.[1]

Except for a brief hysteria during the war years of 1917-18 all this has been done without political compulsion, through the social pressure of a culturally and economically dominant language. It has gone on in the face of a tenacious conservatism of language among the immigrants, a strong reluctance to give up speech habits ingrained from childhood. The immigrant could not be expected to reshape his speech overnight, for habits of speech are rooted more deeply in man's emotional and intellectual life than is generally realized. One's language cannot be tossed aside like last year's bonnet. From his first day in the new land a tug of war between his old and his new self was going on in the immigrant, and nowhere was the struggle more vividly reflected than in his successive linguistic adaptations. It is by slow, incessant attrition that each foreigner has been turned into an American, idea by idea, and word by word. Every language spoken by the American immigrant bears the marks of this conflict and only by recording and analyzing this evidence can we fully understand the processes of immigration. Only through this highly sensitive index can we reach some of the subtlest and most significant aspects of the immigrant's psychological and cultural development. The immigrant straddles two cultures, and if he is homeless in both, it is due in no small measure to his linguistic difficulties.

This approach to the immigrant is one that has received little attention from historians of immigration. The fact is not surprising when we see that even linguists have often regarded the dialects of the immigrant as beneath their dignity. Nevertheless, some studies have been made, and anyone interested in finding them can turn to the appendix of H. L. Mencken's American Language,[2] where the material has been ably surveyed. Mr. Mencken's material reveals that there is a striking parallel between the changes that foreign languages have undergone in America. Each language has parted from the strict purity of its native form, and has taken over elements from American English. Each language has been forced to adapt itself to new conditions, and thereby gives us a vivid picture of the immigrant's struggle for a position within the new nation and his gradual accommodation to its demands.

The usual attitude to this phenomenon, among both lay and learned, has been one of scorn or amusement. The educated foreigner has regarded the lingo of his American compatriots as debased and vulgar, and has struggled against the "demoralizing" influence of his American environment as best he could. He has felt much as did the Norwegian pastor who wrote home from the early settlements in Wisconsin, "Our Norwegian language is so mixed with American words that I was quite disgusted at what I heard when I first came here."[3] If the emigrant later returns to his native land, he is ridiculed because he is no longer a complete master of the old idiom. Among the Norwegians, as among other groups, the cry against language mixture has sounded from the start, with only the faintest of results. The forces that made the immigrant "mix" were too deep-seated to be brushed aside lightly.

In spite of the interesting materials that have been gathered, no immigrant group has had anything like a full or adequate treatment of its linguistic experiences. No general perspective has been reached, and few general conclusions drawn. The collection of linguistic phenomena demands special techniques, and their classification is a slow, difficult task. Without pretending to exhaust the subject, the writer wishes to present some tentative conclusions that grow out of observations he has made on the speech of Norwegians in a variety of American settlements. He has spoken American Norwegian from childhood, and he has long observed and made notes on the speech of Norwegian immigrants. During 1936 and 1937 he collected material in the Norwegian settlements of Dane County, Wisconsin, and from occasional informants born in other settlements, but now living in Madison.[4] It is his hope that students of immigration may find here some intimations of what can be derived from continued researches into the problems touched upon.

That such researches are timely will be clear to all who consider the rapidly diminishing number of foreign speakers in our country. The living sources are drying up, and must be tapped before it is too late. Some little material is available in print; in books, newspapers, and magazines may be found many indirect contributions to the study of the Norwegian language in America. A host of more or less talented authors have depicted life among their countrymen with great vigor, and many of these have included specimens of spoken Norwegian dialects. Writers like Waldemar Ager, Simon Johnson, and O.E. Rölvaag have shown their sensitiveness to language by allowing their characters to speak the Norwegian-American idiom. In print are also a few studies by men with linguistic training, from the pioneer article by Peter Groth in 1897, through a study by Professor Nils Flaten in 1900, to the several contributions by Professor George T. Flom between 1902 and 1931.

But anyone who wants to gain fresh and firsthand material on the spoken language must part from the seclusion of the library. His material is stored in the minds of thousands of immigrants and their descendants who are still capable of forming the linguistic signals taught them by their Norwegian ancestors. But the investigator cannot speak to everyone, and he cannot ask about everything. He must prepare a list of words which will bring out the chief features of the Norwegian dialect of the speaker, so that it may be possible to determine the extent of its change in America, and its relationship to other dialects. He must include words which will give the most valuable information concerning the English influence on the dialect, the words borrowed, the forms they are given, and the meanings they acquire. He must include questions which will bring out the background and linguistic experience of the speaker and the social and historical development of the community. All this must be compressed into a questionnaire which is not so long that it exhausts the patience of the informant or the energy of the questioner. Each answer must be taken down exactly as it is spoken, in as accurate a phonetic spelling as the investigator can muster.

This has been the writer's procedure in gathering the material for future study in this field. During two summers he has sought persons in the most easily available settlements of Wisconsin who could and would answer his questions. He has had many pleasant and interesting experiences in this work. He has uncovered delightful storytellers, historical-minded preservers of tradition, patient men and women with an intense interest in his work. They have sometimes wondered just what his purpose was, but they have always been willing to cooperate. From their thoughtful comments he has gained many an insight into the problems of the immigrant. If any of them read this article, they will perhaps understand what "the professor" was looking for, and they will recognize bits of material drawn now from one and now from another of their accounts.

Lest the value of this material be too dependent on the writer's accuracy of ear and hand, he has also supplemented the written record of his informants' speech with phonograph records. In this way it may be possible for the voices of Norwegian dialect speakers to sound for the benefit of science long after the living tradition of Norwegian speech has vanished in the United States. The writer trusts that the present analysis may be only a first step toward full utilization of the materials thus gathered for the conclusions they will yield in the study of immigration as well as of language and society in general.

II

When emigration from Norway to the United States began a little over a century ago, Norway was overwhelmingly a rural nation.[5] Almost nine-tenths of her 1,200,000 population lived in the country districts, and from this part of the nation came the early emigrants. They came at a time of general agricultural unrest, and they were lured by reports of greater opportunities across the sea.[6] The movement was popular and unorganized, and was met by a general distrust

among the cultured classes, who regarded it as a species of insanity
and usually sought to discourage it. This was a period of social stress
and strain; for the first time the rural population of Norway was beginning to demand a voice in the cultural and political life of the country. Later, as emigration swelled to a peak in the early eighties,
other classes of society were affected. The growing current brought
with it artisans and professional men, and the goal of Norwegian emigration was no longer so exclusively the farm. But these developments
were secondary, and we shall here keep our attention focused on the
main stream. The social and institutional life of the Norwegian emigrant, and accordingly his linguistic development, bear overwhelmingly
the stamp of his rural origin.

Since Norway had achieved an independent form of government
in 1814, her destinies had been guided by a relatively small but able
class, her well-trained bureaucracy. One of the criteria of membership in this class was the ability to speak its language. In its written
form this language was practically identical with Danish, a form it had
acquired during the four-century-long union with Denmark (1397-1814).
In speech, however, it had retained far more of the characteristics
that had long distinguished Norwegian from Danish; its precise form
varied from city to city, with more or less intermixture of Norwegian
elements drawn from neighboring country dialects. But in every case
this language had the status of an upper-class dialect, carefully guard-
ed in its purity within the social group whose medium it was. This
spoken language, which was different from, but tended to seek its
norm in the written Dano-Norwegian, was practically a foreign language to the country folk. It varied in a multitude of ways from the
dialects which served them in their daily lives. It was the language
of schoolmasters, of ministers, and of government officials.

From city to countryside there was a gradual shading off of
dialects, with the lower classes in the cities speaking a language that
approximated more nearly that of the surrounding countryside.
Wherever the influence of city culture had penetrated, there was a
tendency to regard language as an index of social station, and to ridicule the use of forms that smacked of the country. But outside of this
sphere a man's dialect testified to his place of birth rather than to his
social position. The poorest cotter in the farming community shared
his dialect with the rich squire, though the squire would not for a

moment have considered him a fit suitor for his daughter's hand.
Marked differences of dialect existed, however, between the various
communities. As everywhere else in Europe, the common man had
lived on his land through immemorial generations. He had rarely had
much opportunity for travel, and it is not strange that his speech should
take a different course from that of other districts. Within the community group, where contact was frequent, a local dialect grew up,
which became characteristic of people from that district. Neighboring
dialects remained more similar in form than those which were farther
removed, for the more people talked to each other, the more alike
were their dialects. As the country people were largely isolated from
the cultural currents that affected the city people, their language was
also less saturated by Danish and other foreign elements.

The result of this development was a series of markedly different dialects in the various sections of Norway. Although speakers
of any Norwegian dialect can understand speakers of all others—with
a little good will—the differences are quite considerable. They extend
to every aspect of language—intonation, pronunciation, grammar,
phraseology, and word order. A single word like "swallow" varies
from svala and svola in western Norway to svolu and svolo in the Midland valleys, while it becomes almost unrecognizable in the north as
sulu and even solo, with l's that sound like American r. The word for
"pillow" is kodde in one part of the country, and dyna in another, both
of which baffle users of the more general puta. It is clear also that
the varying natural resources and occupations in a country so diverse
would be reflected in vocabulary differences. The technical terms of
lumbering were not current among the farmers, and the fisherman
needed a vocabulary different from that of the hunter. The ever-
changing scenery of the country, from smiling farmlands to desolate
mountain plateaus, also made for a marked variety of expression.

We must not imagine that the relatively secluded culture of
the Norwegian country emigrant meant a poverty of words in his dialects. The number of words at his command was probably not less
than that of the average American citizen in our modern civilization.[7]
The difference consisted in the nature and distribution of the vocabulary, in the cultural items which the speaker was required to manipu-
late. Vocabulary is everywhere responsive to human needs; it accom-
panies man from birth to death, and the more important and interesting

an activity is, the more words he is likely to find for it. In vocabulary man crystallizes the essential elements of his life—his joys and
sorrows, his fears and aspirations, his pleasures and drudgeries.

The application of this to the emigrant becomes clear if we
consider the nature of his culture. With all its variation from seashore
to plateau, it had this in common: it was based on a self-contained and
hand-labor economy. Each freeholder lived with his family on a small
estate that frequently had been in the possession of his ancestors for
centuries. Each member of the household had his duties, at which long
practice had made him adept. Thus the women were past masters in
spinning and weaving, in caring for the cattle and preparation of food;
the men expressed their talents in tilling the soil, in fishing and hunting.
For each of these processes a great variety of words were useful. The
average American may have a large vocabulary for describing the parts
of his automobile, but he is unusual if he can name many parts of a
loom. Nor was a Norwegian of that day at a loss in describing his own
feelings in expressive and picturesque terms that would win a ready
response among his listeners. To some extent he even had a literary
vocabulary, cultivated over centuries in the ballads and folk tales which
constituted his heritage from the past.

In school and church, however, the country folk met a vocabulary that was not derived from the experiences of their daily lives. In
the persons of schoolmaster and pastor they made their chief contact
with the official written language. As the schools were chiefly conducted for the inculcation of Christian doctrine, church and school
were intimately allied. The chief textbooks were Bible stories, the
Catechism, the "Explanation" of the Catechism, and the hymnbook.
All of these were in Danish spelling and composed in a style strongly
influenced by German. Teaching was conducted chiefly by rote, with
advancement measured by the extent to which the pupil could memor-
ize the parts of doctrine. Although the school system was poor by
modern standards, it had succeeded, by the middle of the century, in
teaching most Norwegians to read; but many had not yet learned to
write. And few had discovered the possibilities of reading matter that
lay beyond religious literature; their libraries consisted chiefly of
books of religious instruction and supplementary books of sermons and
devotion. Even this was a long step forward from the eighteenth century; the powerful lay pietistic movement of Hans Nilsen Hauge had

spread the desire to read, so that his followers had been nicknamed
"readers."

The step from dialect to written language was a long one, and
one that was not successfully negotiated by most country people. Even
if they did learn to read the Dano-Norwegian, and came to regard it
as the sacred language of religion and learning, it did not easily become their language. Their pronunciation of it was modeled on the
spelling, and therefore sounded stiff and unwieldy to those whose natural language it was. They had been taught by their betters that their
dialects were vulgar and inferior, yet in their daily lives these served
them best. The same situation prevailed in many other European
countries during these years, for everywhere the nineteenth century
was one of spreading popular education. Country populations were
being brought under the influence of official written languages which
previously had been spoken chiefly in the cities or at court. A Norwegian child from Telemark or Sogn was under no worse handicap
than a Danish child in Jutland, a Scottish child learning English, or
even a child in Hamburg trying to master High German. Everywhere
it was held to be essential that the children be pressed into the jacket
of the official language.

Other ideals have since prevailed in Norway, and the dialects
have had their day. But little of this has been reflected among the
emigrants, who have not moved far from the situation of 1850. Those
who can still speak Norwegian speak a more or less modified country
dialect; those who can write it write the official Dano-Norwegian of
the nineteenth century. There is a spoken language and an institutional
language, and this linguistic dualism is one of the outstanding facts
about the Norwegians in America.

III

When the earliest Norwegian settlers came to Illinois and
Wisconsin between 1836 and 1840, there were no railroads or market
outlets within easy reach. The first settlements in northern Illinois
and in southern Wisconsin were founded at a time when the prairie was
still wild, and chiefly inhabited by the timber wolf, the rattlesnake,
and the Indian. These settlements were the foci of the entire immigration from Norway in the forties and fifties, and for this reason

their dialect was not homogeneous, but included a whole group of districts from which emigration began almost simultaneously: in western Norway the districts of Sogn, Voss, Hardanger, and Rogaland, and in the Midlands the mountain valleys of Telemark and Numedal. These districts are all grouped around the southern half of the great mountain range which divides Norway into east and west, and they reflect the relatively limited economic opportunities offered by beautiful but unprofitable mountain slopes. They also represented some of the most antique and characteristically Norwegian dialects in the country. Though they were far from identical, they had a great deal in common, especially when compared with the lowland East Norwegian, or with the more northerly dialects.

Within these early communities the immigrant was under no serious linguistic or social handicap. He could associate almost exclusively with his own countrymen, exchange advice and repartee with friends and relatives, and he could arrange his work along familiar lines. Before long a social structure was growing up, with groupings of friends and enemies, with drinking groups and praying groups, with a superstructure of school and church showing its first beginnings. In this way the emigrant reduced the shock of his new existence, and was enabled to continue his speech habits from Norway, and make them useful in the new land. Eventually he established newspapers, church synods, and other institutions which knit him more closely to his fellow countrymen in other settlements.

If this growth had continued undisturbed, there would have arisen a New Norway just as there had once arisen a New England. But from the very beginning the influence of American culture insinuated itself upon the Norwegian. Even the most solidly Norwegian community had its neighbors, and was to some degree affected by the attitudes and opinions of those neighbors. Much of the land acquired by the Norwegians in Wisconsin was bought from American speculators, or had been occupied by English or Yankee farmers. There were few merchants among the Norwegians and trade was generally carried on by American storekeepers. Within a few years railroads were extended, markets became available, and a complete change in the farm economy was effected. Each farmer's dependence on the outside world was increased, and accordingly his need for communicating with members of that world. The American public school, which

at first was poorly organized, grew more efficient as attendance was
made compulsory and the length of the school year and the number of
grades extended. In the early years American teachers had to make
rules demanding that the children speak English in school and on the
school grounds. Many people now of middle age can recall when these
rules were openly flouted by the children, who would rather speak
Norwegian. American newspapers and magazines, mail-order cata-
logues, and a flood of other reading matter gradually entered homes
which previously had been devoted to papers and magazines in the
Norwegian language. Norwegians and their children went to work for
Americans, and mixed marriages furthered the process.

These influences, which all tended in the direction of eventually supplanting the Norwegian with the English language, were at
work from the day of immigration. They were universal and pervasive, easy enough to point out in general, often very difficult to spe-
cify for each individual case. In the aggregate they amounted to a
psychic compulsion on the individual, more or less great according
to the amount of his contact with English speech. This psychic compulsion operated on the speech of the individual and of the community
even while Norwegian was still being spoken. From the day of immigration a subtle shift began taking place, with or without consciousness on the part of the individual. Words which he had no occasion to
use were gradually forgotton, only to make way for some of the many
new words and expressions that assailed him from the new language.
The immigrant's vocabulary was thus being constantly atrophied at
one end and renewed at the other.

Such a shift was an inevitable accompaniment of his changing
personality. In learning the new language he was doing more than just
acquiring new phrases. He was absorbing a new social and linguistic
outlook, and this outlook also influenced his native tongue. The bilingual second generation, especially, could not afford to maintain a
Norwegian personality distinct from their American one. It was too
great a strain to keep in mind two complete sets of designations for
everything. And as time went on, the American system naturally
dominated the thinking of the immigrant. In all his linguistic floundering we perceive his struggle to achieve again a unified cultural
personality. His Norwegian approaches his English, because both
are required to function within the same environment and the same

minds. Norwegian becomes a Norwegian-American language, thoroughly characteristic of an intermediate period in the group life of the immigrant. It serves its purpose and passes on. And when that point is reached, the immigrant is no longer an immigrant, and his history becomes that of the general population.

It is possible to trace this parallel development of language and social circumstance in practically every phase of life, and the writer plans to do so in more detailed studies. For instance, the terms of family relationship were more complicated in Norway than in America and reflected the greater significance of the family clan. There were distinct terms, such as farfar and morfar, farbror and morbror, to distinguish maternal and paternal kinsmen. Among the immigrants these usually gave way to the neutral terms bestefar (grandfather) and onkel (uncle), which were standard Norwegian, but not usual in most country districts.[8] In the early days children were named with great reverence for family tradition; grandparents got their proper dues by seeing their names repeated in the second generation. But when the second generation grew up, they gave their children American names with only the initial letters recalling the grandparents' names (as Hazel for Halvor, Tilla for Tore, or Alvin for Anund). In the following generation even this reminiscence of Norwegian custom vanished. In early years the cows had their proper names, rich and melodious descriptions such as Lauvlin, Snøgås, Dagros, Flekkrei, Storigo, Gullsi; but time passed, and names were forgotten as the herds grew larger and the urge to distinguish each cow as a personality was lost.

A common custom in the early years was the popular practice known in New England as "bundling," in Norway as nattefrieri; in many Norwegian communities these nocturnal visits were the only respectable means of "dating." Kristofer Janson mentioned this practice in his Amerikanske forholde[9] as one which gave the Norwegians a bad reputation among the Americans. One of the contributory reasons for its disappearance was no doubt the moral indignation of American neighbors, another form of psychic pressure on the immigrant.[10] Weddings were at first celebrated in Norwegian fashion, as great festive occasions, with drinking and dancing to help seal the marriage. As one informant declared, "It wasn't then as it is now, when they run off and get married without anyone's knowing it, maybe not even they themselves" (Dei springe sta å gifte se' so ingen veit det, kanskje ikkje eigong dei sjøle). Even funerals were not the mere solemn formalities they are today; invitations were issued, there was food and drink after the burial, and a general loosening of spirit before the evening was over.

These are elements of American life which rarely get any consideration in American history. The presence of the "foreigner" is recognized, and to some extent his influence on the body politic. But rarely do we get a study in which his problems are seen from the inside, and in which his efforts to create a group life of his own are regarded with sympathy. Language is one of his most serious problems. In his approach to language, in his employment of this great instrument for the establishment of human contact, we can see the profile of his social progress to the time when his national group gradually diffuses into American society. Many heartaches and bewilderments have assailed the immigrant, and no one can wonder that he has often resisted the melting pot. The social life of his native group has given him a home and a standing in the new nation, and has been a solid protection to his mental health.[10a]

IV

Each immigrant brought with him to America more or less of the roots from which his language had grown. Some emigrated alone, while others brought with them a family. Still others shared in a group emigration from the native district, with common goals and purposes. The lone immigrant sometimes settled among speakers of English or other foreigners, but more frequently he found a place among fellow-Norwegians, preferably of his own dialect. All of these possibilities offer points of interest for the student. But as language is a group phenomenon, it is the fate of the largest group that interests us the most: the immigrants, with or without families, who settled in a farming community largely peopled by members of their own nationality.

The communities from which they came were relatively homogeneous, with a uniform standard of speech. Their dialect was their language, which they took for granted in all relationships to

their fellows. If they heard someone speaking a dialect different
from their own, they sensed him at once as an outsider. They would
be amused or annoyed by his language, and they would find it harder
to concentrate on what he was saying. In this way the dialect became
more than an instrument of practical utility. It constituted an inner
bond between its users. It marked them as members of a group and
helped to establish their position within it. The native dialect, because of its utter familiarity and its associations from the past, was
the perfect and inconspicuous means of comprehension between the
members of a group.

In a classic poem Ivar Aasen expressed this sense of linguistic solidarity:

> Folket og eg er like som eitt.
> Alt kva dei segjer, skynar eg so greidt;
> og aldri er der ord
> på all den vide jord,
> som ganga meg so til hjarta.[11]

In more prosaic terms the linguist might say (to quote Michael West):
"The small group is the natural protection of the individual soul, and
the small language or dialect is the natural and important distinguishing feature of the small group. Anything which, while common to the
group, tends to differentiate it from other groups tends to intensify
the sense of solidarity and of distinctness. Of all instruments for
the intensification of group individuality, language is undoubtedly the
most powerful."[12]

With emigration this whole pleasant state of things was broken; the equilibrium which had permitted language to go unnoticed
was upset, and the emigrant was faced with linguistic problems on
every hand. He was thrown into contact with a babel of tongues from
the other emigrants of his own homeland, assailed on every hand by
strange locutions and sounds; worse yet, he was forced to cope with
persons of whose language he could make neither head nor tail, some
of them emigrants from other countries, and some natives of the land
to which he came. He was in the position described by the anonymous
poet of Wisconsinvisen:

Jau, i fysten da gjek litt paa skakka
daa me landa paa framande jord;
av det maalet som folket her snakka
skyna me 'kje eit einaste ord.

Læra spraaket var nokkot som leita,
ofte stod me mæ skamfulle fjæs.
Ner ein yænki deg spord' ka du heita,
raaka jamt at du svara han "yæs."[13]

He had been drawn out of a normal into an abnormal situation, and it was natural that he should try his best to re-establish a
normal situation, in which he might be a complete master of the linguistic medium. Learning a new language is at best a slow and difficult process. It was simpler and more economical of time and energy
to salvage as much as possible of the old language, by creating a community where it might still function in some degree. It has been noticed that most immigrants show a strong tendency to settle in groups
from the same districts of the homeland, whenever possible. This
has its obvious cause in the desire of friends and relatives to live
together, but it is also a linguistic phenomenon, because of the greater
ease of communication and sympathy of understanding that can exist
between speakers of the same dialect. As one of my informants declared of the early immigrants, "They always preferred to associate
with their own kind" (Dei vilde helst ha å gjera med sine eigne). In
the presence of a large group speaking one dialect, the lone speaker
of another dialect is often made to feel unpleasantly conspicuous.

Yet the circumstances of settlement clearly made such sectional isolation impracticable for the group as a whole. Though Norwegians through their bygdelag organizations have cultivated local
patriotism more ardently than any other immigrant group, even they
could not everywhere maintain the old dialect groupings. Sogning
settled next to Telemarking and Vossing became a neighbor to the
Trønder. There followed a clashing of dialect forms on a scale never
known in Norway. In these settlements ancient dialect boundaries
were shattered overnight, and neighbors made to communicate in
dialects separated by the developments of a thousand years.

In the course of such contact, the peculiarities of the respective dialects were keenly observed, and often associated with the

personalities of the speakers. Any dislike or admiration of the speakers might be transferred to conspicuous forms in their speech. This
was true especially of forms which were limited to small areas in Norway, or which were markedly different from the forms of other dialects, like the mjokk (milk) of the upper Telemarking or the ending -ao
of Sogning in words like jentao (the girl). The difference of the latter
from the jento of the Vossing is small, but it was sufficient to confirm
the judgment of one Vossing informant that Sogning was a more "vulgar" dialect than her own. Such a term is of course socially determined and has its roots not in the sounds and forms themselves, but
in the situations which have called them forth.

    As intermarriages between Norwegians of different breed be-
gan to take place, this dialectal opposition might develop even within
the family. Here constant usage would soon accord each dialect its
place, and only in rare cases would one partner give up his dialect for
that of any other. The smaller these differences, the more likely they
were to continue their independent existence. Several informants have
given me detailed information about the respective dialects of their
parents. O. B. S., born in Koshkonong in 1850, used his mother's
dialect (Morgedal), but could enumerate a great many forms used by
his father from Vinje. A. K. J., born in Perry in 1865, followed her
mother in speaking the dialect of Treongen, but remembered that her
father (from Bø) said øia instead of øugo (eyes) and vinnøi instead of
glas (window). D. A. D., born in Perry in 1857, spoke the Gjevedal
dialect of his mother, but remembered forms from his father's Sanni-
kedal dialect, which "was more like the city language" (Dei snakka
meir ette byens mål). His children, in turn, did not speak the dialect
of Gjevedal, but an East Norwegian dialect from Nannestad, the birthplace of their mother. One couple born in Springdale spoke neighboring
dialects from Valdres, each without hesitation as to his own form
where differences might occur, but frequently uncertain about the
form of the other. Another Wisconsin-born couple spoke Sogning and
Vossing respectively, without obvious mixture. These examples show
that neighboring dialects might live together harmoniously without
seriously affecting each other in the more unconscious parts of the
language.

    There is evidence, however, that when the dialects persisted
in close contact, there was present also a strong tendency toward

mutual modification of the most obvious peculiarities. This is what
happened within both the family and the mixed dialectal community,
when a Telemarking adopted oss (us) instead of okkon, far (father)
instead of fai, golv (floor) instead of tili, or a Sogning modified his
ekkja (widow) to the more common enka, and vetter (winter) to vinter.
If this did not take place within the first generation, it was likely to
do so in the second. With a sufficiently long and undisturbed development, we would have here the basis for a profound modification of the
dialects into a common lingua franca, based on a variety of Norwegian
dialects. That such a common lingo is not more in evidence among the
Norwegians is due to the relatively short period of development, but
even more to the overwhelming importance of the individual family
among the immigrants. The usual unit, both before and after emigration, was the family. The settling on individual farms continued
this tendency, so that the linguistic contacts within the family were
far more significant that the contacts with outsiders. Hence it was
possible for neighboring families to maintain their own dialect, with
only minor modifications due to other dialects. Many informants have
commented on linguistic peculiarities heard from members of neighboring families, and associated in their minds with those families.

     Among the younger generation, however, increasing contact
in school, at play, and at work frequently led to greater modification
of the original dialect. Occasional informants from the Koshkonong
settlement near Rockdale, Wisconsin, and from Coon Valley in western
Wisconsin have spoken forms of Norwegian which corresponded to no
single dialect, and which they themselves recognized as more or less
mixed. The informant from Coon Valley, born in the present century,
stated that her dialect was that of her contemporaries, and different
from that of her parents. T.S., near Mount Horeb, Wisconsin, assured me that "just about everybody around here got to talking Valdres"
(Dæ vart te dæ at mest alle runt her så snakka dei valders). O.B.S.,
from Liberty Prairie, said that Telemarking became the prevailing
speech among the children, even in families that were not from that
district. A prevailing dialect would tend to become universal, and in
mixed communities there would tend to be a leveling of conspicuous
forms. The forms adopted would not be book forms, but such popular
dialect forms as would have the greatest prestige on account of their
wide currency. There was a general aversion to persons who tried to
put on airs and talk the "book language." One informant assured me

that only when the preacher was listening would they say <u>kona</u> for "wife"
instead of the less refined <u>kjering</u>. Another declared that the use of
book forms would make people say, "What a big fellow he thinks he
is" (Kor store han é vorten pao da).

　　　All these tendencies toward leveling have of course been present in Norway also, since the improvement of communications and
the change in farming conditions in late years. As a result many elements in the old dialects have been lost, and these have not always
been the same as those lost in the speech of the emigrants. Both have
altered their make-up to meet new conditions. But one alternative
was open to the emigrant and not to his fellows in Norway: the recourse to English. Whenever the terminology of the Norwegian dialects was mutually unsatisfactory, the emigrant could draw upon the
vocabulary of English.

　　　In American English he met a language practically without
dialectal differences within the area of Norwegian settlement. More
than that, it had the prestige of a governmental, commercial, and
plurality language. Its terminology was already shaped to meet conditions in the new land, and by using it he would not lay himself open
to misunderstanding or ridicule. But he did not need to adopt the
entire language at once. Thanks to his settling among Norwegian-
speaking people he had the opportunity of adopting English piecemeal.
He could take what he needed, as he needed it, and thereby continue
his efficient functioning within the social group. If he needed to designate a blanket, for instance, he might at first refer to it as a
<u>kvitidl</u>, if he happened to come from Voss; but his neighboring Tele-
markings would not understand the word, for many of them called it
<u>tjeld</u>. After a few experiences of this kind, he might well turn to
"blanket" and provide for it a place within his own language.

　　　In the second generation this process went even further, and
in many cases led to all-English speech. A Sogning from Norway
Grove was quoted to me as having said: "When I talk with a stranger,
I don't like to talk raw Sogning" (Naor e ska snakka me ein mann so
lika eg kje te snakka rått sogning), and so he turned to English. A
woman born in Iowa informed me she could speak excellent Gudbrandsdøl. But she was married to a speaker of Sogning, a dialect very different from hers, and she declared that she and her husband spoke

little Norwegian to each other. When I asked her the reason, she
replied (in English), "Well, when my husband talks Sogning, and I
answer in Gudbrandsdøl, it don't hitch so good!" Fear of ridicule
arising either from dialect difference, or from an assumed "vulgarity"
of the Norwegian dialect, has been a significant factor in turning many
a conversation to English. The same tendency is apparent in the relationship of the three Scandinavian peoples in America; though Norwegian and Swede, or Norwegian and Dane can understand each other
without much difficulty they often find it simpler to turn to English.

V

     While the immigrant was thus rubbing off his sharp corners
through contact with fellow Norwegians, he was also being slowly
drawn into the current of American life. The psychic pressure of his
environment frequently made an American out of him without his own
complete awareness of the process. Even while he was learning English, he was unconsciously adapting his Norwegian to be more useful
in the new land. There are three separate aspects of this process:
the Norwegian words which he retained with little or no change, the
Norwegian words which he shifted in meaning, and the English words
he introduced. It has been stated by one early student of the subject
that any English word could get into the Norwegian language that could
"stand the treatment it was apt to get." This is far from true, for
there are many English words that were never adopted as long as the
language was still Norwegian; these include such familiar terms as
"light," "wall," "chair," "elbow," "head," and many others. Yet
many English words were borrowed for concepts which (it seems)
could be adequately expressed in Norwegian. But we must not make
the mistake of condemning speakers for adopting an English term,
just because it seems to us to "mean the same" as a Norwegian word.
The average person's mind is not arranged like a dictionary. The
words he knows are not lined up in alphabetical rows, ready to be fitted together like the parts of a jigsaw puzzle. The speaker uses words
as they come to mind, and he uses them only if they seem appropriate
to the total situation. Even if the speaker knows that in Norwegian
literature the term for grapes is druer, he is not likely to use the
word if it has been of very rare and infrequent occurrence in his previous Norwegian speech, if it is a term associated with situations and

people of a different class from his own, and if (which amounts to
the same thing) he knows it may fail to evoke a response from his
listeners.

　　　Furthermore, two words may be defined in identical terms
and yet not be interchangeable. As suggested above, past associations
of a word may be so strong as to make it inappropriate in a new situation. It may have a different extent of meaning, or it may not fit in
compound expressions which the speaker has to use. An example is
the loss of the Norwegian words for certain bodies of water, bekk
"brook," å "stream," and elv "river." A translator rendering a
literary passage from Norwegian into English might equate these
terms as I have done here. But to the immigrants the situation was
quite different; in America they found neither brooks nor streams.
The Middle West offered them only two choices, "creek" and "river."
Both of these were (relatively) sluggish streams flowing between dirt
banks, and the distinction was between smaller and larger. The first
settlers were frequently compelled to refer to these in the full form
of, say, Fox River or Koshkonong Creek. A literary purist would
have proceeded to do violence to these compounds as well as to the
associations of the Norwegian words by translating the names into
"Foxelven" and "Koshkonongbekken." But a sense of the incongruity
of using bekk and elv, both associated with the rushing waters and
stony brooks of Norway, helped to prevent the pioneers from following
this course. Instead they adopted the terms "creek" and "river,"
which were already associated with the proper names in question,
which expressed exactly and not approximately the distinction that
was useful in this country, and which had the right overtones in the
new situation.

　　　It also happened that an English word entered the language
without displacing its presumed Norwegian equivalent. In this case
it will generally be seen that the English word displaced a part of the
meaning of the Norwegian word, which then continued in its other
meaning. There are so many more things and activities that can be
referred to than there can possibly be words. Hence every word has
to cover concepts which with more exact analysis can be broken down
into smaller units. In Norway lære meant to learn and to teach; in
America it continued its meaning of learning, but formal teaching was
referred to by the English word "teach." The Norwegian hage might

refer to any kind of enclosed garden or orchard; among the immigrants it was frequently restricted to an orchard, while the flower and vege- table garden was called a "garden." The Norwegian kjeller, like English "cellar," referred to a dark, damp place and was obviously inappropriate when referring to a church basement; so English "base- ment" was adopted, but not "cellar." The Norwegian veg (cognate to English "way") was a very inclusive word, as it could refer to any kind of a road or path, and also be used in abstract phrases like the English "away," "in the way of," "on his way." In American Norwe- gian it kept its abstract meanings, its use in phrases, and frequently its reference to cowpaths and minor roads; but important roads and highways were invariably referred to as "roads." These were asso- ciated with traveling to market, perhaps to American neighbors; in many cases, too, they were different in quality and appearance from the corresponding roads in Norway.

That quality and appearance, as well as the less tangible as- sociations of situation, must have played a role in these shifts becomes clear when we observe the fate of the word for "beer." Norwegian øl and American "beer" seem as identical as two words can be, because both refer to the familiar beverage. For some time after their com- ing, the immigrants continued to use the term øl, at least as long as they knew no other drink than the home-brew which they made them- selves. But after a time they ceased their brewing, and bought what- ever beer they wanted from the American dealers. Along with the American beverage came the American word, and "beer" (bir) has since remained the standard term in most country districts. Similarly Vossings have told me that they used the word kvitidl for homemade blankets, "blanket" for factory made or "boughten."

It will be seen that through such changes as these, the voca- bulary was being realigned in the direction of English. Where English possessed a given number of words within a certain field, Norwegian tended to develop the same number, so that the languages might cor- respond point by point.

For this purpose it was convenient that the two languages al- ready had a large number of words of similar form and meaning. These words might seem especially liable to be confused; but we meet here the striking fact that only the meaning and not the form was

confused. Such terms as korn, hamar, kjøken (kitchen), hus (house),
mann, tobakk, potet were never Americanized in form, and appeared
in the pronunciation and with the endings customary in each dialect.
But their meanings gradually approached those of the corresponding
English words which they resembled. Korn acquired all the meanings
of English "corn," even in such compounds as "corn meal." The
regular form for this was kornmjøl, which in Norway would have
meant "grain flour." Mjøl could be adapted to the meaning of "meal"
in this word, because it was no longer used to mean "flour." The
finely ground wheat flour of the new land had brought the word "flour"
into American Norwegian. Similarly, the word "stove" invariably
entered for the object known in Norway as omn, while the latter word
did duty for its English cognate "oven." The Norwegian land is not
an exact equivalent of the English "land"; yet in its American usage
it acquired the same extent as the latter. It lost some of its meanings
through the common use of "country," and took over the sense of
"farmland" for which jord "earth" had often been used in Norway.

Abstract ideas that are not closely tied to specific social conditions always tend to remain Norwegian. A vocabulary from western
Wisconsin prepared by a student native to the community[14] shows that
words for shape (e.g., tall, broad, straight), quantity (big, heavy,
numbers), and time (yesterday, week, Easter) are predominantly
Norwegian. Such words combine a variety of phenomena into one
comprehensive and useful class which tends to persist and frequently
agrees with a similar generalization in English. Other groups of the
same type are place and direction (behind, above, east), character
(lazy, kind-hearted, stubborn), quality (pretty, strange, sweet), noise
(howl, crow, rumble), color (blue, yellow, red), relationships between
man and his environment (use, need, make), relationships between
objects (almost, equally, follow).

There was another group of words which remained generally
Norwegian, even though they were not of this abstract and timeless
character. These were the terms for those activities and institutions
which the immigrant brought with him, and in which there was not or
could not be any essential alteration. His words for the parts of his
body and its functions, and for the mind, with its sensations, emotions,
and thoughts, remained largely Norwegian. His vocabulary for home
and family life, for church and worship, was also wrought from

Norwegian materials. His entire family life from courtship to off-spring was a private concern, into which American influence was slow to penetrate. His church was an institution modeled on the mother church in Norway, and in spite of its stilted Dano-Norwegian language it had succeeded in its task of teaching him the Lutheran way to salvation. The one religious word of English origin with any wide distribution was the term "meeting" for a church service. But on investigation the users of this word turn out to be the "Haugianere," who belong to the more puritanical and pietistic wing of the Lutheran church. Their activities were modeled in part on the reformed and dissenting sects of England and America. Their use of this word marks their differentiation from the Lutheran high church with its <u>messe</u> and its clerical dignity, and reveals their relationship to American practices. Home and church were the social institutions which the immigrant brought with him, just as surely as the parts of his body and the stirrings of his mind, and his language reflects the extent to which he maintained them intact against the inroads of American influence.

VI

But in other spheres of activity American influence was dominant. It is a matter of course that words for all types of machinery that had come into general use since the beginning of immigration were overwhelmingly English, from the reaper and the binder to railroad, automobile, and radio.

Within the terms for city life all but the word for city itself were English. Terms for new sports and games learned in this country (baseball, football) were taken over bodily. Using the list from western Wisconsin alluded to above, we find that two-thirds of all the words for communication and travel, including terms associated with horse-drawn vehicles, and for social affairs and activities (carnival, charivari, convention, fair, merry-go-round, movies, surprise party) were English. The Norwegian American went to a "drug store" to buy his medicines, to a "grocery store" for his food, and to a "saloon" for his drinks.

The predominance of English in these fields is not difficult to understand. The immigrant was unfamiliar with most, if not all, of these activities before coming to this country; along with the activity he learned the words to describe it. He might be quite unconscious of the fact that in his native land, especially in the cities, a parallel development was taking place and words were being found to keep up with it. The relatively few who knew the words for these things were submerged in the mass and compelled to use the words that were generally understood. In Norway a country store was called bu or krambu, and in the cities the general word for store was butikk, a word of French origin. The country word hardly seemed to fit the American store, and the other would have seemed affected. Neither word allowed the kind of compounding that became necessary to describe a variety of store types: hardware, grocery, department, drug. The system of government and politics was of course different, and demanded such words as "sheriff" and "senator" and "governor," "caucus" and "party" and "running for office." In 1880 the Norwegian writer Kristofer Janson was amused to hear a Chicago Norwegian remark, "Jamen vart han nomineta og electa, endaa han inkje var eduketa."[15] Had the speaker chosen to reason out the parallel between the Norwegian and American systems, he could easily have found Norwegian terms. But the natural linguistic tendency is to draw upon the entire vocabulary of a new activity, because the one word fits with the other, and not to analyze each term separately. It seems that in describing any activity that was modeled in part or whole on the activities of Americans, and for which there was no exact parallel in his native experience, the immigrant preferred to make use of the American terms. More than that, if it was an activity in which he frequently came in contact with Americans, such as trade, traveling, or politics, his terminology was likely to draw its significant guideposts from English, regardless of whether his native language might be able to supply occasional needs.

In those fields where the contact was less marked, the vocabulary became strongly mixed. Old and new lived side by side, and admirably reflected the social situation. It seems as if some Norwegian words were thoroughly anchored to the objects they represented, and did not need to be exchanged. Their equivalence with the corresponding English terms was already sufficiently exact to cause no confusion. Golv and vegg were close enough to "floor" and "wall" to keep their places; but tak, with its double sense of "ceiling" and "roof," was occasionally abandoned for the American words. Also, ceilings were of more recent acquisition in the peasant houses of Norway than roofs. In the trinity of knife, fork, and spoon, the fork holds the most uncertain position, due in part to its more recent acquisition and in part to its sound, which assimilated it to the other type of fork—the pitchfork. The vocabulary in these fields can be analyzed into new and old on every hand. New methods of heating and lighting, which required English words (battery, flashlight, wire), did not drive out the old, which remained Norwegian (spark, light, smoke). New tools and implements (monkey wrench, cradle, hatchet) existed beside the old (plane, scythe, auger, saw), new types of food and drink (cake, pie, crackers) beside the familiar (pork, cream, meat, butter). New diagnoses of illness brought such terms as "bronchitis," "gargle," and "chicken pox," but did not make superfluous the Norwegian words for "bleed," "heart failure," "whooping cough," and "tuberculosis." At dances the accordion and the square dance came in to supplement the fiddle and the waltz.

The social-linguistic shift of the immigrant may best be observed by taking a single activity and watching its transformation through the years. Let us see what happened to the grain harvest, which in Norway had been known as skur (or skuronn, vinna).[16] The chief grains raised, in order of importance, had been oats (havre), barley (bygg), and rye (rug), with a small amount of wheat (kveite).[17] The general term which included all of these was korn, though many communities limited this to barley, the chief food grain. Barley and oats were frequently sown together; the resulting mixture was known as blandkorn (or hummelkorn, halvbygg). A sickle (sigd, or skjera) was used to cut (skjera) the grain, in contrast to the hay (høi), which was cut (slå) with a scythe (ljå).

After the grain had been cut, it was tied up into sheaves (band, bundt, bundel) by means of a wisp of straw (bendel). Tall wooden poles (staur, rå, or sneis) were then set up (staura, stappa) in the field. The sheaves were slipped down (sneisa, støyra, festa, etc.) on the poles so that they might be sure to dry before the frost came. If the first sheaf was set up vertically, instead of horizontally like the rest, it got a name of its own (fotband, kjering, staurkjering, stett). In some places the topmost sheaf had a special name (hette, skruv). A stick (stokk, sulu) was sometimes used to prop the sheaves off the ground; a stool (festekrakk, råkrakk, mannauke) was used to stand on while the worker reached up to place the sheaves on the pole; and there might be a forked stick to lift the sheaves on or off (bokskykj, staurkrok, kornskoto).

When the cutting was over, a harvest festival (skurgraut, skurøl) would be held, with certain customary foods and practices. Special superstitions were often attached to the last sheaf; some thought that its size was an omen for the harvest of the following year. When the grain was dry, it was driven into a special barn (låven). In this condition the grain was referred to as lo, and the next step in its preparation was to thresh it (treskja). A flail (tust, treskjestav, flygel, slegel, sloga) was the instrument used for this purpose; the grain was laid on a specially prepared floor (logulv) and beaten until the straw (halm) was separated from the grain. The grain was then stored in bins (kornbingar) until it was needed for household use.

It must not be imagined that these thirty odd terms (counting only one for each object or operation) exhausted the vocabulary of the harvest; only the more significant are included above. But how many of these would function usefully in the American environment? At the very start the immigrant met a new kind of grain, the maize or Indian corn; as "corn" was the name it bore, he used his own equivalent korn to designate it. To take its place he adapted the word grøn, which resembled the English "grain" in sound and was used in many Norwegian dialects in a very similar sense. After the first season the immigrant was ready to plant wheat, which was the chief support of agriculture in the first years of immigration. [18] Oats, rye, and barley were also raised, but in smaller quantities. In spite of the change in proportion, there was no change in the grains themselves, and no reason for abandoning their Norwegian names.

"Wisconsin was settled precisely at the time when new inventions in harvesting machinery began to make their appearance after ages of dependence on implements little more complex than the sickle."[19] The first instrument used in Wisconsin was the "cradle," a scythe with wooden bars to guide the falling grain. This term was at once assimilated by the Norwegians (kridl, krill), while the ordinary scythe (ljå) retained its name together with its function of cutting hay. In this earliest phase, the harvest was still called skur, the men went out to skjera, and they tied their bundles with the same wisps of straw.

But by 1850 the McCormick reaper was in general use, as was the
name, Norwegianized to riper, ryper, ripper, or rippert. The process itself was referred to as ripe (also rype, rippe, riple). It was
still necessary to tie up the bundles, but before long the successive
invention of the Marsh harvester, which raked the grain together, and
the self-binder, which also tied it into bundles, reduced the process
into a single operation. These changes brought with them the noun
harvistar, the verb harviste, and the inevitable harvist for the entire
process. This was no longer skur, as they had known it in Norway,
and the cutting of the grain was therefore not skjera, but katta, from
English "cut." The self-binder was thoroughly assimilated as sjølv-
bindar, in which both parts were accurately translated.

As the summer season was longer than in Norway, there was
small danger of frost before the grain was dry. Hence the elaborate
process used in Norway to insure quick drying became superfluous.
The bundles were set up in small piles known as shocks (sjakkar),
and this work was known as sjakka. If it was necessary to keep these
standing for some time before threshing, so that there was danger of
rain, the bundles might be set up more permanently in stacks (stak-
kar), a process for which there were Norwegian words (stekkja,
stakka), which, however, had been used primarily for hay rather
than grain in Norway. A pole set up to hold this stack was sometimes
known as a sneise, the name used for the pole with the sheaves of
grain in Norway. But the necessity for a special barn to keep the unthreshed grain in, as well as a special name for unthreshed grain,
vanished with the new methods of threshing. The flail was little used
in Wisconsin; almost from the beginning the grain was threshed by
machinery in the field, without the necessity of further transfer. The
term for threshing naturally remained, as its form was practically
identical with that of the English, and the machinery acquired the
obvious name treskjemaskina. The men who worked at the threshing
were treskjarar, and might constitute a treskjarkru (in which the
second half, which takes feminine endings, is the English word
"crew"). After threshing, the grain was deposited in a special building known as a "granary"; the Norwegian-American form for this
became a derivative of grøn: grønneri.

If we make up the balance sheet of the linguistic shift in the
grain harvest, this is what we see: of the thirty-two words connected

with harvesting in Norway, seventeen were also useful in America.
Two of these (grøn, korn) were shifted in function, due to similarity
in sound to corresponding English words. Two Norwegian words
(stakk, stekkja) were adopted from another activity without shift in
meaning, and were also very similar in sound to the corresponding
English words. Two of the Norwegian words retained (høi, treskja)
were so much like the English words that any further anglicizing was
unthinkable. Thirteen English words were introduced to take care of
the new processes and implements. The total number of words in the
new alignment was then very close to that in the old: thirty compared
to thirty-two. But a better than fifty per cent shift had taken place in
the constituents of this vocabulary, which seems a fair index to the
change in the agricultural practices of the immigrants. Each of the
terms now used in their American Norwegian corresponded exactly
to a term used in their American English; they had shortened by one
half the distance between them and the new language. Also they had
practically achieved one term for each concept instead of the wide
dialectal variation of Norwegian exemplified above. The Norwegian
words retained and the English words adopted were understood by all,
no matter what Norwegian dialect they might speak.

VII

The earliest words that entered from English were taken
over and reshaped into completely Norwegian words. The immigrant
was unable to produce the sounds of English as natives produced
them, and so he inevitably made the words fit into his own system of
sounds. In the case of Norwegian this was relatively simple, as there
were many sounds that resembled the English and could easily be substituted for them. American a in "farm," "bar," "car," "barn,"
"honest," was regularly rendered by the Norwegian a. Similarly
there was no difficulty about English i in "brick," "attic," "pink,"
"hitch"; they all became Norwegian short i. But for such a sound as
English u in "cut," "bluff," "brush," "grub," "trunk," there was no
obvious equivalent. So the five words here given were (usually) rendered by five different Norwegian vowels, all of which are close to,
but not identical with the English (katte, blåff, brøsj, grubbe, tronk).

The pronunciation which the Norwegians gave these words
shows that they had picked most of them up from speech and not from

books. When they took over the word "accordion" and pronounced it
kordin (like cordeen´), or when they called a whiffletree hyppeltre,
they were rendering as best they could the common American pronunciation of these words in their neighborhood. But once in a while it
looks as if they were misled by American spelling into a pronunciation which was not that of American speech. When "bran" was adopted,
it should have become bræn (or brenn), but instead it became bran
(or brann, brand), with the a of "father." When "lot" was taken in,
it should have become latt, but instead it became lått, which is the
Norwegian pronunciation of o (not a) in such words. It is reasonable
to assume that the immigrant first met the word "bran" on printed
labels, and the word "lot" in his printed deed. In this way we can
trace one of the channels through which he met the new culture, and
see him eagerly grasping at whatever fragments he could assimilate.

        The adaptation of these words to Norwegian did not cease
with their transformation in sound. They were admitted to that full
membership which consists of receiving the same endings and standing
in the same positions as words of the same class in the original. If
they were verbs, they acquired the endings of past, present, and participle. If they were nouns, they were made to end in the way appropriate for nouns in each dialect. In most Norwegian speech this involved among other things a decision on whether the noun should be
masculine, feminine, or neuter. This decision was generally quite
unconscious and immediate, and for the more common words it agreed
surprisingly well in different dialects and different settlements. The
overwhelming majority of English words in American Norwegian became masculine, while the rest were fitted into the feminine (e.g.
field: ei fil "a field," fila, fili, or filo "the field") or the neuter (e.g.
fence: eit fens "a fence," fense "the fence," fens "fences"). There
is no need of going into the reasons for this particular choice here;
it is a matter of linguistic rather than social significance.

        From the time of their assimilation these words functioned
as part of the immigrant's Norwegian vocabulary. He no longer
thought of them as English; in most cases he learned them from other
Norwegians and not from speakers of English. Some words even suggest by their form that they may have passed through more than one
dialect before reaching some speakers; e.g. the word "pail" does not
rhyme with "mail" in American Sogning, but gets a sound as if it were

pronounced "pile" in English. This seems to be due to the fact that
the diphthong pronounced ei in most Norwegian dialects is pronounced
ai (long i) in Sogning. So the Sognings must have taken it from another
Norwegian dialect and adapted it to their own system. This complete
assimilation is the reason that children could grow up in Norwegian
communities and never suspect that words like "fence," "street,"
"pail," and "road" were not native Norwegian words.

In this development, however, there came a critical point at
which English words began to be introduced without being more than
partly assimilated. American w and r were among the sounds whose
non-existence in Norwegian was most quickly noticed. In the third-
generation speech of Wisconsin the use of these English sounds is
regular in such recent words as "radio" and "weather report." These
and other criteria make it possible (for some speakers) to distinguish
the word for a "poker" game (with Norwegian sounds) from a stove
"poker" (with English sounds), or the whip one beats a horse with
(hyppe) from the whipping one gives an egg (wippe). At about the
same stage English endings, like the plural -s, appear in some words,
and whole phrases begin to bob up in unassimilated form. It is practically certain that these later words are recognized by the speakers
as English, even though they may have acquired some Norwegian
characteristics, and that they are deliberately introduced because the
speaker is unable to recall a Norwegian equivalent. This is a true
mixture of language which can usually be distinguished from the earlier complete assimilation.

The reconstruction of this development is often as exciting
as the geologist's study of layers in the earth's surface. It is possible to find informants whose language dates back to the first generation of Norwegian settlement and who are admirable fossil specimens
of the language of those years. They are usually the children or
grandchildren of the earliest immigrants, and speak excellent English
beside an excellent Norwegian dialect. They mix into their Norwegian
only those English words which were in use in their childhood, for
they can maintain their Norwegian as a holiday luxury, a speech for
special occasions, in all its (relatively) unsullied purity. They look
down on later immigrants, whom they regularly accuse of undue
"mixing." Informants from Koshkonong have described the first generation of settlers (1840-1855) and their children as speakers of "pure"

Norwegian, in contrast to the wave of newcomers who overran the community in the eighties. These last came in as hired men and sharecroppers, and were therefore regarded as inferior by the children of the first emigrants. That the speech of the first generation was only relatively pure is a matter of course; as early as 1853 a poetic immigrant wrote:

> Men dæ døm snakka va vont å skjønne,
> de va så my' Engelst ibland.[20]

The immigrant who was not fortunate enough to be a "first settler" was faced by a bewildering situation. Although settling among compatriots, he was compelled to adapt himself to a partially new vocabulary. Many amusing sayings are recalled to illustrate this. An early settler was talking to a more recent arrival in what he thought was good Norwegian; but the "newcomer" answered in all seriousness: "You'll have to talk Norwegian to me, for I've just come from Norway" (Du lyt snakke norsk te meg for eg e nett kome frå Norge). Professor O.E. Rölvaag, himself such a late immigrant, pictured these difficulties vividly in his first book, Amerika-breve.[21] Rölvaag's "newcomer" was awakened on his first morning in his uncle's home with a call to "breakfast." He had no notion what this might be, but assumed that it referred to syrup, which was served when he reached the table. Again and again he was baffled by the terms he heard his uncle use, and he wrote home to Norway: "This unfortunate practice (uvæsen) makes it more difficult for me than you would believe. When uncle asks me to do something, I stand there like a fool, a regular numskull, and understand nothing."

In his anxiety to conform to his new environment, it is no wonder that the immigrant should overshoot the mark and adopt more English terms than were current in the Norwegian of the older settlers. His adoption of the new terms was a mark of quick learning, and his excessive use a monument to mistaken zeal. Most significant is the fact that because of his ignorance of English, he was compelled to make his Norwegian do double service. When the second generation bilingual felt an expression coming for which he knew no Norwegian, such as "ball bearings" or "wild West show," he could avoid mixture by turning the whole sentence into English. But the "newcomer" had to fill them into his Norwegian, or remain forever silent.

How much English did the immigrants actually mix into their Norwegian before they turned to all English ? This must naturally have varied widely. Persons of subnormal mentality or pidgin tendencies in language might produce specimens of the "gemixte pickles" type which generally pass as immigrant language in the humorous tradition. A second generation Norwegian told of a "newcomer" girl who said, "E va so glad når eg luk ju koming." By the average immigrant such persons are looked on with amusement or contempt. Those who commit the opposite fault of excessive purism are equally suspect. Different degrees of mixture are apparent in different circles, but mixture is nowhere absent. An early immigrant from Voss who thundered against others' use of travla (from "travel") to mean "walk" and who insisted on svidl when everyone else used the English "joist" was himself not above using such English words as "stable" and "lake" in his Norwegian.

If we take a passage of connected speech, or listen to a conversation in this language, we shall see that only a rather small proportion of the words are actually of English origin. For all the most common words are Norwegian, the "ands" and the "buts" of the language, all those words which show the relation between other words and do not themselves carry the meaning of the sentence. These make up at least four out of every five words in any ordinary passage, and leave only one word which is really exposed to English influence.[22] This fifth word is the one that may or may not be English, and if we look at the Wisconsin vocabulary spoken of above, we shall see what happens to it. This vocabulary contains about 4,200 words, and of these about 1,200 are English, or 28 per cent. In other words, onefourth of the words that carry actual meaning may be English in the third-generation speech of that community. If we add another fourth for idioms and changes in meaning, we see that the significant parts of the language are half English. The shell is still Norwegian, but the inward pattern, the spirit of the thing, is American. This is American Norwegian, the language of the Norwegian immigrant.

VIII

Some authentic samples of American Norwegian speech will complete this survey and help to reinforce the conclusions drawn above. All but the fourth are taken from phonograph recordings, and all but the fifth are examples of unprepared narration. The fourth was taken down verbatim by the writer, and the fifth was prepared by a native speaker. These five samples exemplify the four principal dialect areas of Norway—West (2, 3), Midland (1), East (5), and Trønder (4); and three important settlement areas of Norwegians in this country—southern Wisconsin (1-3), western Wisconsin (5), and South Dakota (4). All the samples present bits of cultural lore, and reflect the American adaptation in varying degrees. They are given here in a modified Norwegian spelling, without any indication of finer nuances, and the English originals of borrowed words and expressions are given in parentheses. If the samples are less studded with English terms than some readers might have expected, it is due to the fact that they are authentic, and not made up for humorous effect.

1. Second-generation Telemarking (Morgedal), immigration of 1846 to Koshkonong:[23]

Dæ fyste bryllupe eg va i, då va dæ no skikk og bruk å be heile nabolagje komma. Men te vintern blei dæ nesten alle ihop ongdom. Og når kvellen kom og me hadde hatt søpper (supper) då, så blei dæ te å danse. Dæ va for dæ meste bare ein spilmann og så fele, og lite romm, for stoven (the stove) va i veien og sænjer og alt dæ. Men så gjekk dæ like væl, for vi va lette både i hovui og i føtan for dæ meste. Der på Ramberg, dæ va omtrænt juleti, så kom hormarar ("horners," persons out to charivari or serenade the newlyweds) då når dæ lei på. Fyste me visste så bejynda dei te å skjote av revolverar (revolvers, probably first heard in America) runtom glase og skrike og skramle mæ bjøllur og bar seg fælskeleg åt. Så va dæ mange, dæ var ein par døssen (dozen) av di, trur eg, mestedelen vaksne karar ou, men di fekk ikkje noko traktemente, og dæ va no dæ di reiste etter.

2. Second-generation Vossing, immigration of 1847 to Spring Prairie:[24]

Han far hadde bygt ait lite logghus (log house) so va trettan fot i skvær (square) insaid (inside)—innante—og dar va me fem bodn, og far og mor. Da va ai seng mæ høga føtu, so far og mor laog i, og so va da ai litæ so va stukkjen unde dar, og dar laog ain tre-fyra tao oss og so ain oppi sengjæ jao far og mor. So trefte da se te so at da kom nokke nykommarar ("newcomers"), ait par. Jau, dai skulde fao sleppa inn, og; so vart da to famelia inni detta husi. Men so hadde han far kjøpt ain kostbaru sau, og den skulde fao lamb, og da maotte me ta vare pao, attu me kunde fao behalda da. Ja, so kom far pao at han skulde inn i husi mæ sauen. So tok me ai dør og sette i ai kro på husi tvert yve, og so vart dar ait lite rum fy sauen te væ unde dar. Ja, so va dar sau og to lambu og han far og fyra bodn og so ait anna par. Han far va ain maistar te bryggja, han ha mæ seg sao ifrao Norge og laga te nokso godt øl. Og so fekk me graut so va jord utao helfta kodnmjøl (corn meal) og helfta midling (milling), og stundo va dar ain mole mæ flaur (flour) i, og so vart han bere. So aot me og drakk, og naor me va ferrige, so va me pao ain liten kant og so vo me mette og. So gjekk me dao bortu og la oss i ai kro pao nokre kota (coats), og so laog me so fint og sovu dar um kvelden.

3. Second-generation Sogning (Balestrand), immigration of 1859 to Lodi, Wisconsin:[25]

Da va ain nykommarungdom so kom her mange aor sea frao Norge og so hyrt'n seg ut pao ain farm (farm) og ain kveld naor han og farmaren (the farmer) hadde sytt ifrao seg og kydna sto dar inni banao (the barn), so dai saie her i lande, so saie farmaren ti han Ola, hyrekaren (the hired man), "Denne kyri her, ho tainkje eg kjeme te å bæra ho i kveld. Du e gjedna snilde, du, og ji deg ti her uti banao (the barn), eg e troitt eg og lika å inn og leggja meg, og so snøgt so ho ha bore, so kjeme du inn og vekkje meg." "Ja," sa'n Ola, da skul 'n mair en gjedna gjera, for nykommarfolki dai va so villige og lydige og hjelpsame i adle ting . . . . Jaja, gamlingen raiste inn og la seg og sobna, og naor han vakna, so va dagen kommen og han hadde kje hoirt ifrao 'n Ola. Han klædde seg og ut i banao (the barn) so fort han kunde, og naor han opna døri, so saie han Ola mæ ai gang: "Ho ha kje bore endao!" Og mannen gjekk inn og her laog kyri og han Ola satt pao ain mjelkekrakk bakom kyri. So saie farmaren (the farmer), "Bore! Ho ber alder ho mæ du site dar! Ho ser deg, ho, og trur ho ha bore!"

4. First-generation Trønder (Oppdal), immigration of 1869 to South Dakota:[26]

Vi skull gå tri honnder mil (American miles) tefoss, og så ble vi sårføtte. Så kom vi te et rensj (ranch) en aften, en fransmann

som ha ei skvå (squaw). Hann ha sallon (saloon), og dæ kosta fæm
og tjug sent (cents) glase. Du mått betâl før du fekk fengra i glase,
dæ va itt nå kreddit å få der. Så mått vi stoppe (meaning from "stop")
over natta (phrase: overnight) der. Så sie fransmann, "Vask deres
fødder godt, her er såpe, skur dem godt." Da vi va færdi mæ dæ,
kom hann mæ en stor vaskebolle (combination probably from "wash-
bowl")—hann to visst en par gallona (gallons)—full mæ viski (whisky),
"No ska di vask føten mæ dæ derre." Så sa e te Ole, "Dæ bli en kost-
bar vask. Men dæ ikke nån ann rå, dæ får berre skure, vi må rønne
resken (run the risk)." Vi vaska oss, vi låg der og kvilte godt og
bena ble ål rait (all right). Så sie e te Ola, "Gad vite um han slår
vekk den viskien (that whisky)." Vi så efter, og han slo den ikke vekk.
Hann fyllt den visst i flaska igjen, og nogen fekk dyrt betâl vaskin
vår. Vi betâlt um morgenen for brækfest (breakfast) og seng og
søppel (supper), en dale (dollar, Norwegian form, American meaning)
og en halv på kvar. Så spor e kva viskien skull kost. "Inginteng,"
sa'n.

        5. Third-generation Solør, immigration of 1854 to Trempe-
leau County, Wisconsin:[27]

        Vårona hadde vøri jort, så de att je hadde pleinti (plenty)
ti. Men likevæl så hadde je nåe å drive tia me. De hadde vørti ølløyv
kattonger som var omtreint tre veker gamle da je komm hemm.
Dam ville Goodwin je skülle ha ihæl. Han sa at han hadde veinte
tæll je kom hemm, før han likte itte å jæra de sjøl. Je liker itte å
jæra de je hæll før den delen, men da tenkte je me over (probably
an anglicism from "I thought it over") og sa at je skülle dræpa kattonga før fæm sænt (cents) hedden (the head). De var åtte som skülle
dræpas. Je vart så sørpraisa (surprised) da je fekk fæmti sænt (cents)
før altsammen. Je tog hætsjeten (the hatchet) og jikk bak sjeden (the
shed) me kattonga og høgg hügü tå dam. Kanskje de ser üt stigt å
dræpa dam på dæn måten, men je sinnes de er da bære hæll å stappe
dam i ein gåningssækk (gunny sack) og drokne dam.

                              NOTES

        [1]H. L. Mencken has gathered most of the available material
in The American Language, 150-163 (fourth edition, New York, 1936).
German, Irish, and Spanish appear to have had some slight influence
on American, but even this is insignificant.

[2] See p. 616-697.

[3] A letter from Olaus Duus of July 8, 1856, in Historiografisk Samling Mss. Oslo, copies of which were kindly lent me by Professor Theodore C. Blegen.

[4] These studies have been supported by the research committee of the University of Wisconsin.

[5] Statistisk årbok for Norge, 1934, p. 4.

[6] Cf. Theodore C. Blegen, Norwegian Migration to America, 1825-1860, 154-176 (Northfield, 1931).

[7] Ivar Aasen published a dictionary of the Norwegian dialects with some forty thousand words in it, and his successor Hans Ross another with at least as many more.

[8] Neither Aasen nor Ross list them in their dictionaries, and thereby stamp them as "un-Norwegian."

[9] Copenhagen, 1881.

[10] See a full discussion of the moral problem in the interesting essay on "Immigration and Puritanism" by Marcus Hansen in Norwegian-American Studies and Records, 9:1-28 (Northfield, 1936).

[10a] For similar views, arrived at independently, see the excellent chapter on "Language as a Factor in Social Adjustment," by Leonard Covello, in F. J. Brown and J. S. Roucek, ed., Our Racial and National Minorities, 681 ff. (New York, 1937).

[11] The people and I are just like one.
All that they say I understand so well;
And nowhere on earth are there words like these,
That come so close to my heart.

[12] Bilingualism, 17 (Calcutta, 1926).

[13] Things didn't go right at first,
When we landed in the strange country;
Of the language that people talked
We understood not a single word.

Learning the language was a real task,
And often we were put to shame.
When a Yankee asked you your name,
It often happened that you answered, "Yes."

From Sange og viser, 267 (Decorah, Iowa, n. d.). A variant (and incomplete) version is included in Theodore C. Blegen and Martin B. Ruud, Norwegian Emigrant Songs and Ballads, 344 (Minneapolis, 1936).

[14] Odin Anderson of Blair, Wisconsin.

[15]"He was nominated and elected even though he was not educated."

[16]Material drawn from Ord og sed I, 19-20 (Oslo, 1934), and Ivar Aasen, Norsk maalbunad, 31, 195 ff. (Oslo, 1925).

[17]Proportions in 1890: 56.7 per cent, 33.6 per cent, 7.7 per cent, 2.1 per cent according to Statistisk årbok for Norge, 1934, p. 46.

[18]Much of the information on this point is drawn from Joseph Schafer, A History of Agriculture in Wisconsin (Madison, 1922), especially chapters 5 and 6.

[19]Schafer, History of Agriculture in Wisconsin, 87.

[20]But what they spoke was hard to understand,
For so much English was mixed into it.
From Blegen and Ruud, Norwegian Emigrant Songs and Ballads, 212.

[21]Amerika-breve fra P. A. Smevik til hans far og bror i Norge samlet ved Paal Mørck, 33-34 (Minneapolis, 1912).

[22]Of the thousand most common words in Norwegian, as determined in a word count made by the writer, less than fifty are ever lost in American Norwegian.

[23]O. B. Stephens (Hustvedt), born 1850.

[24]John Pedersen (Hosaas), born 1854.

[25]Robert Nelson, born 1875.

[26]Halvor Aune, born 1846. Told to the author in 1930, with considerable admixture of book forms. The letters italicized are pronounced "thick," i.e., similar to American r.

[27]Odin Anderson, born 1914. The ü is a sound intermediate between ordinary Norwegian u and y.

2 | Problems of Linguistic Research Among Scandinavian Immigrants in America

An American linguist who wishes to devote himself to the stimulating problems of living speech is not at a loss for materials within his own country. He can investigate the languages of our Indian aborigines; he can take up the study of American English, the language of the dominant immigrant group; or he can devote himself to the many tongues that are still spoken by great numbers of later and lesser immigrant groups in this country. Of these three broad linguistic types the last-mentioned is also the most neglected, although one would expect that for the labor expended it would yield the greatest returns.

It has been the writer's experience that every problem of language can find materials for its elucidation among the speech of American immigrants. No practicing linguist should feel himself competent unless he has used an opportunity to acquaint himself with the flux and movement of a living language. No graduate student in linguistics should be permitted to take his degree without a term of field work in the language of his choice or some related tongue. Here phonemic and grammatical systems that are separated by thousands of years of development are thrown into immediate contact within single families or communities. Here the most exigent of social and economic neccessities are forcing language to respond to new and unexpected situations. There is nothing in the linguist's arsenal that cannot be used to advantage here, whether a sharp ear, mechanical laboratory equipment, keen grammatical and syntactic analysis, or an interest in the social functions of language.

Such investigation affords also an opportunity that should not be unwelcome to the linguist, of cooperating with the historian toward a fuller and deeper understanding of the roles played by immigrant peoples in the building of America. This possibility has been most fruitfully and brilliantly exploited by Professor Theodore C. Blegan of Minnesota in the second volume of his great work, Norwegian Migration.[1] In this volume he has included a chapter entitled "Language and Immigrant Transition," which is largely based on material furnished him by linguists. In the following words he stresses the importance to historians of linguistic interpretations of immigrant life: "In according the Norwegian-American speech scientific analysis, [the linguists] have illuminated the processes not only of an interesting linguistic transition, but also of that broader social and cultural re-orientation of immigrant life which the adaptations of language reflect. The issues. . . have a deeper meaning than mere words and phrases, for they center about the adjustment of the mind of the immigrant to the two worlds that his experience encompassed. . . . It appears that what, upon superficial retrospect, has the character of linguistic confusion was in reality a struggle of large numbers of people toward some kind of intellectual, or cultural unity. . . . It is only as such attempts are recorded, as linguists, historians and novelists interpret the immigrant saga, and as popular understanding of American life deepens, that the hidden and surface forces of American culture can be expected to meet and coalesce."[2]

In many parts of America the materials for this study are rapidly vanishing. Before the impact of radio, automobile, and the modern press every little eddy and backwash of American life are being drained of their local flavor. The group life and even the family life of the immigrant are being invaded by the uniforming forces of a mechanized and ruthless civilization. But these have not yet succeeded in eliminating all traces of such factors in the daily life of America. Thousands of churches are still preaching in foreign tongues, and hundreds of newspapers are presenting the news of the day to partially unassimilated groups. Before all of this becomes a part of the America that was, we owe it to linguistics, to ourselves, and to America to gather the evidence and evaluate it for the fuller understanding that it can give.

Most of the studies that have been made of the immigrant tongues are marred by the anecdotal approach. Material of the "gemixte pickles" type can be amusing enough, but it is seldom authentic. Even in the more serious studies that have been made, the tendency is too often one of gathering curiosities of expression which strike the ear because of their variation from the expected. As one who has grown up speaking an immigrant tongue, the writer knows that its forms are no more accidental or irregular than those of any other language. Any one who tries to make up examples of such a mixed language immediately reveals his lack of <u>sprachgefühl</u>, which consists of a habitually acquired sense that certain expressions are customary and certain others are not. This sense of a norm exists even among the unlettered speakers of immigrant tongues, and should be the real object of our study.

The first Scandinavian settlements in this country were those which the Swedes established on the Delaware in the seventeenth century. As Swedish speech died out among their descendants a century or so later, it is too late to make any linguistic observations there; but it is evident from observations made by Swedish travelers in these settlements that the situation was analogous to that in later ones. Peter Kalm, a Swedish botanist, visited his American countrymen in 1749 and reported that their Swedish had deviated widely from that of the homeland. His list of examples is interesting for the parallels it offers with later developments.[3]

As is well known, modern Scandinavian settlements are primarily concentrated in the Middle West. The first to come in considerable numbers were the Norwegians, who established large settlements in Illinois and Wisconsin in the thirties and forties, in Iowa and Minnesota in the fifties, and in the Dakotas in the sixties. Swedish immigration started after most of Wisconsin was settled; it entered Minnesota, and then turned to such states as Nebraska and Kansas. Danish settlements were largely in the same areas, but were smaller in extent. The Icelanders are chiefly in North Dakota.

No study whatever has been made of immigrant Danish, and the only information available of Icelandic is a sketchy article by the explorer Vilhjálmur Stefánsson written in 1903.[4]

Swedish has been more fortunate. The earliest study was made by Dr. Gustav Andreen, when teaching Swedish at Yale University. During a stay in Sweden he lectured to the språkvetenskapliga

Sallskäpet in Uppsala in May, 1899. His lecture, as later printed, devotes about six pages to the subject of American Swedish.[5] In spite of the author's good will, the attitude is the usual one of the educated European, that some loan words are necessary and therefore "excusable," while others are "unnecessary" and are therefore to be condemned. These and other shortcomings were pointed out some years later in a valuable article by Professor A. Louis Elmquist, who showed a wider acquaintance with Swedish-American speech and the social circumstances surrounding it.[6]

In 1904 a native Swedish philologist, Ruben Gustafson Berg, prepared an analysis of unorthodox expressions found in the Swedish American press. This study was somewhat marred by a lack of familiarity with American English and with spoken American Swedish. A series of articles in the same year by a Swedish American pastor, E. A. Zetterstrand, contains much valuable material, but the articles are somewhat vitiated for our purposes by a strong pedagogical-puristic tenor.[8] In the intervening years a number of more or less detailed surveys by journalists and other popular writers have added more material, but no important points of view.[9]

The most ambitious study of American Swedish is an unpublished thesis by Professor Walter Gustafson of Upsala College, East Orange, New Jersey, presented at New York University in 1929.[10] This includes a list of about 700 English loan words, and a chapter-by-chapter treatment of such important aspects as gender, coinages, prepositions and conjunctions, English influence on the meaning of words, translation loans, style, word-order, syntax, personal and family names, place names, and Swedish influence on English.

The weakness of this study lies in its inadequate phonetic observation and analysis. Its indications of pronunciation are based on general impressions of common American-Swedish practice, and there is no attempt to analyze the whole phonetic pattern of transference. The study is practically limited to standard Swedish and its urban subvarietics, taking no account of dialectal and rural speech. The unhappy term 'patois' is used for spoken American Swedish, and throughout we are chiefly made aware of its aberrations from standard Swedish. The strength of the study lies in its many well-taken observations on the syntactical and phraseological shift. On this

point many of the writer's conclusions seem eminently sound, as
when he notes that the borrowing of English terms "is only partly due
to the need of new words to express new ideas; it is mostly due to
the force of new speech habits."[11]

Immigrant Norwegian was first noticed by a Norwegian-
trained philologist, Peter Groth, forced by untoward circumstances
to live in New York for eleven years. In a doctoral lecture delivered
at the University of Oslo in 1897 he discussed what he called 'Some
characteristics of the language of Norwegians emigrated to America.'
This brief but intelligent discussion—the first on any American-
Scandinavian tongue—expressed the hope that 'as Norwegian-American philologists with full scientific training arise, one or more of
them will take this question up for treatment.'

Even as he wrote these words, two young men in the Middle
West had begun gathering materials. The first to publish anything on
the subject was Nils Flaten, now professor of Romance languages at
St. Olaf College. His article in Dialect Notes commented on the language of his native community in Goodhue County, Minnesota. "I
was ten or twelve years old," he wrote, "before I discovered that
such words as paatikkele, stæbel, fens were not Norwegian but mis-
treated English words. I had often wondered that poleit, trubbel,
søppereter resembled the English words so closely. . ."[13] His article consisted of a list of 550 English words used in the Norwegian of
the settlement, and a paradigm of the Valdris dialect to show how
these were treated grammatically.

Two years later a similar, but more thorough article
appeared in Dialect Notes, written by the eminent philologist, Professor George T. Flom. The author was a native of one of the oldest
and most significant Norwegian settlements, located a few miles
southeast of Madison, Wisconsin. He presented a list of about 700
English loan-words (later increased to more than 1000), in which
each word was phonetically transcribed in the Sogn dialect and tagged
with exact grammatical information. Professor Flom also analyzed
the conditions of borrowing and presented statistics on the relative
number of nouns, verbs, etc., borrowed into his childhood dialect.
This article has a double significance, first as an unusually consien-
tious and authentic collection of materials, and secondly for its

stimulus to further research. Similar collections for many dialects will make it possible to formulate general principles.

Professor Flom has used the materials of his list to throw light on various aspects of the problem. He has analyzed some of the principles that operate in the application of gender to loanwords: associations of sound and form, meaning and synonyms. He has shown how the Sognings adapt American vowel sounds to their own pattern. In two articles of a more general nature he has presented surveys of the use and development of Norwegian in this country, both spoken and written. His studies of the Sogn dialect in Norway are not pertinent to this discussion, but they do offer valuable background material for his American dialect. It is clear that although Progessor Flom's articles do not exhaust their theme, they lay an invaluable basis for further study.

In 1931 two of Norway's leading linguists, Professors Didrik Arup Seip (now Rector of the University of Oslo) and Ernst W. Selmer, spent a semester in this country making observations on American Norwegian. But because of the pressure of other work, they have not yet been able to analyze or publish their materials.

Each of the studies listed, except the last-named, has been limited to observations in a single community, that of the investigator's own youth, whose language he shared. All of them are for this reason only partial and incomplete solutions to the problem of immigrant Norwegian.

Before discussing my own work, or plans for the future, it would be well to outline the ultimate goals of this work. Unless we appreciate the full magnitude of the problem, we are likely to be lost in studies of detail.

In its broadest aspect the problem can be divided into four closely related, but distinct fields. First of all, we must have clearly before us the nature of the community in which our speakers are living, its outward as well as inward development. Language in its functional-social aspect is our first object of study. Then there is the technical analysis of the spoken language, its sounds, grammar, syntax, and vocabulary, in relation to the original speech brought over, to the surrounding dialects, and to English. Since every important immigrant group has brought along the art of writing its language, we must also be concerned with the nature of this tradition, whose course of development may often be widely different from that of speech. Finally, there is the problem of names, which carry with them the association of the speech community of which the immigrant was once a part.

 I. The foreign language community. One of the most important bonds of cohesiveness in these communities is the common language, with all of its common assumptions and associations. As Michael West, perhaps with a slight exaggeration, has put it: 'Of all instruments for the intensification of group individuality, language is undoubtedly the most powerful.'[16] A part of our investigation must therefore be the collection of materials on the location, extent, and outward history of the communities in which we are interested. Where this has already been done by historians, we have the advantage of being able to turn to their works for aid. But the subtler aspects of everyday life within the community frequently evade the historian. Knowledge of the affairs and interests of the community is indispensable for a thorough understanding of the language, and certain questions leading to such knowledge must be included in any questionnaire.

 The specifically linguistic problems touching the group life of our speakers include first of all the attitudes of the speakers toward their own language, of which they may either be proud or ashamed. If they have heard other dialects than their own, as most of them have, they frequently harbor interesting attitudes of friendliness or aversion towards them. Their feeling about the traditional schriftsprache is a criterion of social training. Most important for our purposes is their attitude to English, which strongly colors their position on the whole question of linguistic assimilation.

 These linguistic attitudes appear partly in the involuntary expressions of pleasure or aversion with which they accompany their answers to linguistic questions, and partly as a result of direct inquiries.

 In the case of such recent immigration as the Norwegian, the speech of the local community will always be less homogeneous

than that of an English-speaking community. Although there has been
a very strong tendency for persons with the same local dialects to
flock together, no Norwegian community fails to include speakers of
more than one dialect, and some communities are thoroughly mixed.
For this reason it is out of the question to prepare the kind of dialect
atlas that is customary with a long-established population. The most
one can do is to locate on a map those communities which show a high
degree of homogeneity within a larger or smaller area. Instead
another problem comes to the fore: to what extent is a kind of homogeneity, not originally existing, coming into being? This problem
has its bearing on the origin of colonial languages everywhere, including that of American English. Here we can often see this process in
its inception within a generation or two. Hence it is of the greatest
interest to investigate the speech of various members of a single
family, or a single occupational group, or a neighborhood, in order
to find out the actual degree of variation among the various members
of such groups, and the presence or absence of a tendency toward
mutual assimilation.

When we look outside the individual community, as we must
if we are to explain all its linguistic habits, it becomes a problem of
great interest to examine the extent of difference and likeness in the
treatment of the same original dialects in various more or less
remote communities. This gives us material for determining whether
the phenomena of the dialects studied are due to independent, parallel
development, to the influence of the written language, or to something inherent in the languages themselves, or whether the presence
of a wider contact between the various communities speaking the same
language has brought about some of these phenomena.

Finally, the community must be analyzed for its relation to
the surrounding American scene. Who are its neighbors, and what
are the points of contact between the immigrants and the dominant
language? How, and to what extent, do they learn English? How
are English words brought to them? Do young people avoid the old
language, or do they use it? The network of the official American
civilization acts upon the foreign community with a kind of psychic
compulsion, which the community cannot escape even while it is
speaking the foreign language. In many cases it is thoroughly Americanized even before it takes over English as its everyday tongue.

These are all questions on which the linguist and the social historian must work hand in hand, and their results will be mutually enlightening. Some aspects can be elucidated by direct questioning, but others will appear only through the linguistic analysis of community speech, which is the largest part of our work.

II. The analysis of speech. Under this head comes most of the actual labor with which we are here concerned. It is the most exacting and difficult part of our work, and the one that most linguists have been unwilling to undertake. It involves going out into the communities, making patient note of thousands upon thousands of words and phrases, and analyzing these for the information they can give.

One of the most apparent phenomena of immigrant languages is the great vocabulary shift. This is the immediate result of the enormous change in the immigrant's outward circumstances. Two complementary changes have taken place in his vocabulary: he has lost a great number of his native words, which lack a function in his new environment; in their place he has taken over a number of terms from the dominant language, English. His vocabulary is being atrophied at one end and renewed at the other in accompaniment to his changing personality and circumstances. A close analysis of these circumstances will frequently disclose the reasons for the adoption of English terms, which, in principle is exactly parallel to the adoption of loan words by every other language. This phenomenon is the one that has excited most attention because of the large scale on which it takes place, and because of the frequently amusing results to which it leads. No one has studied the complementary process: the words which are lost, and the reasons for their loss. We need analyses, not just of the words taken up, but of their proportion to the native words retained, and their frequency of use in the totality of discourse.

The study of the loaning process in the recent immigrant groups is particularly fruitful because all the forms in question can usually be determined with a high degree of phonetic accuracy. We are not often required to guess at the phonetic form of the word heard by the immigrant, or of the end result in the immigrant's speech, as is true in similar studies of languages of the past. The validity of sound laws as applied to the transfer of words from language to language finds its ultimate tests in this situation. The Englishmen who borrowed Scandinavian words in the tenth and eleventh centuries were, after all, doing exactly the same sort of thing as Scandinavians in the nineteenth century who adopt English words.

In some cases the forms of the immigrant language do not issue from forms now in general use. Even the Scandinavians of the Middle West have preserved forms that are now frequently extinct or obsolescent in the American of their neighbors. For instance, I have heard from older Norwegian speakers the pronunciation fasset for faucet, the word stoop for porch, and buttery for pantry. In such cases the immigrant usage throws interesting light on American speech in these neighborhoods.

The question frequently arises as to whether a given form may not be derived from print rather than from speech. On account of the sharp difference between English speech and spelling, it can often be shown that certain words have come to the immigrants through their reading rather than through their contact with English-speaking individuals.

Once the basic English form in question has been determined, the next goal is to trace the process of adaptation to the native system. This has been the chief object of study in this field, but it is far from attainment. We still need a great deal of material from various dialects and languages to determine the degree of assimilation. As I have pointed out in an article in Language, there seem to be two stages in this assimilation.[17] In the first there is almost complete adaptation, so that the words are made over into Norwegian words phonetically and morphologically. In the second the speakers are familiar with the English system and only partially fit the English words into the Norwegian system. In their speech we can therefore find two strata of loan words, the older ones, which are completely Norwegianized, and the more recent ones, which are partly or wholly English. Within this field there is room for extremely instructive studies of phonetic and phonemic systems, and their relative rigidity under conditions of stress. Similarly, a time comes in the morphological system when the English endings begin to acquire meaning. For example, the English plural -s is at first treated as a singular, but later its plural function is appreciated.

The structural shift is no less apparent in the syntax and semantics of the immigrants. They quite unconsciously are dominated by the word order and meaning patterns of their surroundings; they adopt innumerable English phrases by the process of translating their elements, e.g. well off, right away, it's up to you, etc. Words of clearly cognate form or meaning extend their sphere to include what the corresponding English terms include; e.g. American Norwegians always use their native word for 'corn,' cognate with the English, to mean 'Indian corn' although in Norway it referred to grain in general; they use their cognate to meal, which in Norway means 'flour,' to render English corn meal. These tendencies lead in the direction of a language which in its significant pattern corresponds very closely to English, and constitutes an excellent transitional stage to complete assimilation.

While the English material is being drawn into the native system, this system does not itself remain static. By comparison of the native material in the dialect with corresponding forms in the dialect as originally brought to this country, it is possible to see an evolutionary process in the dialect itself. This is brought on by internal change, as well as by contact with other dialects, with the standard written language as spoken by educated persons, and occasionally by contact with other foreign languages. I might note at this point, however, that there is practically no inter-Scandinavian influence. Where the Scandinavian languages meet, they remain rather strictly apart, unless the meeting takes place within one family. Where dialects and languages stand too far apart for easy, natural communication there seems to be a tendency to turn to English as a ready solution. These are also problems to which no attention has hitherto been devoted.

Altogether the study of immigrant speech offers an infinite variety of problems, which can be solved only by intensive gathering of material and thorough analysis of the results.

III. History of the Written Language. The study of the written traditions of the immigrant points beyond the local community to the whole body of each nationality. The individual contributes to this tradition every time he writes letters in his native tongue, whether back home, to friends in this country, or to the newspapers. These, however, would be currents lost in the sand if institutions did not arise to canalize and preserve the use of the written language. The chief ones of these institutions, at least among the Norwegians, are the church, the press, and the secular societies. In the early years the church maintained summer parochial schools in which children received their training in the Norwegian catechism and in Bible history. The press has been an influential bond between immigrants in various parts of the country, a forum for the group interests of each nationality. Through the press the rise of an immigrant literature has been made possible as well.

There is an abundance of material available for anyone who should wish to take up the study of the role these institutions have played in preserving and developing the foreign written languages in this country. Because these have been borne by men of more or less education, the process has in many respects run a different course from that of popular speech. One would have to investigate the relationship of these men to the written tradition in the native land, on the one hand, and, on the other, their position with respect to the spoken language of their countrymen in America. Authors have frequently depicted their countrymen in action, and valuable information on the spoken language can be garnered from their writings when used with proper caution. Their attitude to English has necessarily been colored by a greater resistance and conservatism than that of their unlettered countrymen, although they simultaneously were more wide-awake to the larger issues of the day. In spite of all conservatism, however, their resistance to English infiltration in vocabulary and syntax has been incomplete, and there are marked differences between their literary style and that of the homeland.

IV. Names. The last great division of our subject, the study of names, is intimately related to all three of the preceding. Names are used in speech and in writing, and they are community phenomena in a very high degree, characteristic of the social development. They supply a very delicate index to the attitudes and relationships of the immigrant toward his American surroundings, and his native tradition.[18]

Among Norwegians the custom of giving each farm a name was preserved in most larger communities. This exactly reversed the

Norwegian custom, by which the inhabitants derived their names from
the farms. Here the farms derived their names from the inhabitants,
and these names would often cling to the farm even though the inhabitants changed. Later owners might very well acquire the name of
the farm. Fields, hillocks, water-courses, and valleys have their
system of nomenclature. Most of these are comparatively imperma-
nent names, tied to the continued existence of the foreign language.
But they throw much interesting light on the folk life of the community.

In many cases the foreign group has left more permanent
memorials of its existence on the American map. It is a matter of
great interest to get the stories of such names noted before their
origin is lost. In most cases Americans had already named the communities in which the Scandinavians now live; but numerous lakes,
townships, villages, and even counties in the Middle West bear testimony to their national zeal. These have been reported on for certain areas by R. W. Swanson.[19]

The naming customs associated with animals are also of
interest. Cats, dogs, and other domestic pets were a part of the
social atmosphere. Horses have regularly been named. Among Norwegians this practice extended also to cows. These names are redo-
lent with old country atmosphere. They gradually gave way to American names or to none at all as the process of assimilation went on.

Most important are, of course, the names of persons. The
custom of given names can be studied advantageously in the local
church records, but these need to be supplemented with personal
interviews since the children who were given unpronounceable Norwegian names frequently refused to abide by them and substituted an
American Julia, or Emma, or Betty. I have found that such an
apparently unimportant question as the number of given names is of
interest. Norwegian custom was to give a single name, American to
give two. Norwegian-American church records show an almost
mathematical rate of progression from one to two.

Given names often yield to nicknames, either American or
Norwegian——a study which opens up the interesting field of folk humor.

The question of Norwegian family names has been given a
preliminary analysis in a doctoral dissertation prepared by Miss

Marjorie Kimmerle under my direction.[20]   This shows some of the
many facets of the subject. Among Norwegians the very custom of
family names was different from that of Americans. Thus we have
added to the purely phonetic difficulties the adjustment to a new way
of naming. This has resulted in differences between members of the
same family, so that four brothers may in America have four different family names. Among the Swedes such problems are less common, but they too faced the necessity of making their names pronoun-
ceable in English.[21]

        These suggestions will bring out some of the valuable results
that can be attained through the study of names, which frequently survive the passing of the foreign group, and have to take up their place
in general American life.

        If we now ask where all these studies lead, I think it will be
clear from the discussion of the various parts that we have in mind
nothing less than a total delineation of the immigrant as a communicating individual. From the moment he steps ashore in America to
the time when he or his descendants are completely assimilated to
the English-speaking community, he is a fit object for our study. All
Americans except the Indians have at one time or another been in
this position, and large sections of our population still are. Our
knowledge of America is not complete until we know what it means to
be an immigrant.

        The goal of our research is a detailed analysis of all linguis-
tic modes of expression and communication employed by members of
immigrant communities in America, with the view of elucidating the
social and psychological forces at work in such communities. This
is no mean or unworthy task, and it calls for every skill and every
method at the command of trained linguists.

        This conception of the goals of investigation is one that has
gradually emerged in my thinking as I have been at work collecting
and analyzing. My first immature attempts at collection began years
ago, when my interest in this subject was first aroused by the appendix to H. L. Mencken's The American Language, Third Edition.[22]
I made as complete a list as I could of all the English and many of
the Norwegian expressions in the American-Norwegian dialect I had

learned in my childhood home in Iowa. There the matter rested
until the summer of 1936, when the Research Committee of the University of Wisconsin made it possible for me to take up field work in
the settlements of the state. Since then I have spent a considerable
part of my spare time pursuing this work along several fronts, trying
to lay as broad a base as possible for future research. Three articles and a volume of lectures delivered at the University of Oslo in
1938 are the only published fruits of the work to date.[23] A great deal
of material has been accumulated, however, and when more time is
available, it should be possible to make rapid progress.

While we cannot here enter upon any questions of technical
detail, I shall sketch in outline my conception of the chief methods of
approach and some of the problems they raise.

Work can and must proceed along four principal fronts which
can be carried on by different workers, but which need careful coor-
dination. These are, the compilation of historical and statistical
material, comprehensive studies of individual speakers, field work
in selected communities or in larger areas, and exerpting of the
written literature.

I. Compilation of historical and statistical material. This
work, which was done for the Linguistic Atlas of New England by the
late Marcus Hansen of Illinois,[24] has been brilliantly carried forward for the Scandinavian group by a number of young scholars,
notably Theodore C. Blegen of Minnesota, whose Norwegian-American Historical Association is the most active and productive group of
its kind in this country. However, beyond the materials on general
Norwegian immigration which its publications, archives, and museum
offer, it is necessary to go to the local histories, and to the official
records of the communities. I have had copied out for Dane County,
in which Madison is located, census records, platbooks, church
records, baptismal records, and other material which has proved
useful both in a general way and specifically for the study of names.
All such records, however, need to be supplemented by personal
interviews with older members of the community, whose view of the
past is less official, but more intimate.

II. Study of individuals. For a number of important purposes
it is essential to have as complete vocabularies of the communities

and family groups as possible. For a field worker to get this would require months, perhaps years of labor; but with the help of word lists and some training, an interested and educated speaker of the dialect can do wonders in this respect. There are nuances in the dialects and aspects of the phonetic systems that only a native can perceive with any confidence. In the case of Norwegian we have two such lists of English loan words in print, produced by students of language born in these communities, the lists by Flaten and Flom mentioned above. I can supplement these with my own unpublished list from Iowa, and the remarkable work of one of my former students, Mr. Odin Anderson, who took the trouble to make vocabulary cards for more than 4000 words in his native American-Norwegian dialect of western Wisconsin, with complete phonetic, grammatical, and lexical information for each. With the help of such educated or educable informants, it is possible to get at aspects of language that would otherwise remain hidden or uncertain.

It is necessary that the subject be trained in the use of phonemic transcription and that a useful system of designating relevant grammatical phenomena be devised. Two tasks can then be set before him: the compilation of a tentatively complete vocabulary of his community, and the dictation or preparation of illustrative texts, as long as possible.

Before one has such material as that described, it is very difficult to create a questionnaire for the use of field workers who approach a community without previous knowledge or contacts. But this is, of course, the next step.

III. Field work by trained workers. My own questionnaire for field work was created on the basis of the word lists I have described above, plus corresponding lists of dialect material in Norway. The general framework of the Linguistic Atlas of New England was adopted because it seemed the most useful way of presenting the material asked about. This meant that once the words and questions were chosen, they were arranged under meaningful heads so that conversation with the informants might proceed along reasonably coherent lines.

The contents of a questionnaire should consist of three broad types of material. First of all, general and cultural questions which

serve two purposes: (1) to learn the subject's own background and
interests and his place within the framework of his group; and (2) to
provide a stimulus to free talk by the subject for observation of
casual speech phenomena and to check the accuracy of his linguistic
statements. Then there must be a number of words and phrases that
serve to illustrate the phonological and grammatical system. These
should, if possible, be chosen from corresponding dialect questionnaires in the homeland, for the sake of convenient comparison with
the dialect work of that country. Then there must be an appropriate
selection of objects and ideas frequently or universally designated by
American loanwords. These should be selected for their value in
elucidating the problems we have set forth earlier, problems of
phonology, gender, aspect, and many others.

It is extremely useful to accompany the questionnaire with a
booklet of illustrations, drawn to show all or most of the objects
asked about. The advantage of this is twofold: to save the field
worker time wasted on roundabout explanations, and to make sure of
what was actually asked about. Such illustrations, however, must
be well and clearly drawn. My own book of illustrations is compiled
from pictures in magazines, Sears Roebuck catalogs, and the like,
and is more entertaining than really effective. But it is a great help.

In the training of field workers it is of course a primary
requisite that they be well schooled in practical phonetics and that
they show a capacity for hearing and retaining sound distinctions.
Beyond this they must have a background of linguistic knowledge
which enables them to judge the value of what they hear. It is preferable that they speak the language in question and ask the questions
in that language, though there is no absolute barrier to asking them
in English, if the informant is bilingual. But it will establish greater
sympathy with the informant if he is able to converse in the native
tongue, even if it is not the dialect of the informant. In my own conversation I approach my Norwegian as closely to that of the informant
as I can.

The problem of finding informants is not always an easy one.
It sometimes requires going around and doing a good deal of informal
listening, or even starting interviews which have to be abandoned.
Not all persons can be made to understand what is desired; some are

suspicious and unwilling, though among Norwegians that is quite rare. More persons are inclined to regard the whole business as foolish and purposeless, or as done with the purpose of eventual ridicule. Within a representative community one can usually find persons who are talkative and genial, who have some spare time, and who are integral and representative members of the community. Whenever possible, I select persons born in this country. I usually get the advice of the local pastor or other persons well acquainted with the community, and then let one informant lead me to another.

It is important to clarify one's purpose to the informants, though this is sometimes impossible. If, as has happened to me, the informant gets the impression that one is interested only in old times or in the 'pure dialect,' as brought across, it is almost impossible to get the current Americanized expressions. The informant will then hesitate when his impulse is to answer with an English loan word, and search his memory for the 'correct' Norwegian word. It is a delight to find an informant who clearly understands that it is his own everyday expression one wants.

The first problem of the field worker is a suitable method of transcription. In my own case I started using the Norwegian dialect alphabet, devised by Johan Storm in 1884, but soon found that it was inadequate for rapid field work. On becoming acquainted with the work of the New England Atlas, I gradually adopted its general framework, based on the IPA alphabet. This would seem the best for all such American work, although each language group will find it necessary to make modifications to suit its own sound system. Since comparisons have to be made with European dialect literature, one does not wish to move too far away from the systems employed in the national literatures.

While most of the work has to be done by hand and ear, the use of a recording apparatus is an invaluable supplement to the handwritten records. A machine provided by the Research Committee of the University has made it possible for me to make a number of records. Even the use of a phonograph has its problems, including that of producing a natural situation in which the speaker will not be inhibited.

When the results of the field work are all in, there is still
the job of compiling and evaluating the results. Each person's record must be worked through to find the phonetic and grammatical
system of his dialect, and its relation to the loan words discovered.
It will often be found necessary to go back and check with the speaker
on the accuracy of certain notations. Shades of sound that are heard
once are not always significant. Many problems of the reliability of
such records arise as one works them over. Native forms given are
frequently older and more Norwegian than the ones in actual use;
there is a tendency to suppress American loan words if the speaker
can think of a corresponding native word; but when one does get the
loan words, they are usually given in a reliable form.

From this point begin the analyses which lead to some of the
results previously indicated as desirable. One thing has been apparent: the making of such records takes a great deal of time and their
analysis even more. My own questionnaire started with about 1000
questions, which I cut down to 800 in the second summer. It still
took anywhere from eight to ten hours, or three evenings. As I have
worked with it, I see clearly that many questions can be solved without so elaborate a questionnaire. I am now planning a shorter questionnaire, which can be completed in about three hours, and will
cover the essentials in the actual loaning process. In this way it
will be possible to cover a greater area and make more confident
generalizations about the extension of certain forms.

IV. Excerpting the written literature. The last task, and
one that fortunately can await the progress of the others, is the study
of the written literature for its linguistic information. This is essential to the third goal above, the history of the written language, but
it will also throw light on the other purposes. I have made one collection of primary material which I expect to work through some
time in the future; namely, the entire correspondence with its subscribers of a leading Norwegian-American newspaper during a period
of three months. These several hundred letters are written by persons with a variety of literary backgrounds, and many of them give
valuable information on the speech of the writers, as well as a strong
impression of their state of literacy. They have the advantage over
printed materials that they have not been edited or proofread, and
hence not subjected to the rulebook of the standard language.

For that aspect of the literary tradition one has to go to the printed literature. Among Norwegians there has been a certain amount of actual dialect literature; but most of the printed matter is in the standard language and the orthography of the time when the immigrants left Norway. Their conservative trend in this respect is a familiar fact. Memoirs, periodicals, and belles-lettres all contain material that is illustrative, as well as directly informative. Discussions of the language situation, both within the Norwegian-American world and in relation to English, are found in these. Imitations of popular speech, with its mixture, are often printed, though they are not too reliable as specimens of speech. But they, too, are part of the story.

This concludes my general remarks about the methods that seem most valuable toward attaining our goals. They are not intended to exhaust the possibilities; there must always be room for further ingenuity. But they cover the field, and apply, I believe, not only to the study of Norwegian, but mutatis mutandis to each of the immigrant tongues of America. With this ground plan it should be possible to work out integrated programs for the analysis of as many such tongues as it seems necessary.

It is clear that each of the topics listed above calls for articles and monographs, depending upon the depth and extent of analysis made; but while we are working on the details, we must not lose sight of the ultimate goals. We are gathering materials for a comprehensive analysis, first, of each significant immigrant group and its problems of expression, then, of the way in which each of these groups feeds into American life and becomes a part of these United States. Beyond the monographs lie the possibilities of building up greater syntheses which deserve a wider public than most of our linguistic studies ever get.

NOTES

[1] The American Transition (Northfield, Minnesota, 1940), pp. 69-99. The first volume was entitled Norwegian Migration to America 1825-1860 (Northfield, Minnesota, 1931).
[2] Kindly submitted to the writer before its publication by Professor Blegen.

[3] See Peter Kalm's Travels in North America, vol. II, 687-89 (Ed. A. B. Benson, New York, 1937).

[4] "English loan-nouns used in the Icelandic colony of North Dakota," Dialect Notes II (1903), 354 f.

[5] Det svenska språket i Amerika. Stockholm, 1900 (Studentföreningen Verdandis Småskrifter 87).

[6] "Ett och annat rörande svenskan i Amerika." Språk och Stil XI(1911), 17-28. The monograph planned by Professor Elmquist and referred to in a footnote to this article has never appeared.

[7] "Svenskan i Amerika. Studier i de utvandrades språk." Språk och Stil IV (1904), 1-21. Errors pointed out in Ungdomsvännen (Rock Island, Illinois) 1904, p. 348 ff. and corrected in a supplement to the original article in Språk och Stil V (1905), 250 ff.

[8] "Engelskans inflytande på det svenska språket i Amerika." Ungdomsvännen (Rock Island, Illinois) 1904, pp. 179 ff., 204 ff., 243 ff.

[9] Vilhelm Berger, Vårt Språk. Rock Island, 1912; Johan Person, "Vårt Språk," in Svensk Amerikanska Studier (Rock Island, 1912); Ernest W. Olson, "Grodor ur svartbacken," in Bläckfisken (published by Swedish Journalists' Association in America), 1920; G. H. Nordqvist, "Svenska Språket i Amerika," in Svenskarna i Amerika, Vol. II (Stockholm, 1925); Vilhelm Berger, "Svensk-amerikanska språket." Nysvenska Studier XV (1935), 1-37.

[10] Swedish in America. 184 pp. Kindly submitted to the writer by Professor Gustafson. The greater number of the titles in the preceding footnote are drawn from Professor Gustafson's thesis.

[11] Op. cit., 43.

[12] "Nogle Eiendommeligheder ved de til Amerika udvandrede Nordmænds Sprog. Prøveforelæsning for Doktorgraden." Morgenbladet (Oslo), April 11 and 18, 1897. (Reprinted in Decorah-Posten, Decorah, Iowa, September 8 and 11, 1931).

[13] "Notes on American Norwegian with a Vocabulary." Dialect Notes II (1900), 115-126. Professor Flaten has returned more recently to this subject with a collection of amusing anecdotes in Norwegian-American: "Valdris-Rispo," Maal og Minne (Oslo, 1939), 30-50.

[14] "English Elements in Norse Dialects of Utica, Wisconsin." Dialect Notes II (1902), 257-267. "The Gender of English Loan Nouns in Norse Dialects in America," JEGP V (1903), 1-31. "Det norske sprogs bruk og utvikling i Amerika," Nordmannsforbundet 1912,

233-250. "English Loan-words in American Norwegian," American Speech I (1926), 541-558. "On the phonology of English Loan-words in the Norwegian Dialects of Koshkonong in Wisconsin," Studier tillägnade Axel Kock (1929), 178-189. "Um det norske målet i Amerika," Norsk Aarbok XI (Bergen, 1931), 113-124.

[15] The only published results appeared in a popular article by Didrik Arup Seip, "Nordmenn og norsk språk i Amerika," Ord och bild, 1932, pp. 253-259.

[16] Bilingualism (Calcutta, 1926), p. 17.

[17] "Phonological Shifting in American Norwegian," XIV (1938), 112-120.

[18] See on the whole problem of names the chapter entitled "Navneskikk i nybygden" in my book, Norsk i Amerika (Oslo, 1939), 60-77. [Now also my Norwegian Language in America, chapter 9.]

[19] "Scandinavian Place-Names in the Danelaw." Swedish-American Historical Bulletin II (1929), 5-17.

[20] Norwegian Surnames of the Koshkonong and Springdale Congregations in Dane County, Wisconsin. Madison, 1938, (unpublished). "Norwegian-American Surnames," Norwegian-American Studies and Records. XII (1941), 1-32; "Norwegian-American Surnames in Transition," American Speech, 17 (1942), 158-165.

[21] Roy W. Swanson, "The Swedish Surname in America." American Speech III (1928), 468-477.

[22] New York, 1923. Greatly enlarged in the fourth edition, New York, 1936, where the Scandinavian section is found between pages 624 and 633.

[23] "Language and Immigration," Norwegian-American Studies and Records (Northfield, Minnesota) X, 1-43 (1938); "Phonological Shifting in American Norwegian," Language XIV (1938), 112-120; "Intonation Patterns in American Norwegian," Language XVII (1941), 40-48; Norsk i Amerika (Oslo, 1939), containing chapters entitled "Det store landnåm." "Bondemål og bygdefolk," "Fra bygdemål til verdenssprog," "Navneskikk i nybygden," "Skrift og tale," "Diktende trang," and five dialect specimens.

[24] See Handbook of the Linguistic Geography of New England (Providence, 1939), p. x.

3 | Problems of Bilingualism

The problems connected with the influence of one language on another have played a large role in the discussions of linguistic science. Such words as 'language mixture', 'loanwords', 'substratum', 'sound substitution' are key terms that bob up everywhere in linguistic studies. Yet there are relatively few who have made this field their primary concern, and we can hardly say that the basic laws of interlingual influence are fully clarified. Investigators who have erected hypotheses to explain some of the results of bilingualism have not always checked their theories by studies of the behavior of bilingual speakers. These are, after all, the carriers of interlingual contagion, and to them we must look for an understanding of processes that must have operated in the distant past as well as in the present. Talk of substrata and superstrata must remain stratospheric unless we can found it solidly on the behavior of living, observable speakers. In the following discussion, the writer wishes to summarize some recent studies made in this field and try to generalize their results in the form of statements that may help us to predict in some degree the behavior of bilingual speakers. While he has kept his own researches in American-Norwegian to one side in this discussion, he has not hesitated to make occasional reference to parallel phenomena personally observed as well as to relevant comments from the literature. [1]

Few countries could be more ideally suited for bilingual study than the United States. According to the census of 1940, there were then still 21,996,240 white Americans whose childhood language had not been English. To these we may add a very considerable Indian population. Most of these several million Americans were by birth predestined to be bilingual speakers. Yet the subject was for many years markedly neglected in this country, and we might say that both

popularly and scientifically, bilingualism was in disrepute. Just as
the bilingual himself often was a marginal personality, so the study
of his behavior was a marginal scientific pursuit. In recent years
there has been a heartening growth of interest, marked not least by
the impulses emanating from the American Dialect Atlas. A conference held at Ann Arbor, Michigan, in the summer of 1940 marked the
first gathering of forces toward a broad-scale attack on the problems
of non-English languages in America, which in effect means the problems of bilingualism.[2] A spate of articles, dissertations, and even
some published books bear witness to the intrinsic interest and importance attributed to the topic.

(1) As the type of an old-established, non-English dialect,
we shall take Pennsylvania German; only Canadian (and Louisiana)
French and Southwestern American Spanish are comparable. Shortly
after the founding of Pennsylvania by William Penn, the Germans
began to arrive. The first settlement was in 1683, the bulk of the
settlers immigrated between 1720 and 1750, and by the time of the
Revolution they constituted about one third of the population of the
colony.[3] For two centuries these thrifty and industrious farmers
have thus been settled fairly compactly and within one area. They
date back to a time before the creation of an American nation, when
the pressure from the English-speaking environment was relatively
small. Their pride of ancestry, their cultural and religious exclu-
siveness, and their economic strength have made them a little island
in the American world. Only the persistent industrialization of this
century has begun to make inroads on them, and it is a minor irony
that just when signs are appearing of a breakdown in the use of PaG,
it has become the object of linguistic attention as never before. Thanks
to the initiative of Hans Kurath while director of the New England Dialect Atlas, we are better informed today about this language than any
other non-English American speech.[4]

Among the several studies of PaG, there are some that deal
primarily with the influence of English on this German dialect of the
Rhine Palatinate. From these we learn that E has scarcely left any
mark on its phonology or morphology, but has enriched its vocabulary
by several hundred loanwords in common use.[5] These include many
terms for objects first met with in America, such as bushel, college,
cracker, county, pie, township, etc. But they also include many terms

for which good German words were available, even in the rural dialects, e.g. bockabuch 'pocketbook', fence-eck 'fence corner'. For
some terms there is vacillation between E and G words: geld beside
'money', disch beside 'table', and schulmeeschter beside 'teacher'.[6]
As Learned noted as long ago as 1889, the use of English words, even
in their native German, was stimulated by the need of transacting business with English-speaking tradesmen and dealing with representatives
of the American government.[7]

The loans have generally been adapted to the sound system
of PaG, but we have the testimony of J.W. Frey that earlier and later
loans can be distinguished according to the extent of adaptation. Thus
E $t > d$ in the early loan 'timothy', but remained t in later words.[8]
They have been fitted into the native morphological patterns, such as
gender and verb tenses, according to principles discussed in articles
by Carroll E. Reed and Lester W. Seifert.[9] Some E material has
been so thoroughly assimilated that new words have come into being
like uff-g'sobered 'sobered up' and Gekick 'constant kicking (grumb-
ling)'. Paul Schach has presented numerous examples of what he calls
'hybrid derivatives', like becksel 'small box', and 'hybrid compounds',
like wasserschpiket 'water spigot' and endschelfutkuche 'angelfood
cake'.[10]

Today, Schach informs us, 'nearly all PaGermans are bilingual'. The youngest generation understands the language, but many
of them 'cannot (or pretend they cannot) speak it very fluently'. This
is confirmed by Reed, of whose 42 informants 25 used English extensively.[11] The E spoken, however, is often phonetically inaccurate,
with occasional German turns of phrase; but on the whole the younger
generation speaks a good English.[12]

(2) As the type of a more recent immigration, we may study
the situation among the Portuguese immigrants of Massachusetts.
This has been described in a recent monograph by Leo Pap.[13] From
his book we learn that the P were first drawn to this country by the
whaling industry. In the first two-thirds of the 19th century it was
common for Yankee whaling captains of New Bedford to replenish their
crews by taking on men in the Azores. Many of these settled in New
Bedford and nearby cities. After the middle of the century womenfolk
and children began to follow the fishermen to New England, and by

1870 mass immigration set in. Whaling was by this time passé, and
the attraction of New England lay in its textile mills. By 1900 'the
bulk of the Portuguese were working in the New Bedford and Fall River
factories.'[14]

Many of them acquired small farms; it came to be said, 'If
you want to see a potato grow, speak to it in Portuguese.'[15] Pap has
shown how the immigrants formed cohesive groups, bound together
by common linguistic and religious traditions, though split by many
internal feuds. Some have wanted to perpetuate the national tradition,
but the younger generation 'appear strongly Americanized in behavior
and outlook.'[16] If they speak P at all, they do so imperfectly, while
their E shows hardly a trace of P influence.

The P language spoken by the older generation, however, has
undergone the same kind of large-scale borrowing from English as
has PaG. Phonology and syntax have remained unaffected, except for
occasional intonational changes and the introduction of E word order
in certain phrases, e.g. Portugues Recreativo Club instead of Club
Recreativo Portugues. Examples have also been noted of the use of
intransitive verbs like marchar 'to march' in transitive connections
as in English, e.g. Fagundes marched his men across.[17] Words for
all kinds of cultural novelties were freely adopted: foods such as
cake, pudding, sandwich; clothing such as slacks, sweater, overalls
(alverozes); terms for housing such as building, cottage, bungalow,
hall; amusements, such as picnic, barbecue, clambake. In general,
terms for politics, sports, diseases, law, school, means of communication, economic life were overwhelmingly American. P remained
the terms for the human body and its functions, for family relations,
and other phases of life in which the immigrants did not come into
immediate contact with American speakers.

Pap points out that in addition to the necessary, cultural loans
there is a massive assortment of terms that are borrowed because they
were associated with a new system of political and linguistic organization. 'Many words frequently heard impose themselves by the sheer
force of repetition.'[18] Words like 'sure', 'O.K.', 'never mind' carry
emotional connotations that could not easily be conveyed by similar
Portuguese expressions. When they go so far as to borrow E words
for potatoes, tomatoes, butter, and milk, he declares that it is nothing

else than 'the plain impact of intimate linguistic contact in an advanced state.'

The loans made are incorporated into the language in two ways: either they are borrowed entire, or else they may influence native words. In some cases the resulting loans are homonymous with native words of totally different meaning, e.g. P bordar 'embroider' acquires also the meaning of E 'board'. Some loans are entirely adapted to P patterns, while others are relatively unadapted. In determining the assignment of gender forms, the most important influence is natural gender, then suffixes, and occasionally a synonymous native word. But there is great vacillation in gender, though nouns that are otherwise unadapted are generally masculine, unless they refer to female beings. Morphological suffixes are sometimes added to loanwords, but not always.

AmP shows certain interesting perculiarities in its vocabulary loans. E 'spring' and 'fall' are borrowed; the year has only two seasons in Portugal. Of the twelve months only July is borrowed, due to the expression fode julaia 'Fourth of July'; Christmas is borrowed. A distinction is made between natural ice, for which P gelo is used, and artificial ice, for which E 'ice' is used.

(3) One group of peoples whose loanword problems have not been seriously considered until quite recently are the American Indians. They were not even included in the previously mentioned conference at Ann Arbor on non-English speech. Yet here are peoples native to the Americas over a far longer period than the Spanish and English invaders. Socially they have been in an even more subordinate position than the most recent European immigrants. An interesting description is available of conditions among the Yaqui, a tribe in Arizona, whose villages were hispanicized by missionaries and political functionaries by the end of the 17th century.[19] Spicer shows how this kind of 'directed culture change' resulted in a one-sided borrowing from Spanish, with very few loan-translations or original inventions. Today 65% of the domestic utensils, social organizations, and religious rituals are named in Spanish terms. Even their term for praying is part Spanish: liosnóoka from Sp dios 'God' and nóoka 'speak'.

Here as elsewhere there are considerable differences in the extent of adaptation of individual words. Spicer believes that the most

markedly modified words were introduced before 1800 when the Yaquis
as a group were not widely familiar with Spanish. Since that time the
tribe has become at least 50% bilingual, and new Spanish words are
admitted freely, without modification. Thus the word for 'stove' was
borrowed from Sp estufa as ehtupa, with a change of f to p; but in the
recent fonografo the f's are not changed. As for the extent of original
creation, the author feels that 'it would seem possible to have invented
descriptive terms which utilized Yaqui roots or to have applied the
names for approximate equivalents', but this was rarely done.

Among the Pima Indians the situation was somewhat different. George Herzog has shown that here a number of descriptive
terms did come into being. They call raisins 'dry grapes', elephant
'wrinkled buttocks', and battery 'lightning box.' He attributes this
activity to a period when the Indians were left pretty much to themselves after the departure of the Spanish and before closer contacts
were established with the Americans. There are, of course, loanwords from the Spanish, and with the establishment of English schools
and a growing bilingualism, English terms are slipping into their
speech with an ease that 'reminds one of what happens to the native
vocabulary of immigrants in this country'. [20]

(4) By way of comparison we may now turn away from the
United States and study a European situation where the contact between
the two languages has been less intimate. In a recent monograph on
E lws. in Modern Norwegian, Aasta Stene has surveyed the conditions
of 'linguistic borrowing in the process.' [21] Through travellers and
tourists, emigrants and sailors a lively traffic has been going on between Norway and the English-speaking world, particularly since the
beginning of the eighteenth century. But in contrast with the situations
described from the United States, most of the words have entered by
way of the written language. Schools have actively taught the language,
giving at least a smattering to most people with a higher education.
English and American books in the original and films with sound have
been spreading it even more widely in recent years. The 'culture
carriers' are Norwegians who have learned English as a foreign language.

The several hundred words that have come in through the
activity of these bilinguals she sums up as 'representative of the age

of the Industrial Revolution.[122]   They are words from the field of
sports: team, outsider, fair play, halfback, knockout, golf, hickory,
splitcane; travel, especially railroad engineering, road building,
motoring and flying: sightseeing, globetrotter, trapper, and wild
west; sailing and shipping: trawler, steward, skylight, deadweight;
trade: boom, check, pool, trademark, bestseller. Highly characteristic are words for dress and fashions: plaid, tweed, pigskin,
smart, up-to-date, sweater, make-up; food and drink: gin, sherry,
cocktail, bar, bootlegger, beef, grill; cultural: film, essay, short-
story, folklore, sketch; government and politics: home rule, boycott,
strike, detective, gangster, revolver, boomerang; society: gang,
mob, gentleman, slum, all right, OK, chummy, rough, square, bluff,
flirt, bum, job, baby, drawback.

In their formal treatment of these words the N behave just as
do other bilingual speakers. Some of the words they pronounce with
some semblance of the English sounds, such as retaining the E diphthongs or the sound of w. This is especially true, says Miss Stene,
of words which 'are felt by the N speaker to be distinctly alien, words
that are mentally given in quotation marks.'[123] In her word list she
marks these with a special symbol, e.g. blizzard, speakeasy, darling,
dreadnought, five o'clock tea. But even those that she does not so
mark are by no means completely assimilated to the N pattern. Miss
Stene has set up a list of synchronic criteria for detecting these, and
excludes (as being no longer 'loanwords' in her definition) words which
show none of these 'foreign' criteria.[24] Among monolinguals who
adopt the new words, the model of pronunciation becomes either the
spelling itself or the E pronunciation of N bilinguals. The greater
influence of the spelling is apparent when one compares the pronunciation of lws. in American Norwegian: E 'bus' > N buss, AmN båss;
E 'check' > N sjekk, AmN kjekk.

The morphology shows a similar range from partial to complete adaptation. While verbs are completely fitted into the pattern,
adjectives often fail to get N suffixes for neuter and plural. Nouns
like 'cocktail' get E rather than N plurals. Some compounds are
adopted in full; some are partially translated, e.g. grapefrukt 'grape-
fruit', filmstjerne 'film star'; others are completely translated, e.g.
fotball 'football'.

As we have seen, there is a high degree of similarity between the phenomena here described, and more examples would only lead to repetition. In each case we have found a bilingual group that served as the vehicle of interlingual influence, and we are probably justified, with Hermann Paul, in regarding such a group as indispensable to any large-scale borrowing. [25]

Our first problem in each case is to discover how such a group came into existence. Why did certain members of one socio-linguistic group learn the language of another? The learning of one language in early childhood is apparently a universal human accomplishment. But the mastery of two or more requires a special explanation in each case. Its practitioners are not indulging in a common group activity, but are developing a special skill, somewhat in the class of acrobatics, woodcarving, or piano playing. In brief, we may say that a bilingual comes into being because he is subject to linguistic pressure from speakers of two languages rather than one. Linguistic pressure is a special type of social pressure which operates to produce linguistic conformity. Such pressure goes beyond the requirements of mere understanding, involving as it does a requirement of identity and identification. In describing interlingual influence, we shall first want to establish the nature, strength, and origin of the linguistic pressure that has brought into being a mediating group of bilingual speakers.

In the United States a rather powerful pressure of an economic, political, and social nature is exerted on minority language groups. These, in turn, set up counterpressures of a frequently religious or cultural nature to maintain their linguistic identity. In the case of modern English in Norway, however, the pressure results from the overwhelming international importance of English, as transmitted by the schools, the radio, the films, the newspapers, and commercial channels. The bilingual group is a minority whose influence will extend only as far as national pride and tradition permit.

One of the most useful quantitative measures of linguistic pressure and counterpressure is to be found in the number and prestige of people who learn the 'other' language. The strength and direction of influence between e.g. English and Yaqui may be gauged by the relative proportion between the number of Americans who learn Yaqui and the number of Yaqui who learn English. But here we must distinguish between various kinds of bilinguals, particularly between childhood and adult bilinguals. The former may roughly be defined as those who learn their second language before their fourteenth year. If the two languages in question are called a and b, we may then distinguish the following types of speakers: A native monolinguals, A_b adult bilinguals, AB childhood bilinguals (who acquired a before b). Within the same community, especially if it is in linguistic transition from language a to b, we will also find speakers BA, Ba, and B. We may even have the type aB, who have learned a in childhood, but lost their facility in it through lack of later practice. A numerical and social analysis of the relative strength of these various groups will tell us much concerning the trends and direction of linguistic pressure within the community.

The tendency of one language to replace the other under such circumstances is a well-known historical phenomenon. But as linguists we are most strongly interested in the mutual influences on the languages themselves. These are in general proportionate to the degree of linguistic pressure. In America it is clearly evident in the relation between English and the many immigrant languages. These have all been profoundly influenced by English, but have had only a local and rather evanescent influence on English.

In refutation of earlier beliefs to the contrary, Bertil Malmberg has recently shown that this is also the case with the Indian languages of South America in their relation to Spanish.[26] Windisch formulated the relationship in terms of the individual learner in his famous thesis of 1897: it is the language of the learner that is influenced, not the language he learns.[27]

The weakness of Windisch's formulation lies in the fact that it obviously does not apply to the mature language learner with whom we are most familiar in our foreign language classes or among adult immigrants. These maltreat the language they learn according to the habits of their own rather than the converse. Windisch's thesis remains a paradox unless we read it in the light of the language learner's total social situation. The learning of a foreign language does not in itself affect his native tongue; but the same force that has caused him to learn the language also causes him to modify his own. The direction of linguistic pressure places him in a stream of influence where he is below the speakers of the other language, but above the speakers of his own. Any pollution he causes will flow downstream to his own countrymen. In more precise terms we may say that he is only an outsider within the group whose language he is learning; but within his own he may often gain prestige by his very knowledge of the other language, so that his innovations have a chance of spreading.

Such a situation must have existed in England at the time of the Norman dominance. We may even suspect that the true originators of that curious patchwork which is modern English were the servants of the Norman-French nobles. The grooms and maids, whose native tongue was English, learned more or less bad French to converse with their masters. Large chunks of this French must have found their way into the English they spoke among themselves, and even to their Anglo-Saxon cousins and aunts. But when their masters gave up French, the English they learned and eventually made into the cultured tongue of the land was the speech they acquired in the nurseries from their own servants.

It is interesting to compare the pressure situations of the American immigrants acquiring English with those of the European intellectual. The English terms acquired by the PaG speakers were of general importance, involving crucial terms of American social and governmental life. But in Norway the terms were of rather special nature, being of greatest interest to only a limited section of the population. The immigrants were thrown into practical day-by-day contact with American life, while the Europeans were largely in indirect contact. The immigrant bilingual lacked social status, and his struggle to acquire it involved the need of accommodating within his language the entire structure of official and economic life in his new homeland. He was under strong pressure to acquire the new distinctions made by native speakers; any others that were provided for by his own language became superfluous and tended to be forgotten.

Most important for the immigrant was the fact that the new situations in which he learned his English were shared by a large number of other speakers of his own language. They were all in the same boat, drifting in the same direction. Without affectation or snobbishness they were speaking an Americanized tongue to each other before they were fully aware of what was happening to them. The needs of understanding and of social solidarity were most effortlessly met by a gradual infiltration of loans. These were not limited to actual cultural novelties or socalled 'necessary' words; the terms most characteristic of the new environment were often impressed on their minds by mere repetition in vivid situations. Their experience in the new language began to outstrip their experience in the old, and the discrepancy set up a pressure which led to linguistic change.

So far we have tacitly assumed that linguistic pressures are determined by social conditions alone. This is not necessarily true, and the question has been raised whether there are innate differences between languages which influence their susceptibility to borrowing. Sapir expressed the opinion that 'the psychological attitude of the borrowing language itself towards linguistic material has much to do with its receptivity to foreign words.'[128] He compares the freedom with which English has borrowed from French to the resistance set up by German, and he attributes the difference to a German desire to have analyzable linguistic units. But the experience of immigrants in this country would not seem to confirm this theory, since there is no marked difference between the languages so far analyzed, when differences of social conditions are taken into account. It seems likely that the difference between English and German in this respect is rather a result of the overwhelming social impact of the Scandinavian and Norman invasions, which set up a presumption in favor of the loanword and a technique for handling them. Yet we cannot overlook the possibility that a well-established technique of borrowing will facilitate further borrowing, and that certain types of similarities between languages may become the foci of linguistic importation.

To settle questions of this kind a far-reaching comparison of lws. in the various immigrant tongues should be helpful. Here a uniform influence has been exerted under reasonably comparable conditions on a multitude of different languages. Even a superficial comparison reveals that some of the words borrowed must be due to special conditions within each language. As mentioned earlier, AmP has borrowed E 'spring' and 'fall'; in AmN these are never borrowed, for the native terms are too well established. AmP has borrowed 'ice' in connection with artificial ice; but the phonetically similar N is has made this superfluous in AmN. The cognates appear to be useful points of contact in such cases. AmN does not import E 'corn' (in the sense of 'maize'), but substitutes its own korn in the functions of the E word. In a study of these rather intricate relationships, we must avoid the historical assumptions involved in such a word as 'cognate'. The speakers are of course unaware of, or unable to determine with any accuracy the historical relationships. We need to use words in this connection that will emphasize the synchronic similarity of sound and meaning which leads to contact and confusion. Instead of 'cognates', we might call such words 'analogues', since they occupy an analogical position within the structures of the two languages being compared. Those that are similar in sound and not in meaning might be called 'homophones', defined as 'interlingual homonyms or near-homonyms'; those that are similar in meaning and not in sound might be called 'homologues', defined as 'interlingual synonyms or near-synonyms'.

The influence of pure homophones on one another in the be-havior of bilinguals can be demonstrated at every turn, though it has not often been mentioned in the literature. In AmN the E words 'field' and 'lake' have received their phonetic and grammatical forms from the semantically unrelated and non-cognate N words fil 'file' and leik 'game'. In AmP the E word 'closet' has acquired the unexpected vowel au in the first syllable, under evident influence from such words as P clausura and claustro. In AmP the prefix 'over-' in such words as 'overshoes' and 'overalls' does not begin with the expected o-, but with al-, from a native prefix of Arabic origin.

The importance of structural relationships is of course un-questionable when we turn to the question of how words have been bor-rowed rather than of why they were borrowed.

Whenever a bilingual speaker draws upon elements from one system to fill in a gap in another, he is compelled to make some sort of rapid adjustment of patterns. This process I should venture to compare to that which a linguist goes through in making a linguistic analysis. The bilingual's behavior may be described as a rough-and-ready, practical operation of comparative linguistics. Perhaps this explains why so many bilinguals become linguists: they already have a natural start toward this kind of activity. In becoming scientists they acquire greater sophistication and superior methods of organiza-tion.

This comparison of loanword adaptation with linguistic analysis does not seem to have been made before. But it is clear that in
becoming bilingual a speaker of language a is required to set up a
competing system b, which covers almost the same ground and serves
similar purposes. The nature of this process is still imperfectly understood, though such studies as Werner Leopold's on infant bilingualism are adding greatly to our insight.[29] In transferring items of behavior from one pattern to the other, some more or less unconscious
analysis must be made of their relative positions in the two patterns.
Each new item will be interpreted as either made up of two or more
items in the other pattern or as being identical with or different from
the items in that pattern.

A speaker of AmN must have gone through some such process
in producing the form beis from E 'basin'. On hearing the final -ən
of the E word, he has automatically analyzed it as a suffixed definite
article, for so it would be in his native language. To form a suitable
root for the adding of other suffixes, such as the plural, he subtracts
the last syllable and comes out with a new plural not warranted by
direct imitation of E 'basins', viz. beiser. A French Canadian would
interpret this final -n in quite a different way. In his language a final
-n is a sign of feminine gender, so any word ending in a nasal group
is likely to be fitted into the category of feminines, e.g. E 'van' >
vanne, 'cent' > senne, 'tongue' > tonne, all feminine according to Ernest Haden.[30] Similarly in phonology, as when a Japanese speaker
interprets the cluster dr- in drama as being syllabic.[31]

The procedure is often described as one of substituting 'the
nearest native sound.' But there is no apparent way of defining 'nearest' except in subjective terms: that is the nearest sound which bilingual speakers choose to substitute. It seems probable that other
factors enter than the purely phonetic ones of sound quality and quantity. We are not yet prepared to state a measure of objective similarity which will enable us to predict the behavior of the bilingual adapter.
So many factors are involved, that only the most complete structural
descriptions are likely to be of much help, going beyond even those
that are possible today.

The problem of description is greatly complicated by the fact
that the very process of learning alters the learner's view of the

relation between the respective structures. He begins by identifying
elements in the new language with rather different ones in his own,
but he ends (in the most favorable conditions) by learning to distinguish
even the most delicate shades of difference between the two languages.
As a result, 'sound laws' are difficult to establish with any confidence.
We have seen the efforts of analysts to distinguish various layers of
sound substitution. Trager in his lw. list in Taos Indian divides the
words into 'oldest', 'more recent', and 'most recent' on the basis of
their greater or lesser similarity to Spanish. [32] But he finds it difficult to distinguish in many cases, as does every student of the subject.
For one thing, there are many words that happen to lack unambiguous
criteria, and for another, the difference is not necessarily one of
time. We usually assume that familiarity with the new language is
one of gradual and steady growth. But this does not always hold;
among the AmP the break has been quick and sharp, while among the
PaG it has been long and slow. When adult and childhood bilinguals
live side by side, they may mutually influence one another's forms in
intricate ways.

        We can thus not be certain in every case that one substitution
is older in point of time than another. If phonemes x and y are substituted in various words for phoneme z in another language, it may
be due to uncertainty of identification in the early stages of learning.
In AmN the E phoneme o is reproduced as N o in 'coat' and 'load', but
as N å in 'stove' and 'road'. It would be hard to say which is the
'nearest' sound, and the behavior of these bilinguals confirms this
opinion. Such behavior is comparable to that of a novice at target
practice, whose shots scatter widely around the target instead of clus-
tering near the bull's eye. We may call this a process of erratic substitution, which is most natural at a strictly pre-bilingual stage.
Further learning may lead the speaker into a habit of systematic substitution, when he settles down to a single equivalent for each of the
foreign phonemes. If he actually acquires the latter well enough so
that he may begin to use them in the loanwords, he may be led into
regular importation of phonemes. But even if he does not go as far
as this—for he may avoid it even if he masters the foreign phonemes—
the process of substitution, of whatever kind, will usually lead to what
will here be called redistribution of the allophones and phonemes of
his native language. This is what Aasta Stene means by her criterion
'native sounds in non-native sequences'; Mathesius has pointed out that

in Czech the voiced allophone of k occurs initially only in lws.[33] Since
this is a change in distribution only, an apt expression for it would
seem to be 'redistribution'. A further possibility may arise through
reborrowing, since a word once introduced in form a may later be
borrowed again in form b by other speakers.

   All of these developments not only make prediction difficult,
but also complicate the possibility of giving a coherent, systematic description of a language at any given moment. A terminological confusion
has here arisen which has made it possible for several scholars to set
up criteria for discovering loanwords, while others have flatly asserted
that 'in a purely descriptive analysis of the dialect of a monolingual
speaker there are no loans discoverable or describable.'[34] The writer has pointed out some of the problems involved in setting up criteria
in a review in Language for 1949.[35] While he hopes to come back to
the problem later, he would like to note here that the technique of setting up such criteria is still largely circular. By comparative-historical analysis certain words are discovered to be lws.; they are found
to have certain structural features that are relatively rare in the language; these features are then said to be lw. criteria. But if one
started without such previous knowledge, would one be able to discover that these features were 'foreign'? Does the behavior of native
speakers who have not been sophisticated by linguistic knowledge in
any way set them off from the more common features? A complete
listing of the features of a language always reveals a gradation from
the very common to the very rare. Just where does one set a limit
between the patterns that 'sound natural' and those that 'feel foreign'?
In any case it is certain that most languages, perhaps all, contain
hundreds of lws. that are in no way revealed as such by any synchronic
criterion. Whatever it is one discovers by means of such criteria, it
is certainly not loanwords in the usual meaning of that word.

   Kenneth Pike and Charles Fries, in the article cited above,
believe that such irregularities can be most easily handled by a technique of 'coexistent systems'. When a single word or group of words
show features which would require a considerable elaboration of the
systematic description, they suggest that the former be regarded as
parts of a coexistent (foreign) system. A case in point might be the
example cited above from Czech; g would then be regarded as an allophone of k in the system of Czech, and the use of g as a separate

phoneme in loanwords would be regarded as part of a coexistent system. The suggestion is welcome as a reaction from the tendency of some linguists to set up monolithic systems of language in which all irregularities were resolved in oversubtle 'higher' formulations. But one wonders whether a consistent application of the principle will not lead to a recognition of all language as a mass of coexistent systems, which are often mutually inconsistent. The very use of the term 'system' tends to suggest that these must be systematic. Language is probably not a closed system at all, but a complex congerie of interacting systems, open at both ends, namely the past and the future. Its 'synchronic' present may only be a function of what it has been and will be. Perhaps a close analysis of these ragged margins of linguistic behavior will yield significant information concerning the nature of language itself.

Certainly the study of loanwords has brought out a great many important facts about language and its degree of internal coherence. Only the infiltration of foreign elements occasioned by interlingual influence has revealed the comparative independence of various linguistic features. In this respect the language may follow quite different courses on the phonological and the lexical planes. It is popular to speak of 'mixed' or 'hybrid' languages, while linguists generally deny that the basic grammatical structures can be mixed and therefore shy away from these expressions. Yet it can be shown and is obvious wherever bilinguals occur that inflections and suffixes can be adopted along with loanwords and then become productive in the new language.[36] As long ago as 1881 William Dwight Whitney in an illuminating article on mixture in language showed that we must be prepared for any kind of a loan.[37] But he also pointed out that socalled phonetic, morphological, or syntactic loans were essentially secondary to lexical-phraseological ones.

Loans, of whatever kind, may be analyzed and described in terms of the extent to which they are imported in extenso and the extent to which they are modified by substitutions of native habits. A wide difference in this respect is seen between phonology, where it is most common to substitute, and the lexicon, where it is most common to import. Speakers are more conservative phonologically than lexically. Tesnière has interpreted resistance to borrowing as correlated to the degree of systematization of a linguistic feature.[38] In terms of

habits, we may suggest that the more automatic and subconscious a
pattern is, the harder it is to change.

The distinction between <u>importation</u> and <u>substitution</u> is important because it can serve as the basis of a typological classification
of loans. Together they constitute the two ways in which linguistic
<u>reproduction</u> can take place. Borrowing may best be defined as an
attempt to reproduce in one language patterns that have previously
been found in another. The reproduction may be more or less exact,
which is determined by the way in which importation and substitution
have been blended. We shall here suggest a division of loans into
three main classes, where the criterion will be the extent to which
native morphemes have been substituted for foreign.

1) <u>Loanwords</u> include, in general, all free morphemes which
have been imported without other morpheme substitution than the mini-
mally essential inflections. These can then be further divided according to the extent of their phonological, morphological, and syntactic
substitution.

2) <u>Loanblends</u> include all loans that involve a partial substitution of native morphemes beyond those of inflection. Native and
foreign morphemes are here blended, producing e.g. PaG <u>bassig</u> from
AmE 'bossy' (with substitution of PaG <u>-ig</u> for AmE '-y') or <u>bockabuch</u>
from AmE 'pocket book' (with substitution of PaG <u>buch</u> for AmE 'book').
They are sometimes called 'hybrids', but the latter term is also used
for native creations from hybrid material.

3) <u>Loanshifts</u> include all loans in which complete substitution
of native morphemes has taken place. The reason for this suggested
name is that the loan appears only as a shift in the usage of the native
term substituted. The speaker who is attempting to reproduce the foreign expression avoids actual importation of its morpheme(s), but in
substituting his native morpheme, he gives it a new range of usage.
This term would include what is usually called 'semantic loans' (such
as AmP <u>humoroso</u> 'capricious' which has acquired the meanings of
AmE 'humorous') and 'loan translations' or 'calques' (such as German
<u>Mitleid</u> for Latin <u>compassio</u>). It would even include such loan homo-
nyms as AmP <u>grosseria</u> 'gross remark' which has come to mean 'grocery' in America. Semantically the two had nothing in common, but
the speakers substituted the native homophone.

It is believed that the terms here suggested (or others, that might cover similar ground) will be less ambiguous than the traditional terms. They are defined in such a way that it should always be possible to apply them to specific cases.[39] They exclude all innovations that are not clearly modelled on patterns in a foreign language. Thus the AmItalian sciainatore 'boot-black' would not be included, since it consists of E 'shine' plus It -tore '-er', and there is no AmE 'shiner' on which it could have been modelled.[40] Similarly with PaG Gekick 'constant kicking (complaining)', for which there is no E model. In both cases we have what can only be called native creations, in which foreign material already borrowed in other forms has been substituted in a native model (e. g. Ital. trovatore or G Gejammer).

If we ask if it is possible to predict for any given bilingual situation just what will be the relative distribution of the types of loans here discussed, we can only say that the task awaits the description of many more situations of bilingual behavior from this point of view. Our goal is full understanding of the speaker's informal analyses which guide his bilingual behavior. It is clear that his activity is shaped in obedience to analogies with previously established habits. But the rules according to which he selects one analogy and not another are still undetermined. Our researches here should enable us eventually to speak with greater confidence about the nature of linguistic behavior and predict more accurately the impact of linguistic pressure on those who are destined to become bilingual speakers.

NOTES

[1] For a discussion of the writer's research plans see American Council of Learned Societies, Bulletin No. 34 (March, 1942), 35-57 (in this volume, pp. 37-58), which also includes a partial bibliography of his writings on the subject; see also Det Norske Videnskaps-Akademi i Oslo II. Hist.-Filos. Klasse 1938. No. 3. The present paper was given as a lecture at the Linguistic Institute in Ann Arbor, Michigan, 1949.

[2] The papers given at this conference are printed in the bulletin cited in footnote 1.

[3] Kurath in ACLS bulletin cited in footnote 1, p. 12.

[4] For a complete bibliography to the date of its appearance see Otto Springer, 'The Study of Pennsylvania German' in Jrnl. of Eng. and Ger. Phil. 42.1-39 (1943).

[5] There are 517 words in Lambert's dictionary; see A. F. Buffington in Studies in Honor of J. A. Walz (1941), 66.

[6] Buffington, loc. cit., 80.

[7] M. D. Learned, The Pennsylvania German Dialect (Baltimore, 1889), 111 ff.

[8] American Speech 17.94-101 (1942).

[9] American Speech 17.25-9 (1942) and 23.239-44 (1949); cf. also Carroll E. Reed (w. introd. by Lester W. Seifert), The Pennsylvania German Dialect Spoken in the Countries of Lehigh and Berks: Phonology and Morphology (Seattle, Washington, 1949).

[10] American Speech 23.121-34 (1948) and Symposium 3.114-29 (1949).

[11] In monograph cited in footnote 9, p. 11.

[12] Hans Kurath in Monatshefte für Deutschen Unterricht 37.96-102 (1945); Struble in American Speech 10.163-72 (1935); Tucker in Language 10.1-6 (1934).

[13] Leo Pap, Portuguese-American Speech. An Outline of Speech Conditions among Portuguese Immigrants in New England and Elsewhere in the United States. New York, 1949. 223 pp.

[14] Pap, 7.

[15] Pap, 13.

[16] Pap, 27.

[17] Pap, 84.

[18] Pap, 122.

[19] Edward H. Spicer, Linguistic Aspects of Yaqui Acculturation, American Anthropologist 45.410-26 (1943).

[20] Language, Culture, and Personality (Menasha, Wis., 1941), 66-74.

[21] Aasta Stene, English Loanwords in Modern Norwegian. A Study of Linguistic Borrowing in the Process. London—Oslo, 1945, 222 pp.

[22] Stene, 204.

[23] Stene, 33.

[24] See the writer's comment on these in his review in Language 25.63-8 (1949).

[25] Prinzipien der Sprachgeschichte (5 Aufl., Halle a. S., 1920), ch. 22.

[26] Studia Linguistica 2. 1-36 (1948).

[27] Verh. der sächsischen Gesellsch. der Wissenschaften 49. 101-26 (1897).

[28] Language. An Introduction to the Study of Speech (New York, 1921), 208.

[29] Werner Leopold, Speech Development of a Bilingual Child. 4 vols. Evanston and Chicago, 1939-1949.

[30] Publ. of the Mod. Lang. Assn. 55. 852 (1940).

[31] See Polivanov's amusing incident of a Japanese who asked his teacher which was the most correct pronunciation, dzurama or dorama. When the teacher said 'drama', the Japanese nodded and said, 'Ah yes, then it's dorama.' Trav. du Cercle Ling. de Prague 4. 79-96 (1931).

[32] IJAL 10. 145 (1944).

[33] Englische Studien 70. 21-35 (1935-6).

[34] Language 25. 31 (1949).

[35] See footnote 24.

[36] Cf. Alf Sommerfelt, Un cas de mélange des grammaires. Avh. NV-Akademi 25 (Oslo, 1926).

[37] Transactions of the Amer. Phil. Assn. 12. 5-26 (1881); this study supersedes Whitney's earlier remark on the subject quoted in Sommerfelt's monograph cited in the previous note.

[38] Lucien Tesnière, 'Phonologie et mélange de langues.' In Travaux du Cercle Ling. de Prague 8. 83-93 (1939).

[39] For further details see the author's article on 'The Analysis of Linguistic Borrowing', in this volume, pp. 79-109.

[40] Here taken from Alberto Menarini, 'Sull' 'Italo-Americano' degli stati uniti' in his Al Margini della Lingua (Firenze, 1947), 145-208; but Menarini erroneously assumes an AmE 'shiner', meaning 'boot-black'. It is occasionally heard in the compound 'shoe-shiner', but is hardly widespread.

4 | The Analysis of Linguistic Borrowing

1. Bilingualism and Borrowing. As early as 1886, Hermann Paul pointed out that all borrowing by one language from another is predicated on some minimum of bilingual mastery of the two languages.[1] For any large-scale borrowing a considerable group of bilinguals has to be assumed. The analysis of borrowing must therefore begin with an analysis of the behavior of bilingual speakers. A vast literature has come into being on the subject of borrowing, particularly in the historical studies of individual languages; but there is still room for discussion of the relationship between the observed behavior of bilingual speakers and the results of borrowing as detected by linguists. Any light that can be thrown on the question by a study of bilingual speakers should be welcome to all students interested in borrowing and in the general linguistic problems associated with this process.[2] In the present article an effort will be made to define more precisely the terminology used in the linguistic analysis of borrowing, and to set up certain hypotheses concerning the process of borrowing. It should then be possible to test these by their usefulness of application to particular studies of bilingualism and borrowing.[3]

2. Mixing the languages. Perhaps the most widely understood term for the phenomena we are here considering is based on the metaphor of 'mixture'. Among speakers of immigrant language in America it is indeed a popular term; cf. the practice of AmN speakers when they say han mikser 'he mixes' or the AmG book title Gemixte Pickles, in which the loanword mix is at once a description and an example of the process. From popular speech it has passed into the usage of linguists, especially of the older generations; Hermann Paul headed his chapter in the Prinzipien 'Sprachmischung',

and the term was regularly used by men like Whitney and Schuchardt. As a description of the process it might seem to have a certain vividness that justifies its use, but on closer inspection it shows disadvantages which have apparently led later linguists, such as Sapir and Bloomfield, to abandon it. Even Paul had to warn against the misunderstanding that it was possible to mix languages 'ungefähr in gleicher menge', as if they could be poured together into a cocktail shaker and result in an entirely new concoction. Except in abnormal cases speakers have not been observed to draw freely from two languages at once. They may switch rapidly from one to the other, but at any given moment they are speaking only one, even when they resort to the other for assistance.[4] The introduction of elements from one language into the other means merely an alteration of the second language, not a mixture of the two. Mixture implies the creation of an entirely new entity and the disappearance of both constituents; it also suggests a jumbling of a more or less haphazard nature. But speakers of e.g. AmN continue to speak a recognizably Norwegian language distinct from their English down to the time when they switch to the latter for good.

So much for the process itself. A further inaccuracy is introduced if the resulting language is called 'mixed' or 'hybrid'. It implies that there are other languages which are 'pure', but these are scarcely any more observable than a 'pure race' in ethnology. The term is ambiguous because it can mean either that the language has adopted elements of foreign origin at some time in the past, or that it shows mutually inconsistent elements in its present-day structure as a result of such adoption. Yet we know that great numbers of words in English which once were adopted are now quite indistinguishable from native words by any synchronic test. Schuchardt insisted that all languages were mixed, but in saying this he gave the word so wide an application that its value for characterizing individual languages would seem to be greatly reduced. In some circles the term 'mixed' or 'hybrid' has actually acquired a pejorative sense, so that reformers have set to work 'purifying' the language without seeing clearly what they were about. For the reasons here given, the term 'mixture' is not used in the present discussion. It may have its place in a popularized presentation of the problem, but in technical discussion it is more usefully replaced by the term 'borrowing,' which we shall now proceed to define.

    3. A Definition of Borrowing. At first blush the term 'bor-
rowing' might seem to be almost as inept for the process we wish to
analyze as 'mixture'. The metaphor implied is certainly absurd,
since the borrowing takes place without the lender's consent or even
awareness, and the borrower is under no obligation to repay the loan.
One might as well call it stealing, were it not that the owner is de-
prived of nothing and feels no urge to recover his goods. The process might be called an adoption, for the speaker does adopt elements
from a second language into his own. But what would one call a word
that had been adopted—an adoptee ? Anthropologists speak of 'diffusion' in connection with a similar process in the spread of non-
linguistic cultural items. We might well speak of linguistic diffusion,
though this would suggest the spread of the language itself rather than
of elements from it. The real advantage of the term 'borrowing' is
the fact that it is not applied to language by laymen. It has therefore
remained comparatively unambiguous in linguistic discussion, and no
apter term has yet been invented. Once we have decided to retain
this well-established linguistic term, we shall simply have to disregard its popular associations, and give it as precise a significance
as we can.

    (1) We shall assume it as axiomatic that EVERY SPEAKER
ATTEMPTS TO REPRODUCE PREVIOUSLY LEARNED LINGUISTIC
PATTERNS in an effort to cope with new linguistic situations. (2)
AMONG THE NEW PATTERNS WHICH HE MAY LEARN ARE THOSE
OF A LANGUAGE DIFFERENT FROM HIS OWN, and these too he
may attempt to reproduce. (3) If he reproduces the new linguistic
patterns, NOT IN THE CONTEXT OF THE LANGUAGE IN WHICH
HE LEARNED THEM, but in the context of another, he may be said
to have 'borrowed' them from one language into another. The heart
of our definition of borrowing is then THE ATTEMPTED REPRODUC-
TION IN ONE LANGUAGE OF PATTERNS PREVIOUSLY FOUND IN
ANOTHER. We shall not here take up the question of what is meant
by 'another language'; Bloomfield has adequately pointed out the
difficulties involved. [5] The term reproduction does not imply that a
mechanical imitation has taken place; on the contrary, the nature of
the reproduction may differ very widely from the original, as we
shall see.

    For our definition it does not matter why the speaker does
it, nor whether he is conscious of what he is doing. We shall

proceed to analyze what he does by comparing the pattern that he is
reproducing with the results that he succeeds in turning out. While
it is true that we shall rarely if ever be able to catch a speaker in
the actual process of making an original borrowing, it is clear that
every loan now current must at some time have appeared as an innovation. Only by isolating this initial leap of the pattern from one language to another can we clarify the process of borrowing.

4. Types of Borrowing. Since borrowing has been defined
as a process involving reproduction, any attempt to analyze its
course must involve a comparison of the original pattern with its
imitation. We shall call the original pattern the MODEL, and recognize that the loan may be more or less similar to it. It may vary all
the way from an imitation satisfactory to a native speaker to one that
the native speaker would not recognize at all. Where the loan is (to
a native speaker) noticeably different from the model, we are faced
with a case of partial learning due to the interference of other factors,
as yet unnamed. If we assume, on the basis of common observation,
that these factors are the previously established patterns of the
speaker's language, we shall be able to separate out two distinct
kinds of reproduction. If the loan is similar enough to the model so
that a native speaker would accept it as his own, the borrowing
speaker may be said to have IMPORTED the model into his language,
provided it is an innovation in that language. But insofar as he has
reproduced the model inadequately, he has normally SUBSTITUTED
a similar pattern from his own language. This distinction between
IMPORTATION and SUBSTITUTION applies not only to a given loan
as a whole but to its constituent patterns as well, since different
parts of the pattern may be treated differently. An AmN speaker who
tries to reproduce AmE whip [hwip] will often come out with [hypp-];
he has imported the whole form itself with its meaning, but he has
substituted his own high-front-round vowel for the E rounded glide
plus lower-front vowel. If the loan contains patterns that are not
innovations in the borrowing language, it becomes impossible to distinguish the two kinds of reproduction. Thus importation and substitution fall together in the initial consonant [h], which are not distinguishable in N and E.

A study of the way these two kinds of reproduction operate
in speech suggests that whenever the patterns of the model are new

to the borrowing language, a compromise is likely to take place between the two sets of patterns. Some kind of adjustment of habits
occurs, whereby the speaker chooses one of his own patterns to stand
for a similar one in the model. A study of the results of this normally unconscious procedure indicates that while there are many
apparently capricious choices, the overall pattern is not unreason-
able. The bilingual speakers who make the first substitutions are in
a rough way carrying on an operation of comparative linguistics.
That substitution is a common phenomenon under such circumstances
has been recognized for phonetics, where the term is well established. That it also applies to elements of inflection, word formation,
and syntax has not been so clearly recognized. Yet when an AmPort.
speaker substitutes the agent suffix -o for English -er in boarder,
producing bordo, he is giving evidence that he recognizes the equivalence between the two suffixes. He would not be able to formulate it,
but his behavior is evidence of some kind of complex reaction which
for brevity's sake we may as well call 'mental', though it can hardly
have been consicous. It is the linguist's task to make the speaker's
procedures explicit, a task for which he has the advantage of a sophistication that comes from having a vocabulary with which to talk
about linguistic behavior. Whether the distinction between importation and substitution can be shown to correspond to mental procedures is uncertain. But it is clear that it is useful in describing the
course of borrowing over a period of time, when there is a growing
tendency to import rather than substitute as the bilingual command
of the languages grows more adequate.

     5. The Terminology of Borrowing. Borrowing as here de-
fined is strictly a process and not a state, yet most of the terms
used in discussing it are ordinarily descriptive of its results rather
than of the process itself. We shall discuss later the question of the
role which loans play within the structure of a language and the extent
to which they can be identified without resort to comparative studies.
We are here concerned with the fact that the classifications of borrowed patterns implied in such terms as 'loanword', 'hybrid', 'loan
translation', or 'semantic loan' are not organically related to the
borrowing process itself. They are merely tags which various writers have applied to the observed results of borrowing. We shall
illustrate their usual meanings with examples and then try to relate
them to the terminology so far proposed and defined.

LOANWORD is the vaguest of the group, since it may include practically any of the others. But it is ordinarily limited to such terms as AmE shivaree 'an uninvited serenade of newlyweds' from Fr. charivari, in which speakers have imported not only the meaning of the form but also its phonemic shape, though with more or less complete substitution of native phonemes. [6] HYBRID is sometimes used to distinguish loanwords in which only a part of the phonemic shape of the word has been imported, while a native portion has been substituted for the rest. Thus PaG has adopted AmE plum pie as [blaumǝpai], in which the morpheme [pai] has been imported, but the native [blaumǝ] has been substituted for plum. [7] In this case the borrowing speakers must have analyzed the compound into its component morphemes while they were borrowing it, or else they could not have made this partial substitution. This distinction puts the process on a different level from the merely phonemic substitution of the preceding type, so that we are required by the evidence to postulate a MORPHEMIC SUBSTITUTION which operates independently of the phonemic.

If we turn now to the LOAN TRANSLATION (known in French as a CALQUE), we encounter such examples as the French presqu'île, German Halbinsel, modeled on Latin paenīnsula; or German Wolkenkratzer, Fr. gratte-ciel, Sp. rascacielos, modeled on E skyscraper. [8] But are these anything more than an extension of the process observed in the preceding 'hybrid' examples? Instead of substituting only one half of the word, the borrowers have here analyzed and substituted both halves. They have imported a particular structural pattern, viz. the combination of the two constituents into a compound expression with a new meaning of its own not derivable by a simple addition of the two parts. [9] Closely related to this is the SEMANTIC LOAN, which is exemplified by the AmPort. use of humoroso with the meaning of the AmE humorous, though it meant only 'capricious' in Portugal. [10] Here no formal structural element whatever has been imported, only a meaning, and the substitution of phonemic shape is complete. To call this a 'semantic loan' overlooks the fact that all the loans described above are semantic; it is merely that in this case the new meaning is the only visible evidence of the borrowing. The morphemic substitution is complete. This is true also of phrasal loans, in which syntactic patterns are involved, such as AmN leggja av 'discharge', modeled on AmE lay off.

If we now try to sum up this discussion, we see that we have succeeded in establishing a division of loans according to their extent of morphemic substitution: none, partial, or complete. Complete morphemic substitution precludes phonemic substitution, but within the morphemic importation there may be a division into more or less phonemic substitution. We thus arrive at the following groupings, based primarily on the relationship between morphemic and phonemic substitution; the terms used to describe them are makeshift expressions, in lieu of an established terminology or better inventions:

(1) LOANWORDS show morphemic importation without substitution. Any morphemic importation can be further classified according to the degree of its phonemic substitution: none, partial, or complete.

(2) LOANBLENDS show morphemic substitution as well as importation. All substitution involves a certain degree of analysis by the speaker of the model that he is imitating; only such 'hybrids' as involve a discoverable foreign model are included here.

(3) LOANSHIFTS show morphemic substitution without importation. These include what are usually called 'loan translations' and 'semantic loans'; the term 'shift' is suggested because they appear in the borrowing language only as functional shifts of native morphemes.

Separate sections will be devoted to the study of each of these types. For all of them it is taken for granted that semantic importation has taken place. It should be noted that the term 'morpheme' does not here include inflectional modifications; when these are applied, they do not affect the grammatical function of the word, but are necessary and therefore non-distinctive accompaniments of its use in the sentence.

6. Loanword Phonology. The simplest and most common substitution is that which takes place when a native sound sequence is used to imitate a foreign one. Complete substitution is characteristic of naive language learners and is heard as a 'foreign accent' by' native speakers. However undesirable this may be when one is speaking a foreign language, it is normal when reproducing foreign materials in one's own. The results may be almost completely unrecognizable to the speakers of the model language, as when Spanish

virgen is reproduced in the language of the Taos Indians as [m'ilxina] or English spade is introduced into AmPort. as [ʃi'peiro]. [11] In many cases the speakers are completely unaware that they have changed the foreign word, as in the story told by Polivanov of the Japanese student who asked his teacher whether dzurama or dorama was the correct pronunciation of the European word drama. When the teacher answered that it was neither one, but drama, he nodded and said, 'Ah yes, then it's dorama.'[12] Hermann Paul and many writers after him have described this process as one in which the speaker substitutes 'the most nearly related sounds' of his native tongue for those of the other language. [13] But neither the speaker himself nor the linguist who studies his behavior is always certain as to just what sound in his native tongue is most nearly related to the model. Only a complete analysis of the sound system and the sequences in which sounds appear could give us grounds for predicting which sounds a speaker would be likely to substitute in each given case. When the Yaqui Indians reproduce Sp. estufa as [ehtúpa], the [h] for [s] is a substitution that occurs only before [t] and [k], where [s] does not occur in their native language; elsewhere they have no trouble with [s]. Polivanov expressed it as follows: [14] 'En entendant un mot inconnu étranger. . . nous tâchons d'y retrouver un complexe de nos représentations phonologiques, de les décomposer en des phonèmes propres à notre langue maternelle, et même en conformité à nos lois de groupment des phonèmes.' Speakers have been trained to react to certain features in the stream of speech and to reproduce these in their own; but they are also trained to reproduce them only in a limited number of combinations and sequences. Loanword phonology is the attempt to recapture the process of analysis that results in phonemic substitution.

    7. Phonological Importation. The problem of description is greatly complicated by the fact that the process of learning changes the learner's view of the language. The more he acquires of the new language the less necessary it is for him to interpret its habits in terms of the old language. So he gradually begins to import into his own language those habits of the other which he has mastered and which are not too incompatible with his previously established habits. Linguists have generally assumed that a scale for the time of borrowing can be set up on the basis of phonological form. Early loans are assumed to be the more distorted words, while the late are more similar to their models. Thus Trager in his list of Spanish loans in

Taos distinguishes between the 'oldest', the 'more recent', and the 'most recent' largely on the basis of differences in loanword phonology.[15] In general the principle is sound, but we need to make certain reservations. First, there are some words that offer us no criteria, since they do not happen to contain the critical sounds. Second, the difference between the most and the least distorted depends not so much on time as on the degree of bilingualism. Bilingualism may come suddenly or slowly; it may persist over many generations, as among the PaG, and words may come in through various members of the community in several different forms. In AmN communities most loanwords may appear in various forms, with more or with less phonemic substitution; but some substitutions are so widespread that they can hardly have been borrowed recently. It is also possible for bilinguals to touch up the form of an older word and introduce a more 'correct' form if they happen to know it.

Since we cannot follow the fate of individual words and expressions from their earliest introduction, we can only guess at the factors that have influenced the form of any given word. We are entitled, however, to make certain assumptions. First, that A BILINGUAL SPEAKER INTRODUCES A NEW LOANWORD IN A PHONETIC FORM AS NEAR THAT OF THE MODEL LANGUAGE AS HE CAN. Secondly, that IF HE HAS OCCASION TO REPEAT IT, OR IF OTHER SPEAKERS ALSO TAKE TO USING IT, A FURTHER SUBSTITUTION OF NATIVE ELEMENTS WILL TAKE PLACE. Thirdly, that IF MONOLINGUALS LEARN IT, A TOTAL OR PRACTICALLY TOTAL SUBSTITUTION WILL BE MADE.

In the case of AmN we are dealing very largely with bilinguals, most of whom learned E in childhood, so that many words may vary from a wholly adapted form to one that is almost wholly unadapted. We shall here reckon with certain characteristic stages, while realizing that these are not always chronological:

(1) A PRE-BILINGUAL period, in which the loans are made by a relatively small group of bilinguals and spread widely among the monolingual majority; the words show (almost) complete native substitution, with great irregularity in the phonetic results. Some phonemes and phoneme sequences will cause the speakers to vacillate, so that they choose now one, now another of their own as substitutes.

In AmN the rhyming words road and load are reproduced with different N phonemes as /råd/ and /lod/. Such behavior may be called ERRATIC SUBSTITUTION, and is comparable to the scattering of shots over the target of a novice marksman.

(2) A period of ADULT BILINGUALISM, when growing knowledge of E leads to a more SYSTEMATIC SUBSTITUTION, in which the same N phoneme is consistently employed for new E loans. This may often be accompanied by the use of familiar sounds in new positions where they were not found in the native tongue. Thus the initial v in E very, vicious, and other words of French origin must once have seemed strange to Englishmen who were used to pronouncing it only between vowels. In modern Czech g is found initially only in loanwords; elsewhere it is only an allophone of k. [16] We shall call this process PHONEMIC REDISTRIBUTION, since it affects the distribution of the phonemes.

(3) A period of CHILDHOOD BILINGUALISM, in which the characteristic process is one of PHONEMIC IMPORTATION, i. e. completely new sound types are introduced. The Yaqui whose first-generation speakers had to substitute p for f in Spanish estufa 'stove', saying [ehtúpa], are by now sufficiently bilingual to produce [fonografo] 'phonograph' without difficulty. AmN speakers acquired E whip as /"hyppa/ in the first generation, but as /"wippa/ in the second period.

8. The Grammar of Loanwords. If loanwords are to be incorporated into the utterances of a new language, they must be fitted into its grammatical structure. This means that they must be assigned by the borrower to the various grammatical classes which are distinguished by his own language. Insofar as these are different from those of the model language, an analysis and adjustment will be necessary here as in the case of phonology, and we observe the same predominance of substitution in the early phases, which later yields to a certain degree of importation. The broadest kind of form classes are those that are traditionally known as the 'parts of speech.' In the case of E and N there is no problem at this level, since their structures are closely parallel: E nouns are adopted as AmN nouns, and so forth. It is reported from Chiricahua, an Athabaskan language, that the Spanish adjectives loco 'crazy' and rico 'rich' are borrowed as verbs. [17] But within the form classes (at least those that have inflections), there are problems for AmN also. N nouns belong to

one of three classes known traditionally as masculine, feminine, and neuter, which differ from each other in inflection and syntactical environment. Since E has no corresponding division, an E noun must be assigned to one of these classes on the basis of analogies which are often difficult to discover both for the speakers and for the analyst. In most languages for which the phenomenon has been studied a clear tendency is seen to assign loanwords to one particular gender unless specific analogies intervene to draw them into other classes. This is even more marked in AmN verbs, where practically every loanword falls into the first class of weak verbs. Such grammatical categories as definiteness, possession, and plurality correspond with sufficient closeness so that little more is involved than a substitution of N forms for E. Again, this would not be true in languages less closely related; the Yaqui have given many loanwords a suffix -um with a singular sense though the suffix is plural in Yaqui.[18]

But even in the relation of E and N there are many cases of erroneous analysis, based on special situations, so that e.g. E -s (plural) may be borrowed with its stem and treated as if it were part of a singular noun. An example is kars 'car', plural karser; similarly in AmItalian pinozzi 'peanuts'. But the next step, correlated to a bilingual stage of learning, is to import the plural suffix for E loanwords. This becomes such a common thing that the N suffixed article may be added to it, producing a hybrid inflection -s- + -a 'the', e.g. kisa 'the keys'. Adjectives and adverbs may also receive N suffixes, but to a much lesser extent. Here the E influence has frequently led to an importation of zero suffixes, i.e. the abandonment of inflection. Aasta Stene has pointed out that this is promoted by the fact that N also has zero suffixes in some positions.[19] The verbs, on the other hand, have invariably a complete N inflection, with practically no substitution from E. This phenomenon has been noted for several languages, and is sufficiently striking to merit some consideration.[20] Miss Stene stresses the opportunity available to nouns and adjectives of appearing in positions where inflection can be avoided, which is not possible for verbs. While this is true, it should not be overlooked that the function of verb inflections is somewhat different from that of the rest. Tense is a necessary feature of every N (and E) sentence in a way that plurality is not; verbs have no inflectional form with the kind of generalized function that the noun singular has. The noun singular not only refers to individuals

of the species, but also to the species itself, and in many cases this
is quite sufficient (e.g. rabbit as a loanword may refer either to a
single rabbit or to rabbits in general). The adjective inflections are
even more secondary, since they have no independent meaning but
are dependent on the nouns which they modify. Thus the importation
of the E lack of inflection is facilitated by the relative unimportance
of the corresponding N inflections and we need not assume any deliberate 'avoidance of inflection', at least by the unsophisticated speakers dealt with in this study.

   9. Loanblends. In reproducing the forms of another language speakers will frequently go farther in their adaptation than
merely to substitute native sounds and inflections for the foreign ones.
They may actually slip in part or all of a native morpheme for some
part of the foreign, as in AmPort. alvachus 'overshoes', alvarozes
'overalls', where the native prefix al- has been substituted for the
E o-.[21] Such substitutions are only discernible when the phonetic results differ from those that derive from phonological substitution.
Thus E -er is reproduced as AmN /-er/; only when it is not, can
one be sure of a suffix substitution, as in /"kårrna/ 'corner' (by
blending with N hyrrna 'corner'). The same would not be true in
AmPort., where Eastern AmE -er [ə] is normally reproduced as /-a/.
Suffix substitution is obvious in such a word as /"bordo/ 'boarder',
since /-o/ is a regular agent suffix.[22] The /-a/ is actually ambiguous, since it not only reproduces E -er, but is added as a regular
suffix to many words which in E end in consonants.[23] In cases like
AmN /"kårrna/, where the suffix is itself meaningless, hardly more
than a gender marker, we are dealing with a BLENDED STEM. Nearest to this is the BLENDED DERIVATIVE, in which native suffixes
are substituted for the foreign. Thus in PaG -ig is often substituted
for E -y, e.g. bassig 'bossy', fonnig 'funny', tricksig 'tricky'.[24]
In AmN it is often hard to distinguish E from N suffixes, since many
of them are phonologically equivalent; e.g. E -y [-i] is homophonous
to N /-i/. BLENDED COMPOUNDS constitute the largest class of
blends in AmN. Compounds may be borrowed about as freely as simple stems, since the two languages have parallel structures in compounding. But about half of the compounds show substitution of one
or both parts. It is conspicuous that in practically every case the
substitute closely resembles the foreign term in sound and has a
meaning not too remote from it. An example from Pa G is bockabuch

'pocketbook', where buch was substituted for E book. The force of
the compounding pattern was such that even some phrases which were
not compounds in E became so in AmN, e.g. black walnut > /'blakk-
val,not/. Only such terms as had direct E models have here been
considered loanblends. Independent AmN formations involving E
morphemes are here regarded as creations which fall outside the process of borrowing.

     10. Loanshifts. Some foreign loans appear in the language
only as changes in the usage of native words. Such changes will here
be classed as 'shifts', which will be made to include all changes that
are not strictly phonological and grammatical. Complete substitution
of native morphemes has taken place. When this occurs in simple
stems, two possibilities result according to the degree of similarity
between the new and the old meanings of the word. If the new meaning has nothing in common with the old, it may be described as a
LOAN HOMONYM. This is the situation when AmPort. has substituted its word grosseria 'a rude remark' for E grocery; the result is
that the word grosseria has two homonymous meanings. In a dictionary they would presumably be listed as two distinct words. When
there is a certain amount of semantic overlapping between the new
and old meanings, one may speak of a LOAN SYNONYM, which only
adds a new shade of meaning to the native morpheme. These can in
turn be distinguished into SEMANTIC DISPLACEMENTS, in which
native terms are applied to novel cultural phenomena that are roughly
similar to something in the old culture, and SEMANTIC CONFUSIONS,
in which native distinctions are obliterated through the influence of
partial interlingual synonymity. It is a semantic displacement when
AmPort. uses pêso 'weight' (from Span. peso) to mean 'dollar'; but
it is a semantic confusion when they substitute the native livraria
'bookstore, home library' for E library instead of using the Port.
biblioteca.[25] This process may be symbolized as follows: if language A has two words a_1 and a_2 which both overlap some meanings of
word b in language B, pressure of B on A will often lead to confusion
of a_1 and a_2; if a_1 resembles b phonetically, it may even displace a_2
entirely.

     The lack of any satisfactory method of classifying degrees
of semantic similarity means that it is not always possible to make
the distinctions here suggested. Thus it would be possible to disagree on the classification of AmPort. crismas 'Christmas'. It is
similar enough to the AmE model so that one might at first imagine

it to be a loanword with phonemic substitution; only the fact that a
word with exactly this phonemic form already exists in Port. requires
us to class it as a loanshift. But is it a loan homonym or a loan
synonym? Pap regards its native meaning, 'oil of sacrament', as
sufficiently similar to the new meaning to call it the latter ('semantic
loan' in his terminolory); but one might well feel that there is no
common 'area of synonymity' between them, so that it should rather
be called a loan homonym.[26] Compounds may also show complete
native substitution, as when N korn 'grain' + krubba 'fodder-rack'
are substituted for corncrib in the sense of a building for storing
unshelled maize. These are the so-called LOAN TRANSLATIONS,
which have played a great role in the development of many languages.
Thus Gk. sympátheia, which was reproduced in E by importation,
was reproduced by morpheme substitution in Lat. compassiō, G Mit-
leid, Dan. Medlidenhed, and Russ. soboléžnovanie.[27] Substitution
may equally well extend to complete phrases, whose parts are reproduced as native words; we may call these SYNTACTIC SUBSTITU-
TIONS, and include such expressions as AmPort. responder para
tras 'to talk back'.[28]

Loanshifts in general occur most readily when there is both
phonetic and semantic resemblance between foreign and native terms.
Terms that are interlingually similar will be called ANALOGUES; if
the similarity is purely phonetic, they will be called HOMOPHONES,
and if it is purely semantic, HOMOLOGUES. All three kinds can become starting-points for a morphemic substitution; in the case of
AmN it is noteworthy how strong the force of pure homophony is.
The similarity of E and N makes it easy to pour new wine into old
bottles—for the old bottles are scarcely distinguishable from the
new.

11. Creation. Loanword lists are often made to include a
number of terms whose existence may ultimately be due to contact
with a second culture and its language, but which are not strictly
loans at all. These did not come into being as direct imitations of a
foreign model, but were secondarily created within the borrowing
language. An example is the Yaqui term liósnóoka 'pray', composed
of the loanword liós 'God' (from Sp. dios) and the native nóoka 'speak'.[29]
Such formations are sometimes confused with loanblends, since they
resemble these in being 'hybrid'. But seen in the light of the borrowing process as here defined, they cannot have come into being

as imitations of a foreign model, for there is no Spanish word of the shape god-speak meaning 'pray'. A parallel from AmN is sjæbrukar 'one who operates a farm for a share of the profits', a technical term much used in the tobacco-raising districts of Wisconsin. The first part is a loanword sjær (from AmE share), the second is a N brukar 'farmer, tenant'. The AmE sharecropper is not in use in these districts; a word shareman is sometimes heard in English. But neither of these can have suggested the AmN word; its origin must be sought in the N word gardbrukar 'farmer (lit. farm-user)', in which the loanword sjær was substituted for the native gard. This kind of REVERSE SUBSTITUTION, in which loan morphemes are filled into native models, is clearly different from the borrowings previously described and should be distinguished from them. PaG has an interesting series of terms of the type Gekick 'habitual kicking or objecting' (e.g. Gekooks 'coaxing', Gepeddel 'peddling', Getschäbber 'jabbering').[30] When classified without regard to the borrowing process, they appear as 'hybrids'; but their starting point is different from such loanblends as blaumepai 'plum pie' previously cited. These do not have a specific E model, for English has no words of this type, implying a habitual or even annoying activity. They appear to be secondary derivatives from the borrowed verbs (e.g. kicken), and are filled into the pattern of the native words of the type Gejämmer 'incessant moaning or lamenting'. The only criterion available for deciding whether a term belongs to this class of native creation is that no model exists in the other language. This may be difficult to ascertain without a rather complete knowledge of the language in question. A doubtful case is raised in the AmIt. word sciainatore 'boot-black', apparently formed by substituting the loanword sciainare 'shine (shoes)' in a native pattern of the type represented by trovatore 'troubadour'. But if, as the Italian scholar A. Menarini supposes, there is an AmE word shiner meaning 'boot-black', it could be a loanblend, in which the native -tore was simply substituted for AmE -er.[31] This writer has never heard or seen such a word (except in the sense of a black eye), the usual word being boot-black, but he recognizes that it does exist in the compound shoe-shiner (also and more commonly shoe-shine).

Since the type of creation here discussed needs a name to distinguish it from the kind of creation that consists entirely of native material, we might dub it HYBRID CREATION, thus emphasizing its bilingual nature. But it must be recognized that it is not a part of the borrowing process; rather does it give evidence of an intimate fusion into the language of the borrowed material, since it has become productive in the new language. The number of hybrid creations seems to vary markedly according to circumstances. PaG appears to have great numbers of them, involving such highly productive suffixes as -erei, -es, -sel, -keet, -meesig, -voll, -weis and the verbal prefix var-.[32] AmN, on the other hand, has relatively few, which may be due to the comparative lack of productive affixes in Norwegian, but also to the briefer period of residence in America. Most hybrid creations are of the type in which loan morphemes have been substituted in the nucleus, while the marginal parts (the affixes) are native. The opposite kind, showing marginal substitution (exemplified by E talkative) is not found at all in the AmN materials.

Occasionally one finds reference in loanword studies to a completely native kind of creation, when this has occurred in response to stimuli from another culture. Examples from the Pima Indians have been presented by George Herzog of such newly created descriptive terms as 'having downward tassels' (oats), 'wrinkled buttocks' (elephants), 'dry grapes' (raisins), 'lightning box' (battery), etc.[33] A solitary example from AmN is the word kubberulla 'oxcart', from N kubbe 'chunk of wood' and rulla 'cart' (the wheels were made of slabs of wood).

12.   Cross-currents of Borrowing. We may assume that unless a number of individuals borrow a word, it is not likely to attain great currency. If they learn if from the same source, and speak the same dialect and have the same degree of bilingualism, the effect will merely be one of reinforcement of the original form. But the situation is rarely, if ever, as simple as this. The speaker of AmPort. in New Bedford, Mass., is not exposed to the same English as the speaker of the same language in California. More important within any one community is the fact that in a bilingual group the same word is liable to variations in reproduction because of the varying degree of bilingualism. The loan is subject to continual interference from the model in the other language, a process which will here be called REBORROWING. It is a commonplace among immigrant groups in America that younger and older speakers will use different forms of the same loanwords. The difference usually consists in the extent of phonological and morphological importations. Some examples from AmN are the following:

Model: whip tavern surveyor Trempealeau crackers mocassin lake
Older: hyppa tavan saver   tromlo   krækkis maggis   lek
Younger: wippa tævern sørveiər trempəlo   krækərs magəsin leik

The forms acquired will also be differently reproduced when
speakers of different dialects attempt them. This follows from our
previous definition of borrowing; but the situation becomes almost
hopelessly confused when speakers of different dialects live together
in the same community, as is the case among immigrants, and the
form is passed from speaker to speaker, many of whom may be monolingual at the beginning. It has been possible in the case of AmN dialects to isolate a few instances that seem reasonably certain evidence
for the transmission of loanwords within the dialects. At least it is
simpler to account for them as INTERDIALECTAL loans than as
directly derived from E models. They are listed in the following
tabulation:

English Model	Original Borrowing	Interdialectally Transmitted Form

(1) E[dl] > WN[dl] > EN [ll]
    cradle (grain harvester) . . . krɪdl   krill
    middling (coarse flour) . . . .mɪddlɪng . . . milling
    peddler. . . . . .peddlar. . . . pellar (1 inf.)

(2) E [eɪ] > EN [ei] > WN [ai]
    lake. . . . . lcik. . . . . . . laik
    pail. . . . . peil. . . . . . . pail
    jail . . . . jeil . . . . jail
    frame . . . . freim. . . . . fraim

(3) E[ɔu] > EN [å] > WN [ao]
    hoe. . . . . hå. . . . . . . .hao

(4) E [au] > EN [æu] > Solør [əy]
                  > Røros [ö]
    flour. . . . . .flæur. . . . . .fløyr, flör

(5) E [ɔ] > EN [å] > Gbr. [öu]
    log. . . . . .lågg. . . . . . .löugg

In each of these cases the variations within the loanword forms correspond to different reflexes from the same Old Norw. originals, found in a considerable number of native words also. But other loanwords with the same E phonemes have different forms, e.g. mail has not become [mail] in the dialects referred to above, but [meil].

A further source of interference with the process of borrowing is the influence of SPELLING. Spelling pronunciations may be suspected wherever the reproduction varies from normal in the direction of a pronunciation traditionally given to a letter in the borrowing language. In any literate community such influence is likely to be present in a number of words which have been brought to the community in writing. Among immigrants this is not true to any considerable extent, but at least in AmN there is a marked tendency to pronounce AmE [æ] as /a/ and [a] as /å/, spelled respectively a and o.

	Eng. Model	Oral reprod.	Spelling pron.
bran	[bræn]	*bræn	brann
alfalfa	[æl'fælfə]	*æl'fælfa	''alfalfa
saloon	[sə'lun]	*sa'lun	''salon
tavern	['tævərn]	'tævərn	''tavan
lot	[lat]	latt	lått
gallon	['gælən]	*gælən	''gallan
			''gallon
battery	['bæt(ə)ri]	'bætri	''battəri

Such words as lot probably come from official documents, bran and alfalfa from sacks, saloon and tavern from signs, gallon and battery from advertisements. The striking part of it is that the spelling pronunciation does not usually affect the entire word, where a choice is possible, so that e.g. gallon may have an /a/ in the second syllable, corresponding to the [ə] of the original. A comparison with the E loanwords adopted in N, as reported by Aasta Stene, shows a much higher proportion of spelling pronunciations in the latter, e.g. buss 'bus' for AmN båss, kutte 'cut' for AmN katta, hikkori 'hickory' for AmN hekkri (or even hikkrill). As one AmN informant commented, when asked for the word for 'battery': 'They just give Norwegian sounds to the English letters.'

   13. Structural Resistance to Borrowing. It has long been
known that some kinds of linguistic patterns are more likely to be
borrowed than others. As long ago as 1881 William Dwight Whitney
set up a scale on which he ranged the various patterns according to
the freedom with which they are borrowed. [34] Nouns are most easily
borrowed, then the various other parts of speech, then suffixes, then
inflections, then sounds. He did not deny the possibility of borrowing
even members of the last two classes, but contended that they are unusual and generally secondary to the borrowing of vocabulary items.
'The exemption of "grammar" from mixture is no isolated fact; the
grammatical apparatus merely resists intrusion most successfully,
in virtue of its being the least material and the most formal part of
language. In a scale of constantly increasing difficulty it occupies
the extreme place. '[35] Emphasis should be laid on Whitney's explanation, viz. that 'whatever is more formal or structural in character
remains in that degree free from the intrusion of foreign material. '
The same view is expressed by Lucien Tesnière in 1939, apparently
without awareness of Whitney's earlier formulation: 'La miscibilité
d'une langue est fonction inverse de sa systematisation. '[36]

     Whatever the explanation, the facts are abundantly supported
by the available lists of loanwords, e.g. for AmN and American
Swedish. The following figures show the percentage of each of the
traditional parts of speech in the total number of loanwords listed:

	Nouns	Verbs	Adj's	Adv. - Prep.	Interj.
AmN (author's word list)	75.5	18.4	3.4	1.2	1.4
AmN (Flom, Koshkonong Sogning)	71.7	23.0	4.2	0.8	0.5
AmSw.	72.2				
(Johnson, Chisago Lake Småland)	72.2	23.2	3.3	0.4	0.8

It is conspicuous that articles and pronouns do not appear in the lists,
though again it would be foolish to deny that they can be borrowed (e.g.
English they from Scandinavian). All linguistic features can be borrowed, but they are distributed along a SCALE OF ADOPTABILITY
which somehow is correlated to the structural organization. This is
most easily understood in the light of the distinction made earlier
between importation and substitution. Importation is a process
affecting the individual item needed at a given moment; its effects
are partly neutralized by the opposing force of entrenched habits,

which substitute themselves for whatever can be replaced in the imported item. Structural features are correspondences which are frequently repeated. Furthermore, they are established in early childhood, whereas the items of vocabulary are gradually added to in later years. This is a matter of the fundamental patterning of language: the more habitual and subconscious a feature of language is, the harder it will be to change.

   This discussion raises the further question whether there is a corresponding difference between languages with respect to borrowing. It would seem that if internal differences exist within a language, similar differences might exist between languages, insofar as these are structurally different. This has frequently been asserted, on the basis of the greater homogeneity of vocabulary in some languages than in others. Typical is the treatment by Otakar Vočadlo, who set up what might be called a SCALE OF RECEPTIVITY among languages, dividing them into the major groups of homogeneous, amalgamate, and heterogeneous.[37] Unfortunately Vočadlo excludes in his definition of 'receptivity' the words borrowed from other languages of the same stock, so that he regards e. g. Danish as a 'homogeneous' language. He is also more concerned with practical problems of linguistic purification, so that the basic question of whether structural or social forces are more important does not emerge too clearly. Kiparsky, in commenting on Vočadlo's paper, declared flatly, 'die Fähigkeit der sog. "homogenen" Sprachen, Entlehnungen aufzunehmen, hängt nicht von der linguistischen Struktur der Sprache, sondern von der politisch-sozialen Einstellung der Sprecher ab.'[38]

   Perhaps one of the most hopeful fields for finding an answer to this question is the situation in the United States. Here a relatively uniform language and culture has exerted a similar pressure on a large number of different languages; much could be learned by comparing the borrowings of immigrant languages of different structures, and by then comparing these with the borrowings of Indian languages, whose structures are even more different than the immigrant languages among themselves. Most of the differences brought out by Vočadlo are not differences in actual borrowing, but in the relationship between importation and substitution, as here defined. Some languages import the whole morpheme, others substitute their own morphemes; but all borrow if there is any social reason for doing so, such as the existence of a group of bilinguals with linguistic prestige.

14. Structural Effects of Borrowing. Closely related to
the preceding is the problem of what borrowing does to a language.
The classic instance of English (with which may also be compared
Danish) leads one to believe that borrowing is at least a contributory
cause of structural reorientation (we avoid as scientifically questionable the term 'simplification'). But if it is true, as pointed out earlier, that the more structural a feature is, the less likely it is to be
borrowed, it will be evident that a corollary is that the effects of borrowing on structure are likely to be small. The instances of new
inflections actually introduced into wide use in the language are few,
cf. the uncertain fate of classical plurals in E words like <u>phenomena</u>,
<u>indices</u>, etc. In the lexicon the foreign patterns may actually pre-
dominate over the native, but the structural elements tend to persist.
The chief danger represented by loanwords is the instability of classification which they bring in. They have been shown to vacillate to a
statistically higher degree than native words, since they often fail to
show criteria that make it possible to classify them immediately in
one or another category of gender, number, or the like.[39] The fact
that they tend to fall into only one class where there is a choice of
several, will strengthen that class at the expense of others. They
will often introduce affixes or other bound morphemes that stand in a
different relation to their stems from that of affixes in native words.
While some of these will not be discovered by the borrowing speakers,
others will, and may even, as we have seen, become productive.

In phonology the effects may consist exclusively of the filling
up of gaps in the native utilization of possible phoneme sequences.
Thus when AmN acquires E <u>street</u> in the form /strit/, no new phoneme sequence is added: words like <u>stri</u> 'stubborn' and <u>krit</u> 'chalk'
exhibit the same types. But sooner or later loanwords introduce
sequences not previously utilized, as when AmFinnish adopted the
word <u>skeptikko</u> 'sceptic', which then became the only word with <u>s</u>
before a stop; words like <u>stove</u> were reproduced as <u>touvi</u>.[40] This
type of change has here been called PHONEMIC REDISTRIBUTION,
since it will require a different statement concerning the distribution
of phonemes and their allophones. There is also the possibility of
PHONEMIC IMPORTATION, though the usual rule is that this does
not extend beyond bilingual speakers. In English the last sound of
<u>rouge</u> is limited to words of French origin, but its importation is
hardly thinkable if English had not already had it as a 'bound' phoneme occurring after <u>d</u> in words like <u>edge</u>.

Very little thoroughgoing study has been given so far to the structural effects of borrowing on the phonemic systems, so that we are still uncertain just how to evaluate contentions like those of Pike and Fries concerning the existence of 'conflicting coexistent systems'.[41] Pike's studies of Mazateco have shown that in this language [d] occurs only after nasals and may there be regarded as an allophone of t. But the Spanish loanword siento 'hundred' is one of a small number of loans in which [t] occurs after nasals, thus setting up a contrast of t and d not found elsewhere in the language. Yet, as Pike has shown, it contradicts the 'sprachgefühl' of the natives to recognize [d] after nasals as a separate phoneme for this reason. It seems probable, however, that this is a temporary and marginal situation in the language; for according to his own evidence, monolingual speakers tend to nasalize the preceding vowel and drop the n, thus restoring the more common native situation. Meanwhile, it is hardly more than a phonemic redistribution which permits voiceless t to occur in a position that is otherwise not known in the language, parallel in effect to that which occurred in English when medial v was introduced in initial position by the entry of French loanwords. As pointed out by Paul Garvin in commenting on a similar situation in Zoque, no new features of articulation are introduced; but it may happen that they are combined in a new way.[42]

15. The Identification of Loans. So far the identification of loans has been taken for granted, but it must not be inferred from the confidence with which such lists are put forward that it is always possible to isolate loan material in each given case. The difficulty, as elsewhere, is that the historical and the synchronic problem have not been clearly distinguished by those who have written about it. Non-scientific writers or speakers show an interesting tendency: if they are monolinguals, they are quite unaware of loans; if they are polylinguals, they suspect them everywhere.

(1) The Historical Problem. As here defined, borrowing is a historical process and therefore to be identified only by historical methods. This means a comparison between earlier and later states of a given language, to detect possible innovations; and thereupon a comparison of the innovations discovered with possible models in other languages. This double comparison is a corollary of our definition of borrowing; its application requires a knowledge of earlier states of the language, as well as of whatever languages may

conceivably have exerted the influences in question. As applied specifically to immigrant speech in America, this means a comparison of
present-day speech with the speech brought to these shores, and then
a comparison of the innovations with AmE as spoken within the areas
inhabited by the immigrants. The complete success of this venture
depends on a number of factors which will be obvious to the reader,
such as the existence of studies of the language in its homeland
describing it at the time of immigration. Certain more special problems which the writer has encountered in treating AmN may be less
obvious.

(a) Pre-immigration Loans. Some E loanwords penetrated
into N speech, even the more remote rural dialects, before immigration. Trade, shipping, and the tourist traffic had led to contacts with
the English-speaking world even in those classes that lacked the educational opportunities of acquiring the English language. Some immigrants may even have picked up their first E loanwords from N sailors on board the immigrant ships, not to mention the fact that there
were many sailors among the immigrants themselves.[43] An example
of a pre-immigration loan is the word træn 'train', apparently introduced by the English builders of Norway's first railroad in 1855. In
cultivated N usage it was soon replaced by tog (a loanshift modeled
on G Zug), but it is still widely known among dialect speakers.[44] A
further complication is introduced by the fact that returning immigrants brought English words back to the homeland.[45]

(b) International Words. A special category of words is
made up of those that are sufficiently common to most west European
languages to have a similar spelling and meaning, in spite of widely
differing pronunciations. Cultivated people in Norway certainly knew
such words as cigar, district, section at the time of emigration, so
that it becomes uncertain whether they should be regarded as loans
even in the rural dialects when they turn up in forms not markedly
different from that of the spelling. It is not always possible to say
whether given words were current in the dialects; and the spelling
pronunciations which they have in AmN might as well have arisen in
America as in Norway. This was certainly true of alfalfa and timothy, which must have been learned in this country since they were the
names of American products first met with over here. On the other
hand, such words as music, museum, and university reveal by a
highly Americanized pronunciation that the words were not in common

use among the immigrants in their Norwegian forms at the time of immigration; yet they can hardly have failed to have heard them in Norway.

(c) Interlingual Coincidences. Where semantic-phonetic similarities exist between two words in different languages, it may be quite impossible to be certain whether borrowing has taken place. Such similarities are of unquestionable importance in causing confusion between two languages spoken by bilinguals. Typical AmN wordshifts are the substitutions of the N korn 'grain' for E corn 'maize', grøn 'food prepared from grain' for E grain 'grain other than maize', brusk 'tuft of straw' for E brush 'thicket'. In each of these cases the fact that we are dealing with the N word in question is confirmed by the variation in phonetic form from dialect to dialect, even though the limited distribution might speak against it in some cases. But when E crew is reproduced as N kru, we have very little to help us decide whether this is a loanword or a loanshift. The N form is identical with a dialect word kru 'crowd, household, multitude'. The AmN word has been identified with this by an AmN writer, Jon Norstog, who asserted that kru was not an English word at all, but a Telemark word which he had known from his childhood. The claim must be disallowed, however; for the N word is highly limited in its occurrence and is always neuter in gender, while the AmN word is widespread in all dialects, is mostly feminine, and has nowhere been recorded over here in its N meaning. Similarly with the AmN travla 'walk', a widely used word. There is a N dialect term travla 'struggle, labor, slave', found only in remote sections of the country; nowhere does it have the meaning of the AmN word. Yet since its meaning is not identical with that of AmE travel, one might be in doubt whether it is a loan at all, were it not for the existence of an English dialect meaning of travel 'to walk' (very widespread according to Wright's English Dialect Dictionary). Even though this is not at present recorded from Wisconsin, it seems most probable that it was used there and acquired by the N settlers in that state. The E word cold with the double meaning of 'a cold spell' and 'an infection' has influenced the meaning of the corresponding N words, which usually meant only 'a cold spell'; yet we find that in some N dialects the N word already had the double meaning.[46] In such cases it has been necessary to weigh the probabilities in the light of our knowledge of the state of the dialects at the time of immigration.

(2) <u>The Synchronic Problem</u>. It appears to be taken for granted, even by some linguists, that a borrowed word somehow occupies a special status within a language. The acute consciousness of the loanword as a 'problem' in certain modern cultures has led to some confusion in the question of what the loanword is and how it is to be regarded in a description of a language at a given time. The rise of synchronic linguistic studies (also called 'descriptive') has led to a renewed consideration of the question whether loanwords can be identified without the kind of double comparison described in the preceding section. Can loanwords be identified by a student who knows nothing of the previous stages of a language?[47] Such a technique, if there is one, would seem to be most useful in dealing with previously unwritten languages; indeed it would be the only one available.

The analyses made so far, however, have applied to languages where the historical facts were at least partially known, and the lists of loanwords to be analyzed have first been determined by historical means. This is true even of Miss Stene's list of E loanwords in modern Norwegian, though she has included in her final list only those words that could be identified by some synchronic criterion as "not in complete agreement with the linguistic system of Norwegian". These represent, she believes, the words that "are felt by the language-conscious speaker to be 'foreign'."[48] She sets up a series of formal characteristics "by which they reveal the fact that they are aliens in the system. " These are: non-Norwegian orthography, pronunciation, correspondence between spelling and pronunciation, musical accent, dynamic accent, morphology, word-formation, and meaning. Unfortunately no one of these is absolutely decisive (expect perhaps the foreign spelling, which is not strictly a linguistic matter), since many of them occur also in words of native origin; and some are so common that it seems very doubtful if they are felt as "foreign" by anyone except the professional linguist.[49] Furthermore, the criteria fail to include some quite obvious loans, such as <u>drible</u> 'dribble', <u>start</u> 'start', and <u>streik</u> 'strike': these have in every respect been assimilated to a common pattern.

Now it would be impossible to deny that, as we have shown in a preceding section, many loanwords have introduced features of arrangement which are numerically less common than certain other

features and which sometimes stand in other relationships to the rest
of the language than the previously existent patterns. But to identify
the results of a historical process like borrowing is simply not possible by a purely synchronic study. What we find when we study a
structure without reference to its history is not borrowing or loans,
but something that might rather be described as 'structural irregularity'. This is not an absolute thing: word counts have shown that
patterns vary in frequency from the extremely common to the extremely rare, with no absolute boundary between the two. Patterns
of high frequency are certain not to sound 'queer' to native speakers;
just how infrequent must a pattern be before it begins to 'feel foreign'?
Very few studies have so far been made in which structural analysis
is combined with frequency determinations.[50] Until a language is
thus analyzed, any statement about the 'aberrations' of loanwords
must remain open to question. Even so it is evident that no synchronic analysis can discover such loanwords as <u>priest</u>, <u>due</u>, <u>law</u>, or
<u>skirt</u> in English. If other words contain sequences that are less com-
mon and are found by synchronic analysis to have a different status,
they will not thereby be revealed as loanwords, but as something else
to which a different name should be given. If confusion is not to be
further confounded, the term 'borrowing' and its kinsmen should be
limited to the uses of historical linguistics.

        This is apparently the conclusion also of Pike and Fries
when they state that "in a purely descriptive analysis of the dialect
of a monolingual speaker there are no loans discoverable or describable."[51] The Germans here make a distinction between the Lehnwort,
a historical fact, and the Fremdwort, a contemporary fact.[52] But it
does not appear just how the line is to be drawn. None of the languages of modern civilization are so simple in their structure that a
single set of categories will exhaustively describe them. Along with
their high-frequency habits they exhibit a great number of 'marginal'
habits which come into play in given circumstances, perhaps only in
given words. Current phonemic theory seems to assume that the
only description of distribution that is relevant in phonology is the
phonetic environment. But it seems impossible to get away from the
fact that individual words and word groups may have habits of their
own, which can only be described in terms of lexical distribution.
This does not surprise anyone when speaking of morphological characteristics: thus the first person singular of the verb occurs only

in one word in English, viz. am. The problem in phonology is not
different in kind, only in extent. Rather than to regard such compli-
cations as 'coexistent systems', it will probably be best to treat
them as systemic fragments occurring under given circumstances—
items of LIMITED LEXICAL DISTRIBUTION.

Summary. An attempt has been made in this article to
establish a precise definition for the term 'borrowing' by describing
it as the process that takes place when bilinguals reproduce a pattern
from one language in another. Two kinds of activity which enter into
borrowing are distinguished, viz. substitution and importation, which
are defined in terms of a comparison between the model and the reproduction. By distinguishing morphemic and phonemic substitution it
becomes possible to set up classes of loans: (1) loanwords, without
morphemic substitution; (2) loanblends, with partial morphemic
substitution; and (3) loanshifts, with complete morphemic substitution.
The second of these includes what are more commonly known as
'hybrids', the third the 'loan translations' and 'semantic loans'.
Various periods of bilingualism are described, involving erratic and
systematic substitution, or importation of phonemes. Loanblends
are classified into blended stems, derivatives, and compounds, while
loanshifts are divided into loan homonyms and loan synonyms. The
process of hybrid creation is so defined as to distinguish it from borrowing, being a reverse substitution, in which the model is to be
found in the borrowing language. Among the cross-currents of borrowing, which sometimes confuse the picture, are the procedures
called reborrowing, interdialectal loans, and the influence of spelling.
The question of structural resistance to borrowing is discussed, and
a scale of adoptability is set up, which is shown to have a correlation
to the structural organization of the borrowing language. It is shown
that the scale of receptivity assumed by some writers is really a difference in the relationship between importation and substitution.
The structural effect of borrowing is found to be largely a certain instability in the categories; in phonology it may produce extensive
phonemic redistribution, but little phonemic importation. The question of identification of loans is shown to be primarily a historical
question, not susceptible to the methods of synchronic analysis. So
far as loans are discovered by the latter method, it is not as loans,
but as residual structural irregularities, which might rather be called 'systemic fragments' than 'coexistent systems'. The historical

problem is difficult enough, fraught as it is with the problems of distinguishing loans made before immigration, international words, and interlingual coincidences from bona-fide loans made during the period of inter-language contact. But the synchronic problem is insoluble without complete analyses of structure which also take into account the relative frequencies of the elements analyzed.

NOTES

[1] Prinzipien der Sprachgeschichte, Chap. 22 (Halle a. S., 1886).

[2] See the writer's article, Problems of bilingualism (Lingua, Vol. 2), for a discussion of the social pressures that lead to bilingualism, and for some recent studies of the problem. [In this volume, pp. 59-78.]

[3] Languages frequently referred to are abbreviated as follows: E English; N Norwegian; PaG Pennsylvania German; AmG American German; AmN American Norwegian; AmPort. American Portuguese. Other abbreviations are standard or obvious.

Examples from AmN are taken from the writer's own materials, collected chiefly in Wisconsin, under research grants from the Research Committee of the University of Wisconsin (1936, 1937), the Guggenheim Foundation (1942), and the Rockefeller Foundation (1949). The substance of the article was presented to students attending the writer's course Problems and Methods of Research in Bilingualism at the Linguistic Institute (University of Michigan, 1949), and to his colleagues of the Linguistic Circle at the University of Wisconsin; the paper has profited from valuable suggestions made by both groups.

The examples from AmPort. are taken from Leo Pap, Portuguese-American speech (New York, 1949).

[4] Paul, Prinzipien 338; Meillet, La méthode comparative 82 (Oslo, 1925); Meillet, Linguistique historique et linguistique générale 76 (Paris, 1921).

[5] Language 445 (New York, 1933).

[6] On shivaree see Alva L. Davis and Raven I. McDavid Jr. in American Speech 24. 249-55 (1949).

[7] Paul Schach, Hybrid compounds in Pennsylvania German, American Speech 23. 121-34 (1948).

[8] Kr. Sandfeld-Jensen, Die Sprachwissenschaft 69 (Leipzig and Berlin, 1915).

[9] Cf. the apt criticism of the term Pap 176-7, note 58.

[10] Pap 87-8.

[11] George L. Trager, IJAL 10.146 (1944); Pap 94.

[12] TCLP 4.79-96 (1931).

[13] Paul, Prinzipien 340-1; George Hempl, TAPA 29.37; Bloomfield, Language 446.

[14] TCLP 4.80 (1931).

[15] IJAL 10.145 (1944).

[16] V. Mathesius, Englische Studien 70.23 (1935-6).

[17] Harry Hoijer, Lg. 15.110-5 (1939).

[18] Edward H. Spicer, Linguistic aspects of Yaqui acculturation. Am. Anthr. 45.410-26 (1943).

[19] English loan-words in Modern Norwegian 164 (London and Oslo, 1945).

[20] Stene 163 (her opinion that borrowed verbs are for this reason fewer than nouns seems insufficiently founded); Pap 106.

[21] Pap 96.

[22] Pap 97.

[23] Pap 101.

[24] Paul Schach, Symposium 3.120 (1949).

[25] Pap 79, 88.

[26] Pap 87.

[27] Sandfeld-Jensen 69.

[28] Pap 89.

[29] Spicer, Am. Anthr. 45.410-26.

[30] Schach, Symposium 3.115.

[31] A. Menarini, Ai margini della lingua 145-208 (Firenze, 1947); reviewed by Robert A. Hall Jr. in Lg. 24.239-41 (1948).

[32] Schach, Symposium 3.115.

[33] Language, culture, and personality (Essays in memory of Edward Sapir) 66-74 (Menasha, Wis., 1941).

[34] W. D. Whitney, On mixture in language, TAPA 12.5-26 (1881).

[35] Whitney's statement in Language and the study of language 199 (New York, 1867) to the effect that 'a mixed grammatical apparatus' is a 'monstrosity' and an 'impossibility' has often been quoted, while his later, more considered statement has been overlooked, e.g. by Otto Jespersen in Language 213 (New York, 1922) and by Alf

Sommerfelt, Un cas de mélange de grammaires 5 (Oslo, 1926).

[36] TCLP 8. 85 (1939)

[37] Otakar Vočadlo, Some observations on mixed languages, Actes du IVe congrès internationale de linguistes 169-76 (Copenhagen, 1938).

[38] Op. cit. 176.

[39] Cf. Stene 5.

[40] J. I. Kolehmainen, Am. Soc. Rev. 2. 62-6 (1907).

[41] Fries and Pike, Lg. 25. 29-50 (1949).

[42] Paul Garvin, Distinctive features in Zoque phonemic acculturation, SIL 5. 13-20 (1947); cf. William Wonderly, IJAL 12. 92-5 (1947).

[43] Unfortunately no study has been made of E words in the N dialects, parallel to Aasta Stene's for the standard language; anyone who has heard Norwegian sailors speak is aware that they have borrowed heavily from English. Cf. Ivan Alnæs, Bidrag til en ordsamling over sjømandssproget (Christiania, 1902); R. Iversen, Lånord og lønnord hos folk og fant (Trondheim, 1939); A. Larsen and G. Stoltz, Bergens bymål (Christiania, 1912).

[44] Evidence on this point was gathered for the writer from the N dialect archives in Oslo by Magne Oftedal and in Bergen by Olai Skulerud. The related term rells 'rails', on the other hand, does not seem to have been known in Norway, though it took root in Sweden; cf. G. Langenfeldt, Språk och Stil 15. 88-110 (1915).

[45] The words river, ticket, coat, surveyor, courthouse, and table knife are reported from Tinn, Norway, as characteristic of returned emigrants by Skulerud, Telemaalet 73 (Christiania, 1918) and Tinnsmaalet (Halle a. S., 1922); cf. similar reports from Sweden and Swedish Finland in Folkmålsstudier 2. 137-40 (1934) and Svenskbygden 1932. 3-5.

[46] Cf. Aasen NO² s. v. kjøld 'Sogn og fler', but not under kulde and the other words.

[47] Cf. V. Mathesius, Zur synchronischen analyse fremden sprachguts, Englische Studien 70. 21-35 (1935-6); B. Trnka, Phonological analysis of present-day standard English 49-53 (Prague, 1935); Stene, op. cit.

[48] Stene 5.

[49] Cf. the writer's review, Lg. 25. 63-8 (1949).

[50] Cf. W. F. Twaddell, A phonological analysis of intervocalic consonant clusters in German, Actes du IVe congrès

internationale de linguistes 218-25 (Copenhagen, 1938); Hans Vogt, Structure of Norwegian monosyllables, NTS 12. 5-29 (1940).

[51] Lg. 25. 31 (1949).

[52] Cf. Eugen Kaufman, Der Fragenkreis ums Fremdwort, JEGP 38. 42-63 (1939). Kaufman wishes to eliminate Fremdwörter from German, but not Lehnwörter.

5 | The Confusion of Tongues

> My friend, if I remember rightly,
> There is a tribe in far Morocco,
> Orangutangs amid the jungles,
> Who have no singers or interpreters.
> Their language sounded malebaric!
>
> Ibsen, Peer Gynt, Act 4 (1867).

The learning of English proved to have a quick and disastrous effect on the Norwegian spoken among the immigrants. We have many testimonials from the very earliest years of settlement to the 'corrupting' influence of English. Ole Munch Ræder, the Norwegian jurist whose comment was quoted earlier,* aptly described the process as a failure to keep the two languages apart.[1] But he was badly informed when he suggested that the Norwegians 'seemed to have a special knack for it'; it was only that he knew them best. His examples were accurate enough, and his observations can be confirmed by studying the letters which some of the earliest pioneers wrote to their relatives and friends at home.[2] They must often have been difficult to decipher for those who knew no English. A Norwegian rural poet who published a poem in 1853 about returned emigrants declared that

Dæ døm snakka va vont aa skjønne, de va saa my Engelst ibland.

(What they said was hard to grasp; They mixed it so with English.[3])

---

*The Norwegian Language in America, p. 13.

The confusion of patterns which resulted in what is popularly known as 'mixing the languages' is so prominent a feature of all immigrant life in America that it has excited endless comment both inside and outside the immigrant group.

In this chapter we shall make a detailed study of the social responses called forth by 'mixing.' This will include the comments of outside observers, which range from the amused to the indignant and very rarely show any understanding of the immigrant's peculiar situation. It will include also the more or less conscious responses of the speakers themselves, those in which they have given expression to certain attitudes toward their own behavior. We shall examine the responses with an eye to answering the question of whether 'mixing' fulfills a social function. Since the chief function of language is communication, we may ask whether the confusion of two linguistic patterns also leads to confused or inadequate communication.

1. Norwegian Observers Speak Their Minds

Those who were freshly arrived from Norway, particularly if they were well educated men, seem to have agreed from the beginning that the speech of their countrymen in America was both barbarous and confusing. Clergyman Olaus Duus shook his head at what he heard in Scandinavia, Wisconsin, and wrote to his father in Norway in 1859, 'Such Norwegian as they talk here! It is so mixed with English phrases that I was quite annoyed when I first arrived. You never hear the word "hvedemeel" any more, just <u>flour</u>; never "gjerde," but <u>fence</u>; never "lade," but <u>barn</u>; never "stald," but <u>stable</u>.'[4] His colleague Johan Storm Munch, who served parishes around Wiota, Wisconsin, from 1853 to 1859 before returning to Norway, wrote in his memoirs: 'The language of the Norwegians over there is famous. They make haste to mix it with English, and the more they can mix the language, the better.' The good pastor was particularly astonished that 'they also freely decline and conjugate the English words with Norwegian endings, not rarely with <u>dialect</u> endings, whereby the most amusing combinations arise.' He exemplifies the practice with such forms as <u>filatn</u> 'the fields,' <u>fencom</u> 'to the fences,' <u>at fide piggom</u> 'to feed the pigs.' In concluding he remarks that many more examples could be found of this 'gibberish' (Kaudervelsk).[5] A rather severe critic of America, the journalist Johan Schrøder, published a description of his emigrated countrymen in which he declared that he often found it difficult to understand them when they 'mix Norwegian and English words'.[6]

Norwegian writers of fiction have occasionally introduced emigrants or their descendants, usually for humorous purposes, and made merry with their language, which they pepper with English expressions in the most unlikely ways. The earliest example of this practice is probably a story by the popular writer Harald Meltzer from 1860 entitled Til og Fra Amerika (To and From America).[7] The narrator visits an American settlement of Norwegians and there meets a character from Hadeland: 'We discovered a tendency in this good man, which later grew more and more visible, or rather audible, namely a zealous effort to mix into his speech as many English words as possible. He had settled land and was now a farmer. He travelled on the railway and on the steamboat. He shot woodpigeons and wild-ducks. He had two dogs and three boys. He sowed 22 bushels of wheat annually and drove seven miles an hour with his horses. In short, he was so far along that it clearly would not take many years before he was a perfect American, and the children were obviously following their father's example.'[8]

The opinion expressed by several of these writers, that the emigrants mixed in as many English words as possible, became the basis of the classic portrait drawn by the Norwegian satirist Jacob Hilditch in his Trangviksposten. This satire of small-town life in Norway would not be complete without a returned emigrant, a Mr. Jens Træby, who impresses everyone with his inevitable American fur coat. But the language he uses is a true hodge-podge, without rhyme or reason; his first words to the editor of the local paper are: 'Do you gjenkjende mig?' (Do you recognize me?). Another sample sentence is this impossible product: 'Well jeg started deirekt for the far West, hvør jeg hæd en Ønkel i Wisconsin, han hæd e Farm hvør jeg tuk tu vork. . .'[9] While this is not the way emigrants usually talk, it may serve as an example of how Norwegian observers think they talk. The writer Bjørnson introduced a returned emigrant in his novel Magnhild (1877); he described her as speaking three languages, viz., English, country dialect, and some standard Norwegian.

But in her conversation he presented her as mingling these in wild
disarray: 'My dear! I am here bærre for di skuld. I wil seje deg,
at all those years I have tænkt meget på denne stund. My dear Magnhild. . . I have spoken norsk bærre a couple of months only og kan
inkje tale godt. . . What hejter'n? Grong. Have you tålå ve'n?. . .
Vil du rejse mæ meg op gjønno lande in this—i denne vogn, Magnhild?
. . . Dine rum up stairs are they to be let?'[9a] In a modern detective
thriller an American of Norwegian extraction is made to talk as follows: 'God damn—min nevø! such rascal—og jeg som tenkte på å
ta that crook in my business—in my business! Never!. . . You kan
la henne gå.'[10] It is significant that all of the writers here cited
attribute the use of the pronoun you to their speakers, something
which has at least not occurred in the experience of this writer, and
which he considers improbable a priori for reasons that will be developed later.

   Some observers have included a note of regret in their comments, with a more or less pointed admonition to their emigrated
countrymen to mend their linguistic ways. In 1893 the Reverend
H. J. S. Astrup wrote that in 'some places they have accustomed
themselves to mix the languages quite terribly. It is not pretty to
hear a conversation like the following: "You'll have to jumpe fencen,
krosse fila, and follow roaden." If this ever comes before the eyes
of my friends in Illinois and other places where such things go on, I
hope they will not be offended if I say that it would be even more pleasant to enjoy their hearty hospitality, their "pie" and their "sas," if
they would make an effort to do somewhat less of this "mixing." It
reminds one a little of "mixed pickles."'[11] A writer of Valdres dialect, O. K. Ødegaard, issued a similar admonition to his emigrated
dalesmen; he expressed his admiration of their success in maintaining their Norwegian speech, but could not refrain from adding 'that I
have also heard a few who, on their visits home, have mixed their
Valdres dialect with American words and expressions, even in the
wrong places. This is sad to hear for one with an ear for his native
tongue; it is sad to see a man making himself small when he thinks
he is making himself big.'[12] The theological professor Absalon Taranger wrote in 1925, after a visit to America, 'It cannot be denied
that the Norwegian-American written and spoken language is nearly
always polluted by English words and expressions. And the Norwegian-American pronunciation of Norwegian is harsh and offensive to
the Norwegian ear.'[13]

In sharp contrast with these loving-severe admonitions is
the all-out criticism of journalist Thoralv Klaveness, who in 1904
lighted into 'that which first attracts a stranger's attention, because
it has both a comic and an unpleasant effect: the language. It is
frightful, particularly in the interior. Strictly spoken, it is no language whatever, but a gruesome mixture of Norwegian and English,
and often one does not know whether to take it humorously or seriously. . . . What have I not seen in letters of this Norwegian-American volapük! They could make even the strongest nerves shudder!
. . . Now there would be no objection if this strange tongue, as yet
undiscovered by the learned, were spoken to Americans. . . . But
the sad fact is that it is used in communication among countrymen.
In other words: Norwegians often use for mutual communication a
language that they do not master. Their own language they do not
seem to consider good enough.'[14]

It seems to be the almost unanimous opinion of educated
visitors from Norway that the emigrants' treatment of Norwegian is
either comical or offensive. They appear to think that the emigrants
adopt English words as a matter of prestige, as an expression of
scorn for the mother tongue. Their efforts to imitate it show that
they think it is done in a haphazard way, without rhyme or reason,
resulting in a hash or gibberish which may be compared with the
chattering of orangutangs, a comparison hinted at by Ibsen in the
passage from Peer Gynt quoted at the head of this chapter. The contemporary poet Herman Wildenvey, who spent some time among his
countrymen in Brooklyn, refers to their speech as 'a linguistic crazy
quilt.' He specifically stated that 'usually there are no laws of language among the city dwellers here.'[15] The laws he appears to be
thinking of are the laws of rhetoric and style which are applicable to
well-established standard languages in the centers of modern civilization. They are certainly not linguistic laws, for as we shall see,
there are underlying regularities in the behavior of bilingual speakers
which determine their linguistic expression, and which certainly deserve the name of laws if any statements about language do. The
view that immigrant language is a comical gibberish is hardly based
upon any real understanding either of immigrant life or the nature of
language.

Among the small number of Norwegian observers who have
perceived this fact we may single out the Reverend S. Sondresen,

who spent the years from 1890 to 1911 as a pastor among the immigrants. His little book on the linguistic development of Norway, cited below, is evidence that he understood more than most people do of the nature of linguistic behavior. In a study of the Norwegian-Americans published many years after his return to Norway, he devoted a few pages to a discussion of the speech of his one-time parishioners. The conclusion at which he arrived was that 'many unthinking judgments have been passed on the poor Norwegian-Americans for their language-mixing.' He declared roundly that the mixing was 'not done in order to be affected, but came so naturally that one simply does not notice it. Even we pastors and others who might regard ourselves as "cultured" often fall into this sin of "mixing." He turned to his countrymen at home and said, 'It is easy enough for us here in Norway to smile at these words and expressions; but when one lives among these people and learns to understand the circumstances under which they live, one will forgive them.'[16]

Sondresen's views are the exception rather than the rule. There can be no doubt that the rise of a special American type of Norwegian created a barrier between the emigrant and his non-emigrated countrymen.

2. The Newcomer's Embarrassment

Those emigrants who arrived in an AmN community after its characteristic speech forms had been established often had a considerable adjustment to make. They had naively assumed that their countrymen would speak the same language as they, and were often shocked to discover the differences. Here are some characteristic samples from the reports of informants. A Madison man who arrived as an immigrant in 1911 called up his brother from the station; he got the following directions: 'Du skal taka stritkarsen til Schenk's Corner' (take the streetcar to Schenk's Corner). He had no idea of what kind of vehicle this might be, so he decided to walk.[17] An immigrant who came to a farm in Crawford County, Wisconsin was told by his uncle to 'ta håltradn og gå ne i pastre ette hestadn' (take the halters and go down in the pasture after the horses). When the lad registered complete lack of comprehension, another uncle said, 'Remember he's a newcomer.' So he translated it for him, 'Ta grimadn og gang ut i havnegangen ette gampadn.'[18]

A late comer to the Coon Valley settlement in Wisconsin reported on some of the troubles she had had as a newcomer: 'They
told me to go over to the <u>fence</u>, chase the cattle away from the <u>fence</u>;
but I had no idea what a 'fence' was, so I walked in the wrong direction.'[19] Several informants have spoken of their difficulties in understanding the terms of everyday life used in the settlements on their
first arrival. One of the most detailed is the following by an immigrant of 1908, who found himself in a farming community of western
Wisconsin where the dialect of his native valley was universally spoken: 'There they were, talking genuine Suldal and they all talked alike.
But whether they talked Suldal or they talked French made no difference at all to me, for I did not understand a word. They were chat-
ting about 'baren' and 'fila' and 'sheden' and 'malkeshantie', 'vinnmøllo' and 'pompo' and all those words. I couldn't understand a single thing they were talking about, even though I understood about
ninety per cent of all the words they used. I couldn't understand it
because all the names were half or wholly English. They talked
about 'mekar' (makes) and 'fiksar' (fixes) and so forth. . . But when
I went to church, the preacher preached so fine, you see, just as
they did in Norway, and I understood every word.'[20]

Just such an experience must have befallen O. E. Rølvaag
on his arrival in South Dakota, for he reproduces it in his first literary effort, <u>Amerika-breve</u>.[21] His central figure Per Smevik is
awakened on his first morning in his uncle's South Dakota farm home
by the call to 'breakfast.' He has no idea of what this might be,
unless it were the syrup on the breakfast table, which is the only
object whose name he does not know. After a number of such experiences, he wrote home that 'this practice makes it harder for me than
you could imagine. When uncle asks me to do something, I stand
there like a fool, a regular numbskull, and understand nothing.'

Everyone agrees, however, that the newcomers learned fast.
Even though they had their troubles at first, they quickly accepted
the new lingo and practiced it with due diligence. Some of those who
had grown up in the AmN dialect even felt that the newcomers went
too far in their readiness to adopt English terms. They were so
eager that they overshot the mark; a woman born in the Koshkonong
settlement averred that where she and her family used the Norwegian
<u>jolegaoena</u> 'the Christmas presents,' the newcomers sometimes said

krismespresense![22] A man from Lodi, Wisconsin, told of a newcomer girl who was heard exclaiming to a friend whom she met outside the church: 'Eg va so glad når eg luk ju koming.'[23] In spite of
such difficulties, however, it appears that they were quickly assimilated, and accepted the norms of the new community. In the meanwhile they acted as something of a brake on the anglicizing tendencies
of the older group.

3. Bilingual Norms

It is time now that we consider the question of whether we
can properly speak of linguistic norms or laws in the bilingual community, and in what sense they may be said to exist. Because of the
constant pressure of English there is a more rapid flux than in older
and more stable communities. Any norms that exist are certainly
more fluid than in an isolated rural dialect in an older country or in a
a standardized literary language. But the careful observer of AmN
life cannot help but discover the remarkably high degree of uniformity
of practice with respect to the adoption of English materials in the
various settlements. There is individual variation, of course, but
the variation cancels out in a common usage which makes it possible
for everyone to be understood.

The writer has to some extent tested this uniformity by sub-
jecting a number of speakers to oral questioning on their usage with
respect to specific words. His questionnaire included several hundred items to which the response might be either Norwegian or English. A comparison of the results for different informants shows
remarkable uniformity of response. For example, three informants
from Coon Valley, Wisconsin, differed on only 30 words.

Informant	11C2	11C1	11C4
Norwegian	17	7	5
N and E		4	1
English		19	24
No response	13		

The most 'puristic' informant, 11C2, was also a speaker of
standard Norwegian with a strong opposition to 'mixing'; but even so

she was unable to produce Norwegian words for more than seventeen of the doubtful thirty.

Another group of informants (all speaking the same dialect) were compared for a specific number of items in the questionnaire for which comparable responses were available. There were 231 words in this investigation; five speakers of Sogn dialect in two different communities agreed in 165 instances, or 72.4% of the cases, in giving a Norwegian word for 47 and an English word for 118. The remaining 69 on which they disagreed were divided as follows:

Informant	17Q2	17Q3	17Q4	12Q1	17Q1
Year of Birth	1873	1890	1886	1884	1874
N responses	42	39	32	31	28

The difference between the most 'puristic' and the least is only fourteen words, or 6% of the vocabulary investigated. Nor is the difference directly related to the age of the informants. It appears, however, that 17Q2 and 17Q3 were less active in their use of Norwegian than the others. One informant commented that she used more Norwegian words in talking to older people, by which of course she meant people who used more Norwegian.[24] But the relatively narrow margin of difference from speaker to speaker suggests that we may have to agree with the informant who said: 'They will all be more or less the same in mixing: if they can't think of the word, they will use the English.'[25]

We may conclude from these examples that there is considerable agreement among speakers of AmN on the words adopted from English, and that any variation that may take place falls within a limited number of words which everyone in the community understands in either language. As we shall see later, there is also a common practice in the technique of adaptation which these words undergo in becoming Norwegian.

One of the forces making for the relative uniformity of speech is the resistance to excessive adoption of English terms by some members of the community. The force of what we may call linguistic purism in the community is hard to measure, but its presence has been reported by some informants. A Koshkonong woman

reported that her father thundered against the use of travla from English travel instead of the proper Norwegian gao; when others spoke
of joists, he clung to the Norwegian svidl.[26] Another Koshkonong
woman asserted that her parents never mixed, 'if they knew it.'[27]
Such awareness was not universal, for I have had informants who did
not become conscious of the English element in their speech until my
questions forcibly called their attention to it. But a number of informants have shown by their unwillingness to answer questions which
required English responses that they felt a certain sense of shame at
not being able to remember the Norwegian word.

        Children growing up in the bilingual community were often
not aware of the situation until someone called their attention to it.
Professor Nils Flaten, who grew up in Goodhue County, Minnesota,
wrote that he was ten years old before he realized that such words
as påtikkele, stæbel, and fens were 'not Norse, but mutilated English.'[28] But the point is that he did realize it during his growing
years. A Koshkonong woman had the same fact brought home to her
by a Norwegian storekeeper when she was still a child. She told him,
'Je vil ha den disjen' (I want that dish). He replied, 'I thought you
were Norwegian.' Only then did she realize for the first time that
she had used an English word in a Norwegian context.[29]

        It seems probable that the greater mastery of English by
most members of the second generation led to a puristic reaction in
their use of Norwegian. Their knowledge of English made them more
conscious of the presence of originally Norwegian words in their
elders' speech. After a discussion of the various words for 'rug',
'carpet', and the like, an American-born informant said: 'There
are a lot of these words I just can't use in Norwegian.'[30] Another
declared that 'to use keep for ha would make me feel ashamed, as if
I were blundering.'[31] A third made the flat statement that 'people
who are born in this country try to keep their Norwegian pure.'[32]
The explanation is suggested by one informant who said, 'We don't
talk enough Norwegian to say "yard".'[33] Paradoxical as this may
sound, it is simply due to the fact that the completely bilingual speakers felt no hesitation at switching to English when their Norwegian
vocabulary was inadequate. Rather than incorporate their lws. singly,
they found it easier to switch to the other language.

4. The Awareness of 'Mixing'

In any case there is no doubt that most adult speakers of
AmN are aware of the need for resorting to English in order to fill
out their Norwegian vocabulary. In his interviews with them the
writer has noted many remarks like the following: 'We mix so much
English into our speech. . .it's terribly mixed up. . .we switch over
so easily. . .you know we have to mix, for nobody can remember all
the Norwegian words. . . .'[34] They comment somewhat scornfully
on their own language as 'Yankee-Norwegian.' Even more characteristic is its localization in some neighboring American state: Iowa-
norsk, Illinois-norsk, Minnesota-norsk.[35] Possibly because most
of his material was collected in Wisconsin, the writer has not happened to hear of 'Wisconsin-Norwegian'; but he has been told of
'Westby-Norwegian' by residents of that town.

The awareness of many speakers of AmN of what they are
doing and the feeling of some that they ought not to be doing it does
not prevent them from actually doing it when necessity arises. Even
the unwillingness of some informants to give an English response to
the writer's inquiry about specific words does not in the least mean
that they would avoid the use of that word in a natural situation where
it was demanded. But it is typical that many pay their respects to
the decencies by making some facetious or apologetic remark when
introducing a particularly flagrant example of English.

Among the typical phrases used in this situation are som me
seier 'as we say' (or dei 'they'), or me kaller 'as we call it,' often
with the addition of 'in English' or 'in this country.' The following
examples are part of a large collection: Eg ha hatt alle—ka di kalla
'taonsjips-embeder' (I have had all—what they call 'township offices').[36] Kek so dai kadla her i Amerika (cake, as they call it here
in America).[37] Då e vart distsjardsja som di seie frå armeen (when
I was discharged, as they say, from the Army).[38] . . .Tok opp som
me sæie kålæksjen (took up, as we say, a collection).[39] Så har vi
lånsosjel dai kalla pao ængelsk (then we have a lawn social as they
call it in English).[40] Some find more original ways of saying it,
calling it 'jænkispråk' (Yankee language); or saying, 'da e vi jenkiar
att' (then we're Yankees again); or adding, 'Dæ engelsk, men vi snur
litt på dæ (it's English, but we twist it a little).[41] The idea of twisting

appears also in these remarks: 'Kattaren—dai ha rængt da'; 'repa-ren—di ha krengt da te sjøle' (the 'cutter'—they have twisted this; the 'reaper'—they fixed this up themselves).[42]

A common whimsy is to apologize for one's use of an English word by pretending it is really Norwegian: 'Ain jænkinabo so me saie no pao gott norsk' (a 'Yankee' neighbor as we say in good Norwegian.)[43] After using an English word, one informant commented 'Da vert no purketysk' (that gets to be pig German).[44]

The informant who has been put to the test by being asked what he says for this or that shows in many cases a deliberate effort to avoid the English word. This appears in some cases where the Norwegian word comes as an afterthought, after he has already given the English word. When the Norwegian word comes to mind first, it is felt as a triumph. Dei svella opp—trotna mao eg vel seia (they swelled up—'trotna' I suppose I should say).[45] Silingen—på ril nosk æ dæ læmen (the ceiling—in real Norwegian it's 'læmen').[46] En røv-ver—elv [er] sjire norsk (a river—'elv' is the pure Norwegian).[47] Hanklæ—dem sier taol mæst ('handklæ'—they say 'towel' mostly).[48] Pao vossamaol kadla mi da fjos, hær kadla mi da barne (in the Voss dialect we call it 'fjos', here we call it 'barn').[49] In these cases we may take it for granted that in most natural situations the speaker would use the English word. As a Spring Prairie informant said after he had uttered the word 'town treasurer': 'Da skulle vel vå pao nårsk, taon-kasserar, men da e nett so atte da inkje høve gått te saia da' (I suppose it should have been in Norwegian, 'town-kasserar,' but it just doesn't seem to fit so well to say that).[50]

The phrases which speakers use to set off some of their loans from English are comparable to the use of quotation marks in writing. Self-conscious speakers may sometimes use the phonetic device of a slight hesitation pause before the word. This is even more common before a switch, which is the term used here to desig-nate a clean break between the use of one language and the other. Such switches rarely occur within a single breath group; it is gene-rally necessary to break the breath group by a pause. An example is the sentence: 'Da venter di på atte di ska få—"treat"' (then they expect to get a—'treat').[51] The dash stands for a momentary hesita-tion, followed by a single word in English. Switching is done with

such frequency and ease by many speakers that we may regard it as
typical for certain stages in the bilingual process. Switching is different from borrowing, in that the two languages are not superim-
posed, but follow one another.

Examination of a few typical recordings made of such speakers shows that the leading factors in switching are the need of quoting
English-speaking people and of using English terms which it is not
desired to adapt to Norwegian. A recording of a Beaver Creek informant lasting about fifteen minutes shows four switches, each time
suggested by quotations from English, but sometimes persisting beyond the quotes.[52] An Iola recording of about the same length shows
four switches also: (1) to show he can speak English; (2) to describe
an illness of his pastor; (3) to describe certain symptoms of his own
health; and (4) to quote an English-speaking person.[53] He needs his
first switch in the middle of a sentence: 'but when it comes right
down to it—nårst æ bæst for mæi' (Norwegian is best for me). Anecdotes are often told in this way: they start in English, but as the
narrator gets under way, he switches back to Norwegian in order to
lead up to the untranslatable and inimitable punch line.

Speakers will often be quite unaware that they are switching
back and forth; they are accustomed to having bilingual speakers
before them, and know that whichever language they use, they will be
understood.

5. Bilingual Humor

The awareness of 'mixing' as a social problem is expressed
also in its use as a humorous device. Many good-natured stories are
current about the use of English in Norwegian contexts which show
that even the ordinary speakers of AmN sometimes find their own language amusing. They do not find it funny in the same way that outsiders do, but there are two ways in which their language amuses
them. We shall give examples of this under two headings: the exaggerated mixture, and the bilingual pun.

The fact that many speakers notice mixture only when it is
exaggerated is in itself evidence that there is a certain norm.

Informants have mentioned certain individuals who amused them by
using loanwords which they themselves did not use, e.g. one who
laughed because a friend of hers said 'garden' for Norwegian have.[54]
Stories were told in the Waterloo Ridge community in Iowa about a
man who used English and Norwegian words side by side, e.g. 'Dæ
sprang en hårrå-ræbbit åver råden-trækken-væien; så bynte fille-
ponien kikke-spænne-slå' (A hårrå-rabbit ran across the road-track-
væi; then the good-for-nothing pony began to kick-spenne-slå).[55]
Most of the anecdotes told about mixing are of this unusual or exaggerated variety, and these form the basis of some of the samples
found in print. They are characterized by a great step-up of frequency in loanwords over that which is normal in everyday speech;
this may be done by picking contexts in which loanwords are naturally
high and by turning into English every word that any speaker might
conceivably anglicize, and even some which they wouldn't. The results are unreal, but funny even to an AmN speaker by virtue of the
exaggeration.

   One sample will suffice; it may be compared with the authentic samples of AmN speech in Chapter 19.* There are no obviously
incorrect forms in it, but the passage as a whole is unlikely; loans
from English are italicised:

   Han Ola, som lever kross raaden fraa mei, hadde bæd
lØkk igaar, saa dæ var funny, han itte lusa live sit. Han
skulle hala noen pigga te toun me kultan. Dæ var keind af
muddy, aa æ regla blizzard, som mæka saa mye nois, atte
han itte notisa træne, som kom runnandes me full spid. Han
var putty klos te trække, da dei visla, aa kultan, som er
skittlis ta sei, blei skærd aa jumpa i ditsen, bØsta leinsa,
kikka ut dasjbore, pulla ut bolten i tanga aa hadde et rægla
smæsop for ei runnaway. Han Ola futta hjem kross fila,
just about saa fort som kultan runne etter raaden. Missis-
sen aa kidsa ble keind af nervØs, men komforta sei me dei
aidien, at det var Guds lØkk, ingen var killa eller hØrta.[56]

   The bilingual pun results when a word is adopted which happens to coincide in sound with a previous Norwegian word of quite

_____

*The Norwegian Language in America.

different meaning, e.g. English clean > AmN <u>klina</u>, which coincides
with Norwegian <u>klina</u> 'smear'. At this point one might expect that
linguistic confusion could arise, but in practice the difficulty is always solved by context, as with other homonyms. Only when the
meanings are grotesquely different and the words can occur in similar contexts does the possibility of humorous confusion arise. Examples are listed below for each of the words that are most commonly
found in such jokes.[57] Even these, which have been worked to death
by would-be humorists, are usually quite inexact and largely based
on spelling rather than sound. Significantly, they are usually presented as having occurred in letters written to Norway; only a person unfamiliar with English could possibly misunderstand the words
in question.

<u>barn</u> n. vs. Norwegian barn 'child'; i America så maler dom alle
    barna røue (in America they paint all the <u>children</u> red)[58];
    eg myste barn min (I lost my <u>child</u>).[59] The lw. is m., the
    N n., and they practically always differ in phonetic form;
    besides, the N word yields to <u>unge</u> in many dialects. The
    pun is thus based purely on spelling identity.

<u>car</u> n. vs. Norwegian kar 'man, fellow'; alt dæi behøvde å jøra nå
    dæi ville ne i byen va å hoppe på ein kar (all they needed to
    do when they wanted to go to town was to jump on a <u>fellow</u>).[60]
    Here, too, the pun is usually inexact, since most speakers
    use <u>kars</u> for English 'car'.

<u>crop</u> n. vs. Norwegian kropp 'body'; sidste harvest blev min krop
    ganske liden, men naar jeg faar brækket mere fil, skal jeg
    kunne sælge saa meget af min krop, at jeg kan klare mig
    (last harvest my <u>body</u> became quite small, but when I get
    more field broken up, I shall be able to sell enough of my
    <u>body</u> so that I can get along).[61] Most speakers pronounce
    English crop as 'krapp', not 'kropp'.

<u>cutter</u> n. vs. Norwegian kattar pl. 'cats'; dæi kjørde te kjærka på
    juledagen me katter (they drove to church on Christmas day
    with <u>cats</u>).[62] The pun is here exact, but quite unusual; the
    cutter was a type of sleigh commonly used in former days.

<u>grease</u> n. and v. vs. Norwegian gris 'pig' and grisa 'make dirty';
    '"Tag Grisen, John, og sæt i Vognen." Hvorpaa Tjeneren,
    efter en Stund at have seet forundret paa sin Husbond, fjer-
    nede sig og kom tillbage med en Gris i Armene.' (Take the

grease, John, and put in the wagon. Whereupon the servant, after having looked wonderingly at his master, went away and came back with a pig in his arms).[63] The servant is supposed to be a newcomer, the master an older arrival. Most speakers use the words in these meanings quite unaware of their collision with the Norwegian homonyms.

lose v. vs. Norwegian lusa 'delouse'; often used with crop (see above): dei syntes de va harmeli, dei måtte sitta der i fire år å lusa kråppen (they felt it was a shame that they had to sit there for four years delousing their bodies.)[64] The writer has heard it seriously used in the phrase lusa presten 'lose one's minister'.

river n. vs. Norwegian røver (-ar) 'robber'; døtter hennes sa at lanne doms låg imellem to røvere (her daughter said that their land lay between two robbers).[65] The pun is purely a spelling pun, for in speech river almost always has short ø, røvar long ø.

6. Confusion of Identity

Once the words were adopted and given a form which did not markedly distinguish them from other Norwegian words, it was not always possible for the speakers to identify them as English. They became as much a part of the Norwegian language as those loanwords which had been accepted into the language in previous centuries in the homeland. The effort to distinguish them was hampered by the great number of cognates already existing in the two languages. Even so, a few informants made shrewd observations concerning the ultimate English origin of such well-disguised words as hyppe from English whip.[66] But most of them were confused by such authentically Norwegian words as potet 'potato', panne 'pan', kløver 'clover', april 'April,' mai 'May'; all of these have been described as English words by one or more informants.[67] The rough-and-ready rule seems to be that when two synonyms or closely similar phonetic forms of the same word are available to the speaker, he identifies the one with the most Norwegian sound as Norwegian. In most cases this works; but the following instances show how it can go astray. Some of them belong to the type of English words now gone out of use.

(1) Near synonyms, the first of which was identified as Norwegian, the second as English (though both words are actually from English):

Norwegian	English	
brendi 'brandy'	viski	5H4
brikkstein 'brick'	brikk	5L4
båttri 'buttery'	pentri	14D3
fæm og tjuge sent '25 cents'	kvart	5G1
grusråd 'gravel road'	grevelråd	5G1
horna 'to horn (shivaree)'	sjøverera	10C1
pæne 'pen'	yard	12R1
slua 'slough'	marsh, fen	5G1
stup 'stoop'	porch	5L2
		5H3 (wife); 15P3
tånga '(wagon)tongue'	wægenpol	19A1

(2) Phonetically adapted lws., described as Norwegian (in contrast to English forms of the same): grønnri 'granary' 14D21; guffert 'gopher' 10C1; karter 'cutter' 10C1; kornfil 'corn field' 10C1; lånmovarn 'the lawnmower' 19A1; røvver 'river' 10C1; saverar 'surveyor' 5G1, 5L5; sjøvring 'shivaree' 20C1; skværil 'squirrel' 10C1.

7. An Interpretation of 'Mixing'

In none of the behavior patterns so far discussed have we seen anything approaching a breakdown of communication. The failure of recent arrivals from Norway to grasp the full significance of AmN speech is similar to that which any speaker of one dialect experiences in having to communicate with speakers of another. The amusement and indignation of some educated observers stems largely from their application of rigid standards of linguistic purity derived from literary and esthetic doctrine. Their shock at finding that their language has had to be adapted to be suitable for American conditions is largely the shock of any linguistic novelty. No native speaker of English feels any esthetic or emotional revulsion over the 'mixed' character of his language, which far exceeds that of most immigrant Norwegian speech. The conclusion by some critics that 'mixing' is an expression of snobbish contempt for the native tongue does not agree well with the fact that the very speakers who borrow are the ones who have clung persistently to the Norwegian language and passed it on to their children. Contempt would rather appear in a refusal to speak the language and an effort to forget it as rapidly as possible.

Reports are sometimes heard of individuals who 'speak no language whatever' and confuse the two to such an extent that it is impossible to tell which language they speak. No such cases have occurred in the writer's experience, in spite of many years of listening to AmN speech. He cannot deny that they might occur, but believes that most of the cases reported are the result of inaccurate observation. He has heard individuals of low-grade intelligence who have larded their Norwegian speech with an excessive amount of English; and Norwegian monolinguals or pre-bilinguals who interpersed Norwegian in their efforts to speak English. There is no reason why pidgin-like sequences could not occur among the immigrants; but they are in no way typical of the AmN community. In a study of 288 letters written by the subscribers to an AmN newspaper, reported on below, he found only two very short, illiterate notes in which a pidginized style occurred.

The fact that neither ridicule nor the admonitions of their betters have stopped the speakers of Norwegian in America from borrowing English patterns should be evidence to support our contention that there is an underlying necessity in the process. In becoming bilingual within the American cultural environment they were forced to modify their Norwegian if they wished to continue using it. At practically every point they maintained the basic phonetic and grammatical structures of their native dialects; but they filled in the lexical content of these structures from the vocabulary of English. This is a time-honored method in all linguistic development, whether bilingual or not. In the immigrant community it was an inevitable part of the assimilation to American life.

As long ago as 1909 this was pointed out by Professor A. A. Veblan (a brother of the famous economist), a mathematician and a connoisseur of Norwegian dialects. After discussing in some detail the reasons for certain loans in the dialects, he concluded: 'Even

the most awful Norwegian-American spoken is a completely natural
growth and development. Words and phrases owe their being to natural, easily explained circumstances and causes. . . .We do not believe that this linguistic confusion is due to scorn of the mother tongue or to any effort to abandon it as quickly as possible so they may
get something better and more resplendent instead. There are, to be
sure, wretched individuals who are foolish enough to think it a great
feat to throw overboard what they have gotten from their ancestors,
particularly in something so everyday as language. But it may be
doubted that such people have had much to say in the matter. This
curious linguistic phenomenon is due quite simply to the fact that it
is so easy and practical a way of getting along. [68]

 Our study of the confusion of tongues in the immigrant community has led us to the conclusion that it is not identical with a confusion of communication. The language used may seem barbarous
and baffling to the outside observer, but those who join the social
group soon discover that they have to follow the customary norm if
they wish to be understood. There exists within the group a general
sense of purism, which keeps the movement from proceeding too
rapidly. Individuals who go too far in the direction of English are
laughed at. A special word was coined to make fun of them: they
were said to be engelsk-sprengt or yankee-sprengt 'anglified' or
'yankeefied', one of the very few original AmN creations. Stories
are current about the excesses of 'mixing,' and the speakers show a
certain self-consciousness about it when they know that potential
critics are listening. But most of them show relatively uniform behavior with respect to the usual loan-words, which means that the
adoption of the words leaves the main structure of their Norwegian
untouched. They think they are speaking Norwegian, even though
they admit it may be a 'Minnesota-Norwegian', and in these contentions they are right. American Norwegian is indeed Norwegian,
though we may wish to designate it as a bilingual dialect of that language.

 In an article published in 1938, shortly after the initiation of
these studies, the writer outlined an interpretation which seemed
then and still seems to him a broader perspective than the one adopted by the critics previously quoted. The great vocabulary shift of
the immigrant was there interpreted as an inevitable accompaniment

of his changing personality. 'In learning the new language he was doing more than just acquiring new phrases. He was absorbing a new social and linguistic outlook, and this outlook also influenced his native tongue. . . . In all his linguistic floundering we perceive his struggle to achieve again a unified cultural personality. His Norwegian approaches his English, because both are required to function within the same environment and the same minds.'[69] In contrast to the writers who have emphasized the rootlessness of the immigrant, his loss of contact with the old home and inability to find a home in the new, it seemed worth while to point out that for the immigrant the hyphenated group has played the role of a home in passage. 'The social life of his native group has given him a home and a standing in the new nation and has been a solid protection to his mental health.'

These ideas were expanded and suggestively developed by Theodore C. Blegen in his chapter on 'Language and Immigrant Transition' in the second volume of Norwegian Migration to America.[70] 'The immigrants,' he wrote, 'did not remain wholly apart from the people they came to—they were not wholly torn off from those they forsook. . . . The immigrant neither gave up his old language nor, though he learned some English, did he master the new, but he was nevertheless not left helpless or frustrated. What he did was to create, by gradual and normal processes of change, adaptation, and growth, something like an intermediate language—Norwegian-American, which combined both languages, broke the shock of his new-world plunge, and on the whole served his needs effectively. . . . He took the English language into his system, not in a mighty gulp, but bite by bite. He adjusted himself to American ways, not by some instantaneous and magical transformation, but idea by idea. . . . It appears that what, upon superficial retrospect, has the character of linguistic confusion was in reality a struggle of large numbers of people toward some kind of intellectual, or cultural unity; in this struggle Norwegian-American played a mediating role.'

NOTES

[1] Gunnar J. Malmin, ed., America in the Forties (Minneapolis, 1929), 33-5.

[2] Cf. examples in Theodore C. Blegen, Norwegian Migration to America, 2.84.

[3]N. R. Østgaard in Blegen and Ruud, Norwegian Emigrant Songs and Ballads (Minneapolis, 1936), 212.

[4]O. F. Duus, Frontier Parsonage, 28-9 (Ed. Blegen, Northfield, Minnesota, 1947).

[5]From the original ms., lent me by the kindness of Dr. Peter A. Munch.

[6]Skandinaverne i Amerika, 233-4 (La Crosse, Wisconsin, 1867).

[7] According to Halvorsen's Forfatter-Lexikon first printed in Aftenbladet 1860, No. 133-167; here cited from the 7. ed., Christiania, 1907.

[8]Op. cit., 80-81.

[9]Trangviksposten, Tredie Samling, 53 (Oslo, Norway).

[9a]Bjørnstjerne Bjørnson, Samlede Verker 6, 131-4 (Oslo, 1932).

[10]Peter Bendow, Det var dengang da, 157 (Oslo, 1935).

[11]H. J. S. Astrup, Blik paa amerikanske Forhold, 77 (Kristiania, 1893).

[12]Valdreser i Amerika, 66 (Minneapolis, 1922).

[13]Absalon Taranger, Inntrykk fra Amerika, 18 (Oslo, 1927).

[14] Thoralv Klaveness, Det norske Amerika, 114ff (Kristiania, 1904).

[15]Intime Forums 10-aars jubileumshefte, 19 (Brooklyn, N. Y.).

[16]S. Sondresen, Norsk-amerikanerne, 146 (Bergen, 1938).

[17]25P3. [This number and the following are code numbers referring to informants; for a key to their names see Norwegian Language in America, second edition, pp. 696-99.]

[18]12R5.

[19]11R1.

[20]13N1.

[21]Amerika-breve fra P. A. Smevik til hans far og bror i Norge samlet ved Paal Mørck, 33-4 (Minneapolis, 1912).

[22]4P1.

[23]6Q3.

[24]6Q1.

[25]6Q3.

[26]4P1.

[27]4H1.

[28]Dialect Notes 2. 115-36 (1900).

[29]4F2.

[30] 6P1.
[31] 4L1.
[32] 6Q3.
[33] 5H1.
[34] 6Q3, 8F1, 14D4, 4F1, 5H4 etc.
[35] 20P2 (letter); 8G1.
[36] 12R6.
[37] 12Q2.
[38] 14L1.
[39] 4Q3.
[40] 4P3.
[41] 5F1; 8L3; 8F1.
[42] 15P4.
[43] 6Q3.
[44] 15P4.
[45] 20Q2.
[46] 12R1.
[47] 8F1; also 4K1.
[48] 10C1.
[49] 6P4.
[50] 6P2.
[51] 9Q1.
[52] 15P1.
[53] 8C2.
[54] 8L3 (wife).
[55] 19A1.
[56] Anders Sylteviken in Numedalslagets aarbok Nr. 7 (1921).
For other printed samples of AmN in the exaggerated style see J.
Meiraak in Norroena, 2.26 (1901); Jan Barvaag, Ibid., 31; C. N.
Remme, Brev til Guri Busterud fra Olava Kampen, Trondhjemsk-
amerikansk, 273-5, Samband 1912; K. G. N(ilsen), Eksempel paa
Amerika-Norsk, Østerdølslagets Aarbok 1925-6, 129.
[57] There are others which involve meanings not ordinarily
heard in polite society; fit v., pool v., sheet n.
[58] 5E1.
[59] 20P2 (letter).
[60] 5E1.
[61] Brev fraa Gullik Uphaug, Valdris Helsing 13.45-6.
[62] 5E1.
[63] H. Meltzer, Til og fra Amerika (here cit. from Smaabil-
leder fra Livet, p. 347).

[64] 5E1.
[65] 5E1.
[66] 11C1; 3C1.
[67] 5L4; 11C4; 4H1; 6Q4.
[68] A. A. Veblen, Svall om sproget o rettskrivningen, Valdris Helsing 26.59-64 (1909).
[69] Einar Haugen, Language and Immigration, Norw.-American Studies and Records 10.1-43 (1938). [In this volume pp. 1-36.]
[70] Northfield, Minnesota, 1940; pp. 69-99.

6 | Language Planning in Modern Norway

During the past century Norway has been the scene of an unusually interesting experiment in language planning. Ideas concerning linguistic engineering have here reached out from the quiet studies of linguists to the market place, where they have affected every citizen and his children. Little by little an avalanche has been set in motion which is still sliding and which no one quite knows how to stop, even though many would like to do so. When the movement began, Norway had a stable written language; today it is blessed with two competing ones, neither of which is stable. One of them claims to be the more civilized, the other the more Norwegian. Whatever truth these claims may contain, they leave the average Norwegian in the confusing position of not being quite sure whether he can manage to be both. [1]

By language planning I understand the activity of preparing a normative orthography, grammar, and dictionary for the guidance of writers and speakers in a non-homogeneous speech community. [2] In this practical application of linguistic knowledge we are proceeding beyond descriptive linguistics into an area where judgment must be exercised in the form of choices among available linguistic forms. Planning implies an attempt to guide the development of a language in a direction desired by the planners. It means not only predicting the future on the basis of available knowledge concerning the past, but a deliberate effort to influence it. In most countries such planning has been distributed over a long period and among many individuals, with little conscious direction. It has usually taken place at a period when the number of writers was small and standards of conformity not rigid. It has been shaped by the speech habits of a social élite which was also a governing class and automatically established its own

patterns as normative for the whole nation.[3] The resulting "standard"
language has had two mutually supporting aspects, on the one hand a
generally accepted orthography, and on the other a prestige dialect
imitated by the socially ambitious.[4]

The Norwegian experiment, however, has been conducted on
a national scale and in recent times. It has been guided by men with
considerable linguistic sophistication, in the full light of social criticism, and under the constant influence and supervision of a democratic public opinion. It has been done at a time of universal literacy
and enforced orthographic conformity through the school system.[5]
The language planners have sought deliberately to upset the status
quo by rejecting the linguistic models of their social élite. Their
goal has been to give the nation a language which should be the unique
expression of its national individuality. The resulting bitterness and
confusion have furnished striking evidence of the problems involved
in such planning. By this time the Norwegians have lived through
two phases of the procedure, whereby one standard language has been
created and another reborn. They are now hopefully but gingerly
entering a third phase in which the claim is made that the two rivals
can be fused into a new, national language embodying the best of both.[6]

In 1814 Norway was politically separated from Denmark,
under whose hegemony she had fallen some four centuries earlier.[7]
As citizens of a young nation, Norwegians began searching for the
cultural roots that had been cut over in the Middle Ages. Among the
several symbols of national individuality and independence, language
was hit upon as one of the most important.[8] Many voices were
raised for a restoration of the Norwegian language, reputedly lost
during the union with Denmark. Norwegians had learned to write
Danish, although their own speech forms were widely divergent from
any of those accepted in Denmark. We may describe the linguistic
situation as one in which the following speech norms could be heard
in the country:[9]   (1) Danish Colloquial from a small number of
immigrated Danish officials and merchants, and from the stage
which was dominated by Danish actors; (2) Literary Standard, a
Norwegian reading pronunciation of Danish used by a small number
of Norwegian-born ministers and other government officials on solemn occasions, as well as schoolmasters instructing the young in

reading; (3) Colloquial Standard, a compromise between reading
pronunciation and local Norwegian speech habits, fairly uniform
throughout the official class in daily speech among themselves, with
only slight local accents; (4) Urban Substandard, varying from city
to city and closely related to the surrounding rural dialects, spoken
by artisans and working-class people; (5) Local Dialect, spoken by
the farming class, different in every parish, with an intricate network of isoglosses crisscrossing the country and falling into broad
dialectal areas determined by the lines of communication. Between
the extremes of the rural dialects and the Danish heard from the
stage there was a gulf which in some cases amounted to complete
lack of communication. As the century wore on, a growing number
of children were being sent to school and put through the discipline
of learning an essentially foreign orthography.[10]

In the middle of the century two divergent responses were
made to the challenge of this situation, both of them by linguist-
schoolteachers, who laid down the principles for the first two stages
and envisaged the third beyond. One of these reformers was Knud
Knudsen (1812-95), a schoolmaster of rural origin, who agitated un-
tiringly for a step-by-step revision of written Danish in the direction
of Colloquial Standard, which he was the first to identify. He produced the first description of this language in his grammar (1856)
and some years later a dictionary of proposed native substitutes for
its foreign words (1881).[11] The other reformer was Ivar Aasen (1813-
96), a self-taught rural linguist, who pioneered the investigation of
Norwegian dialects. From these he distilled what he conceived to be
their "over-all pattern" and wrote a grammar (1864) and a dictionary
(1873) in which he furnished the means for writing his proposed new
language. He called it Landsmål (Lm.) or "national language."[12]
Although both of these men urged the abandonment of the entrenched
Danish orthography, they outlined quite different procedures for
achieving a Norwegian language: Knudsen was a gradualist reformer,
Aasen a revolutionary. Yet such was the similarity of their ultimate
goals that the liberal-nationalistic party of the Left (Venstre) could
sponsor both when it came to power in 1884. In 1885 the Landsmål
of Aasen was voted official equality with Danish. Two years later
schoolteachers were instructed to abandon the reading pronunciation
of Danish in favor of the colloquial standard which Knudsen had first
discovered.[13] From that time on the linguistic situation in Norway

has been a race between the advocates of Aasen's all-Norwegian language and Knudsen's modified Danish, which by 1900 had become a Dano-Norwegian known as Riksmål (Rm.) or "State Language."

The twentieth century has seen a rapid evolution in which the role of government has become ever more prominent. The official acceptance of literary bilingualism, which does not in any way correspond to a bilingualism in speech or otherwise resemble the situation in countries like Finland or Ireland, has inevitably led to the bureaucratic administration of the forms used in both languages. Since 1900 the language issue has been firmly intertwined with the political and social life of the country. As the government has taken over more and more functions in the welfare state, it has also assumed responsibility for establishing linguistic norms. It has rechristened both languages, has appointed numerous committees to investigate the problems involved, and has instituted a series of thoroughgoing changes in the form of each. A system of local option administered through schoolboards has ensured that the voice of the people should be heard and has made these problems part of the daily diet of even the humblest citizen. The process that was begun in the 1880's when the Venstre Party made language reform a plank in its platform, has engulfed all parties, above all the Labor Party which has ruled the country since 1935. Being a socialist party, it could not at first embrace the nationalistic aspects of language reform, but brought to the discussion an emphasis on its democratic aspects. This accounts for the slogan written into the law that the development is to be guided with constant reference to the "folk language," a term that is vague enough to serve as a banner of union for proletariat and peasantry alike.

During the past half century Aasen's Landsmål has been considerably modified in the direction of East Norwegian dialects, accepting forms that Aasen scorned as plebeian and historically corrupt. [14] It has taken a long step in the direction of Substandard Colloquial from its first official norm in 1901 through reforms of 1917 and 1938 to the latest textbook norm of 1958. Known since 1929 as Nynorsk (Nn.) or New Norwegian, it is now (1958) the chief language of instruction in 2,210 school districts, all rural, comprising 23.5 per cent of all school children. [15] This is not too much to show after a century of agitation, but it could be regarded as hopeful of future

growth, were it not that the years since World War II have reversed
an earlier trend and led to a noticeable recession in the number of
communities using it. In spite of its demonstrated serviceability in
both prose and poetry, it has not achieved anything like majority
status, let alone the triumph for which it once looked. Less than 15
per cent of the original books published are written in it, and it is
not the editorial language of any daily newspaper.[16] It is weakened
by its lack of a prestige dialect, since its speakers are limited to a
spelling pronunciation if they do not simply use their native rural
dialect. An important barrier to its success is its puristic resistance
to universally known words of recognizably German origin. It has
had an undeniable impact on the attitude towards rural speakers by
raising their self-esteem and social respect, while creating also
powerful antagonisms among others. Its fortunes are intimately tied
to the cultural self-consciousness of the rural population and the
reaction of the latter to the rapid urbanization of modern times. The
growth of urban or semi-urban centers and suburbs in previously
rural territory has been a serious blow to the advancement of Landsmål. Aasen could not foresee the rapid shift of population to the
cities, nor the growth of a mass culture which by and large has been
inimical to his language. Although Lm. is claimed to be capable of
expressing any cultural phenomenon whatever, it is difficult to dis-
sociate it from values that are widely regarded as primitive, unfash-
ionable, and reactionary. Yet it enjoys considerable sympathy as
somehow more expressive of intimate national sentiments, even
among many who do not use it. And it maintains a devoted following
among many schoolteachers of rural origin, who swing a big stick in
the educational councils of the nation.

        But the chief resistance to the forward march of Landsmål
was the surprising elasticity of Riksmål in the face of a serious
threat to its predominance. Major reforms in 1907 and 1917 brought
its spelling and morphology into substantial agreement with the Colloquial Standard, as Knudsen and his followers had been advocating
for so long. In 1929 it was rechristened Bokmål (Bm.) or "book language," a term surpassed in ineptitude only by the simultaneous
change of Landsmål to Nynorsk (Nn.). Its present government-
administered form was achieved in 1938, with minor adjustments in
the new textbook norm of 1958.[17] But the form of 1938 showed important innovations, following a new policy which first became apparent

in 1917. It had been clear for some time that many disadvantages
were attendant upon the use of two written languages, particularly in
a small and not overly well-to-do nation. The cost in terms of parallel editions of schoolbooks and official documents alone was a size-
able item, not to speak of the highly divisive effects in public life. It
was apparent that neither language was going to be the unqualified
victor, and rather than remain in a kind of cold-war situation, many
embraced a third solution, which called for one of the most delicate
linguistic operations ever undertaken. This was the solution which
has now been declared official policy, namely the fusion of the two
languages into one all-Norwegian language at some not too distant
date. A name for this dreamed-of language was coined in 1909 by the
folklore scholar Moltke Moe: he called it Samnorsk, or "united Norwegian," and declared that what was needed was a "flowing together,"
a "mingling of blood" of the two languages. [18]

        The committee that prepared the spelling reform of 1917
was directed by the Ministry of Church and Education to "open the
way for a development towards national unity, based on the real spoken language of the people." The commission for spelling reform
appointed in 1934, which prepared the reform adopted in 1938, was
directed by the Storting (Parliament) that created it to work for "a
rapprochement of the two languages in orthography, word forms, and
inflections, based on Norwegian folk speech."[19] In 1951 the Storting
authorized the Ministry to appoint a permanent Language Board
(Språknemnd) whose goal should be "to promote the rapprochement
(tilnærming) of the two written languages on the basis of Norwegian
folk speech (folkemål) along whatever lines may be feasible at any
given time."[20] This policy directive was confirmed by the practically unanimous support of four out of five political parties in the
Parliament, the fifth being the Conservative Party which fought a
last-ditch fight against the setting up of the Board. [21] The method
used in promoting the goal established was first of all to regulate the
spelling of all words that differed in purely orthographic features in
the two languages. Where some genuine linguistic difference existed,
the attempt was made to find a middle ground between the two languages. Such forms were often found in the Substandard Colloquial,
itself a compromise between the upper-class Colloquial Standard and
the rural dialects. This is the meaning of the mysterious and frequently attacked key words of the Board directive: "on the basis of

Norwegian folk speech." This has given enemies of the policy a convenient handle for attacking the new norms as vulgar: many of the
forms advocated coincide with forms regarded by upper-class urban
speakers as non-U. But the political parties that support the policy
retort that for centuries rural children were required to learn Danish
forms far more foreign to them than the colloquial forms now being
encouraged among urban children. One of the serious problems fac-
ing planners is the decision on which features of the "folk language"
to promote. Among the arguments advanced are those of regional
spread (as imperfectly revealed by dialect monographs), of structural consistency, and of literary usage.

     The new forms are promoted through officially sanctioned
spelling lists. In these lists most words have only a single permissible form, differing from older spellings in purely orthographic
respects. Where the changes are more radical, alternatives are
often permitted. Some alternatives are designated as equal, either
one being permissible in textbooks. Others are unequal, the secondary one being permissible only in the pupils' written work. [22] In
popular usage the more traditional alternatives are referred to as
"moderate," the proposed innovations as "radical." Even the moderate usages are too radical for some conservatives, who have produced an unauthorized spelling list of their own which eschews most
of the changes that go beyond the purely orthographic. The resulting
confusion has led to a cry for limitation among the alternatives so
as to simplify the task of textbook writers, teachers, and pupils.
The working out of a firm textbook norm on the basis of the spelling
of 1938 was one of the main tasks assigned to the Language Board
after its creation in 1951. This group of 30 members, 15 for each
language, was selected to represent a variety of organizations and
institutions concerned with linguistic problems. Among these were
the universities and teachers' colleges, teachers' and authors' organizations, radio and the press. [23] A permanent secretariat was
established for the Board, consisting of two linguists, one for each
language, who do the actual research and prepare the agenda for
meetings. [24] After six years of intense work, this group succeeded
in presenting a proposal for a textbook norm which was adopted by
the Storting on October 7, 1958, after two days of full-scale debate,
for use in the schools beginning in September, 1959. It is clear,
however, that the effect of the vigorous public discussion stirred up

over the past seven years, much of it a reaction to over-hasty pressure for change, has made the textbook norm a very mild step in the direction of fusion. The trend is there, but the most ardent advocates of fusion have been brought up short before the resistance of established linguistic patterns.

The linguist who studies this development cannot but ask himself: is it conceivable that two distinct languages can be fused, or indeed, that linguistic development can be guided by parliamentary or other governmental action? Can the welfare state extend its paternalistic concern to language, the most intimate of all social patterns? Many would be inclined to deny this a priori, as indeed some opponents of language planning in Norway have done, appealing even to structural linguistics for support. To clarify this problem we must make sure that we distinguish between language and orthography. The government does not pretend to be regulating pronunciation or other spoken usage; it is only concerned with writing. In general it does not prescribe vocabulary or idiom or syntax, only orthography and morphology. But a written language has to draw its models from some form of speech, which for most writers of Bm. has been and still is the Colloquial Standard of upper-class speakers. Insofar as Bm. differs from this norm, it is an artificial language imposed by government edict. This has led to a conservative counter-agitation whereby a distinction is made between Bm. , the government-administered form of Dano-Norwegian, and Rm. , the more conservative form based on the Colloquial Standard. The resistance here is based on the conception that Rm. is a language, a unified organism or structure, which cannot be tampered with by deliberate planning. Against this stands the conception of the planners that the Colloquial Standard itself is not firm, but is changing under the pressure of the growing democratization of society, and that this change will be accelerated as the schools adopt forms in writing that encourage the more popular speech forms, now often regarded as plebeian by many speakers of Rm. A form that is used in writing thereby gains prestige, and it is believed that little by little the Colloquial Standard itself will become more Norwegian and more democratic by accepting these elements. There can be no doubt that a process of liberalization in speech has been going on. Urban parents no longer exercise the control over their children's speech that they once did, particularly since the schools began counteracting their influence. But the

forms of the spoken Rm. appear too deeply entrenched to yield to
much more than a superficial infiltration of folk speech. The prestige of the Colloquial Standard is rooted in the entire social structure,
which in spite of all socialism and government regulation is still
basically class structured. For each folk form that is admitted,
there are numbers of people who pass over from the use of dialect to
Colloquial Standard when they move to the city, or get a better job,
or go to an advanced school. It is thus a situation in which the government is trying to push a language in one direction by authorizing
certain forms as prestigious, while the prestiges of private life are
trending in the opposite direction. Though the result may be a relax-
ing of older standards, with a widespread adoption of some folk forms,
it is hard to be sure just how much of this is due to the schools and
how much of it is due to a more general social development found in
other countries as well.

    None of the planning for fusion which has here been briefly
sketched would be conceivable if the two written norms with all their
subvarieties were genuinely distinct languages. Bm. and Nn., particularly in their government-administered forms, have a very large
common core: (1) They have identical phonemic systems, though
the phonemes are of course differently distributed in many obviously
cognate words. Aasen's Lm. was based on the phonemic system of
certain West Norwegian dialects with a different and more conservative structure, but this has been largely eliminated. (2) They have
virtually identical syntax: word order is so similar that in nearly
every case translation requires no change whatever; Nn. differs
primarily in requiring gender agreement in the anaphoric pronoun
(as in German), while Rm. has a combination of sex and gender; and
in eschewing the possessive -s wherever possible in favor of a prepo-
sitional construction. (3) They have most of their vocabulary in
common, though Nn. draws more freely on the rural dialects and
doggedly replaces words of German origin with newly coined terms.
Many of its advocates have been realizing the futility of this procedure and have suggested that this barrier between the languages
might well be cleared away. (4) The chief difference today is in
morphology, and it is at this point that interpenetration of the two
languages is most difficult, since the forms of Nn. are more complex, and it seems unlikely that any of its distinctions will be introduced unless they are widespread in usage. But if they are

widespread, they often occur as socially marked forms, with a stamp
of rusticity or vulgarity. Only a long period of written usage will, it
is hoped, gradually eliminate this association and dignify them as
part of the future Samnorsk language.

The conflict of the two languages in Norway is thus today
reduced to a conflict over the writing of forms that are either felt by
many to be vulgar or rustic or that are simply unfamiliar and strange,
being either coined or otherwise of limited usage. The two languages
are not really distinct languages, but might rather be called stylistic
norms, each one a syndrome of features that have no inner structural
connection other than the fact that they are associated respectively
with certain speakers and certain occasions.[25] There is no linguistic
or structural reason why the use of diphthongs in bein, stein, rein,
sein, (vs. ben, sten, ren, sen) should be connected with the use of
-a in the weak preterite of verbs like kasta, hoppa, elska, hata (vs.
kastet, hoppet, elsket, hatet), or with the use of a feminine gender
in boka, døra, natta, dronninga (vs. boken, døren, natten, dronning-
en). Both sets of forms are familiar to all, and much of the planning
consists in deciding which of the forms commonly heard is to be selected as normative. In a democratic country this cannot be done by
fiat, but must be carried on in a way that will win general assent. If
a given "radical" form shows signs of finding favor among younger
writers, it is seized upon by the planners and made obligatory in the
schoolbooks. In this way the coming generation is being made the
object of a stylistic re-education through forced obsolescence of
older forms. This raises immense problems for the appreciation of
the classic authors, who are being antiquated more rapidly than in
any other country. It has reached the point where Ibsen and Bjørnson
require rewriting to be read by the younger generation, and this procedure raises new problems for educators and educated alike.

In conclusion: The Norwegian experience shows that social
pressure for linguistic change can be created and channeled through
official organs. Although linguists generally bridle at the suggestion
that language can be tampered with, it is here shown that given sufficient motivation, written and possibly spoken language like any
other social phenomenon can be deliberately guided and changed.
Whether the effects of government planning in this field, as in other
parallel fields of social life, will be permanent and thoroughgoing,

or only superficial, remains to be seen. About all the government
can do is to create an atmosphere favorable to certain kinds of linguistic change, and recognize that there are forces that escape
government regulation. One of these is the cohesive force of the
Colloquial Standard, which is not easily counteracted. It still seems
likely that this dialect will form the backbone of the future language,
as it is today of the Bm. But it will probably be essential to the linguistic peace of Norway that further concessions be given to the supporters of Nn. They have earned the satisfaction of feeling that it
was they who saved the Norwegian language, even if they should have
to give up the main sector of their battlefront.

An earlier version of this article appeared as: Planning for
a Standard Language in Modern Norway. Anthropological
Linguistics, I; 3, 1959.

NOTES

[1]See Arne Garborg's Vor Sprogudvikling (1897), 10: Et
selvstændigt norsk Kulturmaal er ikke opnaaet. Derimod har vi
faaet to Sprog. Deraf er det ene norsk, men endnu intet udformet
Kulturmaal, medens det andet vistnok er Kulturmaal, men endnu ikke
"selvstændigt norsk."

[2] Linguists tend to look askance on normative linguistics,
because it brings in an element which is not purely scientific. Some
of them even have emotional reactions to it like that suggested by the
title of Robert E. Hall Jr.'s Leave Your Language Alone! In Bloomfield's Language (e.g., 496 ff.) one will find expressed a distaste
for the "authoritarianism" of the usual school norm, particularly
when it is based on erroneous observation of good usage. Linguistics
as such is obviously not equipped to deal with these problems, which
belong in the realm of social and political values. But linguists will
no doubt continue to have opinions on the subject.

[3] For a valuable discussion of the rise of European standard
languages, see Otto Jespersen's Menneskehed, Nasjog og Individ i
Sproget (Oslo, 1925), 36-77, e.g., p. 58: "The standard language
is often to a high degree a class language, an upper class language. . ." See also Bloomfield, Language, 48-52, for an excellent
discussion of the various types of language within a complex speech
community.

[4] In the United States schools have taught the orthography and with it some kind of standard pronunciation as "correct." This teaching has unquestionably had a considerable influence on American pronunciation, though linguists are inclined to discount "schoolmarm" English (while generally following it themselves quite closely). In the absence of a true social élite, schoolteachers have felt called upon to exercise its linguistic functions in a democratic society.

[5] The Ministry of Church and Education prescribes the orthography used in the schools, following a Danish tradition that goes back to 1775 (Rolf R. Nygaard, Fra dansk-norsk til norsk riksmål, Oslo, 1945, p. 14). A number of changes were authorized in 1862, which led to the working out by Aars of his first book of spelling rules in 1866; its 9th edition was officially authorized in 1885, after which this came to be standard practice.

[6] See Marie Skramstad's unpublished M.A. thesis Reform and Reaction in the Linguistic Development of Modern Norway (University of Wisconsin, 1958). The only authoritative account in English is Alf Sommerfelt's The Written and Spoken Word in Norway (Oxford, 1942). A good perspective is found in Einar Lundeby and Ingvald Torvik, Språket vårt gjennom tidene (Oslo, 1956). The fullest source of information for the earlier phases is Achille Burgun, Le développement linguistique en Norvège depuis 1814 (Oslo, 1919). Numerous useful brochures have been published by Didrik Arup Seip, e.g., Fornorskingen av vårt språk (2 ed., Oslo, 1947), Omstridde spørsmål i norsk språkutvikling (Oslo, 1952), Gjennom 700 år (Oslo, 1954).

[7] For details, see Karen Larsen's History of Norway (New York, 1948).

[8] The arguments of German romanticists from Herder on were repeated in Norway, but most of the arguments advanced were of a more practical nature: that school children were being seriously penalized in their education by the wide gulf between Danish writing and Norwegian speech, particularly in the countryside. This motivation has been important for the widespread support language reform has won among schoolteachers. The growth of democratic political movements was also significant, since the "folk language" was conceived as a means of diminishing the prestige and power of the official class. See Willard M. Overgaard's unpublished M.A. thesis Political Aspects of the Language Controversy in Norway (University of Wisconsin, 1955).

[9] The terminology here used is adapted from that of Leonard Bloomfield in Language, 52.

[10] Norwegian pronunciation dominated the stage after the 1860's, but the last Danish actor did not leave until 1899 (Nygaard 39). While reading pronunciation was officially abolished in 1887, it was still flourishing in many schools as late as 1904 (Nygaard 72).

[11] Knudsen first advanced his ideas publicly in 1845. In his grammar, Haandbog i Dansk-norsk Sproglære (Christiania, 1856), he used the term Byfolkets Talesprog "the spoken language of city people" (urban colloquial). In 1876 he called it Den landsgyldige norske uttale "the nationally used Norwegian pronunciation." See my account in The Norwegian Language in America (Philadelphia, 1953), 103-8.

[12] The grammar: Norsk Grammatik (Oslo, 1864); the dictionary: Norsk Ordbog (Oslo, 1873). Before his time Landsmål had been used chiefly to mean rural dialects, but his use of it suggested an extension to the other meaning of Land, viz. "entire country."

[13] See Nygaard 36, where it is shown that both Aasen's and Knudsen's "målstrev" were included in the thinking of the politicians. The instructions to the teachers were: "The norm for pronunciation and reading is the 'cultivated colloquial,' i. e. , that pronunciation which in each part of the country is the usual one in careful, but natural everyday speech. "

[14] Aasen rejected many East Norwegian dialects because their form seemed to him to be influenced by urban speech, which he regarded as un-Norwegian. In addition, he gave his language an orthographic form which should have the same dignity as neighboring Swedish and Danish, chiefly shown by silent letters and other etymological spellings. Some of this was eliminated when Nn. was given an official spelling norm in 1901. See my article "The Linguistic Development of Ivar Aasen's New Norse," PMLA, 48:558-97 (1931).

[15] Norsk Statistisk Årbok 1960. In 1952-53 (according to Lundeby-Torvik 96) the percentage was 28.

[16] The figure counts only book titles and includes a great many officially subsidized items, such as school textbooks and public documents; also there is no doubt that the average circulation of Nn. books is lower than that of Rm. books, so that if it were possible to get figures in terms of actual number of books sold and read, the position of Nn. would be still weaker. For this figure and others on recent book production, see Kaare Haukaas, Litteraturspråket i tidsromet 1946 til 1955 (Oslo, 1957); the author is favorable to Nn. ,

but his figures appear reliable. Note that nearly all translations from foreign languages are in Bm., so that if these are included the figure falls to about 11 per cent Nn.

[17] For a brief list of the major changes in these spellings, see my Spoken Norwegian (New York, 1947), 238-39. Also Lundeby-Torvik 80-91.

[18] Moltke Moe had been writing in this vein for some years, see, e.g., his essay "Retskrivning og Folkedannelse" (1900) and "Norsk og dansk Sprogdragt" (1906), in his Samlede Skrifter, 1, 219-59, 2, 64-85. The term Samnorsk occurs in his "Nationalitet og kultur" (2, 252-64). An important book at this time was H. Eitrem's Samarbeide mellem Landsmaal og Riksmaal? (Oslo, 1908); the author that year became a member of an official commission which published a report in 1909 entitled Utredning av spørsmaalet om et mulig samarbeide mellem landsmaal og riksmaal i retskrivningen.

[19] The quotations are taken from the Bill prepared for the Storting by the Ministry of Church and Education St. prp. nr. 1 Tillegg nr. 3. Norsk Språknemnd (Oslo, 1950), pp. 2, 3, 21.

[20] Each one of the terms in this directive has been fought over and argued so much that is is difficult to translate it into English without a loss of connotation. In particular the term "Norwegian folk speech" (norsk folkemål) is a dubious one, since there is no single linguistic form which can be so designated. It is a cover term which includes all rural dialects and the urban substandard, in short, all that is not standard or "upper class." This was calculated to appeal to the voters supporting the Labor and Agrarian parties, since speakers of the standard are characteristically Conservative. But the term "folk" is ambiguous, including as it does the concept of the whole people; hence it has been argued that since Colloquial Standard is also spoken by a segment of the Norwegian people it should be taken into account in planning. For a defense of the term see a brochure from Norsk språknemnd entitled Svar på kritikk av "Framlegg til læreboknormal 1957," pp. 4-6.

[21] The final vote on the establishment of a Language Board Dec. 14, 1951 was 95 to 24, the latter votes being those of the entire Conservative Party plus two from the Labor Party. All others voted in favor of the measure, which envisages eventual fusion of the languages: the Labor Party, the Liberal Party, the Christian Peoples' Party, and the Agrarian Party. Most of these had specific planks in their platforms favoring Samnorsk.

[22] The terminology was (1) jamstilte former "alternative
forms" (e.g., tru or tro "believe") and (2) hovedform "principal
form" vs. sideform "secondary form," the latter being placed in
brackets in the spelling lists, e.g., seter [sæter] "chalet." See Lundeby-Torvik 85 ff. for details.

[23] The Ministry chooses from two sets of nominations made
by each group and in addition appoints six members on its own initiative. The Board is purely advisory. Its whole membership gathers
usually only once or twice a year, while its working or executive
committee meets about once a month. The chairmanship rotates
annually between the two languages. The bylaws are to be found in
the records of the Storting for 1950 (St. prp. nr. 1. Tillegg nr. 3).

[24] The first secretaries were Einar Lundeby for Bm. and
Ingvald Torvik for Nn. They published annual reports since 1953, a
survey of Norwegian language history in 1956 (Språket vårt gjennom
tidene), and prepared the Board's proposal for a textbook norm in
1957 (Framlegg til læreboknormal).

[25] The stylistic syndrome is a collocation rather than a structure, if we assume that a structure must show some statable relationship between its parts, e.g., sg. plus the morpheme $-Z_1 = pl$ (in
English). A collocation shows no statable relationship between its
parts other than a purely spatial or co-existential selection, e.g.,
the co-occurrence of the phoneme $/ \check{z} /$ and preterites in $-D_1$ in English.

7 | Schizoglossia and the Linguistic Norm

When I received the invitation to participate in this panel on bilingualism, I decided to take as my topic the kind of bilingualism which exists in every complex civilized community, and which I decided to call schizoglossia. While we are all familiar with it under various other names, it has not usually been considered in this connection. This led me on to ponder the conflict which arises within the individual speaker when he becomes uncertain as to what he ought to say and write because the same linguistic item is presented to him in more than one way. This raised the question of a linguistic norm and its place in society, a question which has occupied me recently in connection with a book I am writing on language planning in Norway. Not until I got the printed program of the conference did I discover that a whole section was being devoted to such problems. By this time I was stuck with my title, and if this paper would seem to belong rather in tomorrow's than today's panel, you will now understand the reason why.

Schizoglossia may be described as a linguistic malady which may arise in speakers and writers who are exposed to more than one variety of their own language. Under favorable or more precisely, unfavorable conditions, the symptoms may include acute discomfort in the region of the diaphragm and the vocal chords. If the patient refuses to "leave his language alone," we are assured by Robert A. Hall that he may also be afflicted by general insecurity, which expresses itself as "false humility" and "needless self-depreciation." The damage to his character, we are told, may be "incalculable."[1] Pursuing this thought, I may add that the victims of schizoglossia are often marked by a disproportionate, even an unbalanced interest in the form rather than the substance of language. In extreme cases

they may even turn into professional linguists, just as schizophrenics
sometimes become psychoanalysts in order to study in others the symptoms of their own ailment.

   Schizoglossia is endemic in American society, which was
founded by speakers from various parts of the British Isles. It flares
up at times, especially when new editions of standard dictionaries are
published. Sufferers are especially common in a society where most
people are socially mobile and very few know exactly where they stand.
Since its germ or virus has not yet been isolated, its cure, like that
of the common cold, has mostly been undertaken by quacks and other
well-meaning but financially interested persons. A flourishing industry exists for the purpose of supplying the country with remedies,
ranging from pocket handbooks to improve your English through evening courses in diction to huge and costly tomes of scholarship. Dr.
Noah Webster diagnosed the malady to his own interest in the early
years of the Republic, and set himself to rescue the populace from its
Babylonic babble. With patriotic devotion this Noah of our linguistic
deluge followed in the footsteps of Dr. Johnson, who in 1755 had expressed the hope that by his dictionary he might "retard what we cannot repel, palliate what we cannot cure."

   The malady which Dr. Johnson wished to cure was not precisely schizoglossia, but linguistic change in general. He was realistic enough to see that codification would not inhibit it completely.
The medical metaphor which I have been developing was anticipated
in his Preface, where he wrote: "When we see men grow old and die
at a certain time one after another, from century to century, we laugh
at the elixir that promises to prolong life to a thousand years; and
with equal justice may the lexicographer be derided, who being able
to produce no example of a nation that has preserved their words and
phrases from mutability, shall imagine that his dictionary can embalm
his language and secure it from corruption and decay, that it is in his
power to change sublunary nature, and clear the world at once from
folly, vanity and affectation." Nevertheless, he stoutly declared his
desire to make an effort: "Life may be lengthened by care, though
death cannot be ultimately defeated: tongues, like governments, have
a natural tendency to degeneration: we have long preserved our constitution, let us make some struggles for our language."

This point of view, so typical of the eighteenth century, is one which few American linguists would endorse today. In fact, the prevailing attitude is rather the opposite, that not only is schizoglossia not a problem, but that it is positively harmful even to try to eliminate it. Bloomfield's remarks in the last chapter of <u>Language</u> pointed the way, which has been well-trodden by his followers, including such eminent scholars as Charles C. Fries and Robert A. Hall, Jr. Hall exhorted his readers in the previously cited book to "abandon entirely the old dogmatic, normative, theological approach of traditional grammar and of social snobbery; and to substitute the relativistic, objective approach of scientific study and analysis."[2] In another passage he makes an even more sweeping condemnation of the concern of the rhetorician with what is "right" and "wrong:" "The merit of what a person says or does is not in any way affected by the way in which they say or do it, provided it is the most efficient way of saying or doing it; and to accept or reject someone just because of 'correct' or 'incorrect' speech is to show oneself superficial, lazy, and snobbish."[3]

It will be my contention in this paper that the case of linguistic relativism has here been vastly overstated, and that there is no warrant in linguistic science for the wholesale condemnation here made of normative grammar. In his eagerness to neutralize the ill effects of Miss Fidditch's rigidity, Hall has thrown out the baby with the bath. It takes only a modest amount of discourse analysis to show that in these two passages the word "normative" has been associated rhetorically with pejorative terms such as "dogmatic," "traditional," and "snobbery," while "relativistic" has been associated with favorable terms like "objective" and "scientific." It also seems unrealistic to declare that merit is unrelated to the way in which something is done. Many would hold that the manner of doing may be more important than the doing. "Correctness" may not be synonymous with grace or charm, but together with these it is a significant element in what we think of as civilized behavior. For linguists as a group to put themselves in a position of opposing normative standards is to invite a charge of cultural barbarism. In recent discussion of Webster's Third New International Dictionary it has even been contended that "structural linguistics" is behind its supposed betrayal of standards.[4]

It needs to be clearly understood that "scientific" is not necessarily identical with "tolerant." A plea for tolerance may be laudable

from a moral or ethical point of view, but does not of itself follow
from the premises of science. A botanist may have private opinions
about the plants he studies, such as that some taste better or are
more sightly than others, but in expressing these he is not speaking
as a scientist and his opinions have no more validity than anyone else's.
The problem of linguistic correctness involves dimensions of human
behavior that are not provided for in the models which linguists usually build. I venture to go so far as to maintain that when Robert Hall
tells the non-standard speakers that "there is nothing inherently
wrong with your language," he is no more scientific than Miss Fidditch.
He is doing his bit to eliminate snobbishness, which does honor to his
good heart, but he is not being either objective or scientific.

        The conflict between the dual role that linguistic scientists
are sometimes called to play has been painfully evident in recent
years in Norway, where schizoglossia is not endemic, but epidemic.
Although there are two official written languages, it is rather a case
of schizoglossia than of diglossia, since these are little more than
divergent dialects of one language. The official government policy
during the past 25 years has been to promote the fusion of these two
languages into one compromise norm. In 1952 a Language Commission was established by act of parliament which should advise the
government. The directives given to this Commission declared that
its function should be to give this advice "on the basis of scientific
research" and thereby "promote the mutual approach of the two written languages on the basis of Norwegian folk speech." The humanis-
tic faculty of the University of Oslo at first refused to nominate representatives to the Commission on the plea that this formulation committed them to a particular linguistic policy which would be inconsistent with their freedom as scientists. In its comment on this stand
the Ministry of Education emphasized that "a distinction must be made
between linguistic research and linguistic normalization and guidance.
The latter has to build on scientific research and take its results into
account, but is not in itself a purely scientific problem. It is in equal,
or greater, degree a national, social, or practical-pedagogic problem."[5]

        The distinction made by the Ministry of Education's adviser
is one that it would be hard for any linguist to reject once he thinks
more closely about it. In countries where he is asked to assume

partial responsibility for language normalization, he has to face the
same conflict of conscience as the atomic scientist in our country.
No matter how well versed he may be in linguistics, he cannot then
plead that everyone's language is equally good or that it does not matter how a thing is said or written. Every dialect or every language
may be equally entitled to exist in a historical sense and equally capable of expressing what its users wish to say. But within the nation
Hall's goal of "the most efficient way of saying or doing" something
is precisely promoted by uniformity of code rather than by diversity.

It is along this dimension that our understanding of linguistic
normalization must proceed. If we do not keep our gaze one-sidedly
turned on the linguistic structure itself, but lift up our eyes to see the
society in which we really live, I think we have a model on which we
can build. Linguists seldom consider the nature of the pressure that
creates the high degree of uniformity among the speakers of what
Bloomfield called a "speech community." Anyone who has observed
the process of child learning of language will not fail to note the numerous instances of mutual ridicule and intolerance on the part of the
still untutored savages. Schizoglossia is rooted out among them by
constant correction, which goes far beyond the minimum needs of
communication and virtually insists on identity of code. If it were not
for this kind of insistence, there would be no language structure and
no language history.

The introduction of writing made possible the infinite extension of the language community beyond the immediate reach of the
voice. It made possible the building of nations and empires, which in
their turn became extended speech communities. Within these the
pressure against schizoglossia was directed above all at the normalization and standardization of writing, but with the growth of other means
of communication through travel, it came to embrace also speech at
least of those who travelled. Only by reducing what Hockett has called
the noise of the code could the institutions of modern societies be built.
From the prime community of children and savages over the secondary
communities of classes and professions to the great states of modern
times the basic model of communication remains the same, and the
need for uniformity of code wherever communication is to be rapid
and unimpeded is constant. The role of the written word in this connection has barely begun to be understood. Perhaps even the much

reviled "spelling pronunciations," which Bloomfield (p. 501) called
"ugly," may be found to have their virtues.

It seems to me that all the activities of rhetoricians and
normative grammarians, from Samuel Johnson to the lowliest schoolmarm in American rural schools, need to be reevaluated in terms of
this model. Dialects, whether regional or social, have their charms,
but they hamper communication by calling attention to features which
either are or ought to be irrelevant to the message. They label their
man by his social history, and their maintenance is often advocated
precisely by those who wish to maintain a snobbish distinction of class.
If dialects are to be tolerated, the teaching of tolerance must begin
with other and more basic features of inequality in society than the
purely linguistic one. In spite of the evidence piled up in Fries's
American English Grammar* concerning the failure of the schoolmarm
to impose her norm in certain areas, I am convinced that the comparative uniformity of American linguistic usage has been greatly facilitated by her activities. There is no nation in the world where the dictionary has entered daily life to the extent of ours, or where the teaching of "correct" grammar has touched as many lives. It is not difficult to see in this activity a reflection of the basic faith of Americans,
however unrealistic it may have turned out to be, in equality of opportunity for all. In other countries one could learn the best usage only
by associating with an aristocracy, which generally meant being born
into one; here culture could be learned from a book.

There is an interesting difference of attitude among the Scandinavian countries in this respect. In Sweden the firmness of the written standard language has led to its dominance over speech. While
the colloquial standard in many ways escapes from this dominance,
the formal standard is strongly marked by it. While there are regional
varieties, a recent investigation of the school practices showed that
they were being reduced. Those pronunciations which come closest
to the spelling are favored. In Norway the opposite condition prevails.
The fluidity of the written standard has led to widespread toleration
of dialectal speech on the stage and in private life. But the effects of
widespread communication are nevertheless apparent in the mutual

---

*Charles C. Fries. American English Grammar. New York:
D. Appleton-Century Co. 1940.

adjustment of speakers from various parts of the country to one another. And one may surmise on the basis of various tendencies that
if once the written norm is unified, a concerted effort will follow
through the schools to impose a common standard of pronunciation.

In conclusion, then, I note that there are two courses one can
follow to meet the problem of schizoglossia in modern society. Linguists who do not regard it as a problem may of course take a laissez-
faire attitude to it. But they cannot claim that they do so because this
is the scientific position. The scientific position is to recognize that
a problem exists, that it needs research and study in terms of social
goals, and that mere toleration is not really a remedy. Normalization, which aims to provide a common code for those who need one,
is a remedy, and linguists can make a contribution by seeing to it
that it is a good one. It would be nice if we could persuade polite society to accept Eliza Doolittle as she is, but in our heart of hearts
most of us would prefer to associate with her after Dr. Higgins has
straightened out her aiches.

NOTES

[1] Robert A. Hall. Leave Your Language Alone. (Ithaca,
New York, 1950) p. 236.
[2] Op. cit. , 248.
[3] Op. cit. , 236.
[4] Dwight MacDonald. New Yorker, 10 March 1962.
[5] Stortingstidende 1950, St. prp. nr. 1, Tillegg nr. 3.

DISCUSSION

J. C. THOMPSON: (U. S. Government) I want to add one more
possible way of looking at this. After Henry Higgins had straightened
out Eliza Doolittle's pronunciation, he had to correct her dress and
her manners before she was acceptable in polite society. I think that it
is both accurate and illuminating to consider linguistic norms in the
same light as we consider norms in dress and etiquette. They are very
definitely there and if you don't observe them you will find yourself
with a very bad social black eye. But Miss Fidditch has always considered that the norms of grammar were much more immutable than

the norms of etiquette, and it is perhaps an attempt to correct this attitude which led Hall[1] and others to over-correct it, by, as you say, throwing the baby out with the bath water.

CHARLES BIDWELL: (University of Pittsburgh) I think Prof. Haugen has quite correctly stated that the question of normalization vs. laissez faire with regard to regional social variations of speech is not a question of scientific attitude. But I can't see that he has proven that there actually is a question here. He apparently has an aesthetic preference for normalization. I have an aesthetic preference for diversity. I think this is perhaps a question of individual philosophies.

MR. HAUGEN: I don't have any comment on Mr. Thompson's statement, but I do have a comment on Mr. Bidwell's. I think I said that dialects have their charms, and this indicates my aesthetic preference for diversity, but I prefer it to be, in some ways, an individual diversity, rather than a dialectally determined diversity. In other words, I prefer the inevitable diversity of individuals within a group, rather than an individual's membership in a group, which exposes him to the prejudices of other groups with whom he comes into contact. However, it is evident that this is not just a matter of aesthetics. I was trying to suggest that the development of norms, and whatever fumbling efforts have been made by Miss Fidditch or by Miss Fidditch's teachers to create such norms, is simply an extension of the normalization that goes on in every speech community, whether a relatively primitive one, or a more civilized one. Where people talk together they talk alike if they continue long enough. This is clearly a result of a basic feature of communication, which we can study in Hockett's book[2] by studying the models and the theory of communication, namely that uniformity of code leads to more rapid encoding and decoding than is possible when we are uncertain what the person said because we did not hear it. I have that difficulty, when listening for example, to British stage plays, and I lose a great deal of what is said because there is a deviation, a difference in code between British English and my English.

PAUL GARVIN: (Thompson Ramo Wooldridge) One of Bloomfield's great contributions was, among others, to have pointed out that sub-standard varieties of a language deserve study. The great virtue of the present paper is that it points out that the study of sub-standard

varieties does not exclude normative varieties of the language as a
fit subject for study. I think that the role of the linguist in the normalization process, is, perhaps, one of attempting to bring about a
certain realism in the sense that the norm which one would like to see
taught in the schools should be one which is actually in use and not one
which exists merely in the imagination of certain people. This, I believe, is a scientific problem because it is a matter of ascertaining
what exactly is good usage in appropriate sources from which the norm
is to be taken. It involves more than just linguistics. It also involves,
as was properly pointed out, sociology, and anthropology, just to mention two.

WILLIAM STEWART: (Center for Applied Linguistics) It is
true that Hall has been criticized time and again, and this is not the
first time that he has been accused of having thrown the baby out with
the water, in his book, Leave Your Language Alone.[3] However, his
comments are more to the point in another book which is less read,
but is a good book, that is, Hands Off Pidgin English![4] It still has
the admonishing attitude which is so typical of Hall, but it brings out
a point which should be well taken. Namely, that it is one thing to
say that, in an area which is already linguistically unified to a certain
extent, maximum unification under the norms of a single, prescribed
set of linguistic norms may be desirable. But it is another thing again,
in a linguistically pluralistic situation, to try to apply indiscriminately
a single set of norms to what are structurally fairly autonomous linguistic forms. Attempts of this type have led to attacks on most of
those pidgin and creole languages which are lexically related to European standard languages, but which, in fact, have grammatical structures which make them different enough from the latter to require
separate formalizations. This is, for example, what Hall describes
as having happened with Melanesian Pidgin English in the book I refer
to.

RALPH ALLEN: (Department of the Army) Prof. Haugen
needs no defense from me, but in this matter of normalization, we,
the people identified with the Armed Services, have a special problem.
That is, the codes of large and sophisticated groups of speakers of
English are the codes of British English, not American English, and
we find it very definitely necessary to create a reflex response identification in American English as opposed to British English. My asso-
ciates from the Air Force can bear testimony that when you are in a

jet trainer headed for something large and solid at about 450 knots, there is no time to go into an analysis, syntactic or otherwise, to determine what the British English phrase means in American English or vice versa.

MR. HAUGEN: I am grateful for this example. If we all are going to be reduced to traveling at jet speeds, we obviously will have to have one common language for the entire world, one code in which we can communicate. Whether this is British English or American English will remain for the future to determine.

I would like to comment on Mr. Stewart's point with regard to Hall's Melanesian book which I will grant that I have not read so that I am handicapped in commenting on it. But I accept his statement, and I think that in a down-to-earth discussion, Hall and I would not disagree very seriously. It is more the aggressive tone in his other book Leave Your Language Alone to which I reacted, and which I think should not be allowed to stand as the last word of scientific linguistics' comment on this problem. I think the problem is far subtler than Hall presents it, far more difficult to handle. I was particularly driven to this problem by the review in The New Yorker[5] of the Webster's Third New International Dictionary in which structural linguistics is specifically the villain of the piece in "the betrayal of English," "the string untuned." I agree that Miss Fidditch's norm was not always realistic, as Paul Garvin pointed out. Nevertheless it was a norm, and most people, I think, can be taught anything as long as you teach it to them in simple terms. If you tell them that 'ain't' is wrong, this is a much more effective way to teach it than to say, "well, over in Pennsylvania there are a few cultured people who say 'ain't' in the first person but never in the third." This is essentially what Webster's new dictionary says, namely, that a number of cultured people in various parts of the country say 'ain't' in the first person, but in the third person, or second person, it is non-standard or sub-standard. Perhaps it is a large question to decide whether a dictionary should be normative or scientific in such cases and just what the difference is between the two.

NOTES ON DISCUSSION

[1]R. A. Hall, Jr. Leave Your Language Alone! Ithaca, N.Y.: Linguistica, 1950.

[2] Charles F. Hockett. A Course in Modern Linguistics; Mac-Millan, 1958.

[3] op. cit.

[4] R. H. Hall. Hands Off Pidgin English; Pacific Publications, Sydney, Australia, 1955.

[5] Dwight MacDonald. New Yorker, 10 March, 1962.

8 | Linguistics and Language Planning

1. Introduction

1.1. The problem of correctness in language has been a topic of absorbing interest to a number of writers in the United States for many years. The issue has arisen once more since the appearance of a third edition of Webster's New International Dictionary, hereafter referred to as Webster's Third. Some estheticians of the English language, chiefly self-appointed guardians of its purity, have associated the policies of Webster's Third with the name of structural linguistics. We are told by one notorious critic of Webster's Third, Mr. Dwight MacDonald (1962), that its lexical method is based on "the theory of Structural Linguistics." Now there is no evidence either in the editor's statements or in the practice of the dictionary to support this surprising claim. Nevertheless we are informed by Mr. MacDonald that the dictionary is an example of "the infiltration of Structural Linguistics into places it doesn't belong." If only to protect the good name of linguistics, I believe we should examine the relationship between the science of language and the problem of linguistic norms. Without attempting to refute the absurd accusations here made against structural linguistics, we shall try to formulate once again, for our generation, the nature of linguistic normalization and the potential role of the linguist in codifying norms and giving them the sanction of authority.

1.2. Prior to the nineteenth century it is safe to say that ALL LINGUISTICS WAS NORMATIVE. The much-admired Pāṇini was a linguistic law-giver, whose work served the purposes of religious continuity. The Greek and Latin grammarians were textbook writers, who wished to establish immutable norms for the correct

writing and speaking of their languages, the <u>ius et norma loquendi</u>.
Perhaps this is the reason their work is regularly referred to in
slighting terms as "pre-scientific." But even in the nineteenth century many of the distinguished founders of the new linguistic science
were deeply involved in problems of normalization. The Danish
Rasmus Rask spent a great deal of time in devising a more rational
spelling for his native tongue and published a whole book on the subject (1826). German founders of the historical school of linguistics,
like Jakob Grimm and August Schleicher, wrote extensively on the
subject of correctness in German. In the second half of the century,
when the Neo-Grammarians dominated linguistics, they too made
important contributions to the problem. Hermann Paul devoted a
whole chapter of his <u>Principien</u> to the "Gemeinsprache" or standard
language (1886: 350-68), while Adolf Noreen wrote a penetrating study
of the problem of correctness in language (1892). In England the
great founder of phonetics, Henry Sweet, was active throughout life
in the Spelling Reform Association. In the twentieth century Antoine
Meillet considered the problem in great detail (1928), while Otto
Jespersen devoted two full chapters of his <u>Mankind, Nation, and
Individual</u> (1925) to the subject of "standards of correctness." Jespersen also took active part in the work for international auxiliary
languages, creating one of his own called Novial.

　　　　1.3. In our own country two of the best-known founders of
linguistics, Edward Sapir and Leonard Bloomfield, both took an
interest in the subject. Sapir worked for the International Auxiliary
Language Association (Sapir and Swadesh 1932). Bloomfield wrote
an article on "Literate and illiterate speech" (1927) and devoted several pages in his book <u>Language</u> (1933) to the application of linguistic
science to problems of correctness and standard language, as well
as to those of English spelling and international languages. In his
conclusion he wrote: "It is only a prospect, but not hopelessly
remote, that the study of language may help us toward the understanding and control of human events" (Bloomfield 1933: 509). Even
the anti-normative pronouncements of Robert A. Hall, Jr. represent
a vigorous concern with the problems of a normative linguistics.
Urging people to "leave their language alone" (Hall 1950) or to keep
their "hands off pidgin English" (1955) is in itself an evaluation of competing policies with respect to linguistic innovation. In our discussion
here we propose to be neither pro- nor anti-normative, but to insist

that correctness in language is a linguistic problem, and that as such it is worthy of the attention of linguistic science. The anti-normative attitude is by no means original with American linguistics. In the nineteenth century linguists early began making the distinction now accepted between descriptive and prescriptive linguistics; Esaias Tegnér, the Swedish linguist, wrote (1874:104) that the business of linguistics was "not to prescribe the laws of language, but to describe them" (inte att skriva språkets lagar, utan att beskriva dem). However, the line between these two activities is a thin one. And in our day of social science, the description of norms and values and the process by which they are arrived at is not regarded as an entirely unscientific procedure. Our problem today will be to distinguish these activities and see just what linguistic science and scientists can contribute to them. Even if this is not a pure science, it is unquestionably an application of linguistic technology which will classify as one branch of applied linguistics.

2. The Nature of Language Planning.

     2.1. Normative or prescriptive linguistics may be regarded as a kind of management or manipulation of language, which presupposes what I shall here call "language planning" (hereafter written LP). PLANNING is a human activity that arises from the need to find a solution to a problem. It can be completely informal and ad hoc, but it can also be organized and deliberate. It may be undertaken by private individuals or it may be official. Social planning is an activity with a well-defined scope in our society, though various countries find it palatable to varying degrees in particular areas. If planning is well done, it will include such steps as extensive fact-finding, the consideration of alternative plans of action, the making of decisions, and the implementation of these in specified ways.

     2.2. This suggested model is applicable to LP also. LP is called for wherever there are language problems. If a linguistic situation for any reason is felt to be unsatisfactory, there is room for a program of LP. In an earlier paper I defined LP as "the activity of preparing a normative orthography, grammar, and dictionary for the guidance of writers and speakers in a non-homogeneous speech community" (Haugen 1959:8). I would now prefer to regard this as one of the outcomes of LP, a part of the implementation of the decisions made by the language planners. The heart of LP is rather what I referred to as the "exercise of judgment in the form of choices among available linguistic forms." Even more concisely, I think we can define LP as THE EVALUATION OF LINGUISTIC CHANGE. This is the opinion also of the Indian scholar P. S. Ray, whose stimulating book on Language Standardization has been invaluable in preparing the following paper. He describes prescriptive linguistics as "the search for reasonableness in the discrimination of linguistic innovations" (Ray 1963:18).

2.3. It is of course possible to deny all scientific value to the process of evaluation and choice, since linguistics proudly declares itself to be a descriptive science. Without getting entangled in the problem of free will and determinism, however, we can safely say that the question of choice in language is still completely open. The fact that each individual has to learn language anew, and never learns precisely the language of his teachers, and that people can and do change their language in the course of their lives, is sufficient to guarantee that there must be some area of choice. In so far as this is true, we can speak of LP as an attempt to influence these choices. Like any evaluation, it assumes that there are standards against which different linguistic innovations can be evaluated.

2.4. We must not in advance, however, assume that we know what these standards are. LP is not committed in advance either to PROMOTING or PREVENTING change. It is not committed to advocating either UNIFORMITY or DIVERSITY among different speakers or groups. It is not committed to either resisting or encouraging borrowing between languages: it may work either for PURIFICATION or HYBRIDIZATION. It may advocate either EX- PANDING or RESTRICTING the resources of a language. It is not committed to EFFICIENCY at the expense of BEAUTY; it may work for ACCURACY as well as EXPRESSIVENESS. It is not even committed to the MAINTENANCE of the language for which it plans: it may work for a SHIFT to some other language.

2.5. In presenting the following systematic account of LP, we shall adopt a plan that is suggested by the general approach of DECISION THEORY. The study of decision making is one of the

favorite pursuits of social theorists in our day, and there can be no
doubt that the general pattern of decision making holds for LP also.
Without pretending to master the intricacies of this field of study, I
would like to suggest that the data here presented fit well into a
sequence which we may call a decision procedure. To take a definition at random: "Decision-making results in the selection from a
socially defined, limited number of problematical, alternative pro-
jects (i. e. course of action) of one project to bring about the particular future state of affairs envisaged by the decision-makers" (Snyder 1958:19).[1] We shall consider the kind of PROBLEMS that give
rise to LP, the kind of DECISION-MAKERS that have been involved,
the ALTERNATIVES that have been proposed and the limitations on
these, the principles of EVALUATION that have been applied, and
the IMPLEMENTATION by means of which policies have been enforced. In a short paper like the present one, we can only hope to
sketch the outlines of what is obviously a very large subject.

     2. 6. Before considering the problems that give rise to LP,
it will be important to establish the respective roles of SPEECH and
WRITING. It will be quite impossible even to enter upon the subject
if we maintain the usual position of linguists as expressed in Bloomfield's famous dictum (1933:21) that writing is "merely a way of
recording language by means of visible marks." The aggressively
pejorative form of this statement is understandable in the light of
Bloomfield's didactic purpose. No one can deny the overwhelming
importance for linguistic science of the realization that writing is
historically secondary to speech, as well as in the learning and the
life of an individual. However, in the study of LP we shall have to
reverse this relationship. We shall have to consider writing primary
and speech secondary. This may be one reason for the comparative
lack of interest among linguists in LP: to them it turns things upside
down. It considers as primary what the linguist regards as secondary
and assigns value to something which the linguist considers only a
shadow of reality. The reason for the reversal is given by the function of writing as the medium of communication between speakers
separated in time and space. Its permanence and its importance for
the community permit and require a different kind of treatment from
that which is accorded natural speech. Instead of remaining a mere
record, it comes to embody a code of its own, which can influence
the community speech.

2.7. The relation of a written language to the idiolectal codes of its users can be analyzed into a dual translation. If we start with any given idiolect, a linguist can apply his techniques and come up with an accurate and exhaustive record of the idiolect in the form of a standard linguistic description. We may call this the speaker's GRAPHOLECT, a precise record of his idiolect. Even in the most favorable case there are perceptible differences between them. The grapholect differs from the idiolect in being (a) edited, (b) analyzed, (c) delayed, and (d) stabilized. That it is EDITED means that it contains none of the innumerable and unpredictable erroneous utterances and false starts of the real speaker (Hockett 1958:142). That it is ANALYZED means that such sequential units as the phonemes and the words are separated instead of being fused: /wàyncə télmiy/ appears as five or six successive units in any orthography I could imagine of English: why didn't you tell me? That it is DELAYED means that it is learned as a second language and will therefore call for greater reflection and elaboration than the idiolect. that it is STABILIZED means that it has greater storage capacity and carrying power, and therefore encourages repetition and stability in its forms. In applying these principles to the idiolect, the linguist has translated the idiolect into a new medium, with consequent change of techniques and loss of information. The user of the grapholect must do the same in learning to read and write.

2.8. But the grapholect is not yet an orthography. A second translation must take place to adapt it to the needs of other idiolects, or in short, A COMPROMISE OF GRAPHOLECTS. As pointed out by Martin Joos (1960:257) an ideal orthography should provide some degree of morphemic stability by being morphophonemic; it should permit alternate interpretation of the symbols so that different idiolects can read their own sounds into it; and it should be uniform so that diverse speech habits can be translated into it. But this means that a standard orthograpny is to some extent independent of the speech habits of its users; it becomes a language of its own, not just a reflection of speech. Its learners have a double learning problem: the gap between speech and writing purely as an encoding technique, and the gap between their idiolects and those reflected in the writing. This second gap is the one that can lead to actual linguistic change under the influence of writing, for writing can generate its own speech by being read aloud. By applying the translation rules he

has learned, the reader can produce an idiolect different from his
own to the extent that the grapholect is not identical with his. This
effect is possible no matter how phonemically a language is spelled.
In fact, a completely phonemic spelling will promote uniformity of
pronunciation, so that spelling pronunciation is rather more likely in
German than in English. Spelling pronunciations are unpopular
among linguists, but a language like High German is inconceivable
without them. [2]

2.9. The problem of STYLE in language is also important
in a consideration of LP. While this, too, is closely associated with
the distinction between speech and writing, it goes back well beyond
the invention of writing. The distinction of styles according to situation has been documented by students of American Indian languages,
who have used the term 'non-casual' speech for what I would prefer
to call by its traditional term, 'formal' style. [3] We can identify certain genres of discourse which promote linguistic formality even in
non-literate societies, such as LAWS, RITUALS, and EPICS. In
these the language departs from that of everyday speech by being
more dignified, distinct, and memorable. The reason is quite simply
that these are of such importance to the life of the community that
they must be memorized and passed on unaltered from generation to
generation. They are entrusted to the LAWMAN, the PRIEST, and
the BARD, who thereby become at once the conservers of tradition
and its potential innovators. The language which in this way comes
down from the past is public and official, in a way that everyday talk
is not. It is based on the situation of one speaking to many and for
many; it is the voice of the group itself. If this is true in a non-
literate society, it becomes increasingly so in a literate society,
since writing enormously extends the size of memory storage as well
as its accuracy. It would be most surprising if this did not have linguistic consequences in the form of a growing gap between casual and
formal discourse, with the consequent high level of vocabulary retention over time (Zengel 1962).

2.10. Having now established the primacy of writing over
speech for purposes of LP, we may make it into a general statement:
LP refers primarily to the formal rather than the informal styles of
language, especially in their written form. Any influence of the formal style on the informal is a secondary effect; the primary purpose

is to influence the formal through changes in its written expression.
This is the setting and background for all LP.

3. Problems of Language Planning

3.1. If we now consider the first aspect of LP, the PROB-
LEMS that give rise to it, they are all special cases of the problem
of NON-COMMUNICATION. LP is in principle conceivable wherever
there is failure of communication. But failure is not an either-or
concept; it ranges along a scale from complete success to complete
failure. If we take the extremes and the mean of this parameter, we
may establish three kinds of communicatory situations: that of the
face-to-face PRIMARY SPEECH-COMMUNITY where the only differences between speakers are idiosyncratic, or in linguistic terms,
idiolectal; a SECONDARY SPEECH-COMMUNITY where there is partial understanding; and a TERTIARY SPEECH-COMMUNITY in which
there is none, so that interpreters are required. Among political
units we may instance Iceland as a primary speech-community, England as a secondary speech-community, and Switzerland as a tertiary
speech-community. We cannot here be concerned with the overlap-
pings of these concepts, but merely point out that the secondary
speech-community is ripe for a NATIONAL language, the tertiary
for an INTERNATIONAL, or AUXILIARY language. Both are instances of situations where LP can be called on for assistance and
development. More generally, each of these needs a common code,
an auxiliary language, which will enable those who wish to communicate with the members of other primary speech-communities than
their own to do so (Gumperz 1962).

3.2. By emphasizing the importance of the spoken language
and the individual informant, linguistics has singled out the primary
speech-community as its special concern. In such a community LP
is superfluous, since the immediate necessities of communication
have provided the corrective to individual anarchy. Each learner is
corrected on the spot by other learners and his older models, often
by the bitter expedient of mockery, until he has learned to conform
to the best of his ability. The linguistic code is internalized by each
member of the community. In this way the interference with communication which has been referred to as 'code noise' is reduced to

a minimum. It seems to me that the model which is here suggested, on the basis of information theory, as most adequately describing the face-to-face situation of primary speech communication, can also be applied to the secondary and even tertiary speech communities. Mutatis mutandis, the larger speech community, in which communication must be mediated, is best served by a common code. This code lacks the immediacy of the speech situation; it must be more consciously shaped, and in so far as writing is involved, there is ample room for LP. The main point is that a written language lacks the self-correcting feature of speech; it needs a specialized class of guardians to provide this therapeutic effect.

3.3. In practice the problematical situations vary widely. At one end of the scale is the illiterate population without any written tradition or centralized government whatever, a situation that is rapidly growing rarer throughout the world. Where writing has been introduced, a number of distinct situations can be distinguished. Ferguson (1962) has proposed a scale for describing these, using W0-W2 as a scale for the extent of WRITING, and St0-St2 as a scale for the extent of STANDARDIZATION. W2 represents languages in which "original research in physical sciences is regularly published" and St2 languages which have "a single, widely accepted norm which is felt to be appropriate with only minor modifications or variations for all purposes for which the language is used." Even these "ideal states" are of various kinds and require subclassification; for example, Swedish, which he considers an example of St2, covers an area in which there are living dialects that are quite incomprehensible to each other and to speakers of the standard. For speakers in Dalecarlia there are many occasions when Swedish is not felt to be appropriate. Countries like the United States or Iceland, to take one large and one small example, are much closer to the "ideal state" of St2 (Benediktsson 1962). Whatever the situation with respect to writing or standardization, there are problems for the language planner.

3.4. If the language is unwritten, there is the problem of providing an ORTHOGRAPHY. If it has an orthography, it may be or have become INADEQUATE for the needs of its users; or there may be COMPETING ORTHOGRAPHIES. Even if the orthography is adequate or is so well established that there can be no reasonable hope of change, there may be VARIATIONS within the standard which are subject to evaluation. These may affect pronunciation, grammar,

syntax, or lexicon. Opinions can differ on which if any is either
desirable and therefore to be promoted, or undesirable and therefore
to be discouraged. It appears that such judgments are made in all
speech communities, from the simplest to the most complex. They
are not even limited to literate communities. Bloomfield (1927)
found that his Menomini informants in Wisconsin, much to his surprise, had strong opinions concerning the quality of language used by
their fellow speakers. He concluded that "by a cumulation of obvious
superiorities, both of character and standing, as well as of language,
some persons are felt to be better models of conduct and speech than
others."

4. The Role of the Language Planner

4.1. This suggestion leads us now to consider the PLANNER
himself, as DECISION-MAKER. Or in Dwight MacDonald's loaded
form (1962: 259): "What kind of authority, if any, should attempt to
direct and control change?" Prior to the Renaissance the care of
language was in the hands of the grammarians and rhetoricians.
Quintilian in his De Institutione Oratoria (ca 95 A.D.) defined one of
the functions of grammar as that of "forming right speech" (recte
loquendi scientiam) (1875: 29). The grammars of Greek and Latin
came, predictably, well after the classical periods of these languages,
and were essentially CODIFICATIONS of an already accepted norm.
Codification is usually assumed to be one of the marks of a standard
language, but it makes a difference whether it is merely a linguist's
description of an accepted norm, say in literature or polite speech,
or is conceived of as fixing or even creating that norm. The term
codification means simply the explicit statement of the code, in the
form of an ORTHOGRAPHY, a GRAMMAR, and a LEXICON. But the
attitude towards the codifier and his own conception of his role has
changed sharply through time, along with the meaning of the word
"code." To those who thought of language as having divine origin,
the codifier was a pundit, dispensing God's truth to the people. Suc-
cessively the code has been regarded as law and the codifier as law-
giver, as etiquette and the codifier as arbiter of fashion, as national
symbol and the codifier as a national hero. To estheticians he has
stood as a champion of the norms of beauty, to logicians as the up-
holder of rationality, to the philosopher as interpreter of the laws of

thinking. Now that information theory has given us a new meaning of "code," we are prepared to think of a codifier as a linguistic technician. But as social scientists we must be prepared to recognize that all the meanings of code and all the roles of the codifier which I have suggested still exist and enter into the complex function of language planning in human society.

4. 2. It is noteworthy how the first grammars and dictionaries of the modern languages coincided with the rise of their countries to wealth and power in the fifteenth and sixteenth centuries. A typical instance is the first Spanish grammar, Nebrija's Grammatica de la Lengua Castellana of 1492, which he dedicated to Queen Isabella and called "a compañero del imperio" (Daube 1940:31). The first academy devoted to winnowing out the "impurities" of a language was part of the same movement, in this case the establishment of Florence and its Tuscan dialect as the model of Italian. This was the Accademia della Crusca of 1582, which was the model of Cardinal Richelieu's Académie Française of 1635. The canny cardinal dictated the statutes, no doubt as part of his policy of political centralization, asking its members "to labor with all the care and diligence possible to give exact rules to our language and to render it capable of treating the arts and sciences" (Robertson 1910:13). The example was followed, among others, in Spain (1713), in Sweden (1786), and in Hungary (1830). The chief visible fruits of the academies were dictionaries, beginning with the first known monolingual dictionary, the Vocabolario degli Accademici della Crusca (1612). There was great agitation in England on the part of many notable writers of the 17th and 18th centuries, such as Milton, Dryden, Defoe, and Swift, calling for an English academy (Flasdieck 1928). But the English resisted any French idea, especially one in which they could sniff the odor of authoritarianism, and in the long run they accepted instead the decrees of a private citizen, Samuel Johnson, whose dictionary (1755) became the first important arbiter of English. The United States declared its linguistic independence of England by substituting another private citizen, Noah Webster, for the English Johnson.[4]

4. 3. The heaviest demand for codifiers arose, however, in the nineteenth and twentieth centuries, primarily as a consequence of the American and French Revolutions and the spread of literacy. Reaching the masses was a problem of teaching, and books were the

instruments of instruction. The technological demands of the printing press required standardization. Some populations awoke to the
fact that they were being pressured into a new language, and were in
fact second-class citizens in their own country. Political upsets led
to the rise of new nations, or the revival of old ones, and we see in
country after country the establishment of new languages as the result of codifications by individuals, by government commissions, or
by academies. Names like Korais in Greece, Aasen in Norway,
Štur in Slovakia, Mistral in Provence, Dobrovsky in Bohemia, Aavik
in Estonia, and Jablonskis in Lithuania come to mind. These men
were part linguists, part patriots, and their work left something to
be desired as pure linguistics. Yet some of them contributed strongly
to the growth of the science; for example, Aasen was also the founder
of Norwegian dialectology. In all European countries with a universal
public school system the Ministries of Education exercised control
over the orthography and grammar of their language. In Turkey the
dictator Kemal Atatürk established a semi-official Turkish Linguistic
Society in 1932, filled it with party members and school teachers,
and gave them the job of planning the reformation of Turkish after he
had officially abolished its Persian script and substituted Roman
(Heyd 1954). Between the extremes of private initiative and dictator-
ship, there is a wide range of organizations which have undertaken
LP on behalf of some linguistic form, whether churches, societies,
or schools of literature and science.

5. Alternatives in Language Planning

    5.1. Let us now consider some of the ALTERNATIVE
COURSES OF ACTION that are open to a program of LP. We shall
here confine our attention to the secondary speech community, and
of these particularly to the nation, since as Ferguson justly observed
(1962:25), this linguistically neglected entity is after all the usual
basis for "communication networks, educational systems, and language 'planning'". There are sub-national groups like the Welsh and
trans-national groups like the Jews who have language problems of
the same order as nations, but lacking official organs of support must
get along as best they can in their language planning efforts. Much of
what is here said applies equally to them, and only space prevents me
from discussing their special situations.

5.2. In considering courses of action we need first to ponder some of the GOALS of linguistic behavior. We have so far assumed that this is rapid and effortless communication. But the basic model of communication, as suggested by Bühler and elaborated by Jakobson (1960), makes it clear that communication is not limited to purely referential conveying of information. There is that expression of ego which Jakobson calls EMOTIVE and the appeal to the listener which he calls CONATIVE; beyond these are such minor functions as the PHATIC, the METALINGUAL, and the POETIC. In terms of the social situation there is here involved an intricate interplay between the speaker and his audience, who may be taken to represent the community. He is expressing himself, but only that can be expressed which his community is ready to accept. Language does not merely serve as a means of social coöperation, but also as a means of individual expression. The first leads to UNIFORMITY of code, the second to DIVERSITY. The actual result has to be some kind of balance between the two.

5.3. For this reason we cannot, as stated earlier, identify the goal of planning as necessarily an absolutely uniform code, either in time or space. This is one of the errors that some would-be planners make: they wish to fix a language for all time, or to impose a single standard on speakers with the most diverse dialects. But planning can either envisage the replacement of MANY BY ONE or of ONE BY MANY. There can be planning for diversity as well as for uniformity, for change as well as for stability. Havránek (1932, 1938), in defining the nature of a standard language, described it as having STABILITY with FLEXIBILITY (cf. Garvin 1959). This is nothing peculiar to a standard language; it is the definition of any language norm, even that of the primary speech-community. Stability is the diachronic correlate to uniformity, while flexibility is the diachronic correlate to diversity. While a living language norm is predominantly stable and uniform, it provides for its users a varying margin of elasticity and diversity. As Hoenigswald has pointed out (1960: 27 ff.), all language change can be defined as REPLACEMENT, which may be either a split or a merger or neither. Evaluation follows the same course: it may decide in favor of many rather than one or one rather than many.

6. Limitations on Language Planning

6.1. Before making any such decisions, however, it is
necessary to establish the LIMITATIONS OF CHANGE. The planner
enters the situation at a given point in time and space. His first task
will be to identify the language in question. This may not be an easy
thing to do. When the Norwegian language reformer Ivar Aasen set
out to recover the Norwegian language from its eclipse in the Middle
Ages, he had to identify the language as a norm existing only in a
variety of rural dialects, which most people assumed were degenerate varieties of Danish. Prior to the work of Štur in Slovakia, at
about the same time, the dialects of that country had been identified
as varieties of Czech, a language with a much longer written tradition.
One way for the planner to identify a language is to establish its history. By a combination of internal reconstruction and comparative
linguistics, these men created norms which took their places as apparently lineal descendants of older languages spoken or written in
these areas. In this way linguistic geography and history combine to
fix limits to the possible proposals that can be made.

6.2. There is a further limitation on the projections of the
planner. This is constituted by the state of the spoken and written
traditions which he proposes to reform. If the standard proposed is
for a previously illiterate nation, he need consider only the speech
norms of his community. If there is only one norm, his problem is
largely the technical one of providing an orthography, as we have
noted earlier. If there is more than one, he is faced with a set of
choices which will call forth the whole panoply of problems and the
need for the kind of evaluations which we will shortly discuss. If, in
addition, there already is one or more orthographies in existence,
his task is further complicated, unless he chooses to build on one of
these and merely patch it up in some way or other. In any literate
community with some tradition behind it there is a whole set of con-
victions and rationalizations concerning speech and writing, against
which the planner may turn out to be powerless, unless he can turn
them to account for his own purposes. However irrational they may
seem, they generally turn out to bolster the status and convenience
of those who have invested effort in learning the social traditions.

6.3. In view of the sharp limitations on the alternatives, one might despair of ever securing any change, if it were not that people and societies do change and their languages with them. In evaluating the possible solutions to the problems we have broached, there is need of a decision procedure which classifies the alternatives. The alternatives must be classifiable in terms of some objective CRITERION, e.g. as longer or shorter, as older or younger. These in turn must be associable with some PURPOSE of wider concern, such as communication, self-enhancement, or group stability.

7.   Criteria for Language Planning

7.1.   Those who have written extensively on this topic have offered a variety of criteria of evaluation. Adolf Noreen (1892) rejected the classical view that the models are to be found in the past and the organismic view that language is an evolving organism beyond the control of man's reason. He proposed a set of criteria for "wrong" language based on what he considered a reasonable approach: that is wrong which is misunderstood, or not understood, or understood only with difficulty; also that which is hard to pronounce or to remember, or is longer or more complicated than necessary, or is novel without adding anything to the langue.

7.2.   Most of these criteria are aspects of what we may more concisely sum up as the criterion of EFFICIENCY. The earliest formulation of it which I happen to know was made even before Noreen, under the impact of modern science, by the Swedish linguist Esaias Tegnér, who wrote (1874:104) that the best language was "that which, most easily uttered, is most easily understood" (cf. also Noreen 1892:113, Jespersen 1925:88). The important part of this dictum is that it recognized clearly that the interests of the speaker may not be identical with those of the hearer. In practice, communication is achieved by a precarious balance between the speaker's economy of utterance and the hearer's economy of perception. Writing lacks the immediate correction of an audience and therefore requires that the writer anticipate the reader's needs. It lacks a number of the devices of speech for securing clarity, such as intonations and gestures, and must make up for these by explicit signals. For the experienced reader some of this may even be supplied by

unphonemic spellings, which are so unpopular among spelling reformers and children.

7.3.   There is a clear conflict of interest here between the
haves and the have-nots, in this case those who have learned and
those who have not. A system that is simple for those who have
learned it may be extremely difficult to learn. Chinese characters
are said by those who know them to be more rapid to read than alpha-
betic representations of the same units; but the cost of learning is
clearly very high. English spelling bears only an imperfect relationship to any kind of English pronunciation; but its very unphonemic
quality gives it morphemic identity, and for other European learners
a greater familiarity and ease of learning than if it were phonemic.
Efficiency must therefore be interpreted in terms of the relative cost
of LEARNING to that of UNLEARNING. Since those who would have
to unlearn generally control the social apparatus, while those who
would learn are school children or foreigners, it is obvious that we
have here a very strong brake on any form of change. But the general principle is still valid: a form is EFFICIENT if it is EASY TO
LEARN and EASY TO USE.

7.4.   We must above all avoid such facile notions as that
shorter words are necessarily more efficient than longer words, or
that a grammar without case endings is more efficient that one with.
As P. S. Ray reminds us (1963:41), there is a real economy in having text-frequent words as short as possible, and in natural languages we find that the function words usually are. Rare words, on
the other hand, which are likely to be missed by the hearer, are more
efficiently coded as long words since this makes them more redundant.
Such words are also more usefully complex and therefore grammatically transparent than the more frequently used words. A language
like English which for Indo-European has a minimum of inflectional
endings has on the one hand an extremely complex system of prepositions, on the other a rigid word order which requires its written
style to be more explicit than other languages of the same family in
the introduction of such empty fillers as "do" and "one" (e.g. "I do
say," or "the young one").

7.5.   It should be a sufficient warning of caution, in the
establishment of the efficiency of one linguistic form as compared

with another, to recall that during the nineteenth century two diametrically opposite judgments were made of the change-over in English from a so-called synthetic to analytic structure. The Romantics called it DEGENERATION, while the Evolutionists called it PROGRESS. Today we call it merely CHANGE. We have learned that one cannot take isolated bits from a structure and judge its efficiency from these; one has to evaluate each item in terms of the whole structure, and we still have far to go before our opinions in this area can become much more than speculations.

7.6. Another criterion which is the special concern of LP, wherever it occurs, is one that I shall call ADEQUACY, a term I prefer to that of Ray, who calls it "linguistic rationality" (1963: 45 ff.). It includes also what Garvin (1959), following Havránek, calls "rising scale of intellectualization." Both of these writers were thinking primarily of the capacity of the language to meet the needs of its users as an instrument of referential meaning. This is one of the points at which LP is brought into play, for example, in creating terms to correspond to the needs of modern science. In the primary speech community devices are always available, either through borrowing or creation, to extend the lexicon as far as its speakers need for everyday purposes: we all know that Arabs are concerned about camels and Eskimos about snow and therefore have highly developed vocabularies in these areas. In the secondary speech community such needs are often stimulated by contact with other nations and translations from their languages.

7.7. But there is another kind of adequacy which is nourished within the nation. This is less likely to affect the purely rational area, but rather fall within the more intimate personal life of its users. A language is extended in adequacy not only by an extensive terminology of science and philosophy, but also by a well-developed terminology of emotional and poetic expressiveness. LP may call for the encouragement of words from rural dialects, in order that a more vivid and homely flavor be imparted to its writing. This has actually been the case in Scandinavia, where language planners in all the countries long have regarded a study of the dialects as a stimulus to enrichment of the standard languages. The rule for adequacy is that a form must convey the information its users wish to convey WITH THE DESIRED DEGREE OF PRECISION.

7.8. The third criterion is ACCEPTABILITY, by which I
mean much the same as Ray when he sets up the criterion of "linguistic commonalty. " This is the sociological component of evaluation.
It corresponds to what previous students of the subject have called
USAGE, as a standard of correctness. Jespersen (1925:133) pointed
out that there are three types of usage: the INTELLIGIBLE, which
meets the barest minimum of communication; the CORRECT, which
meets all the conventional requirements of the language norms; and
the GOOD, which meets certain higher standards of either clarity or
beauty, and therefore stirs the admiration of its audience. Actually,
these differences refer to varying degrees of acceptability within the
secondary speech-community. Since this community is neither homogeneous nor completely heterogeneous, it shows a complex pattern of
disjunctions which build up usage differentials and consequent drifts
in language. The terminology developed by Ray (1963:61) for this
situation is useful: there is a sub-set of users called the "lead, "
who are regarded as imitation-worthy and therefore have "prestige. "
The other users may imitate their usage to the extent that they have
"access" to it, which will produce the "spread" of their usage.

7.9. This corresponds to the observation made, for example, by Antoine Meillet (1928) concerning the standard languages of
Europe: "They are languages created by and for an élite. " The
whole problem is an extremely intricate one, of course, since the
presence of an élite, even for some centuries, does not in every case
lead to the triumph of its language. Classical languages like Greek,
Latin, and Arabic washed across the shores of the Mediterranean in
successive waves, absorbing populations of other language groups.
Turkish did much the same, but in the end retreated and was con-
fined to a relatively small area, as was Greek (Brosnahan 1963).
Even in ancient times some populations developed resistances to the
spread of major languages. In modern times this resistance is bol-
stered by the growth of linguistic NATIONALISM. While Meillet
deplored what he called the "linguistic balkanization" of Europe in the
twentieth century, there are grounds for thinking that linguistic
nationalism is one of the more attractive aspects of nationalism.
Indeed, a revaluation of nationalism itself appears to be taking place
among younger American scholars, who are beginning to realize that
nationalism is a step in the direction of internationalism rather than
the reverse (Geertz 1963). It means in the first instance an

encouragement to the individual citizen to think not only of his personal or local concerns, but also of those which affect his larger community. Nationalism has welded together the people of many primary
speech-communities into secondary speech-communities, and thereby counteracted the parochialism and narrowness of the former.
This function of the national standard is one reason for its value as a
symbol of the nation. It forms an instrument of communication, not
only by rulers to subjects or citizens, but also among the citizens
themselves. They become part of a larger network, even if they also
yield some portion of their linguistic distinctiveness.

7.10. At the same time the standard forms a CHANNEL OF
COMMUNICATION with the outer world, at least to the extent that
translations from other languages are made into it. While its user
may be excluded from direct participation in the life of other nations,
he gains greater access to them than he otherwise would, simply by
having a language which is capable of rendering the ideas of other,
possibly more significant, nations. The national standard is thus
under influence from the outside world, at times even threatened in
its distinctiveness by the languages of that world. Like the nation, it
wears two faces: opposing disunity within and absorption from without.

7.11. Whether the planner is setting up a national standard
or attempting to modify it, he is faced with choices as to whose usage
he is to follow in so far as he chooses to build on speech. In most
European nations it is accepted that the "lead" is an élite which is
marked either by wealth, power, birth, education, or all four together. In newer nations and more recent times, however, it has come
to pass that this élite is either non-existent or is deliberately bypas-
sed. Those who advocate Demotike in Greece, Gaelic in Ireland, or
New Norwegian in Norway have set themselves against the current
élite and made themselves a counter-élite, whose usage is built either
on rural dialects or on everyday urban speech. The problem is sometimes envisaged as one of NUMBERS (the most widespread usage) or
QUALITY (the best and most genuine forms) or of SOCIAL JUSTICE
(reducing the learning handicap of the poor). But it may also be a
conflict of geographically separated dialects, each claiming its rights
as a language. The rule of acceptability is that a form must be
ADOPTED OR ADOPTABLE BY THE LEAD of whatever society or
subsociety is involved.

7.12. The three rules of efficiency, adequacy, and acceptability may either diverge or converge in any concrete instance.
They overlap to some extent and interact in various ways, and their
relevance differs according to circumstances. But they should
enable anyone who contemplates a program of LP to make certain
decisions.

8. Implementing Language Planning

8.1. In all such programs there comes the time when the
decisions are to be implemented. How exactly has this been done?
The linguist with his grammar and lexicon may propose what he will,
if the methods that could assure acceptance are missing. Research
on this problem is essentially one of mass media and would perhaps
be more appropriate for a student of advertising than of linguistics.
In the end the decisions are made by the users of the language, the
ultimate decision-makers.

8.2. PRIVATE INDIVIDUALS have no other weight than
their personal or professional authority. Those who attack such
authority are prone to regard it as "authoritarian," while those who
favor it will prefer the word "authoritative." The economy of being
able to appeal to authority for decisions on matters that in themselves are too trivial to compel attention is very considerable. Norm-
deviant spellings draw attention away from the subject matter, but in
certain kinds of literature (e.g. light verse) this may be precisely
what is desired. Without a norm, such deviations are meaningless,
becoming mere free variation. A Samuel Johnson or a French Academy are alike in establishing a norm which by virtue of being explicit gives meaning to linguistic behavior. Style is understandable
only in terms of deviation from norms, and the rise of subnorms.

8.3. GOVERNMENTS have the advantage over private individuals of having control over the school system, through which it is
possible to train or retrain a population in its writing habits. The
success of such programs varies greatly, according to the extent of
need which they fulfill in the population. Atatürk was successful in
changing the script of his language, but his attempts to purify it of
Arabic and Persian words met solid resistance and had to be

soft-pedaled. Languages like Lithuanian (Hermann 1929) and Estonian (Ross 1938) have had great success in the coining of new words
for intellectual phenomena, while similar attempts in modern German or Danish have fallen flat (Tauli 1948).

8.4. If we consider the implementation of LP as a problem
in language learning, we see at once that it resolves itself into the
usual dilemma of the language teacher. Language teaching has basically only two kinds of instruments at its disposal: (a) models for
imitation in the form of spoken or written texts, provided by INFOR-
MANTS; and (b) a set of rules known collectively as grammar, provided by LINGUISTS. One can learn a language best from informants,
who provide models of behavior; but for adults it is helpful to supplement this with explicit rules. The reverse is not true: one may
learn ABOUT a language from rules, but without informants and their
texts one is not likely to learn a language at all. The best planner is
therefore the one who not only codifies but also produces text. For
this reason authors are necessary in the case of a written language,
just as speakers in the case of speech. The Norwegian Aasen did not
only codify his language, but also wrote poetry and prose which
established the possibility of writing it and inspired others to follow
his example. Interested organizations can provide incentives and
sanctions, from authors' subsidies and prizes to the elimination of
potential linguistic rivals by official fiat. Prestige must somehow be
established, and opportunity ("access") provided for those who wish
to learn. The most important thing is to make sure that those who
are to do the learning are motivated by some genuine advantage which
will accrue to them in return for their effort. At the very least it
must strengthen their self-respect, by making them better and more
valuable members of the society in which they live.

8.5. The simplest STRATEGY is to introduce the reform in
the schools and let it gradually grow up with the children; but this
may only result in social confusion. If English spelling were to be
reformed, I think we should pray that it be a sudden rather than a
gradual change. But this would require the act of a dictator like
Atatürk, or else total consent in advance, neither of which appears
to be in the offing.

9. The Role of Linguists

9.1. We are now ready to provide what answers we can to
the question of the role that linguists can play in a program of LP.
It must be granted that linguists are not necessarily equipped to pur-
sue language planning. Their sensitivity to linguistic nuances may
be dulled by excessive preoccupation with the mechanics of language.
But even a Linnaeus could love flowers, and there is nothing to prevent a linguist from loving his language. Literary men rarely possess the technical knowledge of linguistic patterns to be able to say
exactly what they are doing with language. One might as well ask
a great dancer or violinist to explain his art. Ability to perform is
not necessarily coupled with ability to analyze. If language planning,
as suggested earlier, is "the evaluation of linguistic change," it is
necessary to know just what change is and how it relates to the past
and present structure of the language. The great task of nineteenth
century linguistics was to make clear the fact of linguistic change:
all languages change and in regular ways. The regularity proved to
be so great that many linguists became determinists, who denied the
possibility of influencing change. Since language planning involves
the deliberate direction of linguistic change, it will be rejected by
anyone who takes a consistently deterministic position. On the other
hand, the fact that other social institutions can be and have been
changed by formal planning has given hope to those who find inade-
quacies in their language or its writing. The real problem comes in
the evaluation itself: for the literary man's hunch, the linguistic
scholar attempts to substitute explicit rules. Here twentieth century
linguistics has supplied precious information on the nature of language
as a functioning medium of human communication. Only a full understanding of this aspect can provide the knowledge necessary for a
useful evaluation.

9.2. There is also the historical fact that linguists have par-
ticipated in all successful programs of LP in the history of the world,
either as technical consultants or as prime movers. The urgent need
for such planning by linguists in the developing nations of Africa is
strongly emphasized by the Conference Report of the Leverhulme
Conference held at University College, Ibadan, Nigeria, in 1963:
". . . There is an urgent need [in Africa] for information on which
practical decisions concerning language can be taken. . . . If, in
these circumstances, linguists maintain a critical, detached,

'ivory-tower' outlook on the language situation and the language problems, they will certainly be detached from any role in some of the
greatest experiments in the twentieth century, and lose the opportunity of contributing to the general development of the continent, in
those fields in which they can make a more useful contribution than
any other group of workers" (Spencer 1963:136).

9.3. What are some of the special types of information linguists can and must bring to the problem? I would say there are
four ways in which they can help; there may be others I have overlooked. The linguist can contribute as 1) historian, 2) descriptivist,
3) theoretician, and 4) teacher.

As HISTORIAN, the linguist can establish the history of the
language. His studies make it possible to trace the continuity in
speaking or writing by a group as far back as records or reconstruction can go. He can distinguish native from borrowed elements in
the language, thereby providing a basis for purification or hybridization, as the case may be. For whatever value is placed on tradition,
he can provide it. Some periods, such as the Romantic era, feel
their self-respect enhanced by an honorable ancestry; others, perhaps more realistic, are less excited by it.

As DESCRIPTIVIST, the linguist can provide accurate descriptions of actual present-day practice, both in speech and writing,
of the community involved. As a dialect geographer he can gather
information about variety and unity in the popular speech; as a
modern student of social dialect he can establish the prestige value
of various forms. He can observe and classify the phenomena associated with standard speech and writing, so that the actual practice
of the community may be known. He can embody the results of his
research in an orthography, a grammar, and a dictionary.

As THEORETICIAN, he can establish some of the guide lines
for an understanding of language in general. More specifically,
through his knowledge of linguistic techniques of analysis and the uni-
versals of language typology, he can make statements about the
design of languages. His understanding of the relation of speech to
writing enables him to say what one can expect from the manipulation
of either one. He realizes the importance of unitary structure for

efficient communication at the same time as he allows for individual deviation. He has studied previous programs of language planning and observed the extent of their success, so that he can distinguish the "natural" from the "artful" changes.

In so far as he is also a TEACHER, the linguist keeps an eye open for problems that are likely to be involved in the training or retraining of language users. His experience and training should enable him to judge whether a particular project is pedagogically feasible and desirable. He can estimate the amount of effort currently expended on learning, and can feed back information to himself and other planners on the attitudes of his pupils toward the project involved.

9.4. Lest it be thought that we are proposing either that linguistics be identified with LP, or that LP needs only employ linguists in its project, I hasten to add in conclusion that linguistics is NECESSARY but not SUFFICIENT. In so far as LP is a kind of language politics, it needs the insights of POLITICAL SCIENCE concerning the art of what is possible and the ways of winning the consent of the governed. Since it is deeply involved in man's behavior as a social animal, it needs the support of an intelligently conceived ANTHROPOLOGICAL and SOCIOLOGICAL theory of linguistic behavior. For whatever contribution PSYCHOLOGY can make concerning learning behavior and modes of perception, there is more than enough room in LP. Nor can we overlook the contributions of the ESTHETICIANS and the PHILOSOPHERS. Even though a Dwight MacDonald may be badly informed about linguistics, he voices a point of view which cannot be disregarded if we would not wish to be considered barbarians. Even if linguistics in its pure or MICROLINGUISTIC sense can narrow its view to the microcosm of language, an applied linguistics which claims to be included in MACROLINGUISTICS cannot overlook the macrocosm of society in which we actually live, speak, and write.

NOTES

This paper is a by-product of my work on language planning in Norway (cf. Haugen 1959, 1964).

[1]I owe this reference to Charles Moskos, and others to Carl Hempl (both Fellows at the Center for Advanced Study in the Behavioral Sciences, 1963-64).

[2]Pyles (1952:241 ff.) writes: "Pronunciations based upon spelling, when these involve a change in the traditional pronunciation of a word in popular use, are a pretty sure indication not only of a spiritual arrogance which it is difficult to admire in the abstract but also of an ignorance of the relationship between writing and language."

[3]See Voegelin 1960, and other contributions to the same symposium.

[4]On Webster's views see his Errors of Grammars (1798) (quoted in Leonard 1929:223), where he objected to adopting "the practice of a few men in London." Cf. also his preface to An American Dictionary (1828), reprinted in Sledd & Ebbitt 1962:32-39.

REFERENCES

Benediktsson, Hreinn, "Icelandic dialects," Íslenzk Tunga, 3 (1962), 72-113.

Bloomfield, Leonard, "Literate and illiterate speech," American Speech, 2 (1927), 432-39.

_____ Language (New York, Holt, 1933).

Brosnahan, L. F., "Some historical cases of language imposition," Language in Africa, ed. by John F. Spencer (Cambridge, 1963), pp. 7-24.

Daube, Anna, Der Aufstieg der Muttersprache im Deutschen Denken des 15. und 16. Jahrhunderts (= Deutsche Forschungen, vol. 34) (Frankfurt a. M., 1940).

Ferguson, Charles A., "The language factor in national development," Anthropological Linguistics, 4:1 (1962), 23-27.

Flasdieck, Hermann M., Der Gedanke einer englischen Sprachakademie in Vergangenheit und Gegenwart (= Jenaer Germanistische Forschungen, 11) (Jena, 1928).

Gallis, A., "Buk Karadžić, Jugoslavias Ivar Aasen," Det Norske Videnskapsakademi i Oslo, Årbok 1949 (1950), pp. 20-21.

Garvin, Paul L., "The standard language problem—concepts and methods," Anthropological Linguistics 1:3 (1959), 28-31.

Geertz, Clifford, "The integrative revolution: primordial sentiments and civil politics in the new states," Old Societies

and New States, ed. by C. Geertz (New York, 1963), pp. 105-57.
Gumperz, John J. , "Types of linguistic communities," Anthropological Linguistics, 4:1 (1962), 28-40.
Hall, Robert A. , Jr. , Leave Your Language Alone! (Ithaca, N.Y. , Linguistica, 1950).
_____ Hands Off Pidgin English! (Sydney, Pacific Publications, 1955).
Haugen, Einar, "Planning for a standard language in modern Norway," Anthropological Linguistics, 1:3 (1959), 8-21. Reprinted, in revised form, as "Language planning in modern Norway," Scandinavian Studies, 33 (1961), 68-81. [In this volume, pp. 133-47.]
_____ Language Conflict and Language Planning: The Case of Modern Norwegian (Cambridge, Mass. , Harvard University Press, 1966).
Havránek, Bohumil, "Úkoly spisovného jazyka a jeho kultura," Spisovná Čeština a Jazyková Kultura, ed. by B. Havránek and M. Weingart (Prague, 1932), pp. 32-84. Translated in part, as "The functional differentiation of the standard language," in A Prague School Reader on Esthetics, Literary Structure, and Style, by Paul L. Garvin, 3rd printing (Washington, Georgetown University Press, 1964), pp. 3-16.
_____ "Zum Problem der Norm in der heutigen Sprachwissenschaft und Sprachkultur," Actes du Quatrième Congrès International de Linguistes (Copenhagen, 1938), pp. 151-6.
Hermann, Eduard, "Die litauische Gemeinsprache als Problem der allgemeinen Sprachwissenschaft," Nachrichten der Gesellschaft der Wissenschaften zu Göttingen, 1 (1929), 65-125.
Heyd, Uriel, Language Reform in Modern Turkey (= Oriental Notes and Studies, no. 5) (Jerusalem, Israel Oriental Society, 1954).
Hockett, Charles F. , A Course in Modern Linguistics (New York, Macmillan, 1958).
Hoenigswald, Henry, Language Change and Linguistic Reconstruction (Chicago, University of Chicago Press, 1960).
Jakobson, Roman, "Linguistics and poetics," Style in Language, ed. by Thomas Sebeok (Cambridge, Mass. , M.I.T. Press, 1960), pp. 350-77.

Jespersen, Otto, Menneskehed, Nasjon og Individ i Sproget (Oslo,
        1925). English version: Mankind, Nation and Individual
        from a Linguistic Point of View (London, 1946; Blooming-
        ton, Ind., 1964.).
Johnson, Samuel, A Dictionary of the English Language. 2 vols.
        (London, 1755).
Joos, Martin, Review of Axel Wijk, Regularized English, in Lan-
        guage, 36 (1960), 250-62.
Leonard, Sterling A., The Doctrine of Correctness in English Usage,
        1700-1800 (Madison, Wisc., 1929).
MacDonald, Dwight, "Three questions for structural linguists, or
        Webster 3 revisited," Dictionaries and That Dictionary, by
        James Sledd and Wilma R. Ebbitt (Chicago, 1962), pp. 256-
        64.
Meillet, Antoine, Les Langues dans l'Europe Nouvelle (Paris, 1928).
Noreen, Adolf, "Über Sprachrichtigkeit," Indogermanische
        Forschungen, 1 (1892), 95-157. (Translated from Swedish,
        with substituted German examples, by Arwid Johannson;
        cf. also Johannson's commentary, "Zu Noreens Abhandlung
        über Sprachrichtigkeit," Indogermanische Forschungen,
        1, 232-55).
_____ Abriss der Altnordischen Grammatik (Halle, Niemeyer,
        1896).
_____ Vårt Språk (Lund, Gleerup, 1903).
Paul, Hermann, Principien der Sprachgeschichte. 2nd ed. (Halle,
        1886).
Pyles, Thomas, Words and Ways of American English (New York,
        Random House, 1952).
Quintilian, De Institutione Oratoria. Quintilian's Institutes of Ora-
        tory, trans. by J. S. Watson (London, 1875).
Rask, Rasmus Kristian, Forsøg til en Videnskabelig Dansk
        Retskrivningslære, med Hensyn til Stamsproget og Nabo-
        sproget (Copenhagen, 1826).
Ray, Punya Sloka, Language Standardization: Studies in Prescriptive
        Linguistics. (The Hague, Mouton, 1963).
Robertson, D. Maclaren, A History of the French Academy, 1635-
        1910 (New York, 1910).
Ross, Alan S. C., "Artificial words in present-day Estonian,"
        Transactions of the Philological Society, 1938, pp. 64-72.

Sapir, Edward, and Morris Swadesh, The Expression of the Ending-
    Point Relation in English, French, and German (Baltimore,
    1932).
Sledd, James, and Wilma R. Ebbitt, Dictionaries and That Dictionary
    (Chicago, Scott, Foresman, 1962).
Snyder, Richard C., "A decision-making approach to the study of
    political phenomena," Approaches to the Study of Politics,
    ed. by Roland Young (Evanston, 1958), pp. 3-37.
Spencer, John (ed.), Language in Africa (Cambridge, 1963).
Tauli, Valter, "Om språkvårdsproblemet," Språkvetenskapliga
    Sällskapets i Uppsals, Förhandlingar (Bilaga G), 1948,
    pp. 113-31.
Tegnér, Esaias, "Om språk och nationalitet," Svensk Tidskrift,
    1874, pp. 104 ff. Reprinted in Ur Språkets Värld, 1922,
    p. 137.
Voegelin, C. F., "Casual and non-casual utterances within unified
    structure," Style in Language, ed. by Thomas Sebeok
    (Cambridge, Mass., M.I.T. Press, 1960), pp. 57-68.
Voegelin, C. F., and John Yegerlehner, "Toward a definition of for-
    mal style, with examples from Shawnee," Studies in Folk-
    lore for Stith Thompson (Bloomington, Ind., 1957), pp. 141-
    49.
Zengel, Marjorie S., "Literacy as a factor in language change,"
    American Anthropologist, 64 (1962), 132-39.

DISCUSSION

BIRNBAUM: I was interested in your reference to L'udovít
Štúr and his achievements with Slovak, and I think there are very
interesting and important parallels with the creation of Landsmål by
Ivar Aasen. On the other hand, there's a slight difference, since in
the Slovak case we have to do with the attempt to create a literary
standard language on the basis of a number of dialects which up to
that time were considered only varieties of Czech. A similar situation is actually prevailing even today in Poland, but leading to almost
the reverse result. We have the case of Kashubian; attempts were
made to establish Kashubian as a literary language separate from
Polish, but today I would think the tendency is rather not to allow
Kashubian to emerge as a literary language, but to consider it as a
more remote type of Polish dialect.

HAUGEN: As far as Štúr is concerned, there's one especially interesting parallel, namely that before Ivar Aasen's work, it
was commonly assumed that the Norwegian dialects were degenerate
forms of the Danish language. They were degenerate because they
were spoken by peasants, and they were a form of Danish because
Danish was the official language. This was of course a common
European assumption, and still is in many circles. The very term
'dialect' is created out of that concept. This is one reason I don't
like it as a scientific term at all, because it normally has this pejorative sense.

BIRNBAUM: In the context of Slavic parallels we should
emphasize the parallelism with Serbo-Croatian, where the achievements of Vuk Karadžić to a very high degree parallel the situation
with Ivar Aasen. Aasen tried to create a literary language on the
basis of dialects, even though the official language in the area was a
foreign language—though it was a closely related language, namely
Danish. Something very similar happened in the Yugoslav territory,
where Karadžić actually tried to create a new language, primarily on
the basis of one dialect. The previous literary standard, if any such
did exist at that time, was something that didn't have the same roots.

HAUGEN: I am quite aware of Karadžić's work, although I
confess it is only recently I have been learning about it. But Professor Gallis at the University of Oslo has written some excellent material on the Serbo-Croatian situation, including an article called "Vuk
Karadžić, the Yugoslav Ivar Aasen" (1950).

P. IVIĆ: In connection with Aasen and Karadžić, there is
really a strong parallelism between the two cases. I remember that
as a schoolboy, in high school, I read an article in a Yugoslav publication, with the title "Ivar Aasen, the Norwegian Vuk Karadžić."

In connection with Karadžić, I wanted to discuss the principles of orthography given by Martin Joos (1960). None of them seems
to me universal. All of them are necessary only for languages with
certain types of structural or sociolinguistic complexities. There
are morphophonemic complexities in languages like English, making
necessary a morphophonemic orthography. But without alternations
which can deform the shape of morphemes, you don't need

morphophonemic orthography, so that phonemic orthography suffices;
and this is exactly what Karadžić introduced in Serbia. As to the
principle that an orthography should permit alternate interpretation
of the symbols, so that people with different idiolects can read their
own sounds into it—this is connected with another complexity, with the
co-existence of two or more acceptable pronunciations of the standard language. If this does not exist, this condition too is unnecessary. The third condition is that the orthography should be uniform
so that diverse speech habits can be translated into it. This again is
connected with a type of diversification which is not necessarily present everywhere. Thus it seems to me that conditions for an ideal
orthography vary greatly from language to language. In the case of
a language like Serbo-Croatian, the ideal solution was that of Karadžić, simply a phonemic orthography.

HAUGEN: I think that your point is very well taken, because clearly the difference in structure between different languages
will be a determining factor. Finnish, for example, seems to have
no problem with a phonemic orthography because each morpheme is
just there. Although there are complicated morphophonemic rules,
they are not reflected. On the other hand, a simple example in Norwegian is the word dag / dag / "day" and its genitive dags / daks / .
It is perfectly possible to argue that this should be written daks,
because this is what people say, and since / k/ and /g/ are in opposition within the language. But writing g in the genitive keeps the
forms of the word together. This shouldn't be carried too far, for it
does create problems. There are other words, like the word for
"scissors," which is written saks and rhymes with dags. For the
children who write it, this is a complication. But in general there
are many advantages in writing morphophonemically.

BIRNBAUM: Do you have any conclusions as to the desirability of this merging of Nynorsk and Bokmål into one common language in Norway? Are your feelings that this is something worth-
while supporting, or something rather detrimental?

HAUGEN: It would require a whole new lecture and paper
to justify any opinion I could give on it. Personally all I can say is,
I don't like it. But this doesn't mean anything at all, because whether I like it or not, some such form of fusion is going to take place.

How fast it takes place is another problem. It may not take place for a hundred or two hundred years. But it may also take place much more rapidly, depending on the possibility of indoctrinating the young people into the concept of a common language. But it is a very difficult process, because all the traditionalists are against it—and as I indicated here, the traditionalists are always in a majority in any social group.

BIRNBAUM: I understand that today the people who take the students' exam have to write two compositions, one in Nynorsk, one in Bokmål.

HAUGEN: Yes, this is a matter of national tradition, insisting that everyone must at least know, passively, both languages, even if he doesn't actively use either one. In the long run, this can't help but result in an informal fusion, a kind of pidginization whereby, on the one hand, the standards of the educated classes are broken down because their children no longer are forced to submit to them, and on the other hand the education of the country people comes to a point where they will be using a standard form. So they will meet somewhere, but I would not be so rash as to predict when, where, or how.

GUMPERZ: I'm interested in the role of linguists as language planners, and this morning we have suggested that possibly our own cultural heritage has something to do with the way we do linguistics. I think a very good example of this is found in modern Asian societies. Since Panini's time, Indian linguists have become more and more conservative. Their main concern has been the preservation of pre-existing grammatical conventions and literary tradition rather than the creation of new styles. It seems to me that this conservative role of Indian linguists creates some difficulties in the context of Indian modernization. At the present time India faces the problem of converting Hindi into a standard language, capable of serving as a communication medium in a modern nation-state. If this is to be accomplished, a new style will have to be created which, while uniform in spelling and grammar, is at the same time intelligible to a maximum number of people. When linguists have been called in to aid in this process, they seem sometimes more concerned with reviving Sanskrit forms than with facilitating communication. It

is interesting to see the changes they advocate and to observe the
effect that these changes have had. In one group of commonly accepted Sanskrit borrowings, such as raaj "government," they have advocated the addition of a nominalizing suffix -y, thus reviving a final
consonant cluster which no longer exists in modern Hindi and creating literary raajy, with the same meaning as raaj. Since uneducated
speakers of Hindi have difficulty in learning the new cluster, innovations of this type have the effect of increasing the language distance
between spoken and literary Hindi. This type of change cannot be
justified on the grounds of communicative efficiency. Therefore, we
might wonder whether linguists advocating this type of change are not
confusing their role as language planners with their well-established
role as preservers of the older literary traditions.

        HAUGEN: The matter implies a value judgment, obviously,
and that puts us right in the midst of a difficult problem. Something
like what you described happened in France, in the Renaissance,
when the natural French was interlarded with hundreds of loans from
Latin, which of course was the language of law and of government,
and was therefore thought of as superior to the broken-down forms of
Vulgar Latin, which had developed into French. And so we get these
contrasts within French which are reflected in English borrowings,
e. g. "king" versus "royal" and "regal."   This situation in present-
day Hindi is very similar.

9 | Construction and Reconstruction in Language Planning: Ivar Aasen's Grammar

Linguists have traditionally been more concerned with the analysis than with the synthesis of languages. Nevertheless, there is a long tradition of linguistic activity in the field of language planning.[1] When we speak of "applied linguistics," we should not overlook language planning as one of the fields where linguists have made and are still making a contribution. Rasmus Rask, one of the founders of modern linguistic science, devoted years of effort to promoting a much-needed reform of the spelling of Danish, his mother tongue.[2] One of Rask's illustrious Danish successors, Otto Jespersen, applied himself to the construction of an international language, which he called Novial.[3]

The growth of language planning has gone hand in hand with the growth of linguistic science. Practical problems of communication in new and developing nations have stimulated linguistic thinking ever since the late eighteenth century. New orthographies were needed for new languages, and many of the old were felt to be unsatisfactory. When school systems were first established for whole populations, the governments that conducted them had to take a hand in regulating the language in which they were taught. Many groups awoke to discover that they were second-class citizens in their own country, excluded from public life by their unfamiliarity with the dominant standard. In some cases this led to the establishment or reestablishment of competing standards, and in this activity the services of linguists were in demand. Devoted individuals came to the fore in many countries, who felt themselves called upon to apply the best linguistic knowledge they could muster to the solution of the national problem.

One of the earliest of these reformers was the Greek Adamantios Korais (1748-1833), who established the conservative norms of

the Katharevousa, or "pure language," beginning in 1788.[4] His model
was the religious and academic version of modern Greek, retaining
as much as possible of New Testament Greek. His ideal was a restoration of the classical Greek grammar and vocabulary, purifying away
the many loanwords which modern Greek had acquired during the sub-
jection of the Greeks to the Turks. The result of his choice was a
deepseated language split in Greek life, which eventually forced the
emergence in writing of a more popular form of the language, known
as Demotike. In Serbia, on the other hand, a rather different procedure was followed by the first great reformer of the language, the
celebrated Vuk Stefanovïc Karadžić (1787-1864).[5] Vuk rejected the
Old Slavonic church language in favor of the folk language, and succeeded in rallying around his Grammar of 1814 and his Dictionary of
1818 not only the Serbs, but in 1850 the Croats as well (with the aid of
Ljudevit Gaj, a Croatian grammarian). This became the foundation
of the Serbo-Croatian language, which is the major language of Yugoslavia. While Greek became a prime example of what Ferguson has
labeled "diglossia," Serbo-Croatian is a reasonably well-integrated
standard in spite of the deep cultural and religious cleavage between
Serbs and Croats. Ferguson has labeled it a case of "bimodal standardization," along with Hindi-Urdu and Armenian.[6]

The recent interest shown by some linguists in the problems
of language standardization and the classification of languages by their
sociolinguistic type has encouraged me to take up for renewed consideration the work done a century ago in Norway by the linguist and
language reformer Ivar Aasen (1813-1896), creator of the landsmål
(nynorsk) language.[7] The interplay of linguistic theory and its application is particularly interesting in the case of his work as a construc-
tor of a new Norwegian language norm in the middle of the nineteenth
century. There is as yet no comprehensive account of the work done
by such language makers, although a great many names come to mind:
Štur in Slovakia, Aavik in Estonia, Jablonskis in Lithuania, Ben Yehuda
in Palestine, and others.[8] Norwegian scholars have recently been re-
assessing the work of Aasen as a linguist in the light of the perspective
offered by a century of living with the movement for language reform
which his work inspired.[9] Many new materials have come to light
which make it clear how deeply grounded his thinking was in the new
science of comparative and historical linguistics of the early nineteenth
century. His complete correspondence and diaries have been published

in three massive volumes, under the editorship of Reidar Djupedal.[10]
These make it possible to trace the growth of Aasen's thinking on linguistic matters from his early youth to the end of his long life. It will
not be the purpose of this paper to exhaust the topic, or to identify
the sources of Aasen's ideas in any detail. There is still much research to be done before this can be fully clarified. But I do plan to
present some of Aasen's basic principles, and show how they are related to linguistic theory, particularly as reflected in his grammar of
1864, which bears the deceptively unassuming title of Norsk Grammatik.

        Unfriendly critics have often spoken of Aasen's work as if it
had been the result of an arbitrary and indiscriminate mixture of dialects. Johan Storm, a distinguished Norwegian linguist, wrote in
1896 that Aasen's Landsmal was "an artificial and arbitrarily constructed dialect language."[11] Antoine Meillet, the well-known French linguist, included it among the new, superfluous languages of Europe,
which he declared were a result of the takeover of the peasantry,
mere calques on the cultured languages.[12] Arnold Toynbee, the English historian, took notice of it only to condemn it as an example of
the unfortunate archaizing of modern Europe, the striving of new nations to provide themselves with ancestors.[13] There is no denying
that Aasen's language had some archaic traits, but it will be one of
the theses of this paper that these are a direct consequence of the
theory of standardization on which it was based. It will also be shown
that the procedures which Aasen applied in implementing his theory
were fully in harmony with the teachings of the founders of comparative and historical linguistics. There was nothing either arbitrary or
unsystematic about his approach. On the contrary, the classic quality
of his language resulted in a great degree from his concern with structural consistency. Rather than a constructed language, we should call
it a reconstructed language, based on the rigorous application of the
methods of comparative linguistics.

        Mary Haas has recently pointed out that Bloomfield's com-
parative grammar of the Algonquian languages was in fact a descriptive grammar of Proto-Algonquian.[14] Bloomfield himself wrote in
his book Language that a reconstructed form "is a formula that tells
us which identities or systematic correspondences of phonemes appear
in a set of related languages; moreover, since these identities and

correspondences reflect features that were already present in the parent language, the reconstructed form is also a kind of phonemic diagram of the ancestral form. "[15] Aasen's creation of a written Norwegian language came as the culmination of a comparative study of the Norwegian dialects. In trying to find the "overall pattern" of these dialects, what he did in fact discover was a proto-Norwegian, related by precisely statable correspondences to the existing dialects, to its sister languages in the rest of Scandinavia, and to their common ancestor, Old Norse. [16]

The magnitude of Aasen's accomplishment is the greater when we consider the difficulties he had to overcome. Even though there were enthusiasts and visionaries who had loudly proclaimed the necessity of reviving the dead language of ancient Norway in the newly founded nation, no one was really inclined to do anything radical about dislodging the written Danish. It was a language hallowed by religion and taught by the state, successfully used by Norwegians high and low, in practical affairs and in belles lettres. Aasen himself was a country lad, early orphaned, without funds of any kind, in a remote mountain valley. [17] Yet he proposed to create a national language for Norway by a comparison of the spoken dialects, which he believed were the true heirs of the defunct language known as Old Norwegian. He brought to this task a genius for languages, infinite patience and determination, and an unflinching sense of personal and national integrity.

Aasen's reputation as a scientist has been somewhat obscured by the controversies raised on account of his activity as a language maker. It has long been appreciated that he was the founder of Norwegian dialectology, though his work has sometimes seemed primitive to his more phonetically and geographically oriented successors. What is only now beginning to be realized is that in constructing a language, he was a providing a check on the methods of linguistic reconstruction. He was also, and more importantly, showing one of the practical uses of such reconstruction. He was exemplifying one of the ways in which a standard language can be brought into being where there is previously nothing but dialectal diversity and confusion.

We should not exaggerate the handicaps under which Aasen suffered, although they have always seemed impressive to his admirers

and biographers. He did live in a country where an elementary education was available to everyone, and he was fortunate enough to be
living in a place where private libraries were available to a young
bookworm. He began keeping a diary at the age of 17, so that we know
the titles of virtually every book he read. He wrote poetry before he
turned to prose, and some of his poems are today Norwegian classics.[18]
For two years he was housed by the local Dean, who tutored him in
Latin and Greek; for seven years he was himself a tutor to the children
of a local captain. But when the Dean, who perceived his promise,
offered to help him get a university education, he quietly refused,
declaring that he wished to remain within his own class and devote
his life to its benefit.[19] This significant but extraordinary decision
was probably a blessing in disguise for his scientific progress. He
was relieved from the folderol of courses and examinations, which
were supposed to fit him for some educational or ministerial position.
He was freed to devote himself to his own studies and to embark on
the research work which was to be his chief claim to fame, probably
much earlier than would otherwise have been possible.

Aasen was only 22 years old when he conceived the idea that
was to be his guiding star through life. Between 1832 and 1835,
leading Norwegian writers had proposed two possible methods of
creating a medium of expression that would reflect the recent restoration of the old kingdom of Norway. One method was to retain the
Danish framework, since this was already implanted in the educated
classes, and to enrich it chiefly with lexical borrowings from the
spoken idioms. The other method was to set up an entirely new language, with a grammatical framework corresponding to that of the
rural dialects.[20] Aasen experimented with both approaches, but rejected the first as inorganic.[21] The stimulus of his growing insight
into grammar led him to emphasize the morphology as the really crucial criterion of a language. From Danish and Latin grammar he
worked his way into Greek, German, French, and English. As he put
it later, "the idea then came to me that I would make the experiment
of investigating and treating a language on my own. This was the language which I properly could call my mother tongue and which I did
not find treated in any grammar."[22] He used himself as informant
and began to work out a sketch of his native dialect, the first such attempt for any Norwegian dialect. This was to be the first step in a
plan which he wrote down in 1836: to create a national language on

the basis of the folk dialects.[23] "It is not my purpose," he wrote,
"to promote any one of our dialects; no, the chief language (Hovedsprog)
should not be one of them, but a comparison of, a basis for all of them."
He proposed that grammars and dictionaries be prepared for each dialect and that a society of linguists should collect these and construct
a language by comparing them. As it turned out, however, he would
do the job single-handedly, thanks to a set of fortunate circumstances
which brought him into contact with men who appreciated his talents
and approved of his purpose.

        This crucial turn in his life came in 1841, when he had com-
pleted a revision of his dialect sketch. While working on it, he had
set about learning Swedish and Icelandic, as the neighboring languages
which he felt would offer the key to his problem. Instead of taking the
new linguistic science secondhand, he went to the sources and read
Rasmus Rask's Guide to the Icelandic or Old Norse Language.[24] The
comparison of Swedish, Icelandic, Old Norwegian, Danish, German,
and Latin enabled him to find the fixed points in the field of his study
and to see the correspondences which it became his task to establish
in the years ahead. In the first version of the grammar the material
was organized in relation to Danish, but in the revision it was oriented
to Old Norse.[25] Twenty-eight years old he timidly presented himself
to the learned bishop of Bergen diocese, Jacob Neumann, and asked
him if he would read a manuscript he had brought with him.

        Bishop Neumann was not only a learned, but also a patriotic
man, and he read this pioneer effort with interest and even enthusiasm.
He wrote an article in the paper about this remarkable young farm boy,
who had risen forth as it were from the depths of society with a precious contribution to the national welfare. Through his mediation
Aasen was employed by the Royal Scientific Society in Trondheim as
the country's first dialect investigator. His field work was supposed
to extend primarily over the West Norwegian dialect area, which his
employers conceived would be "of the greatest importance for our lost
tongue."[26] From 1842 until his death in 1896 Aasen was supported
either by this society or by the Norwegian government for the purpose
of investigating the dialects. He set off from his native community,
moving southwards down the coast. Eventually he was to cover virtually the entire country, though with less emphasis on those areas
that he found uninteresting for his ultimate purposes. His first major

results were published after five full years of travel in the form of a grammar entitled Det norske Folkesprogs Grammatik (1848), followed by a dictionary entitled Ordbog over det norske Folkesprog (1850). He had here expanded the framework of his grammar and vocabulary of the local dialect to encompass all the so-called "genuine" dialects of the country. He called the resulting language a "folk language," or in other words the language of the common people, which in the Norway of that day meant essentially the dialects of the country folk.

These works were still avowedly dialect studies, in spite of the underlying concept of language unity. His purpose was the purely scientific one of "reporting only what had been found and nothing beyond."[27] Where the dialects differed, he presented all the forms he had found, using one more or less arbitrarily as the head, but without deliberately selecting or constructing any common form. He later called his grammar "an enumeration of dialect forms without a unifying model form (Mønsterform)." "The unity and independence of the language were not sufficiently emphasized. . . ."[28] Even while he was preparing these works, however, he was getting ready for the next step. As far as can be seen, he mentioned his plan to create a new Norwegian language to a colleague for the first time in 1845.[29] He even sketched his plan for the vowel system in this letter, a plan to which we shall soon return. After the publication of the grammar and the dictionary he was ready to go ahead with his revolutionary scheme. He mentioned it publicly for the first time in a book review of 1852, and in 1853 he presented his first sample texts in a small book called Prøver af det norske Landsmål. This included dialect specimens together with a section of texts in a generalized Norwegian language which he called "et almindeligt Landsmål," i.e. a general national language. After a period of experimentation with various forms of this language, he modified it into the form presented in Norsk Grammatik (1864) and Norsk Ordbog (1873). His thinking had now progressed to the point where this was no longer a folk language nor even a national language, but the Norwegian language, sans phrase. After this time Aasen made few changes in his norm; this became the classic statement of his language, as it issued from the hand of its creator.

Prior to Aasen's generation there had been no clear understanding of the historical relations of the Scandinavian languages, either internally or externally. As the first great connoisseur and enthusiast for Icelandic, Rasmus Rask established its tremendous importance as a key to the problem. He even exaggerated it by erroneously identifying modern Icelandic with the Old Norse language.[30] His view was corrected by Jacob Grimm, who in his <u>Deutsche Grammatik</u> made it clear that the old pronunciation must have been quite different from that of the modern Icelanders.[31] Aasen first read Grimm in 1846 and in the same year Bopp's <u>Vergleichende Grammatik</u>.[32] In the following year Munch and Keyser's grammar of Old Norse appeared, which first brought Grimm's views to the attention of Norwegian students of the subject.[33] He quickly recognized that at least with respect to the vowel system Norwegian dialects had retained a more archaic structure than modern Icelandic. The picture of a Scandinavian mother tongue from which all the modern idioms were descended was beginning to emerge. It was clear that there were two branches, an easterly one, with extensive innovations, including Swedish and Danish, and a westerly one, with less innovation, including Icelandic and the newly normalized Faroese. Although the two latter issued from Norway and had been written in Norway prior to the dynastic union with Denmark in the fourteenth century, there was no counterpart to the other languages in the place where Norwegian ought to have been in the family tree alongside Icelandic and Faroese, except for the rural dialects which Aasen had begun to study. While Aasen never drew any tree diagrams, we may represent his conceptions as follows:

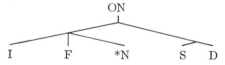

ON

I   F   *N   S   D

    Icelandic had been written continuously since Old Norse times, but the late eighteenth and early nineteenth century saw an extensive renewal and restoration of its orthography, including the writing of accents to mark the old long vowels, which were now qualitatively different from the lengthened short vowels.[34] Rask contributed to this reform, and his follower, N. M. Petersen, was influential in the normalization of Faroese undertaken by Hammershaimb in 1846.[35] Both of these languages were politically and linguistically dominated by Danish, as was Norwegian, and Aasen had a similar goal of liberation and purification in mind. In Norwegian, as in Faroese, there was no continuous tradition of normalized writing, and his problem was how to make use of the dialects in filling the hole in the Nordic pattern

represented by the starred N on the family tree. His academic advisers, Munch and Keyser, wanted him to follow the example of Icelandic
and Faroese; but Aasen knew that Icelandic was an unreliable guide
for Norwegian, and he strongly felt that Hammershaimb had gone too
far in removing the written norm from speech in the direction of Icelandic.[36] His Norwegian norm had to build first and foremost on a
comparison of the Norwegian dialects, in order to bring out all the
basic features of Norwegian structure. This was essential if it were
to have an independent form, distinguishing it from its neighbors.[37]
At the same time, these neighbors formed fixed points of comparison,
including the mother tongue Old Norse and the sister tongues to the
west and east. The position of Norwegian among them required that
it fulfill the same functions and have a comparable dignity and value
as a standard language. His comparison was therefore not only internal, but also external. In his hierarchy of values the dialects were
primary, Old Norse was secondary, and the sister languages were
tertiary. Among the latter he valued Swedish especially, since its
forms were clearly more conservative and closer to those of Norwegian.[38]

    In evaluating the dialects he also established a hierarchy of
more or less "genuine", according to the degree to which they preserved the structural rules of the older language. He divided them
into three groups, the western (which included his own), the northern,
and the eastern:

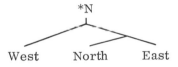

The most genuine offspring of Old Norse was the Western group,
which also fits into our previous tree by being closer to Faroese and
Icelandic.[39] In the East there were some dialects that were not only
less "genuine," being closer to Swedish and Danish, but some that he
regarded as downright illegitimate, being the bastard offspring of
Norwegian speech and Danish writing.[40] He would not have objected
to a description of the cultivated speech of Norway as a kind of creolized Danish. In using the tree model for presenting Aasen's views,
I think I am doing justice to the fact that he thought of each dialect as
in some sense a unity, distinct from its neighbors. Each language

and dialect was its own node in the tree, and the later concept of the
wave theory had not entered to disturb it. Johannes Schmidt's wave
theory came in 1872, well after Aasen's grammar.[41] While Aasen
recognized that neighboring dialects resembled one another, he still
felt that influence which spread from place to place reduced the independence of the dialects and made them less "genuine." The most
"perfect" dialects were those that preserved most faithfully the structural traits of the mother tongue.[42]

Since he did not find any one dialect that could be described
as perfect and be made the basis of a national language, his recourse
was to a technique that has been called "comparative dialectology."[43]
He established for each dialect the correspondences among cognate
words which made it possible to find the forms of greatest generality.
His word for the correspondences was "Overgang," a term he drew
from Rask, where it appears to have been a translation of Latin mu-
tatio or permutatio.[44] These "permutations" included indifferently
what we have learned to call sound changes as well as morphophonemic correspondences, or even what are now called transformations
by some. Thus he included both Umlaut and Ablaut as "permutations,"
even though he understood that Umlaut was also a historical change,
but had no clear notion of the origins of Ablaut. For each new dialect
that he studied he noted the permutations which it showed in relation
to his basic model and added its vocabulary to his collection of lexical
forms. Finally, in his grammar of 1864 and his dictionary of 1873 he
was ready to launch a full-fledged "Middelform" for Norwegian, which
should be for the Norwegian dialects what he conceived Swedish and
Danish to be for their dialects, a kind of Platonic noumenon amidst
the phenomena, to which he would contribute phenomenal substance.[45]

We shall now quickly survey the organization and contents of
Aasen's Grammar. In the Preface he set forth his arguments concerning the existence and value of his language. He stated his purpose of
"presenting the basic rules which occur in the Norwegian language in
its present state and at the same time to give the necessary information about its relationship to its nearest kinsmen."[46] It is a conspicuous quality of the book that it is simply, precisely, and clearly written, in a style that would do honor to any grammarian. The first of
its five chapters is a phonology (Lydlære), divided into three parts:
the individual sounds, their combinations, and the prosodic features,

including stress (Betoning) and tone (Tonelag). The second chapter
is entitled "Word Forms" (Ordformer) and corresponds closely to
what we might call the morphophonemics. This chapter was new in
this edition of the grammar. In it he analyzes the phonemic shape of
the morphs, and divides them into bases (Grundformer) and suffixes
(Endelser). The rules for Umlaut and Ablaut are presented as rules
of alternation within the grammatical forms of the language. In a
section called "Adapted Word Forms" (Tillempede Ordformer) he lists
the phonemic changes from Old Norwegian and the differences between
Norwegian and its related languages in the Germanic family, especially Swedish and Danish. Finally he presents the sound changes
(Overgangsformer) which distinguish the dialects from his norm. In
the third and longest chapter he presents the inflections (Bøiningsfor-
mer) by word class, with paradigms for each distinct inflectional category, the Old Norwegian and dialectal correspondences, and lists
of words exemplifying each.

The fourth chapter presents the rules of word formation
(Orddannelse), under the three heads of derivation without a suffix
(Overførelse), suffixation (Afledning ved Endelse), and compounding
(Sammensætning). After this purely formal classification he organizes
them by semantic criteria and word class, showing how nouns, for
example, are derived from verbs and by what means. Aasen regarded
this section as of great importance because he was anxious that users
of his language should utilize its resources of word formation to the
exclusion of the borrowed suffixes and prefixes which had entered
from German. The last chapter is a syntax (Sætningslære), in which
he outlines the rules for the formation of sentences. This is systematically arranged under nominals (nævnende Led), verbals (fortællende
Led), particles (Partikler), word order (Ordfølge), complex sentences
(Sammensatte Sætninger), phrases and incomplete sentences (Tale-
maader og afvigende Sætninger).

There are two appendices, the first a survey of the dialects
and their chief divisions and characteristics (Om Landskabsmaalene),
the second about the national language (Om Landssproget). The last
includes a summary of the characteristics of his language as compared
respectively with other Germanic languages, with other Scandinavian
languages, and with Old Norwegian. He discusses also the nature of
its vocabulary and the problem that faces the users of a language in

attempting to make it over from a language spoken by peasants to one
that shall fulfill the functions of a cultivated standard language.

This leads naturally over to his dictionary, in which close to
40,000 words are listed in the orthography he established in his gram-
mer, with precise and full information on the inflections, meanings,
and dialect forms of each word. Together these two books constitute
a description of the language. Although it had been "non-existent"
until he called it into being, Aasen made it probably one of the best
described languages then in existence. Even aside from this aspect,
his grammar can still be read with great profit as an introduction to
the study of Norwegian dialects. For his language the two books fur-
nish all one needs to write it, provided of course one knows a Norwegian dialect and applies the rules of correspondence. Even though its
terminology at times seems old-fashioned and traditional, it meets
the basic requirements of a descriptive grammar. Not being one-
sidedly limited to phonology and inflection, it covers every level fully,
if not exhaustively, from the sounds to the stylistics. For every rule
it provides the evidence on which it is based in the dialects and the
reasoning which led the author to set it up in just the way he did.

In calling Aasen's norm a reconstruction, I should make it
clear that he rarely resorted to forms which had no real existence in
the dialects. ON rules which no longer applied, such as the case
system of the nouns, the personal endings of verbs, or the distinction
of t and th (thorn) he rejected, however regretfully. His academic
advisers, Munch and Keyser, urged him to make the language much
more like Old Norse than he did.[47] Aasen emphasized above all the
importance of establishing correct basic forms of the words, what we
might call canonical shapes. He regarded the shape of the grammatical suffixes as secondary in importance, and purely graphic problems
as unimportant.[48] On such matters he made many concessions to
contemporary Danish, e.g., the use of Gothic type and the capitali-
zation of nouns. He did not wish to frighten away potential adherents
by the adoption of orthographic innovations which did not affect the
basic structure of the language.

In order to illustrate his method and support my contention
that his is a language reconstructed according to the methods of comparative linguistics, I shall present his handling of two different

phonological problems, the vowel system and the so-called "silent" consonants.

Even though Aasen's work preceded that of the modern school of phonetics, his terminology was quite adequate to clarify the phonemic relations of his basic units of phonology.[49] From the start of his dialect researches he began setting up vowel and consonant diagrams which in every essential respect corresponded to those we might find in a modern textbook on phonology, from Trubetzkoy to Hockett. In the grammar he presents his vowel system in terms of the nine symbols available in the Danish alphabet (which adds to the basic Latin a e i o u the Umlaut symbols y æ ø aa, later changed to å).[50] But he makes it clear that his system consists of six additional vowels and three diphthongs, the latter written ei, øy, and au. In his grammar the additional vowels are what he calls "intermediate" or "open" vowels and are designated by a following apostrophe because the Gothic type permitted no accents above the letters. But in his own notations these vowels were always written with a grave accent, a practice which his successors have followed, and which we shall adopt here.[51] In order to make the table look a little more familiar, we shall turn it upside down, so that a is at the bottom instead of the top. I have also added a modern phonetic transcription of the approximate values intended and some examples furnished by Aasen himself. He was careful to give minimal or near-minimal pairs for most of his distinctions, but of course it would be impossible to find a single environment for all the vowels.

ei [ɛi] bein 'bone'	øy [œy] høy 'hay'	au [æu] draum 'dream'
i [i] vin 'wine'	y [y] fyr 'fire'	u [u] lut 'lye'
ì [ɪ] vìn 'friend'	ỳ [Y] fỳre 'before'	ù [U] lùt 'lot'
e [e] ven 'pretty'	ø [ø] føra 'lead'	o [o] stol 'chair'
è [ɛ] vèra 'be'	ǿ [œ] fjǿra 'beach'	ò [ɔ] stòlen 'stolen'
æ [æ] vær 'pillowcase'	a [a] fara 'go'	aa [ɒ] staal 'steel'

Each of the vowels occurs either long or short, in inverse correlation with the length of the following consonant, when the syllable is stressed.

Each of the units in this surprisingly large inventory was
established by sets of correspondences between cognates which Aasen
identified in the dialects. The diphthong ei, for example, appeared
in cognate words in different dialects as [ai], [æi], [ɛi], or [e]. In
normalized Old Norse and Icelandic it was spelled ei; in Swedish and
Danish it corresponded to e. Aasen's decision to adopt ei was founded
not only on the normalized Old Norse writing, but also on the rule for
palatalization of velar stops. These were palatalized before [e], but
not before [a], which established the greater antiquity of the higher
vowel.[52] The correspondence of the Norwegian diphthongs to Danish
and Swedish monophthongs became one of the major criteria of Aasen's
Norwegian norm; where these wrote ben 'bone', sten 'stone', he established bein and stein as Norwegian, in spite of the fact that some
of the "less genuine" dialects in the East also had the monophthongs.

But the most striking innovation in Aasen's system was his
full set of intermediate vowels, which he designated with the grave
accents. Since each of these matched a vowel one step above it, he
called them "open" vowels and contrasted them with the corresponding
"closed" ones. Aasen discovered that in his own and other conservative dialects of western Norway oppositions like vin: vìn corresponded
closely to the Old Norse opposition of vín: vin(r). In most dialects
the word vìn had become ven (or even vænn). But to write the next
lower vowel, which was the usual practice in Danish also, would obscure the correspondences, since the vowel e would then have both
[ɪ] and [e] as its counterpart in the western dialects. In order to state
the rules so that they were in consonance with Old Norse and the more
conservative dialects, it was necessary to set up an extra level between the "closed" vowels.

What Aasen did not fully realize was that his "open" vowels
were in reality Old Norse short vowels, which had been lengthened in
the late Middle Ages in open syllables, as in most other European
languages. He was right, however, in assuming that they were more
"open" than the corresponding longs, since in general the short vowels
were lax. In the more conservative dialects the lengthened short vowels remained phonemically distinct even when they were lengthened.
It did not matter to Aasen that they generally accomplished this by
diphthongizing the old longs, e.g., by making long i of vin into [ᵉi],
which can be regarded as a phonemic cluster /ij/. This kept it apart

both from the old [ei] and the new long [ɪ], but provided scant justifi-
cation for an 18-vowel system.[53] In other dialects the short vowels
simply coalesced with the long vowels of the next lower level, so that
vèra became væra, fỳre became fø̧re, and so forth. In such dialects
the long vowels usually remained monophthongal and the old system
of nine vowel qualities was reconstituted on a new basis. Aasen noted
that most dialect words borrowed into Dano-Norwegian were written
with the lower vowel, so that, e.g., his bìl 'while' was written bel and
his bròte 'brush' braate. He condemned this practice as being defen-
sible

> only so long as one writes for uninformed readers in a dialect
> which one does not consider of any special significance. But
> when the language is to be treated as the language of a whole
> country, higher considerations must be taken into account,
> and the vowel system must be returned to the form which is
> found to be the right one according to the most established
> old spelling and which still has perfect support in many good
> dialects. Only in this way can the words receive that form
> whereby their origin and kinship can most precisely be shown
> and by means of which their alternations by Umlaut and other
> mutations can best be explained.[54]

As this passage shows, Aasen wished his orthography to reflect the set of maximal distinctions in his dialects in such a way that
it would be possible to state clear rules for both phonemic and morphophonemic alternations. Dialects which did not maintain all the distinctions could then be described as having undergone merger. He
could write, for example, that in Telemark i̧ "comes too close to i,"
or that in the Eastern dialects "it often changes to ȩ."[55] In the Danish
spelling Umlaut was confused by the fact that æ could represent the i-
Umlaut of both a and aa, e.g. mand 'man', plural mæ̧nd; gaas 'goose',
plural gjæs. In Aasen's system the rule was that the Umlaut of a was
è, as in mann, mènner, while that of aa was æ, as in gaas, gjæser (ON
menn, gæss).[56] While Aasen was guided to this reconstruction by his
knowledge of Old Norwegian, he refused to archaize it to the extent
that Icelandic and Faroese had done. His academic advisers wanted
him to mark the closed vowels with an acute accent, as do reconstructed
modern Icelandic and Faroese. He followed their advice in the first
grammar, but not in the second. His grounds were that for Norwegian

readers accustomed to Danish spelling, the new and unexpected vowels were the long open ones and that therefore these should be marked.
In one set of words he even accepted the lower vowels against the practice of ON, since he found that all the dialects agreed in lowering i
before historical d. Hence he wrote <u>fred</u> 'peace', <u>smed</u> 'smith', <u>ved</u>
'wood', in happy agreement with Danish as against Old Norwegian
<u>friðr, smiðr, viðr.</u>[57]

The examples I have just given also illustrate his practice
with respect to what is ordinarily called the writing of silent consonants.[58] Most Norwegian speakers do not pronounce the postvocalic
d in such words as these, except as spelling pronunciations. This is
contrary to the practice of standard Danish and Swedish. When dialects were transcribed, it was therefore customary to drop the final
d, and the same with loanwords from the dialects, such as <u>hei</u> 'heath',
<u>sau</u> 'sheep', <u>ski</u> 'ski' (ON <u>heið, sauðr, skið</u>). Aasen himself did so
in his first, dialect-oriented grammar and dictionary. But in his
standard form he not only accepted the d in words where Danish had
it, but wanted it reintroduced in words like the ones I have just given,
where standard practice left it out. Aasen insisted that the d was an
essential part of the word stem, that omitting it would obscure certain
distinctions (e.g. <u>flod</u> 'flood' and <u>flo</u> 'high tide'), and would be dis-
criminatory against the Norwegian words as compared with those that
Norwegian and Danish had in common ("there is as much reason for
writing <u>lid</u> as <u>tid</u>"). Not only did he want d written, but in keeping
with Norwegian practice at that time in reading Danish, he wanted it
pronounced, at least in formal style.

As in the case of the vowel system, Aasen's practice here
was dictated on the one hand by the necessities of reconstruction, and
on the other by the previous habits of his potential readers. At least
there is no evidence in his writings of the kind of pseudo-psychologiz-
ing which some of his contemporaries indulged in when they wrote,
e.g., that "when one of our peasants says 'anna' for 'annat' or 'mykje'
for 'mykit', the consciousness of an omitted final d or t is certainly
present in them."[59] Aasen's academic advisers wanted him to reintroduce the Old Norse ð, as had been done in Faroese, which also
has lost this phoneme. Aasen rejected this symbol as unfamiliar to
Norwegian readers, but he granted the importance of maintaining a
symbol in this position. The evidence from the dialects was slight,

but decisive: (1) one dialect area maintained a d̲ or ð in most words
(including his own native dialect); (2) many dialects maintained a d̲
intervocalically in some words (e.g. Orkdalen s̲l̲a̲a̲d̲a̲a̲ 'sled', ON
sleði), especially before certain affixes (e.g. t̲i̲d̲i̲g̲ 'early' from t̲i̲d̲);
(3) preterite verb forms after consonant stems retained a d̲ (e.g.
r̲u̲d̲-d̲e̲ 'cleared' from r̲y̲d̲-j̲a̲, the latter often pronounced r̲y̲a̲). For
these reasons he not only wrote the d̲ in stems, but even in suffixes
like the weak preterite -a̲d̲e̲ and the participle -a̲d̲. On this latter
point he could adduce the model of Swedish, which also wrote it in this
manner even though most Swedes did not pronounce the consonant.
Aasen was reluctant to admit that the d̲ was not pronounced in Norwegian, and his statement of the situation is characteristically under-
stated: "The complete form with 'ade' is probably not distinctly heard
anywhere, but is nevertheless quite necessary in writing, since it is
precisely the consonant which is the prime marker of the preterite
form."[60]

It would be possible to go on at great length about the reasoning which Aasen applied to each of the many decisions he made in setting up his new Norwegian language. But it is unnecessary for our
purpose, which has been to place his methods in the history of linguistic thinking. In detail Aasen was not committed to Old Norse as a
model; he also had in mind the practical problems of his potential followers, and he frequently considered one form preferable to another
for reasons of beauty and clarity, or as we might say today, elegance.[61]
But the basic decisions were dictated by what he had learned of the
methods of linguistic reconstruction. One could even show that these
were ultimately responsible for his lexical purism, which led him to
exclude from his norm a large number of German-derived words commonly used in the Danish language and even in most Norwegian dialects.
The rules of correspondence made it feasible for the first time to separate out the native elements from the borrowed ones. Aasen's position on this problem was a moderate one, as on most others. He recognized that Norwegian, like any other language, was entitled to enrich its vocabulary by borrowing. But he rejected it as "the right way
to develop and enrich a language," primarily because it complicated
the phonological and derivational rules of the language and made the
common man's path to learning excessively difficult. "We may wonder just how well English people are served by the innumerable Romance words which they are compelled to learn even in their earliest

religious training, such as 'grace', 'pardon', 'remission', 'trespass', 'doctrine', 'commandment', 'baptism', etc. [62] In this connection it is interesting to note his comment on English loanwords in Norwegian: "Because of their pronunciation, they may be difficult enough; but fortunately only a few of these are known in our country." [63] Times have changed, and today these are held by some to be the chief menace to Norwegian linguistic independence!

Aasen believed that he had found a language, while others said he had made it up. I think we can now identify it as a reconstructed, classical standard for the Norwegian dialects. [64] One critic has written that Aasen's language was "born wrinkled." [65] We may agree that it is archaic in relation to the spoken dialects, though no more so than most written languages. [66] If it had been created for an illiterate population, there is no obvious reason why it would not have been immediately accepted. The fact that the Norwegian people had already learned to read and write Danish and that the ruling élite spoke a variety of it made the future of Aasen's Norwegian uncertain indeed. The currents of social prestige ran strongly against it, since the "best" dialects were also the least populous and the most remote from the centers of power and influence. Even so, a modernized form of his language (under the name of nynorsk) is recognized as one of the two official languages of the Norwegian government. One fifth of the school children of the country receive their primary education in it under a system of local option, and there exists in it a respectable body of literature in all fields. When I say a "modernized form," I mean that pressures which Aasen foresaw but was powerless to resist have caused his followers to abandon some of the internal consistency and harmony which he built into his norm. [67] The open vowels proved to be a real stumbling block for speakers whose nine-vowel system had no room for them. The silent d has remained silent and is written chiefly in words which traditionally have it in Danish writing. In the weak verbs it has vanished completely. Experience, as well as the scientific insights of such disciplines as dialect geography and linguistic normalization, have brought out some of the deficiencies of a starred language as a practical national orthography.

However, we are not here concerned with the problems which his language had to face in gaining acceptance. I hope I have succeeded in my purpose of calling attention to Aasen's contribution to the theories of language planning. His grammar has not won the attention I believe it deserves, because of its purely local concern with an internal Norwegian problem. Its controversial results have at times overshadowed its scientific merits even within Norway. But I think we may be more ready to listen to its message today when linguists are no longer exclusively intent on bringing orthographies into biunique relation with the phonemics of the language. A new approach to language is bringing out the remarkable correlation between the ordered rules of a morphophonemic description and the sequence of historical changes. Aasen's approach was comparative and historical, but it led him forward to an insight into the morphophonemic rules of his language and the need of representing these in the orthography.

NOTES

I wish to express special gratitude to the editor of Aasen's correspondence and diaries, Reidar Djupedal, for his kindness in answering my questions and furnishing me with otherwise inaccessible materials for this study.

[1] For the term "language planning" see the writer's article "Linguistics and Language Planning" in Sociolinguistics, ed. by W. Bright (The Hague: Mouton, 1966), pp. 50-71 [in this volume, pp. 159-90], and his book Language Conflict and Language Planning (Harvard University Press, 1966). The term was used by Uriel Weinreich as the title of a seminar at Columbia University in 1957.

[2] Rasmus K. Rask, Forsøg til en videnskabelig dansk Retskrivnings-lære med Hensyn til Stamsproget og Nabosproget (Copenhagen, 1826).

[3] Otto Jespersen, An International Language (London, 1928).

[4] The Greek restoration was held up as a model for the Norwegians by P.A. Munch in his articles of 1832 on "Norsk Sprogreformation."

[5] Charles E. Bidwell, "Language, Dialect, and Nationality in Yugoslavia." Human Relations XV (1962), 217-225; Arne Gallis, "Skriftspråk og dialekter i Jugoslavia," in Skriftspråk i utvikling (Oslo, 1964), 187-195. Vuk's grammar was translated into German by Jacob Grimm in 1824, but there is no evidence that it was known in Norway.

[6] Charles A. Ferguson, "Diglossia," Word XV (1959) 325-340; "The Language Factor in National Development," Anthropological Linguistics IV (1962), i, 23-27.

[7] For an earlier treatment by the author see "The Linguistic Development of Ivar Aasen's New Norse." PMLA XLVIII (1931), 558-597.

[8] For references see the author's Language Conflict and Language Planning (above, fn. 1).

[9] Trygve Knudsen, "Sprogforskeren Ivar Aasen," Maal og Minne 1963, 135-153; Reidar Djupedal, "Ivar Aasen, målgranskaren og målreisaren," Halvtanna hundreår med Ivar Aasen (Oslo: Noregs Mållag, 1964), 9-21; Gustav Indrebø, Norsk Målsoga (Bergen, 1951), 437ff.; Alf Hellevik, "Ved Aasen-minnet," Syn og Segn 1963, 3-15; Alf Hellevik, "Om tilhøvet mellom skriftmål og talemål," Syn og Segn 1945, 271ff.; Aasen's development as a scholar was first outlined by Halvdan Koht in Ivar Aasen, Granskaren, maalreisaren, diktaren (Kristiania, 1913); see also Trygve Knudsen, P.A. Munch og samtidens norske sprogstrev (Kristiania, 1923).

[10] Ivar Aasen, Brev og Dagbøker, ed. Reidar Djupedal, 3 vols. (Oslo, 1957-1960).

[11] Johan Storm, Norsk Sprog (Copenhagen, 1896), 115.

[12] Antoine Meillet, Les langues dans l'Europe nouvelle (Paris, 1928), 182, 241-243.

[13] Arnold Toynbee, A Study of History (Oxford, 1934-1954), Vol. 6, p. 63.

[14] In a lecture on historical linguistics at the Linguistic Institute held at Bloomington, Indiana, Summer 1964.

[15] Leonard Bloomfield, Language (New York, 1933), 303.

[16] Cf. Wallace Chafe, "Internal Reconstruction in Seneca" (Language XXXV [1959], 477-495), p. 478: "Most of historical linguistics is fundamentally dependent upon the technique of comparing cognate forms"; p. 479: "The first step is the discovery of recurrent phoneme correspondences." For other recent statements on the methods of historical linguistics see Henry Hoenigswald, Language Change and Linguistic Reconstruction (Chicago, 1960); W.P. Lehmann, Historical Linguistics: An Introduction (New York, 1962). For an older, but still useful introduction see Antoine Meillet, La méthode comparative en linguistique historique (Oslo, 1925).

[17] For Aasen's life see Halvdan Koht, op. cit., and now Brev og Dagbøker, ed. R. Djupedal (above, fn. 9).

[18] Ivar Aasen, Skrifter i Samling, 3 vols. (Kristiania, 1911-12); and Skrifter, 2 vols. (2nd ed.; Oslo, 1926). All quotations here are from the 2nd ed.

[19] See Skrifter I, 9-14.

[20] For the discussion conducted by P. A. Munch, Jonas Anton Hielm, and Henrik Wergeland see Trygve Knudsen, P. A. Munch og samtidens norske sprogstrev (Kristiania, 1923), 6-19.

[21] See his experiments with a reformed orthography in Brev og Dagbøker I, 38ff.

[22] Skrifter I, 13.

[23] Skrifter II, 48-50, written in January, 1836 (cf. Brev og Dagbøker III, 415).

[24] According to Aasen's own diary notation he read Rask's "Iislandske Grm." in February, 1838 (Brev og Dagbøker III, 21), but the edition is not identified. It could either have been the fuller Vejledning til det Islandske eller gamle Nordiske Sprog (Copenhagen, 1811) or the abbreviated Kortfattet Vejledning til det oldnordiske eller gamle islandske Sprog (Copenhagen, 1832). The only one he is known to have owned is the latter, which he was given by Rev. J. P. Berg on December 12, 1841 (Brev og Dagbøker III, 34); see also Lista yver Ivar Aasen-boksamlingi (Volda, 1946), 13, and his report of September 1, 1842 (Brev og Dagbøker I, 49). His diaries and papers show that his plan for a Norwegian language and his first Sunnmøre grammar preceded his reading of Rask; but in letters of 1863 and 1874 he claimed that Rask had stimulated him to the study of his own dialect (Brev og Dagbøker II, 19, 140).

[25] According to Trygve Knudsen, Maal og Minne 1963, 138.

[26] The citation here is from Knudsen, Maal og Minne 1963, 140.

[27] Norsk Grammatik, Introduction, p. xiv. (Hereafter cited as NG, by the numbered paragraphs).

[28] Ibid.

[29] To Andreas Faye, Brev og Dagbøker 1.102.

[30] See his Vejledning til det Islandske eller gamle Nordiske Sprog (Copenhagen, 1811), esp. the Intr. p. xviff.; also his Undersøgelse om det gamle Nordiske eller Islandske Sprogs Oprindelse (Copenhagen, 1818), 64: "det gamle nordiske Sprog, som nu kaldes Islandsk."

[31] Jacob Grimm, Deutsche Grammatik, Vol. 1 (2nd ed.; Göttingen, 1822), 280-330.

[32] Franz Bopp, Vergleichende Grammatik des Sanskrit, Zend, Griechischen, Lateinischen, Littauischen, Gothischen und Deutschen (Berlin, 1833ff.).

[33] C. R. Unger and P. A. Munch, Det oldnorske Sprogs eller Norrønasprogets Grammatik (Christiania, 1847).

[34] See Jón Aðalsteinn Jónsson, "Ágrip af sögu íslenzkrar stafsetningar," Íslenzk tunga I (1959), 71-119.

[35] Chr. Matras, "Det færøske skriftsprog av 1846," Scripta Islandica II (1951), 5-23; Reidar Djupedal, "Litt om framvoksteren av det færøyske skriftmålet," Skriftspråk i utvikling (Oslo, 1964), 144-186.

[36] On Faroese see his letter to Landstad on April 16, 1852 (Brev og Dagbøker I, 232).

[37] His basic view was expressed in his 1845 plan for the dictionary (Kgl. Videnskabers Selskabs Skrifter, Vol. 4): "Det gamle Sprog bør ellers overalt haves for Øie, dog saaledes, at man ikke derfor taber det nuværende Sprogs Beskaffenhed af Sigte." He repeated similar ideas several times, especially in his discussion with Landstad over the spelling of the ballads (e. g. , July 22, 1848, Brev og Dagbøker I, 159). For discussion see Trygve Knudsen, P. A. Munch, 54ff.

[38] Cf. his remark in a letter to Marius Nygaard (9 June, 1859): "Hvordan vi snoe og vende det, komme vi dog i mange Stykker til at ligne Svensken alligevel, og dette er da egentlig ikke nogen Skade heller." (Brev og Dagbøker I, 371).

[39] In NG 7n he praises the pronunciation "som er almindeligst i den sydvestlige Deel af Landet og især i Bergens Stift og de nærmeste Fjeldbygder østenfor."

[40] In his report to the Scientific Society June 26, 1845, he wrote: "Dialekten i Mandals og Nedenæs Fogderier er ikke af nogen Vigtighed, da den omtrent falder sammen med den Mellemart af Norsk og Dansk, som sædvanlig forekommer i Kjøbstæderne og hos conditionerede Folk paa Landet. Det samme er, med adskillige Forandringer, ogsaa Tilfældet med Sprogarten i de nedre Dele af Bratsberg og Budskeruds Amter." (Brev og Dagbøker I, 111).

[41] Holger Pedersen, Linguistic Science in the Nineteenth Century (Cambridge, Mass. , 1931), 314.

[42] His reason for praising the western dialects (above, fn. 39) was that they "come quite close to the model (Mønsterform) which one can infer from the orthography of the old language." Dialects of the northern group he described as belonging to "the poorer or more distorted" because of their deviation from the norm and the difficulty of setting up rules for them (Report to the Scientific Society Dec. 31, 1846, Brev og Dagbøker I, 133-135).

[43] Reidar Djupedal, "Ivar Aasen, målgranskaren og målreisaren" (cf. fn. 9), 4: "Vi kan gjerne seia at Aasen grunnlegg ein ny vitskap, den jamførande målføregranskinga."

[44] Cf. Paul Diderichsen, Rasmus Rask og den grammatiske tradition (Copenhagen 1960), 66ff., where quotations from the Latin of G. J. Wachter (1737) show both terms. Note that Aasen did not speak of "Bogstavovergange," as did Rask, but of "Lydovergange."

[45] Cf, NG 377 for his use of the term "Middelform" and a definition.

[46] NG 6.

[47] Cf. Trygve Knudsen, P. A. Munch, 47ff.

[48] For a succinct statement of his principles see his letter to Marius Nygaard, Brev og Dagbøker I (9 June, 1859), 364.

[49] The earliest available statement of his vowel system is in a letter to Andreas Faye of January 15, 1845 (Brev og Dagbøker I, 103). The three columns are here distinguished by acoustic terms, strangely reminiscent of Roman Jakobson's contrast of grave and acute. The back round vowels are called "hollow but not sharp," the front round "hollow and somewhat sharp," the front unround "sharp but not hollow" (i. e., plus grave, plus-minus grave, minus grave). In the 1848 grammar an articulatory terminology has been substituted, describing what he calls "Fremskydning of Stødepunktet," according to which the "least advanced" are what we would call "front"; apparently the term refers to the protrusion of the lips, without regard to tongue position. This terminology is carried over into the 1864 grammar. The rows are distinguished by degree of opening as "broad" and "narrow." The "open" vowels are called "Mellemlyd" in 1845, but the term "aaben" enters in 1848 and is the only term used in 1864.

[50] The vowel chart is in NG 20. For further information on the vowel systems of the dialects see Einar Haugen, "On the Stressed Vowel Systems of Norwegian," Scandinavian Studies Presented to George T. Flom (Urbana, Illinois, 1942), 66-78.

[51] Grave accents only are used in the vowel chart of 1845. For details on his discussions with academic advisers in Oslo see his letter to Olaus Vullum (9 November, 1847) in Brev og Dagbøker 1, 146; also his report to the Scientific Society (7 October, 1847) ibid., I, 139-141 and letter to F. M. Bugge (7 October, 1847), ibid., I, 141. He gave up the grave and adopted acute on the old long vowels in the 1848 grammar. As a result of this discussion he gave up any marking of vowels in the 1864 grammar and 1873 dictionary, but placed instead

either a double vowel (for the closed vowels) or an apostrophized vowel (for the open vowels) in parentheses after the word where he found it necessary to distinguish (usually only when long).

[52]NG 26n.

[53]Cf. Aasen's statement in NG 20n: "Det synes ogsaa ellers at være et Slags Regel, at naar den aabne Vokal nærmer sig meget til den lukte Lyd, da vil netop den lukte Lyd fraskille sig ved en bredere eller mere diftongisk Form. "

[54]NG 29n.

[55]NG 15n.

[56]He did not write the grave accent over short vowels, as a rule.

[57]NG 15.

[58]NG 33n.

[59]P. A. Munch, Den Constitutionelle, 1845, cit. Trygve Knudsen, P. A. Munch, 52ff.

[60]NG 228n.

[61]For references to euphony (Velklang) and clarity (Tydelighed) see, e. g. , NG 233n, 234n, 343n.

[62]NG 390n.

[63]NG 392n.

[64]For a typology of language functions see William A. Stewart, "An Outline of Linguistic Typology for Describing Multilingualism," in Frank A. Rice, Study of the Role of Second Languages (Washington, D. C. , 1962), 15-25.

[65]Moltke Moe, in a review of Garborg and Mortenson's reader (Vor Ungdom 1886, 75-93).

[66]Cf. Aasen's own statement in a letter to V. E. Lidforss (7 March, 1873): "Mange af vore Landsmænd sige rigtignok, at det er 'lavet Sprog', men noget lignende kan man vistnok ogsaa sige om flere af de moderne Sprog . . . . Forøvrigt ere de allerfleste Former i virkelig Brug, og allesammen ere de historisk givne, saa at intet kan siges at være opfundet eller vilkaarlig opstillet. " (Brev og Dagbøker II, 128).

[67]For a vigorous critique of later changes in Aasen's norm see Gustav Indrebø, Norsk målsoga (Bergen, 1951), 457: "Visst er òg at Aasens ettertid hev vore for snar til å riva ned og riva sund ymist av verket hans. "

10 | Semicommunication: The Language Gap in Scandinavia

The Problem

      Communication does not require the participants to have iden-
tical languages. Despite the growing loss of efficiency in the communication process as language codes deviate, it is often astonishing how
great a difference speakers can overcome if the will to understand is
there. The elasticity of mutual comprehensibility is one of the reasons
for the difficulty of setting up any acceptable scale of language distance.
There is a popular impression that dialects are mutually intelligible,
while languages are not. Experience with actual dialects and languages,
as these are commonly defined by linguists, contradicts this idea. All
the major languages of Europe have dialects that are mutually incomprehensible without a considerable amount of experience. Americans
tend to be baffled by Cockney English and completely floored by broad
Lancashire or Scots. A Berliner is lost in the Bavarian Alps, as is a
Parisian in Gascony, or a Piedmontese in Sicily. There are related
languages, on the other hand, whose speakers can communicate by
using their own languages, given only a little good will. From the historical linguist's point of view, these may be dialects, but in their
present-day function they are languages, standardized for use by a
particular nation. This certainly is true of Czech and Slovak, of Bul-
garian and Macedonian, of Ukrainian and Russian, and, to some extent, of more distantly related languages such as Spanish and Italian
or Czech and Polish.

      The question of how people communicate across such language
gaps has not challenged linguists to any great extent until the last decade or so, when a number of anthropological linguists (e.g. Wolff)
have begun to explore it.[1]

One of the multilingual areas to which Wolff[2] referred is the culture area popularly known as Scandinavia, where both languages and dialects constitute barriers to but do not wholly block communication. Danes, Norwegians, and Swedes expect to be understood by fellow Scandinavians when they use their own languages. At times, however, they are disappointed in their expectations; and the region as a whole offers many examples of what we may call semicommunication, the trickle of messages through a rather high level of "code noise."

Although there is some disagreement on the meaning of "Scandinavia," all Scandinavians agree that their own term, Norden, includes the five sovereign states of Denmark, Finland, Iceland, Norway, and Sweden. These have a common cultural heritage which unites them to some extent and distinguishes them from other nations but does not make them identical. This heritage of the past is constantly being renewed by cooperation and adaptation in the present. The sense of unity is strongest when threatened from the outside; at other times independence tends to be emphasized. Iceland and Finland are marginal and will be excluded from this discussion, since they offer entirely different language problems. Finland shares her type of government, social organization, religion, and the like with the rest of Norden, but differs linguistically in having Finnish as her chief language, a non Indo-European language which is completely unintelligible to other Scandinavians. Swedish is also recognized as one of Finland's languages. For many centuries it was the only language of government, but today it has shrunk to being the native speech of only 7.4 per cent of the population according to the 1960 census. The other languages, excluding Lappish, are all Indo-European; they are descended from the Germanic branch, to which English also belongs, by way of a Common Nordic language.[3] Icelandic is also excluded here, because it is not mutually comprehensible with the rest of its kinsmen. Icelanders are taught Danish as a second language and normally expect to use it in making themselves understood. In spite of a common linguistic heritage, each language has its own history and its own more or less independent standards. Danish and Norwegian have a large part of their vocabulary in common, but differ sharply in pronunciation; Norwegian and Swedish have a similar pronunciation, but differ greatly in vocabulary; Danish and Swedish have to contend with both problems. These languages tend to diverge like the branches of a tree, since many changes take place independently. The cultural leaders of

Scandinavia are understandably concerned over the threat of complete
linguistic separation which hangs over these countries and have made
many proposals which aim to remedy the situation. These range from
multiple language teaching in school to deliberate language reform in
order to promote linguistic convergence.

While on a Fulbright research year in Norway in 1951-1952,
this writer devoted some time to studying the literature written on
this problem. He quickly found it to be either narrowly linguistic or
broadly agitatorial. The linguistic writings were largely historical,
outlining the development of each language or dialect and rarely em-
bracing either the Scandinavian languages as a whole or making detailed comparisons of their present-day structures. The popular versions were uninformed attacks, for the greater part, on the unwillingness of Scandinavians to read each other's writings or to accept each
other's speech. There seemed to be no bridge provided between the
linguistic approach, on the one hand, and the sociopolitical approach,
on the other, by any sort of research into the actual attitudes and experiences involved in inter-Scandinavian communication. The writer's
personal observations led him to believe that the first task should be
the collection of statistically valid information concerning the functions
and problems of language within the social setting of inter-Scandinavian
communication. Being a linguist and having no sociological team behind him, he naively set to work preparing a questionnaire which was
to bring out the kinds of information he thought might be useful. Although the sample to which it was submitted was small and the results
only suggestive, the resulting figures turned out to be very interesting.
Since they have not previously been published in English, the writer
takes this opportunity to make them known to sociologists, whose field
he intrepidly invaded at a time when most other linguists were totally
disinterested in their kind of enlightenment.[4]

The Questionnaire

There were 45 questions in all, grouped into four sections.
The first consisted of personal questions, intended to identify the informants' sex, age, birthplace, present and past residence, marital
status, nationality, occupation and title, education, and political affi-
liation. The second section contained questions about the informants'

willingness to change certain spelling rules in their own language in order to accommodate inter-Scandinavian communication. The third and fourth sections consisted of 15 identical questions designed to test the informant's linguistic relationship to each of the two sister countries. The informant was asked how often and for what length of time he had visited each country or how many persons of that nationality he had met, how well he had understood the other language, and how well he had been understood. He was asked to report any cases of misunderstanding he had experienced. He was asked whether he made any changes in his own speech to improve understanding. A crucial question was: "How do you like the sound of language X, (a) compared with Y, (b) compared with Z ?" He was further asked to indicate the approximate amount of instruction he had received in the languages, how much he read in each, whether he enjoyed inter-Scandinavian radio programs, and whether he listened to broadcasts from the neighboring countries. Finally he was asked whether he thought Scandinavian books ought to be translated for the Scandinavian market, a burning problem for many publishers. Most of the questions could be answered by simple underlining of alternatives.

The questions were written in English originally and then translated into each of the three languages.[5] The questionnaire was mailed to 300 persons in each country, whose names were selected at random from the national telephone directory.[6] The reason for choosing this source was simply that it was the only nationwide list of names that was readily available. That the sample was skewed in favor of certain classes will be obvious from the results. One can only defend the choice by saying that telephone subscribers are more likely to be interested in communication than is the population as a whole. Even so, the response rate was not overwhelming, though adequate for the very general survey purpose which the writer had in mind. A total of 252, or 28 per cent, of the questionnaires were returned, 81 from Denmark, 117 from Norway, and 54 from Sweden. The low Swedish rate resulted from failure to send followup letters to those informants. A supplementary mailing of 60 questionnaires went to people in each country whose names were taken from that country's Who's Who. These social and intellectual leaders were more enthusiastic; here response rates were as high as 50 per cent of those asked. But their answers did not differ in general from those in corresponding social position in the larger group, and they have therefore not been included in the figures given below.

The Informants

Telephones are usually listed in the names of men; thus 88 per cent of the sample proved to be male. The age range was from 30 to 70, with the average just under 50. Most of the informants, 87 per cent, either were or had been married. These figures were virtually identical for all three countries.

The questions on occupation, education, and politics made it possible to sort the informants roughly into four social classes: farmers, workers, middle class, and university-trained. Table 1 shows their distribution by country.

The figures do not correspond in any way to the actual distribution of these classes in the population, in any one country, or in Scandinavia as a whole. The middle class and the university-trained are vastly overrepresented, although it is quite likely that the figures are not out of line with the actual influence which these groups wield in society. Workers are clearly underrepresented in view of the strength of the labor movement in the political life of these countries, though it must be recalled that most labor leaders would be classified here as middle class or university-trained.

TABLE 1
Socioeconomic Composition of the Sample, by Country

Socioeconomic Class	Country		
	Denmark %	Norway %	Sweden %
Farmers	14	15	15
Workers	9	9	22
Middle Class	48	57	41
University-trained	27	16	17
Other	2	3	5
TOTAL	100	100	100
(N)	(81)	(117)	(54)

TABLE 2
Travel in Other Scandinavian Countries

Infor- mants	Country Visited	Per Cent with Designated Degree of Contact						
		Never	Once	More Than Once	Have Lived There	No Re- sponse	Total	(N)
Danes	Norway	47	16	26	7	4	100	(81)
	Sweden	22	4	51	19	5	101	(81)
Norwe- gians	Denmark	51	10	32	6	1	100	(117)
	Sweden	31	15	40	13	2	101	(117)
Swedes	Denmark	33	15	43	7	2	100	(54)
	Norway	48	15	35	2	0	100	(54)

Most of the farmers had only elementary school education, except that in Denmark a number of them had attended a "folk high school" (folkehøjskole). The same was true of workers, except that some had gone to vocational schools. The middle class was a heterogeneous group, including businessmen and functionaries without university degrees. Most of these either had high school or vocational school education. The university-trained class included architects, lawyers, doctors, educators, high government officials, and business leaders. They were all what might be called "professional" men.

As we shall see, there are consistent differences in attitude towards language among these groups.

Social Contact. The informants were asked how often they had visited one of the other countries. Table 2 shows the results.

The figures suggest that the Danes are the most traveled of the Scandinavians: three quarters of them have been in Sweden, and half of them in Norway. Norwegians and Swedes are about even, but the direction of their travel is different: two thirds of the Norwegians have been in Sweden, but only half of the Swedes have been in Norway; half of the Norwegians have been in Denmark, whereas two thirds of

the Swedes have been there. Sweden clearly exerts the greatest attraction. It must be remembered, however, that these figures reflect
the situation immediately after World War II; there have been great
changes since that time. Even so, the figures correspond with the
geographical accessibility of each country to prospective travelers
from the other.

If we look more closely at the figures, however, and break
them down by classes, we find that virtually none of the farmers or
workers have been across the border. Of 17 Norwegian farmers not
one had been in Denmark and only three in Sweden. Of eleven Swedish
workers only three had been in Norway and three in Denmark. The
university-trained persons, on the other hand, had nearly all been in
the other countries. In the Who's Who group all 32 Norwegians had
been in Sweden and all but two in Denmark; of 36 Danes all but three
had been in Norway and all but one in Sweden; of 23 Swedes all but
one had been in Denmark and all but four in Norway. A question designed to bring out the amount of contact experienced by stay-at-homes
revealed that of 38 Danes who had not been in Norway, 23 had spoken
to less than ten Norwegians, while of 18 who had not been in Sweden,
13 had met less than ten Swedes. The conclusion is clear: professional men and the better situated members of the middle class have
far more outside contact than others. It may be added that the tremendous expansion of automobile ownership and tourism since World
War II has probably altered these figures greatly.

It is doubtful, however, that they have greatly altered the
proportion of people who read the publications of the other countries.
Table 3 shows the answers to questions on reading patterns over the
preceding year.

If we consider only those who claim to have read "some" or
"many" books and periodicals, we discover that more Danes seem to
read Norwegian than read Swedish (47 per cent compared to 42 per
cent), but the proportion is still less than half. About the same proportion of Norwegians read Danish, but rather more seemed to read
Swedish (47 per cent compared to 53 per cent). The Swedes, on the
other hand, appear to be content with their own literature, since only
about a quarter of them read the writings of either neighbor. Once
more the less academic class lagged behind: of eight Swedish farmers

TABLE 3

Readership of Books and Periodicals from Other Scandinavian Countries

Informants	Publications of	Per Cent Reading Designated Number of Publications in Preceding Year											Total		(N)
		None		One		Some		Many		No Response				Total		
		Books	Per.	Books	Per.	Books	Per.	Books	Per.	Books	Per.	Books	Per.		
Danes	Sweden	43	47	6	1	27	27	15	14	9	11	100	100	(81)
	Norway	46	38	1	6	36	40	11	7	6	9	100	100	(81)
Norwe-gians	Denmark	51	40	5	3	35	42	6	11	3	4	100	100	(117)
	Sweden	43	29	6	0	38	53	7	9	6	9	100	100	(117)
Swedes	Denmark	72	52	7	9	15	26	2	6	4	7	100	100	(54)
	Norway	61	54	7	7	19	22	4	4	9	13	100	100	(54)

TABLE 4

Ability to Understand Other Scandinavians Upon First Meeting

Informants	Other	Ability to Understand						Total	(N)
		Not At All	With Great Difficulty	Had to Listen Intently	All But a Few Words	Every-thing	No Response		
Danes	Swedish	1	32	38	16	2	10	99	(81)
	Norwegian	0	7	14	58	14	6	99	(81)
Norwegians	Danish	0	15	41	32	10	3	101	(117)
	Swedish	0	5	13	64	12	6	100	(117)
Swedes	Danish	2	37	31	19	4	7	100	(54)
	Norwegian	0	2	7	63	24	4	100	(54)

only one and of eleven Swedish laborers only four had read anything at all in the other languages. Of the three countries Sweden is clearly the most self-sufficient, intellectually as well as economically. This is even more striking in the figures for radio listening. While 41 per cent of the Danes and 52 per cent of the Norwegians said that they listened to the Swedish radio "often," only nine per cent of the Swedes said the same for Danish radio and 13 per cent for Norwegian radio.

Two questions sought to explore the informants' membership in inter-Scandinavian organizations, of which there are many. The answers showed significantly higher than average membership in Denmark and in the academic group, reflecting a long academic tradition, particularly in Denmark, of inter-Scandinavian activity. The Society Norden, created purely for the purpose of promoting Scandinavian contact, included 17 per cent of the Danish informants, seven per cent of the Norwegians, and only two per cent of the Swedes. The proportions were much higher in the Who's Who sample: Denmark, 37 per cent; Norway, 16 per cent; and Sweden, 43 per cent. Others belonged to a variety of Pan-Scandinavian organizations, from philatelists and geologists to administrators and dentists. In the Who's Who group 31 per cent of the Danes belonged to such organizations, 17 per cent of the Swedes, and 16 per cent of the Norwegians.

These figures do not have any significance in themselves, since such memberships are more likely among those who responded to the questionnaire at all. The results do show that such contacts are largely among the educated; this does not diminish their importance as promoters of unofficial links across national borders.

Mutual Comprehension. Five questions were designed to explore the informants' opinion concerning the problem of mutual comprehension:

(1) When you met an X for the first time, how well could you understand him? (not at all—with great difficulty—had to listen intently—all but a few words—understood everything.) (2) Do you now understand X speech without difficulty? (No. Yes. Fairly well.) (3) When you speak with X, how well do they understand you? (Same alternatives as under 1.) (4) Have you had any experiences of amusing or serious

misunderstandings ? In that case, please write on the back.
(5) Do you usually make any changes in your own language
when you speak with X, in order to ease comprehension ?
Speak more slowly ? Avoid words that can be misunderstood?
Mix in words from X ? Change your pronunciation ? Adopt
the other language ? Adopt a non–Scandinavian language, and
if so, which one ?

Tabulation on Table 4 of the answers to the first question
shows the basic dimensions of our problem. The first observation to
be made is that only three respondents claimed not to understand at
all. These were involved in the most difficult leg of the three-way
relationship, that between Danish and Swedish. The answers for this
relationship show almost perfect symmetry: Danes and Swedes find
one another's language difficult to about equal degrees. The relation
of Norwegian to Swedish is clearly the easiest; and it is also almost
symmetrical, with only slight skewing in the direction of Swedish
optimism in thinking they understood everything. The relation of
Danish to Norwegian appears to be intermediate in difficulty, but with
marked skewness demanding explanation. Danes claimed to understand
Norwegian at a greater rate than the reverse: only 14 per cent had to
"listen intently," while 41 per cent of the Norwegians had to do so to
understand Danish. Since standard Norwegian and Danish have a very
high degree of lexical communality—which results from the long dominance of Danish in Norway—difficulties of understanding must
largely be due to marked differences in pronunciation. In general one
can say that Norwegian pronunciation agrees with Danish spelling better
than does Danish pronunciation. Hence it is possible, if the figures
are valid, that Danes can understand Norwegian pronunciation by referring to spelling, while the Norwegians are completely at a loss in
listening to Danish pronunciation (e.g. røg, meaning "smoke," is pronounced and written røk in Norway, but pronounced [Roj] in Denmark).
But also involved is the fact that persons from rural Norway are less
adept at Danish because of the greater distance between their dialects
and Danish; 78 per cent of the Norwegian farmers found Danish difficult.

The marked difference between the three relationships is
brought out more clearly if we combine frequencies in the first three
columns and compare them with those with the sum of the next two.

The first sum represents those who found the other language "difficult" (a number of informants even underlined both the second and third responses), the second those who found it "easy." The following figure results if we place the languages in rough geographical relationship to each other and draw arrows along the sides of a triangle to represent per cent finding their neighbors' language easy on first encounter.

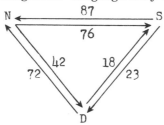

It is evident that Norwegian occupies the favored position of being most easily understood by both Swedes and Danes. As one Danish wit put it, "To a Dane Swedish is a difficult language pronounced in Norwegian, while to a Swede Danish is Norwegian pronounced in a difficult way (Mogens Brøndsted)." This is confirmed by the answers to the question on current understanding, where only three alternatives were permitted, "yes," "no," and "fairly well." If we consider only those who replied "yes" (meaning that they now understood the language without difficulty) the triangle will look as follows:

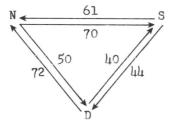

Here the figures reach what is probably reasonable stability with fair symmetry within each relationship. The number claiming ease of understanding was much lower, however, among the less educated classes. Almost 100 per cent of those who were university-trained claimed to understand all three languages.

A useful check for these questions on understanding was the one which explored being understood. It appeared that informants generally thought themselves to be understood better than they themselves were able to understand. There was little such difference for situations in which own understanding was virtually complete, as in the Norwegian-Swedish relationship. Only 50 per cent of the Norwegians would admit to understanding Danish easily, but 76 per cent of the Danes thought they were easily understood by Norwegians. Only 40 per cent of the Danes would admit to understanding Swedish easily, but 87 per cent of the Swedes thought they were understood by Danes. When the latter situation is reversed, however, the rates were in agreement: 44 per cent of the Swedes claimed that they understood the Danes, and 42 per cent of the Danes felt that they were understood in Sweden.

It is clear that the Danes are in the most difficult Nordic communication situation. Individual informants provided a good deal of anecdotal material to illustrate this point. A Danish school principal told about a lecture she had given to a Stockholm audience from a manuscript which had virtually been translated into Swedish:

> "They understood me very well. Then I fumbled for an expression, and the audience cried out, 'Just talk Danish, you are so easy to understand.' I switched to Danish, to the great surprise of the Swedes, who understood nothing! They had thought I was talking Danish all along."

A Danish journalist wrote about the situation with some bitterness, attributing it to Swedish contempt for the Danes:

> "This is not true of academic people, who as a rule are very good at understanding and reading Danish and often make honorable efforts from pure politeness to speak Danish to the Danes. But if you talk with the man in the street in Stockholm, you feel as if you were in Moscow, for example. He just shakes his head as if to show that he doesn't understand anything and, alas, doesn't really care to know, for of what concern is a creature from such a distant, uncultured land to him!"

To the linguist it seems obvious that the true explanation lies in difference of pronunciation, but as Wolff[7] has pointed out, attitudes also count heavily. Among the anecdotes reported was one of a

Norwegian who asked for directions in Copenhagen. What he heard
sounded to him like Yæeeeeee, but when he finally made his way to
the place, it turned out to be spelled Ryesgade. Another Norwegian
asked for bløtkaker ("pastry") and got blødkogte ("soft-boiled" [eggs]).
There are a number of common words which can be used in identical
contexts but with quite different meanings: among the most frequently
mentioned are rar, which means "nice" in Denmark and Sweden but
"peculiar" in Norway, and rolig, which means "quiet" in Denmark and
Norway but "amusing" in Sweden. But there also are more subtle differences. A Norwegian schoolboy asked, "Do I have to undress out
in the yard?" at a Danish resort. The modal auxiliary må means
"have to" in Norwegian, but to the Danish inspector it meant "may";
and he kindly replied, "Yes, you may," which the Norwegian boy interpreted as a command.

Linguistic Attitudes. Even though mutual comprehension is
basically a matter of language distance, we cannot entirely discount
the effect of mutual social attitudes in reducing or enhancing the will
to understand. We have already noted a certain skewness in the relationship of Danes to Norwegians, the former being more willing to
understand the latter than vice versa. In order to explore the sphere
of attitudes, tentatively at least, a purely evaluative question was introduced: "How do you like the sound of Y?" The response alternatives were: (a) "Compared with X (the informant's own language), Y
is: more beautiful, equally beautiful, less beautiful." (b) "Compared
with Z (the third language), Y is: More beautiful, equally beautiful,
less beautiful."

It is clear that one might set up some kind of abstract beauty
scale for all languages considered purely as sound and ask musicians,
poets, or art critics to judge them. Some languages (like Italian) are
popularly considered to be "musical," others (say German) to be "guttural," etc. It is reasonably clear, however, that such clichés are
heavily biased by particular historical circumstances and accomplish-
ments. Italian spoken by an uneducated, careless speaker with a harsh
voice is no esthetic pleasure, while German spoken by a trained actor
reading a lyric by Goethe or Heine is a thing of joy. Such attitudes
have changed demonstrably over time without any corresponding changes
in the languages themselves. For example, Danish was the only pronunciation tolerated on the Norwegian stage in the early nineteenth
century; today this would be quite unacceptable.

TABLE 5
Perceived Beauty of Scandinavian Languages

Informants	Language X	Language Y	Prefer X	X and Y Equal	Prefer Y	Total	(N)
Danes	Danish	Swedish	29	29	42	100	(81)
	Danish	Norwegian	18	42	41	101	(81)
	Norwegian	Swedish	37	33	30	100	(81)
Norwegians	Norwegian	Swedish	10	58	32	100	(117)
	Norwegian	Danish	73	25	2	100	(117)
	Danish	Swedish	2	19	79	100	(117)
Swedes	Swedish	Danish	86	14	0	100	(54)
	Swedish	Norwegian	18	63	20	101	(54)
	Danish	Norwegian	6	16	78	100	(54)

We may therefore take it for granted that a simple judgment of beauty contains a strong component of social and national attitude. Further studies would be necessary to disentangle these, and the results to follow are presented with full realization that they fail to explore the root of the matter. Nevertheless, they do correspond closely to the experiences the writer has had in his association with Scandinavians over many years, both in the homeland and in the United States.

A few informants felt themselves to be superior to the question and quite properly refused to answer it. Most informants were, however, willing to reveal their prejudices, and their preferences appear on Table 5.

Given strong nationalism in these countries, one might suppose each nation to prefer its own language to that of its neighbors. This did not prove to be the case. Again Danish is the underdog in Scandinavian linguistic opinion. Only two per cent of the Norwegians and not a single Swede preferred Danish to their own language, while 41 per cent of the Danes preferred Norwegian and 42 per cent preferred Swedish to their own language. This least-favored position is confirmed in the more disinterested comparisons made in the other two countries: Norwegians voted 79 to two for Swedish over Danish, while Swedes voted 78 to six for Norwegian over Danish. Only a modest 29 per cent of the Danes ventured to prefer their own language to Swedish, and only 18 per cent preferred it to Norwegian. To be sure, those who thought it equal to the others brought the number supporting Danish to a majority.

Informal comments by Danes revealed part of the problem. A Danish doctor wrote that "Danish can be pretty when it is spoken clearly and purely, but it is greatly corrupted even by the 'cultured' class, and sounds flat and tiresome." On the other hand, one Danish lady quoted a Swedish professor and his wife who found the Danish language very beautiful, " . . . . . like music in their ears!" A Swedish professor wrote that Danish is " . . . . . charming when ladies speak it, but is less suitable for men." The most crushing judgment is that of the Norwegian who repeated an ancient cliché by writing that "Danish is not a language, but a throat disease!"

The phonetic basis for these judgments is quite clear, since Danish has developed a strongly guttural quality through its uvular r,

its glottal stop, and its velar spirant, all of which are rarely heard
in non-Danish Norden. Extensive transformation and loss of postvocalic consonants and weak vowels has also made it less comprehensible to its neighbors. Considered together with the growth of nationalism in these countries, these factors decrease willingness to make
the effort of understanding Danish, until its very "otherness" has become a target of ridicule instead of a mark of distinction. Moreover,
the prestige of Danish pronunciation is directly traceable to the fortunes of the Danish crown, which have steadily been on the wane since
the Reformation.

The relations between Norwegian and Swedish are of a different order. Here one can only speak of a mutual admiration society.
A majority in each country regards the other's language as equal in
beauty to its own; most of the remaining 40 per cent in each country
prefer that of the other, though Norwegians display the greater tendency in this direction, voting 32 to ten for Swedish, with the Swedes
voting only 20 to 18 for Norwegian. The Danes appear objectively unable to make up their minds, voting about one third for each point of
view, with a slight preference for Norwegian. One reason may be
their inability to draw auditory distinctions between Norwegian and
Swedish. Both have a strong musical accent which is distinguishable
only by natives, usually not by outsiders. A Norwegian informant
writes, "Can't stand Danish, but Swedish is beautiful." A Swedish
physician writes, "Norwegian sounds 'heroic' and sometimes quite
'dramatic' . . . . Many Swedish words can be recognized, but in a
more vigorous form at times, at others transformed into slang."

Practical Applications

Thoughtful Scandinavians have been concerned for the past
century and a half with the problem of averting what appeared to be inevitable divergence among the languages and consequent mutual incom-
prehensibility. Some form of applied linguistics has been called for,
with two favorite solutions predominating, those of language teaching
and language planning.

The questionnaire sought information about the extent of
school instruction given in the Nordic languages. There has been

vigorous growth of such instruction in recent years, but only ten per cent of the Swedish and Norwegian informants could remember having read one another's language in school. About 13 per cent of the Swedes had read Danish, while 40 per cent of the Danes had read Swedish. Another source of instruction resides in the radio programs which are exchanged between the three countries. A majority of the informants favored this, but opinion in Sweden favored translation or adaptation of Danish programs. Publishers have made numerous half-hearted efforts to sell books printed in the other languages. Until this century Norway and Denmark constituted a common literary market, but the numerous reforms of Norwegian have made it almost imperative that Norwegian books be translated for Danish consumption and vice versa. Figures which show what the informants thought about translation appear on Table 6.

Opinion was obviously strongly divided; and unfortunately the figures are meaningless, since it turned out that the question was ambiguous. Some took it to mean that books from the other countries should be made known in their country, a practice of which they approved. Those who understood the question as it was meant often commented on the absurdity of translating closely related languages. These were academic persons, whose position was determined by the fact that they themselves adapted their reading habits; they condemned the general reading public for not doing likewise. Farmers, workers, and citizens tended to favor translation, however, in the words of a Danish farmer, "Otherwise they won't be read whether this is wrong or not." A question which requested the informants to name Scandinavian authors from other countries whose works they read since leaving school was not very productive. Two thirds of the Danes, 54 per cent of the Norwegians, and 46 per cent of the Swedes could name at least one such author, but a high percentage had read them in translation. Without further detail it is clear that facility in reading the other languages is limited largely to university-trained people and that the publishers were right to issue most books in translation. Only further education which includes specific training in reading the other languages could alter this situation.

The idea that growing barriers between reading publics could be somewhat reduced by deliberate changes in the languages, above all in spelling, already found expression in a conference held in 1869.

TABLE 6

Opinions About Translating Books from Other Scandinavian Countries

Informants	Publications of	Per Cent Saying Books Should Be Translated	(N)
Danes	Norway	35	(81)
	Sweden	54	(81)
Norwegians	Denmark	26	(117)
	Sweden	43	(117)
Swedes	Denmark	33	(54)
	Norway	43	(54)

At least one of the proposals of this conference has been adopted by now: the Swedish symbol å has been substituted for the Danish and Norwegian aa. Most other reforms arose out of the internal considerations of each language, however, and often have separated rather than united the languages. Before 1906 all three languages wrote the word for "what" unphonetically as hvad; today only Danish retains this feature, while Swedish has dropped the h and Norwegian the d! Two questions sought to learn whether the informants were willing to take Scandinavian unity into account when new reforms were considered. But the results of these questions were inconclusive. Many did not answer, and those who did were fairly evenly divided pro and con. Here again there was a solid phalanx of general support among the professional men. But in practice some of the proposals were not found to be acceptable or only mildly so.[8]

There have been more radical proposals, one of these having been advocated by Danish author and jurist Professor Sven Clausen for the decade during and immediately after World War II. He proposed that each language consciously adopt words from the other in order to lessen the gap; he was also strongly in favor of retrieving words from dialects, all in order to reduce the German element in these languages. Although promoted with great talent, this plan was too Utopian to win solid support. But several of the informants still alluded to the idea of a pan-Scandinavian language as a solution to the

problem of Nordic communication. The problem is thoughtfully and
regretfully considered as follows by a Danish minister: "In my view
it is good that the written languages are brought close enough together
so that one reads each other's languages without difficulty. But it
must not be done in such a way that the delicate nuances and finesses
of the individual languages suffer injury." The field in which practical cooperation can really take place along these lines is in science
and technology, in government, and commerce. In these and other
modern activities there is constant coinage of new terms, and commissions are now at work in the Scandinavian countries to do what
they can to coordinate terminology.

          Most of the changes in any language, however—and this
probably applies to a literary standard as much as to a spoken norm—
stem from the unplanned needs of its users. Present-day languages
did not arise as the result of any one event or anyone's conscious
planning. Their separate development was closely tied to the fact
that Scandinavia fell apart into distinct political units, within each of
which life was lived independently to some extent from that of the
rest. Any convergence in the languages can therefore only come
about in the same way, through political union or, failing that, through
intense social contact on a country-to-country basis. One question
was included to learn if the informants were aware of the adaptations
which they made in order to ensure understanding by their interlocutors across the border. It appeared that when speaking to Danes, two
thirds of the informants found it necessary to slow up their speech.
About one third made an effort to avoid words that could be misunderstood.[9] About one fourth admitted using words from the other languages
when they spoke. Very few admitted changing their own pronunciation,
the highest proportion being 22 per cent of the Danes when they spoke
to Swedes. Virtually no one admitted to adopting the other language
in toto, only about six per cent of the Swedes and Danes doing so in
relation to one another. In most cases even these rare instances may
have been along lines noted by one Danish professor, who wrote that
in talking to the rural residents of Sweden he made use of a "home-
knit Swedish," where he mixed in "as many Swedish words as possible and pronounced Danish words with a 'Swedish' accent." As a result farmers would comment on "how easy it is to understand Danish."

          The desperation course is occasionally taken of using a non-
Scandinavian language as the medium of communication. This is only

mentioned sporadically by the informants and always in relation to
Danish. A Norwegian school man said, "When I am in Copenhagen,
I ask the waiters to speak German."

Conclusions

The tentative nature of the questionnaire and its inadequate
statistical validation do not permit other than tentative conclusions.
To some extent the results have confirmed the author's observations
and hypotheses, and to some extent they have brought new ideas into
the picture.

1) Nordic cooperation is an activity which is of primary concern and interest to members of the academic class and part of the
upper middle class. These are the ones who travel in other countries,
learn their languages, read their books, and belong to Nordic organizations. Other social classes, especially farmers and workers,
have fewer opportunities and interests in this direction. Any change
in this respect will have to come through improved Nordic instruction
in the common school, which is their chief medium of education.

2) Danes show the most active interest in Nordic cooperation,
having traveled more, read more, and listened more to the radios of
their neighbors. Swedes, on the other hand, show the least interest,
being from a country that is larger, wealthier, and more self-sufficient than either of its neighbors. One reason for activism by Danes
may be that they are the ones who stand to gain the most, since they
are generally less well understood than the rest. Denmark's exposed
position vis-à-vis Germany has for more than a century made Danes
painfully aware of the necessity for Nordic cooperation.

3) Phonetic developments which have created a cleft between
Danish and its Nordic neighbors do not only constitute bases for incomprehension, but also for irritation and general distaste for Danish on
the part of the other countries. While minor efforts have been made
recently to bring Danish modes of spelling in line with others, it is
improbable that any amount of conscious planning can affect pronunciation. The only conceivable remedy is one that makes use of inten-
sified social contact and mutual instruction, whereby the naturally divergent tendencies can be held in check and possibly be reversed.

4) It is suggested that research of this kind can form a valuable and needed bridge between purely linguistic description and the life problems of language users. Here the relationship between language and sociopolitical development has been explored. Languages that are closely related and mutually comprehensible serve as media of a partial understanding which is constantly felt to be fragile and on the verge of collapse. Attempts are made to counteract linguistic divergence, often without clear realization of the problems to be faced. The ideal of total convergence is resisted in the name of national sovereignty by all, and yet the desire exists for channels to remain sufficiently open to avoid that complete form of segregation which is translation.

5) The next research step should be to check these data against the following two kinds of information: (a) differential descriptions of the structures and vocabularies of the languages, and (b) a battery of comprehension tests to be administered to a representative sample of speakers in each country. The first would permit examining differences which cause the difficulties against a background of common elements. Some comparisons have been made, but so far there are no contrastive grammars for the entire area. Predictions made on the basis of such studies could then be tested in the field to examine their validity. Suggestive leads can be derived through familiarity with such popular attitudes and beliefs as we have explored in this paper.

6) As we have mentioned above, the problem of semiunderstanding, or communication across language gaps, may be found in many parts of the world. In countries like Germany and Italy they are referred to as dialect differences, while in countries like India, Pakistan, Yugoslavia, and Czechoslovakia they are recognized for what they are, language differences. Within the Romance, Slavic, Arabic, Turkic, and Bantu areas there are many cases of partially understandable languages. Information is scarce concerning the extent of semicommunication in such areas and the problems it causes. This should be a field of great concern to students of language and society, since language differences are not only marks of differential group membership, but also powerful triggers of group attitudes.

NOTES

[1] One may now read Hans Wolff's stimulating 1959 article on "Intelligibility and Inter-ethnic Attitudes," which has been reprinted in Dell Hymes, editor, Language and Culture in Society, New York: Harper and Row, 1964. His bibliography, it is interesting to note, goes back no farther than 1952. The problem is, however, one of central importance to sociolinguistics, since it is intimately involved with the social organization of many multilingual areas.

[2] Ibid.

[3] For further information see e. g. Gösta Bergman, A Short History of the Swedish Language, Stockholm: The Swedish Institute, 1947. The cleavage between the two written languages of Norway will be disregarded in the discussion to follow; "Norwegian" invariably will mean "Dano-Norwegian," the language of culture which is spoken and written most widely.

[4] The only previous publication was in the writer's article "Nordiske språkproblemer—en opinionsundersøkelse," in Nordisk Tidskrift, 29 (1953), pp. 225-249. The research was supported in part by the Social Science Research Council. Some of the calculations were performed by Lloyd Hustvedt.

[5] The Swedish version was prepared in Stockholm by Docent Gösta Bergman, the Danish one in Copenhagen by Director Franz Wendt, and the Norwegian one by the author.

[6] The writer is grateful to the Society Norden, whose facilities were made available for mailing and receiving the questionnaires.

[7] Wolff, op. cit.

[8] Details may be found in my 1953 article.

[9] This was Gösta Bergman's proposal in Särsvenskt och samnordiskt, Stockholm: Nämnden för svensk språkvård, 1947.

11 | Dialect, Language, Nation

The taxonomy of linguistic description—that is, the identification and enumeration of languages—is greatly hampered by the ambiguities and obscurities attaching to the terms "language" and "dialect." Laymen naturally assume that these terms, which are both popular and scientific in their use, refer to actual entities that are clearly distinguishable and therefore enumerable. A typical question asked of the linguist is: "How many languages are there in the world?" Or: "How many dialects are there in this country?"

The simple truth is that there is no answer to these questions, or at least none that will stand up to closer scrutiny. Aside from the fact that a great many, perhaps most, languages and dialects have not yet been adequately studied and described, it is inherent in the very terms themselves that no answer can be given. They represent a simple dichotomy in a situation that is almost infinitely complex. Hence they have come to be used to distinguish phenomena in several different dimensions, with resultant confusion and overlapping. The use of these terms has imposed a division in what is often a continuum, giving what appears to be a neat opposition when in fact the edges are extremely ragged and uncertain. Do Americans and Englishmen speak dialects of English, or do only Americans speak dialect, or is American perhaps a separate language? Linguists do not hesitate to refer to the French language as a dialect of Romance. This kind of overlapping is uncomfortable, but most linguists have accepted it as a practical device, while recognizing, with Bloomfield, "the purely relative nature of the distinction" (1933:54).

The two terms are best understood against the perspective of their history. In English both words are borrowed from French.

<u>Language</u> is the older, having partially displaced such native words
as "tongue" and "speech" already in Middle English. The oldest
attestation in the OED is from 1290: "With men þat onder-stoden
hire language." The French word is itself late, being a popular derivative of Latin <u>lingua</u> with the probable form *<u>linguāticum</u>, first
attested in the 12th century. <u>Dialect</u>, on the other hand, first appears
in the Renaissance, as a learned loan from Greek. The oldest OED
citation is from 1579 in reference to "certain Hebrue dialectes,"
while the earliest French I have found (in Hatzfeld and Darmesteter's
dictionary) is only 16 years earlier and speaks of Greek as being
"abondante en dialectes." A 1614 citation from Sir Walter Raleigh's
<u>The History of the World</u> refers to the "Aeolic Dialect" and confirms
the impression that the linguistic situation in ancient Greece was both
the model and the stimulus for the use of the term in modern writing.

There was need for some such term in Greece, since there
was in the classical period no unified Greek norm, only a group of
closely related norms. While these "dialects" bore the names of
various Greek regions, they were not spoken but written varieties of
Greek, each one specialized for certain literary uses, e.g., Ionic
for history, Doric for the choral lyric, and Attic for tragedy. In
this period the language called "Greek" was therefore a group of distinct, but related written norms known as "dialects." It is usually
assumed that the written dialects were ultimately based on spoken
dialects of the regions whose names they bore. These spoken dialects were in turn descended by normal linguistic divergence from a
Common Greek language of an older period, which can be reconstructed by comparison of the dialects with each other and with their
Indo-European kinsmen. In the postclassical period, however, the
Greek dialects disappeared and were replaced by a rather well-uni-
fied Greek norm, the <u>koiné</u>, essentially the dialect of Athens. So, in
the Hellenistic period "Greek" became the name of a norm that resulted from a linguistic convergence. The differences among the dialects were eliminated in favor of a single, triumphant language,
based on the dialect of the cultural and administrative center of the
Greeks.

The Greek situation has provided the model for all later
usage of the two terms "language" and "dialect." Much of the uncla-
rity in their application stems from the ambiguities present in that

situation. This has become evident with their extension to other
countries and with their adoption into the technical terminology of
linguistics. In a descriptive, synchronic sense "language" can refer
either to a single linguistic norm, or to a group of related norms.
In a historical, diachronic sense "language" can either be a common
language on its way to dissolution, or a common language resulting
from unification. A "dialect" is then any one of the related norms
comprised under the general name "language," historically the result of either divergence or convergence.

     Since this historical process can be indefinitely repeated,
the two terms are cyclically applicable, with "language" always the
superordinate and "dialect" the subordinate term. This is also clear
from the kind of formal structures into which they can be placed: "X
is a dialect of language Y," or "Y has the dialects X and Z" (never, for
example, *"Y is a language of dialect X"). "Language" as the superordinate term can be used without reference to dialects, but "dialect"
is meaningless unless it is implied that there are other dialects and
a language to which they can be said to "belong." Hence every dialect is a language, but not every language is a dialect.

     In addition to the ambiguities provided by the synchronic and
diachronic points of view distinguished above, increasing knowledge
concerning linguistic behavior has made the simple application of
these two contrasting terms ever more difficult.

     In French usage a third term developed, patois, which
applied primarily to the spoken language. The term dialecte is defined in the dictionary of the Académie française and other French
dictionaries as "variété régionale d'une langue." Littré (1956) expli-
citly requires that a dialect "include a complete literary culture"
(comportant une complète culture littéraire). As pointed out by
André Martinet (1964), this usage reflects the special French situation, in which there were a number of regional written standards,
which were then superseded by the written standard of Paris. The
French dialects were regional, like the Greek, and literary, but not
functionally distinguished like the Greek. When the dialects ceased
to be written, they became "patois": "Après le XIVe siècle, il se
forma une langue littéraire et écrite, et les dialectes devinrent des
patois" (Littré). Even more succinctly, Brun (1946) writes: "Un

patois est un dialecte qui s'est degradé." A patois, then, is a language norm not used for literary (and hence official) purposes, chiefly limited to informal situations. Thus Provençal might be considered a French dialect, but its local, spoken varieties are all patois. This distinction introduces a new dimension in our discussion: the social functions of a language. In terms of the language-dialect distinction, we may say that a patois is a dialect that serves a population in its least prestigious functions. The distinction of patois-dialect is therefore not one between two kinds of language, but between two functions of language. The definition in Littré (and others like it) clearly suggests a pejorative attitude toward the patois, since it no longer carries with a "a complete literary culture."

In English the term "patois" has never been seriously adopted in the description of language, and "dialect" has carried the full burden of both scientific and popular usage. Older writers, cited in the OED, often used it for any specialized variety of the language, e.g., "the lawyer's dialect." Samuel Butler (Hudibras, 1663) railed against "a Babylonish dialect, which learned pedants much affect." General usage has limited the word largely to the regional or locally based varieties, such as "Lancashire dialect" or "Irish dialect" in reference to varieties of English. It is less customary to speak of "London dialect" or "Boston dialect," except in reference to the lower-class speech of those cities. Nor is it common to speak of "British dialect" in reference to cultivated English speech, and Americans are generally resentful of being told they speak "American dialect" when reference is had to the speech of educated people. Martinet is therefore beside the mark when he writes that in America "the term denotes every local form of English but without any suggestion that a more acceptable form of the language exists distinct from the dialects" (1964:146). It is quite different with the word "accent": an American may inoffensively be described as having a "New England accent" or a "Southern accent," and, of course, all Americans speak of the English as having an "English accent." "Dialect" is here as elsewhere a term that suggests informal or lower-class or rural speech. In general usage it therefore remains quite undefined whether such dialects are part of the "language" or not. In fact, the dialect is often thought of as standing outside the language: "That isn't English." This results from the de facto development of a standard language, with all the segregation of an élite and the pyramidal power structure that it has usually implied.

As a social norm, then, a dialect is a language that is excluded from polite society. It is, as Auguste Brun (1946) has pointed
out, a language that "did not succeed." In Italy, Piedmontese is
from every linguistic point of view a language, distinct from Italian
on the one hand and French on the other, with a long tradition of writing and grammatical study. But because it is not Tuscan, and Tuscan became the standard language of all Italy, Piedmontese is only a
"dialect," yielding ground to Italian with every generation and kept
alive only by local pride and linguistic inertia (Clivio 1964). Only if
a "dialect" is watered down to an "accent"—that is, an intonation
and a set of articulations, with an occasional lexical item thrown in
for color—does it (say in Germany or Italy or England) become
"salonfähig." As a complete structure it is out in the cold limbo of
modern society. In America the stigma is placed not so much on
local dialects, since these are few and rarely heard, as on "bad"
English, which is quite simply lower-class dialect. The language of
the upper classes is automatically established as the correct form of
expression. They cannot only say, "L'état, c'est moi," but also "Le
langage, c'est le mien."

In trying to clarify these relationships, linguistic science
has been only moderately successful. Even in the Renaissance it was
perfectly clear to serious students of the subject that the term "language" was associated with the rise of a nation to conscious unity and
identity. George Puttenham wrote in his book The Arte of English
Poesie (1589): "After a speach is fully fashioned to the common
understanding, and accepted by consent of a whole country and nation,
it is called a language." This kind of historical development, by
which convergence was achieved at the expense of deviating varieties,
was familiar to the men of that age. But the arbitrary tower-of-
Babel approach to linguistic divergence was dispelled by the discovery,
in the early 19th century, of historical regularity. The realization
that languages have resulted from dialect-splitting gave a new content to the terms and made it possible to begin calling languages like
English and German "dialects" of a Germanic "language."

But in the mid-19th century, when scientific study of the
rural and socially disadvantaged dialects began, a generation of research was sufficient to revolutionize the whole idea of how a dialect
arises. The very notion of an area divided into a given number of

dialects, one neatly distinct from the next, had to be abandoned. The idea that languages split like branches on a tree gave way to an entirely different and even incompatible idea, namely, that individual linguistic traits diffused through social space and formed isoglosses that rarely coincided. Instead of a dialect, one had a "Kernland-schaft" with ragged edges, where bundles of isoglosses testified that some slight barrier had been interposed to free communication. Linguistics is still saddled with these irreconcilable "particle" and "wave" theories; this in effect involves the differing points of view from which any linguistic structure can be seen: as a unitary structure (a "language"), or as one of several partially overlapping structures (the "dialects").

Without going into the problems raised by this conflict, we may simply state that the "particle" theory of language as a unified structure is a fruitful hypothesis, making it possible to produce an exhaustive and self-consistent description. But it excludes as "free variation" a great many inconsistencies within the speech of any informant, and it fails to account for the fact that communication is possible between users of identifiably different codes. Comparative grammar succeeded in reconstructing the common structure from which "dialects" could be derived. Contrastive grammar has tried to program the differences between languages in order to ease the learner's task or, on a higher theoretical plane, to arrive at a linguistic typology. But there is still no calculus that permits us to describe the differences between languages in a coherent and theoretically valid way.

Our discussion has shown that there are two clearly distinct dimensions involved in the various usages of "language" and "dialect." One of these is structural, that is, descriptive of the language itself; the other is functional, that is, descriptive of its social uses in communication. Since the study of linguistic structure is regarded by linguists as their central task, it remains for sociologists, or more specifically, sociolinguists, to devote themselves to the study of the functional problem.

In the structural use of "language" and "dialect," the overriding consideration is genetic relationship. If a linguist says that Ntongo has five dialects, he means that there are five identifiably different speech-forms that have enough demonstrable cognates to make it certain that they have all developed from one earlier speech-form. He may also be referring to the fact that these are mutually understandable, or at least that each dialect is understandable to its immediate neighbors. If not, he may call them different languages, and say that there is a language Ntongo with three dialects and another, Mbongo, with two. Ntongo and Mbongo may then be dialects of Ngkongo, a common ancestor. This introduces the synchronic dimensions of comprehension, which is at best an extremely uncertain criterion. The linguist may attempt to predict, on the basis of his study of their grammars, that they should or should not be comprehensible. But only by testing the reactions of the speakers themselves and their interactions can he confirm his prediction (Voegelin and Harris 1951; Hickerson et al., 1952). Between total incomprehension and total comprehension there is a large twilight zone of partial comprehension in which something occurs that we may call "semicommunication."

In the functional use of "language" and "dialect," the overriding consideration is the uses the speakers make of the codes they master. If a sociolinguist says that there is no Ntongo language, only dialects, he may mean that there is no present-day form of these dialects that has validity beyond its local speech community, either as a trade language or as a common denominator in interaction among the various dialect speakers. A "language" is thus functionally defined as a superposed norm used by speakers whose first and ordinary language may be different. A "language" is the medium of communication between speakers of different dialects. This holds only within the limits established by their linguistic cognacy: one could not speak of Ntongo as a dialect of English just because its speakers use English as a medium of intercommunication. The sociolinguist may also be referring to the fact that the "language" is more prestigious than the "dialect." Because of its wider functions it is likely to be embraced with a reverence, a language loyalty, that the dialects do not enjoy. Hence the possibility of saying that "Mbongo is only a dialect, while Ngkongo is a language." This means that Ngkongo is being spoken by people whose social prestige is notoriously higher than that of people who speak Mbongo. When used in this sense, a dialect may be defined as an undeveloped (or underdeveloped) language. It is a language that no one has taken the trouble to develop into what is often referred to as a "standard language." This dimension of functional superiority and inferiority is usually disregarded by linguists, but it is an essential part of the sociolinguist's concern. It becomes his special and complex task to define the social functions of each language or dialect and the prestige that attaches to each of these.

What is meant by an "undeveloped" language? Only that it has not been employed in all the functions that a language can perform in a society larger than that of the local tribe or peasant village. The history of languages demonstrates convincingly that there is no such thing as an inherently handicapped language. All the great languages of today were once undeveloped. Rather than speak of undeveloped languages as "dialects," after the popular fashion, it would be better to call them "vernaculars," or some such term, and limit "dialect" to the linguist's meaning of a "cognate variety." We are then ready to ask how a vernacular, an "undeveloped language," develops into a standard, a "developed language." To understand this we will have to consider the relation of language to the nation.

The ancient Greeks and Romans spread their languages as far as their domains extended, and modern imperialists have sought to do the same. But within the modern world, technological and political revolutions have brought Everyman the opportunity to participate in political decisions to his own advantage. The invention of printing, the rise of industry, and the spread of popular education have brought into being the modern nation-state, which extends some of the loyalties of the family and the neighborhood or the clan to the whole state. Nation and language have become inextricably intertwined. Every self-respecting nation has to have a language. Not just a medium of communication, a "vernacular" or a "dialect," but a fully developed language. Anything less marks it as underdeveloped.

The definition of a nation is a problem for historians and other social scientists; we may accept the idea that it is the effective unit of international political action, as reflected in the organization of the United Nations General Assembly. As a political unit it will presumably be more effective if it is also a social unit. Like any unit, it minimizes internal differences and maximizes external ones. On the individual's personal and local identity it superimposes a national one by identifying his ego with that of all others within the

nation and separating it from that of all others outside the nation. In
a society that is essentially familial or tribal or regional it stimu-
lates a loyalty beyond the primary groups, but discourages any conflicting loyalty to other nations. The ideal is: internal cohesion—
external distinction.

Since the encouragement of such loyalty requires free and rather intense communication within the nation, the national ideal demands
that there be a single linguistic code by means of which this communication can take place. It is characteristic that the French revolutionaries
passed a resolution condemning the dialects as a remnant of feudal society.
The dialects, at least if they threaten to become languages, are potentially disruptive forces in a unified nation: they appeal to local loyalty.
This is presumably the reason that France even now refuses to count the
number of Breton speakers in her census, let alone face the much greater
problem of counting the speakers of Provençal. On the other hand, a
nation feels handicapped if it is required to make use of more than one language for official purposes, as is the case in Switzerland, Belgium,
Yugoslavia, Canada, and many other countries. Internal conflict is
inevitable unless the country is loosely federated and the language borders are stable, as is the case in Switzerland.

Nationalism has also tended to encourage external distinction,
as noted above. In language this has meant the urge not only to have
one language, but to have one's own language. This automatically
secludes the population from other populations, who might otherwise
undermine its loyalty. Here the urge for separatism has come into
sharp conflict with the urge for international contact and for the advantages accruing both to individual and nation from such contact.
Switzerland is extreme in having three languages, no one of which is
its own; Belgium has two, both of which belong to its neighbors. The
The Irish movement has faltered largely under the impact of the overwhelming strength of English as a language of international contact.
The weakness of the New Norwegian language movement is due to the
thorough embedding of Danish in the national life during four centuries
of union; what strength the movement has had is derived from the
fact that Danish was not one of the great international languages.

Whenever any important segment of the population, an élite,
is familiar with the language of another nation, it is tempting to make

use of this as the medium of government, simply as a matter of convenience. If this is also the language of most of the people, as was the case when the United States broke away from England, the problem is easily solved; at most it involves the question of whether provincialisms are to be recognized as acceptable. But where it is not, there is the necessity of linguistically re-educating a population, with all the effort and disruption of cultural unity that this entails. This is the problem faced by many of the emerging African and Asian nations today (Le Page 1964). French and English have overwhelming advantages, but they symbolize past oppression and convey an alien culture. The cost of re-education is not just the expense in terms of dollars and cents, but the malaise of training one's children in a medium that is not their own, and of alienation from one's own past.

The alternative is to develop one's own language, as Finland did in the 19th century, or Israel did in the 20th. Different languages start at different points: Finland's was an unwritten vernacular, Israel's an unspoken standard. Today both are standards capable of conveying every concept of modern learning and every subtlety of modern literature. Whatever they may lack is being supplied by deliberate planning, which in modern states is often an important part of the development process.

It is a significant and probably crucial requirement for a standard language that it be written. This is not to say that languages need to be written in order to spread widely or be the medium of great empires. Indo-European is an example of the first, Quechua of the Inca Empire an example of the second (Buck 1916). But they could not, like written languages, establish models across time and space, and they were subject to regular and inexorable linguistic change. It is often held that written language impedes the "natural" development of spoken language, but this is still a matter of discussion (Zengel 1962; Bright and Ramanujan 1964). In any case the two varieties must not be confused.

Speech is basic in learning language. The spoken language is acquired by nearly all its users before they can possibly read or write. Its form is to a great extent transmitted from one generation of children to the next. While basic habits can be modified, they are not easily overturned after childhood and are virtually immovable after puberty. The spoken language is conveyed by mouth and ear and mobilizes the entire personality in immediate interaction with one's environment. Writing is conveyed by hand and eye, mobilizes the personality less completely, and provides for only a delayed response. Oral confrontation is of basic importance in all societies, but in a complex, literate society it is overlaid and supplemented by the role of writing.

The permanence and power of writing is such that in some societies the written standard has been influential in shaping new standards of speech. This is not to say that writing has always brought them into being, but rather to say that new norms have arisen that are an amalgamation of speech and writing. This can of course take place only when the writing is read aloud, so that it acquires an oral component (Wessén 1937). There is some analogy between the rise of such spoken standards and that of pidgin or creole languages (Meillet 1925:76; Sommerfelt 1938:44). The latter comprise elements of the structure and vocabulary of two or more languages, all oral. They have usually a low social value, compared to the oral standards, but the process of origin is comparable. The reawakening of Hebrew from its century-long dormant state is comprehensible only in terms of the existence of rabbinical traditions of reading scripture aloud (Morag 1959). Modern Hebrew has shown a rapid adaptation to the underlying norms of its new native speakers, so that it has become something different from traditional Hebrew. Similarly with the standard forms of European languages: one is often hard put to say whether a given form has been handed down from its ancestor by word of mouth or via the printed page. "Spelling pronunciations" are a well-known part of most oral standards, even though purists tend to decry them.

While we have so far spoken of standard languages as if they were a clear and unambiguous category, there are differences of degree even among the well-established languages. French is probably the most highly standardized of European languages, more so than, for example, English or German. French, as the most immediate heir of Latin, took over many of its concepts of correctness and its intellectual elaboration. French in turn became a model for other standard languages, and its users were for centuries nothing loth to have it so considered. When English writers of the 18th century debated whether an English academy should be established to regulate the language, the idea of such an institution came from France. The proposal was rejected largely because the English did not wish to duplicate what they regarded as French "tyranny."

In France, as in other countries, the process of standardization was intimately tied to the history of the nation itself. As the people developed a sense of cohesion around a common government, their language became a vehicle and a symbol of their unity. The process is reasonably well documented in the histories written for the older European languages. But the period since the French Revolution has seen a veritable language explosion, which has been far less adequately studied. In many countries a process that elsewhere took centuries of effort on the part of a people and its writers has been compressed into a few short years or decades. In a study of the new standards developed since 1800 for Germanic languages, Heinz Kloss has suggested that there may be a typical profile for what he has called the "Ausbau" of a new language (Kloss 1952: 28). First comes its use for purely humorous or folkloristic purposes. Then lyric writers may adopt it, followed by prose narrators. But it has not reached a crucial stage of development until success is achieved in writing serious expository prose, or what he calls "Zweckschrifttum." Beyond this comes the elaboration of the language for purposes of technical and scientific writing and government use. Each of these "domains" (as Fishman [1964] has called them) constitutes a challenge for the language in its attempt to achieve full development.

While making a survey of the world's standard languages, Ferguson proposed (1962) to classify them along two dimensions: their degree of standardization (St. 0, 1, 2) and their utilization in writing (W 0, 1, 2, 3). Zero meant in each case no appreciable standardization or writing. St. 1 meant that a language was standardized in more than one mode, as is the case, for example, with Armenian, Greek, Serbo-Croatian, and Hindi-Urdu. He also included Norwegian, but it is at least arguable that we are here dealing with two languages. St. 2 he defined as a language having a "single, widely accepted norm which is felt to be appropriate with only minor modifications or variations for all purposes for which the language is used." W 1 he applied to a language used for "normal written purposes," W 2 to one used for "original research in physical sciences,"

and W 3 to one used for "translations and résumés of scientific work
in other languages."

These categories suggest the path that "underdeveloped"
languages must take to become adequate instruments for a modern
nation. The "standardization" to which Ferguson refers applies primarily to developing the form of a language, i.e., its linguistic structure, including phonology, grammar, and lexicon. We shall call this
the problem of codification. Ferguson's scale of "utilization in writing" applies rather to the functions of a language. We shall call this
the problem of elaboration, a term suggested by a similar usage of
Bernstein's (1962) and corresponding to Kloss's Ausbau. As the
ideal goals of a standard language, codification may be defined as
minimal variation in form, elaboration as maximal variation in function.

The ideal case of minimal variation in form would be a hypothetical, "pure" variety of a language having only one spelling and
one pronunciation for every word, one word for every meaning, and
one grammatical framework for all utterances. For purposes of
efficient communication this is obviously the ideal code. If speakers
and listeners have identical codes, no problems of misunderstanding
can arise due to differences in language. There can be none of what
communication engineers call "code noise" in the channel (Hockett
1958: 331-332). This condition is best attained if the language has a
high degree of stability, a quality emphasized by many writers on the
subject (e.g., Havránek 1938). Stability means the slowing down or
complete stoppage of linguistic change. It means the fixation forever
(or for as long as possible) of a uniform norm. In practice such fixation has proved to be chimerical, since even the most stable of norms
inevitably changes as generations come and go. At all times the
standard is threatened by the existence of rival norms, the socalled
"dialects," among its users. It is liable to interference from them
and eventually to complete fragmentation by them.

Apparently opposed to the strict codification of form stands
the maximal variation or elaboration of function one expects from a
fully developed language. Since it is by definition the common language of a social group more complex and inclusive than those using
vernaculars, its functional domains must also be complex. It must

answer to the needs of a variety of communities, classes, occupations, and interest groups. It must meet the basic test of <u>adequacy</u>. Any vernacular is presumably adequate at a given moment for the needs of the group that uses it. But for the needs of the much larger society of the nation it is not adequate, and it becomes necessary to supplement its resources to make it into a language. Every vernacular can at the very least add words borrowed from other languages, but usually possesses devices for making new words from its own resources as well. Writing, which provides for the virtually unlimited storage and distribution of vocabulary, is the technological device enabling a modern standard language to meet the needs of every specialty devised by its users. There are no limits to the elaboration of language except those set by the ingenuity of man.

While form and function may generally be distinguished as we have just done, there is one area in which they overlap. Elaboration of function may lead to complexity of form, and, contrariwise, unity of form may lead to rigidity of function. This area of interaction between form and function is the domain of <u>style</u>. A codification may be so rigid as to prevent the use of a language for other than formal purposes. Sanskrit had to yield to Prakrit, and Latin to the Romance languages, when the gap between written and spoken language became so large that only a very few people were willing to make the effort of learning them. Instead of being appropriate for "all purposes for which the language is used," the standard tends to become only one of several styles within a speech community. This can lead to what Ferguson (1959) has described as "diglossia," a sharp cleavage between "high" and "low" style. Or it may be a continuum, with only a mild degree of what I have called "schizoglossia," as in the case of English (Haugen 1962). In English there is a marked difference between the written and spoken standards of most people. In addition, there are styles within each, according to the situation. These styles, which could be called "functional dialects," provide wealth and diversity within a language and ensure that the stability or rigidity of the norm will have an element of elasticity as well. A complete language has its formal and informal styles, its regional accents, and its class or occupational jargons, which do not destroy its unity so long as they are clearly diversified in function and show a reasonable degree of solidarity with one another.

Neither codification nor elaboration is likely to proceed very far unless the community can agree on the <u>selection</u> of some kind of a model from which the norm can be derived. Where a new norm is to be established, the problem will be as complex as the sociolinguistic structure of the people involved. There will be little difficulty where everyone speaks virtually alike, a situation rarely found. Elsewhere it may be necessary to make some embarrassing decisions. To choose any one vernacular as a norm means to favor the group of people speaking that variety. It gives them prestige as norm-bearers and a headstart in the race for power and position. If a recognized élite already exists with a characteristic vernacular, its norm will almost inevitably prevail. But where there are socially coordinate groups of people within the community, usually distributed regionally or tribally, the choice of any one will meet with resistance from the rest. This resistance is likely to be the stronger the greater the language distance within the group. It may often be a question of solidarity versus alienation: a group that feels intense solidarity is willing to overcome great linguistic differences, while one that does not is alienated by relatively small differences. Where transitions are gradual, it may be possible to find a central dialect that mediates between extremes, one that will be the easiest to learn and most conducive to group coherence.

Where this is impossible, it may be necessary to resort to the construction of a new standard. To some extent this has happened naturally in the rise of the traditional norms; it has been the aim of many language reformers to duplicate the effect in new ones. For related dialects one can apply principles of linguistic reconstruction to make a hypothetical mother tongue for them all. Or one can be guided by some actual or supposed mother tongue, which exists in older, traditional writings. Or one can combine those forms that have the widest usage, in the hope that they will most easily win general acceptance. These three procedures—the comparative, the archaizing, and the statistical—may easily clash, to make decisions difficult. In countries where there are actually different languages, amounting in some African nations to more than a hundred, it will be necessary either to recognize multiple norms or to introduce an alien norm, which will usually be an international language like English or French.

Finally, a standard language, if it is not to be dismissed as dead, must have a body of users. <u>Acceptance</u> of the norm, even by a small but influential group, is part of the life of the language. Any learning requires the expenditure of time and effort, and it must somehow contribute to the well-being of the learners if they are not to shirk their lessons. A standard language that is the instrument of an authority, such as a government, can offer its users material rewards in the form of power and position. One that is the instrument of a religious fellowship, such as a church, can also offer its users rewards in the hereafter. National languages have offered membership in the nation, an identity that gives one entrée into a new kind of group, which is not just kinship, or government, or religion, but a novel and peculiarly modern brew of all three. The kind of significance attributed to language in this context has little to do with its value as an instrument of thought or persuasion. It is primarily symbolic, a matter of the prestige (or lack of it) that attaches to specific forms or varieties of language by virtue of identifying the social status of their users (Labov 1964). Mastery of the standard language will naturally have a higher value if it admits one to the councils of the mighty. If it does not, the inducement to learn it, except perhaps passively, may be very low; if social status is fixed by other criteria, it is conceivable that centuries could pass without a population's adopting it (Gumperz 1962, 1964). But in our industrialized and democratic age there are obvious reasons for the rapid spread of standard languages and for their importance in the school systems of every nation.

The four aspects of language development that we have now isolated as crucial features in taking the step from "dialect" to "language," from vernacular to standard, are as follows: (1) selection of norm, (2) codification of form, (3) elaboration of function, and (4) acceptance by the community. The first two refer primarily to the form, the last two to the function of language. The first and the last are concerned with society, the second and third with language. They form a matrix within which it should be possible to discuss all the major problems of language and dialect in the life of a nation:

	Form	Function
<u>Society</u>	Selection	Acceptance
<u>Language</u>	Codification	Elaboration

NOTE

This paper was written as a contribution to the work of the Seminar
on Sociolinguistics, held at the Indiana University Linguistic Institute
in the summer of 1964, under the direction of Charles A. Ferguson.
It has profited from extensive discussion with the members of the
Seminar.

REFERENCES

Bernstein, Basil. 1962. Linguistic codes, hesitation phenomena
        and intelligence. Language and Speech 5: 31–46.
Bloomfield, Leonard. 1933. Language. New York, Holt.
Bright, William, and A. K. Ramunujan. 1964. Sociolinguistic varia-
        tion and language change. Proceedings, IX International
        Congress of Linguists. The Hague, Mouton. Pp. 1107–1114.
Brun, Auguste. 1946. Parlers régionaux: France dialectale et
        unité française. Paris, Toulouse: Didier.
Buck, C. D. 1916. Language and the sentiment of nationality.
        American Political Science Review 10: 44–69.
Clivio, Gianrenzo. 1964. Piedmontese: a short basic course.
        Mimeographed ed. Center for Applied Linguistics, Washing-
        ton, D. C.
Dictionnaire de l'Académie Française. 1932. Paris, 8th ed.
Ferguson, Charles A. 1959. Diglossia. Word 15: 325–340.
_____ 1962. The language factor in national development.
        Anthropological Linguistics 4, 1: 23–27.
Fishman, Joshua. 1964. Language maintenance—language shift as
        a field of inquiry. Linguistics 9: 32–70.
Gumperz, John. 1962. Types of linguistic communities. Anthropo-
        logical Linguistics 4, 1: 28–40.
_____ 1964. Hindi-Punjabi code switching in Delhi. Proceed-
        ings, IX International Congress of Linguists. The Hague,
        Mouton. Pp. 1115–1124.
Hatzfeld, A., and A. Darmesteter. 1920. Dictionnaire général de la
        langue française. Paris, 6. ed.
Haugen, Einar. 1962. Schizoglossia and the linguistic norm. Mono-
        graph Series on Languages and Linguistics. Georgetown
        University, Washington, D. C. No. 15, 63–69. [In this
        volume, pp. 148-58.]

Havránek, Bohumil. 1938. Zum Problem der Norm in der heutigen
    Sprachwissenschaft und Sprachkultur. Repr. in A Prague
    school reader in linguistics. J. Vachek, ed. Bloomington,
    Ind. Pp. 413-420.
Hickerson, H., G. D. Turner, and N. P. Hickerson. 1952. Testing
    procedures for estimating transfer of information among
    Iroquois dialects and languages. IJAL 18:1-8.
Hockett, Charles F. 1958. A course in modern linguistics. New
    York, Macmillan.
Kloss, Heinz. 1952. Die Entwicklung neuer germanischer Kultur-
    sprachen von 1800 bis 1950. Munich, Pohl.
Labov, William. 1964. Phonological correlates of social stratifica-
    tion. In The ethnography of communication. John J. Gum-
    perz and Dell Hymes, eds. American Anthropologist 66,
    No. 6, pt. 2:164-176.
Le Page, R. B. 1964. The national language question: linguistic
    problems of newly independent states. London, Oxford
    University Press.
Littré, E. 1956. Dictionnaire de la langue française. Paris.
Martinet, André. 1964. Elements of general linguistics. Chicago,
    University of Chicago Press.
Meillet, Antoine. 1925. La méthode comparative en linguistique
    historique. Oslo, Institutet for sammenlignende kultur-
    forskning.
Morag, Shelomo. 1959. Planned and unplanned development in
    modern Hebrew. Lingua 8:247-263.
Oxford English Dictionary. 1888 ff. James A. H. Murray et. al.,
    eds. Oxford University Press.
Sommerfelt, Alf. 1938. Conditions de la formation d'une language
    commune. Actes du IV Congrès international de linguistes.
    Copenhagen. Pp. 42-48.
Voegelin, C. F., and Z. S. Harris. 1951. Methods for determining
    intelligibility among dialects of natural languages. Proceed-
    ings of the American Philosophical Society 95: 322-329.
Wessén, Elias. 1937. Vårt riksspråk: Några huvudpunkter av dess
    historiska utveckling. Modersmålslärarnas Förenings
    årsskrift. Pp. 289-305.
Zengel, Marjorie S. 1962. Literacy as a factor in language change.
    American Anthropologist 64:132-139.

12 | National and International Languages

It is one of the features we take more or less for granted about our world that each nation has a language of its own. In France they speak and write French, in Italy Italian, in Germany German, in Russia Russian, and in England English. Yet it takes only a moment's reflection to realize that there are many nations of which this is not true. On the one hand, there are some that have no language of their own, and on the other are those that have more than one. We Americans have no language of our own, in spite of some assertions to the contrary; at most we have an American variety of the English language. We share this language not only with its motherland England, but also with England's many former colonies. Countries like Belgium and Switzerland are in the same situation of having no language of their own: there is no Belgian or Swiss language. Instead they share two or more languages with their neighbours: Belgium has Dutch and French, while Switzerland has German, French, and Italian. A country like Yugoslavia has three languages of its own, with Serbo-Croatian as the most important, Slovenian in the north and Macedonian in the south. India has fourteen official languages, one of which, Hindi, is supposed to become the national language; but English, the language of India's former masters, is still the most widely used in official communications.

When we look around the world, we find that in fact very few nations have one and only one language. Even the countries which come closest to this situation have minority populations that speak other languages: in France there are German speakers in Alsace-Lorraine, Breton speakers in Brittany, and Basque speakers in the Pyrenees. Not to speak of the fact that each region of France has its own local dialect; in southern France the dialects are so different from Standard French that they can be regarded as a separate language, which has been written under the name of Provençal. Every European country of any size has both of these deviations from its national language: lumps of unassimilated "foreigners," and regional variations in speech which may create an almost total gap in understanding between the users of the national language and the users of the local dialects. In the newly created nations of the world, whose experience with nationhood is very fresh, there may be so great a variation in language that there is not even any accepted national standard. It is one of the most acute problems of many newly created African nations that their tribal languages are so diverse and so little cultivated that none of them can be used as a common medium of communication for modern purposes. In such situations their rulers are forced to continue the use of the language of their former masters, usually English or French. They are put into the uncomfortable position of having to use languages that are not the mother tongues of anyone in their own population, and that are so remote from their own that they require years of schooling for their mastery.

The most impressive thing about the language situation in the world is its tremendous complexity. People who are looking for easy solutions to the world's problems have advocated that everyone should learn English, or if not English, then some artificial and neutral language like Esperanto. But the fact is that there are enormous resistances to both of these solutions, and it is not at all certain that either one would be a good solution. In any case it can be asserted with some confidence that the world is not ready for any such solution and that it would be Utopian to try to put it into effect. Instead, we need to understand a little better how the present situation came to pass and how language actually works in the life of the community.

The problem is the extremely unequal distribution of man's languages: of the three thousand or more languages in the world the vast majority are spoken by tiny groups of people scattered in remote places. Only a few have any great number of followers. In language as among nations there are the haves and the have-nots. We find some areas where there appear to have been a great variety of languages spoken within a very small area over a long time; these are often bordered by other areas where one language has

spread widely at the expense of others. One region of high density
is California, where over a hundred languages were spoken by the
Indians at the coming of the white man. The Great Plains, on the
other hand, were dominated by two or three major languages, such
as the Algonquian and the Sioux. Central Africa, a land of dense
jungles, has a patchwork quilt of languages to this day, while South
Africa is almost entirely dominated by one language family, the Bantu. New Guinea is crowded with languages, while the islands around,
from Indonesia to Hawaii, are dominated by one language family, the
Malayo-Polynesian. In Europe the Caucasus is a region of high density of mutually incomprehensible and unrelated languages, while
most of Europe to the west of it and a great protion of Asia to the
east are dominated by the Indo-European family of languages, which
probably spread out over its present area some four thousand years
ago.

In each case it is clear that in areas where small populations
could easily isolate themselves from each other and live their lives
untroubled by their neighbors, they tended also in the course of time
to develop their own language. This process of gradual and unconscious differentiation of language over a period of time is one of the
most characteristic features of language, one which has been much
studied by linguists. It attracted the attention of the ancient Jews,
who invented the story of the Tower of Babel to account for it. While
the Lord's dramatic intervention made a good story, the facts show
that the process itself is usually quite undramatic. People who do
not communicate with each other, simply drift apart. One reason is
that every person has to learn the language anew, and therefore does
not learn it quite the same. The cumulative changes of all the new
learners in every generation constitute the basis for linguistic change
and gradual splitting off. If we could imagine a world in which all
human beings were living in small tribal communities, each one completely independent of the other, we would probably find that each
such community would in a few thousand years speak its own language, completely incomprehensible to every other community. This
certainly is the reason that in Europe practically every town or country parish has its own dialect; these are only a few hundred years
old, and yet they often show tremendous differentiation. This kind
of gradual and unconscious splitting is often presented in the image of
a tree, with branches dividing off from a trunk and twigs from the
branches.

In actual fact, however, very few communities are left alone to this extent. In all areas where the possibilities for defense and isolation have been low, populations have been more mobile. They have communicated with their neighbors in daily life; they have conquered or have been conquered by them, and have entered into larger communities with a social organization of higher and lower strata. The results have been that language changes have not all been unconscious drifts away from a common source, but have also been spread far and wide by the movements of ideas, of goods, and of people. They have been like waves, which have washed away barriers to communication and have made large populations share a language instead of falling apart into dialects. If we wish to continue the image of the tree, we may say that some trees have been pruned, so that most of their twigs have been eliminated in favor of a few major branches. In some cases even, grafts have been performed, so that essentially new languages have been imposed on old trees.

This is the process that underlies the creation of all those languages that we now refer to as national or international languages. They are not the result of a gradual differentiation only, but also of a deliberate unification and cultivation. They are steps on the path towards a universal world language, in contrast to the numerous spoken languages of local tribes and the innumerable local dialects still used in the world. They are everywhere the result of a concentration of political power, which establishes dominion over an area in which it is convenient for that power to have a single language for communicating with its subjects. Over and above the face-to-face communication of the local groups, there are networks of communication among officials and leaders, who adopt a language as a means of maintaining their position and facilitating the business of government.

This was already true in the ancient world. Greek did not become a single language until the time of the conquest of the Greeks by Philip of Macedon and the establishment of his empire. Before that time each city state had its own dialect of Greek, which it jealously preserved as a symbol of its identity. Similarly, Latin was a creation of the Roman state, originally based on the speech of the tiny area of Latium and developed by the early rulers of Rome as an instrument of government. Throughout its existence as an official

language of government and literature it was a highly artificial product of intellectual activity. The Romans spread its use throughout
the western part of their empire, so that the Italians, the Frenchmen,
the Spaniards, and the Portuguese today speak varieties of Latin.
But the language did not take root in the eastern part of the empire,
where Greek remained dominant because of its cultural strength
(only Romania remains of the eastward thrust of the Latin language).
The Roman intellectuals even learned Greek and imitated its forms in
Latin. This increased the gap that had always existed in Rome between the cultivated Latin of writing and the daily speech of the average
Roman. We have no direct evidence on the way the Romans spoke,
but we can tell from inscriptions written by bad spellers and from
dialogue in plays, as well as by comparing the daughter languages
among themselves. The word for 'head' in official Latin was caput,
but in daily speech it was testa, clearly a slang word for the head,
meaning originally a 'pot;' this is the word in modern French, tête.

Latin continued to be used as the language of government and
culture in Europe long after the fall of the Roman empire. Not only
was it used in the countries where a form of Latin was spoken, but
also in those countries where the Roman Catholic Church established
its form of Christianity. Thanks to this fact, Latin became to some
degree the model of how a language should be, if it were to serve as
a vehicle of national and international culture. Both Greek and Latin
belong to the kind of languages which can be referred to as normalized,
or standardized, or for short, as standard languages. This means
that they have been codified, or in other words, that they have been
analyzed in writing and turned into a set of rules which can be taught
in school. In the process of codification a number of decisions have
been made as to which of various competing forms should be regarded as correct. Wherever there is human speech, there is certain
to be differing pronunciations, disagreements on grammatical forms,
and different opinions on the names of things. These disagreements
are small within a small community, and the standard languages
have usually come into being in a small community, often an élite
which was recruited from various parts of the country or the empire.
The standard languages have therefore nearly always been clique languages, either grown up in or regulated by the ruling network of a
country. Very seldom can one say that the grammarians who wrote
the grammars have made the languages: they have only acted as
arbiters of taste.

Most of the major European languages were not normalized
until the time of the Renaissance. This means that until the sixteenth century they occupied only a secondary position within their
countries, since Latin was the universal language of learning. This
did not mean that great literature was not written in them: Dante
created Italian literature in the first half of the fourteenth century,
and Chaucer at least greatly developed English literature in its
second half. Both of these writers did an enormous service to their
languages when they proved that they could be used as vehicles of
great poetry. But they did not create these languages: they only
helped to make the selection that eventually became the standard.
Dante chose the language of Florence and Chaucer the language of
London because these were centers of government and culture. English did not become what it is today until near the end of the sixteenth
century, when men of learning and culture had worked for some centuries on it to make it as useful for all kinds of writing as Latin had
been. French came into its own in 1539, when it took the place of
Latin in the courts of France. The German we know today was
shaped as the government language of Upper Saxony, where the Holy
Roman Empire had its seat at one time. When Luther adopted it in
the 1540's for his Bible translation, this became the vehicle for
carrying it into areas which had never before used High German.

It was also in this period that the first grammars were written for these languages, an acknowledgement of their importance and
a necessary part of their normalization. The close connection between grammar and politics is shown in the fact that the first Spanish
grammar appeared in 1492 and was dedicated to Queen Isabella; it
was intended to be a companion of the empire, the author wrote, and
should spread Spanish along with the rule of the Spaniards. In Florence was established the first language academy in 1582, which
published in 1612 one of the first one-language dictionaries in the
world. This model was followed in France, where Cardinal Richelieu
cannily formed an academy in 1635 as part of his plans for unifying
the country. It is hard to be sure of just what role the French Academy actually has played in the regulation of the French language,
but there can be no doubt that French is the most highly regulated and
normalized language of Europe. The French take a fierce pride in its
correctness, although a famous French linguist, Antoine Meillet, has
written that in its fixed form it "has never been the language of any

but a few people and is today not the spoken language of anyone."
English writers of the seventeenth and eighteenth centuries agitated
for the creation of an English academy, but failed to overcome an
English distaste for this kind of official regulation. One of those who
opposed it was Samuel Johnson in the name of "the spirit of English
liberty;" however, his dictionary of 1755 had very much the same
effect as an academy would have had. But it is typical that in England the regulation has always been informal and based on private
enterprise; this tradition was passed on to the United States, where
Noah Webster and his successors became the unofficial arbiters of
English usage. This feeling is so strong that when a new edition of
Webster's dictionary made some mild changes in its judgments a
few years ago, there was a tremendous outcry among the literary
critics.

One of the major factors in the setting up of these and other
standard languages in Europe was the invention of printing. This
made it possible to multiply the number of copies of all forms of writing. It led forward to the common public school, through which
every citizen could learn to read and write and participate in the
affairs of state. In Greece and Rome the standard language had been
the possession of small, ruling cliques; in modern Europe it could
spread to an entire population. What had only been taught to the children of the élite could now be taught to everyone. The ideal of demo-
cracy could only be realized through an educated citizenry. This became clear in the eighteenth century, which ended with the American
and French Revolutions. These established the right of each nation
to rule its own affairs, including the right of everyone to participate
in a common language in which those affairs were conducted. When
we add to this the enormous mobility of modern man, and the wide
spread of international means of communication, it is clear that even
the nation is not an adequate framework of contact. Many look beyond
the borders of their nations to an international brotherhood of man.
At this point they envisage the time when the national languages will
give way to international communication.

The period of history that has intervened between us and the
French Revolution is a short one, and it is hard to evaluate it in the
long term. But it has shown two opposing developments, both of
which are likely to continue and which may bear within themselves the
possibilities of a fruitful solution of the language problem of the world.

On the one hand each political unit has seen it as a vital part of its national policy to cultivate and strengthen its national language. This means that as new nations came into being in the nineteenth and twentieth century each one emphasized its own language. When Greece was liberated from Turkey, it reestablished a form of Greek as nearly like that of ancient Greek as possible. When Norway was liberated from Denmark and Sweden, it bent its best efforts to the development of a Norwegian language which had been lost during its union with these countries. The map of Europe today is dotted with literary languages which were never heard of in 1800: Slovak, Ukrainian, Macedonian, Esthonian, Faroese, Catalan, Romansch, and so forth. Outside Europe the most spectacular rise of a new language is the establishment of Modern Hebrew in Israel, truly a new graft on an old stem. Almost as remarkable is the creation of Indonesian, a special form of Malayan which is now the official language of Indonesia. Minority populations even in long-established countries are refusing to accept the language of the majority, and rebel against notions of the inferiority of local speech habits, notions which have reduced them in the past to second-class status and excluded them from the best jobs. This is conspicuous in the restlessness of the French in Canada, of the Flemish in Belgium, and of the Dravidian and Bengali speakers in India, to mention a few.

In each of these countries a language has become part of the struggle for national identity, which means that it is a great deal more than just a practical problem of utility. However convenient it may be for the rulers to have a single language, they must also take into account the feelings and attitudes of the users of this and other languages. If there is a national language with which the citizens of the nation can identify themselves, they are in luck. Then the work of national academies and committees for the cultivation of the language can bear fruit, and the youngsters in school will grow up as loyal supporters and users of that language. Their emotions are involved with the language because it truly gives voice to their inmost experiences and does not reduce them to inferior members of society. The culture of the world and of their own nation comes to them through a single, well-developed and consistent medium, which is close enough to their mother tongue so that it feels familiar. But if this is not true, there are inevitable conflicts and problems, which can only be solved by intelligent, reasoned, understanding policies of language teaching.

If we transfer this situation to the international scene, we see that the world as a whole is in much the same state as were the nations of Europe, at the time of the Renaissance and as many new nations are today. In a period when the masses of Europe were illiterate, it was easy to establish such languages as French or English in the usage of the élites. As the population was gradually educated, the norms that were already established could be passed on to the masses. In the course of time this had led to the weakening and partial disappearance of local dialects, especially in the areas within easy reach of capital cities like London and Paris. Some languages, like Cornish, have disappeared entirely, and others, like Scottish Gaelic, are strongly threatened. But a few have managed to survive and create many important cultural values for themselves and others, because of the intense devotion of their supporters to the cause of their language. In such cases the rulers must either face the possibility of a divided nation, or else adopt a policy of patience and tolerance toward minorities. If the minority is sufficiently aware of the need for learning the majority language, it will do so for purely practical reasons. The learning of a second language is no calamity; on the contrary, it can be made an experience of great value. It is important that any group should have a written, standard language of its own, in which it can take pride; this contributes to its dignity and its awareness of self. But if this is a language with few adherents, there is also need for a second language of wider communication.

It seems to me that the nations of the world today stand in this situation: there are a few languages, like English, French, Russian, Chinese, and some others, which are rivals for the future standard language of the world. Every standard language of the past has acquired its strength from the power of the nations that used it. The necessity for a single world language does not arise unless and until a single world government is established. Anyone who needs to learn the world languages of today will do so; we need only observe the tremendous increase in the teaching of Russian in American schools since World War II. In the meanwhile each national language must strive to make itself as rich and responsive to the culture of our day as possible. The diversity of language is part of the interesting diversity of culture which characterizes man in various parts of the world. Any attempt to legislate this diversity out of existence is not only futile, it is culturally crippling. Any attempt to substitute an artificially created language for these languages is equally futile and dangerous.

By the natural political trends of the world we have moved from local tribes to regional unions to nation states, and along with these from the natural diversification of language to a pruning and grafting which has given us the relatively small number of standard languages now existing in the world. When the day is ripe, we will move beyond the nation, into world government, and with it we will find our way to a world language.

NOTE

This paper was written for the Voice of America Forum Series on linguistics, at the request of Archibald A. Hill, who directed it.

REFERENCES

Deutsch, Karl W. 1953. Nationalism and social communication. Cambridge, Mass.: M.I.T. Press.

Haugen, Einar. 1966. Language conflict and language planning: the case of Modern Norwegian. Cambridge, Mass.: Harvard University Press.

Kloss, Heinz. 1952. Die Entwicklung neuer germanischer Kultursprachen von 1800 bis 1950. München: Pohl,

Lieberson, Stanley (ed.) 1966. Explorations in sociolinguistics. Sociological Inquiry, 36:2.

Ray, Punya Sloka. 1963. Language standardization. The Hague: Mouton.

Rice, Frank A. (ed.) 1962. Study of the role of second languages in Asia, Africa, and Latin America. Washington, D.C.: Center for Applied Linguistics.

13 | The Scandinavian Languages as Cultural Artifacts

In the Early Modern period following the Reformation, the Scandinavian countries were developing nations, and the creation of national languages was a significant part of their development. It appears to me that the history of these languages offers a valuable opportunity to study the elaboration (what Kloss calls the "Ausbau") of standard languages in a region of minimal language distance ("Abstand") (Kloss 1952). Scandinavia is a single dialect area with gradual rather than sharp transitions from country to country (we are disregarding here the Finno-Ugric languages of the area, Finnish and Lappish). Yet within this area there are six standard languages, each with a respectable literary tradition and a group of enthusiastic users: Danish, Swedish, Dano-Norwegian, New Norwegian, Faroese, and Icelandic.

Problem

Our study will be devoted primarily to the initial problem of standardization, the selection of a norm, and secondarily to its acceptance (for these terms see Haugen, 1966a, in greater detail 1966c). There are two rival hypotheses concerning selection: (a) than an SL (standard language) is (or should be) based on a single dialect, that is, someone's vernacular; (b) that an SL is (or should be) a composite of dialects (the nature of the composition being left unspecified). We may call the first the unitary thesis and the second the compositional thesis. This problem was much debated in Renaissance Italy, where some writers maintained that Italian should be based on Tuscan, whereas others (e.g., Dante) held that it should be a supralocal norm based on all the dialects. Both theses have been argued in Scandinavia

as well, with inconclusive results. It will be suggested here that both
theses are true—and false—in varying degree according to time and
place. However, by the time a norm has been codified and elaborated
by its users, it has become virtually impossible to identify its base.
It has become an independent artifact in the culture, one of the devices
by means of which a particular group, usually a power elite, manages
to maintain or assert its identity and, when possible, its power. [1]

    The acceptance of a norm is also a problem of power and
identity. Language distance is not the only factor in identification.
Unless it agrees with other cultural norms, it may easily be overrid-
den. But when it is allied with a whole complex of traditional differences, it becomes a high-level symbol of that complex. I shall trace
in a quite informal and anecdotal way some of the political constellations that have determined the rise of new SLs in Scandinavia, suggesting what the reasons may have been for the differential reactions
to the establishment of these. In the Early Modern Period Norway
accepted Danish, Iceland did not; Northern Jutland accepted Danish,
Southern Jutland did not; Scania accepted Swedish, Finland did not.

    If we think of the spread of languages and their gradual differ-
entiation through time as a "natural" or "inevitable" phenomenon, we
still need to account for the tremendously convergent linguistic trends
that have led to the spread of SLs. From the point of view of the comparative linguist, this is a disturbing and unpredictable factor, which
is likely to throw his reconstructions off. If we adopt the metaphor
of the traditional family tree for languages, SLs are artifacts that result either from pruning or grafting the tree. The gardeners are a
special priesthood of taste and learning, who are entrusted by society
with the codification and elaboration of a code that is part of the conscious heritage of the social establishment.

    Although it has been asserted that standardization can take
place without writing (Stewart 1962, p. 24), the evidence for this is
slender. Languages can obviously spread over large areas without
writing and can achieve a relatively homogenous norm (Eskimo, Indo-
European). Non-literate tribes have various types of formalized discourse as well as standards of correctness. Unless the rules are ex-
plicitly formulated, however, it is questionable that this should be

regarded as standardization. All the known standards have had the technical support of writing; even the Greek koiné is known to us primarily as a written language. It is clear that before the spread of writing through the printing of books and newspapers and the common school, the influence of writing made itself felt only within very restricted circles of literate élites. I shall therefore distinguish between a writing tradition, which is passed on by hand, and a standard language, with explicit codification of its orthography, grammar, and lexicon. Only Iceland among the Scandinavian countries has a medieval grammatical literature, so that its writing tradition may also be regarded as a standard language.

Survey

Scandinavia is here understood to include the present-day nations of Denmark, Finland, Iceland, Norway, and Sweden; my chief interest here is Danish. A history of the Scandinavian languages may well be called "The Rejection of Danish." Danish is the ugly duckling of Scandinavia, with humble beginnings under the shadow of Latin and Low German, with tremendous potentialities for becoming the SL of all Scandinavia, and with the most brilliant development in modern times as the language of Hans Christian Andersen and Søren Kierkegaard. In spite of this it has suffered a continual restriction of area and rejection by its neighbors, which has made it the least Scandinavian, although in some ways the most developed of the Scandinavian languages (Haugen 1966b). At least Danish has one advantage over the others for our purposes: it is the only one to have received full historical treatment not only of its internal development but also of its changing social context (Skautrup 1944-1970). [2]

The writing traditions of Scandinavia fall into three distinct historical periods, which we may name "ancient" (third to tenth centuries), "medieval" (eleventh to fifteenth centuries), and "modern" (sixteenth to twentieth centuries). As Table 1 indicates, the ancient and medieval periods include an epigraphic tradition of runic writing. We shall here disregard this tradition, in spite of its value for linguistic history, because there is no significant relationship between the runes and the development of the modern SLs. The history of the SLs is closely linked to that of the Latin alphabet, which came to Scandinavia

TABLE 1
Scandinavian History: A Sociolinguistic Aperçu

	Periods		
	Ancient (third to tenth centuries)	Medieval (eleventh to fifteenth centuries)	Modern (sixteenth to twentieth centuries)
Society	Tribal	Monarchic	National
Religion	Pagan Norse	Roman Catholic	Lutheran
Writing	Epigraphic	Epigraphic Manuscript	Printed
Script	Runic	Runic Roman	Roman
Language	Unified ("Common Norse")	Dialectal ("Old Norse")	Standardized (in six varieties)

with the Roman Catholic church in the tenth century. Although the
foundations of the medieval monarchies were laid in the ancient period, even the Middle Ages did not see the rise of "nations" in our sense
of that word. The kings were often weak, the nobility unruly, and the
people untouched by national affairs. Borders were still fluid, but
there was a clear trend toward the centralization of power throughout
the area. This seemed to have achieved its historical goal in 1397,
when the kingdoms of Norway (including Iceland, the Faroes, and
Greenland) and Sweden (including Finland) joined in a dynastic union
with Denmark (including Schleswig-Holstein) under the leadership of
the Danish monarch, Queen Margaret. Denmark was by far the strongest of the Scandinavian countries, having under its immediate rule the
greater part of Scandinavia's arable soil, from the Eider River just
north of Hamburg and Bremen to the border of Småland in what is today central Sweden. All of Scania (plus the shires of Halland and Blekinge and the island of Gotland) were Danish. Since archeological
times, Denmark had been the wealthiest Scandinavian country, the
closest both geographically and culturally to the European continent.

The Middle Ages

The nature of manuscript writing was substantially the same in all western countries in the Middle Ages. Latin as the universal tongue of religion and learning was the language of wider communication used by the clergy and the royal houses, and eventually by all men of learning. Within Scandinavia the Latin tradition was strongest in Denmark, the last country to adopt the native language in legal documents issued by the royal chancery. This adoption occurred in 1371 under Queen Margaret, 30 years later than in Sweden and nearly two centuries later than in Norway (Seip, 1955, p. 96). The native tradition was stronger in Norway and Iceland, no doubt because of their having been converted from England where (thanks to Irish influence) the native language had long been used in writing. It is characteristic that the Icelander Snorri Sturluson wrote his History of the Kings of Norway in Icelandic, whereas his Danish contemporary Saxo Grammaticus wrote his History of Denmark in Latin (Gesta Danorum).

In all these countries the oldest preserved monuments of the native language are laws, which were transcribed from oral recitation. Since these were only superficially changed at the time of conversion, their language is formulaic and archaic, but thoroughly native. Their style is in marked contrast to that found in the flood of translations with which the clergy supplied Scandinavians for edification and enlightenment, occasionally even for entertainment. Favorite types were saints' legends, Bible paraphrases, homilies, leech books, tax lists, rhymed historical chronicles, and romances of the order of Tristan and Isolde or Flores and Blanchefleur.

Translations and original documents alike were written and copied in scriptoria attached to important centers of church and state. In Denmark there were such centers in Jutland, at Copenhagen, and at the archbishop's seat in Lund, in Scania. In Sweden there were centers in Western Guthnia, in Eastern Guthnia (at Vadstena Monastery, seat of St. Birgitta), at the archbishop's seat in Uppsala and the royal chancery in Stockholm. In Norway there were centers at the archbishop's seat in Trondheim, the older royal residence in Bergen, and the younger royal residence in Oslo. In Iceland there were centers at the bishop's seats in Holar and Skálholt and at the chief's estate of Oddi. Each of these centers wrote without much regard for the practices of others, and there were marked changes from century to century. It is clear that the spoken dialects were diverging, but it is extremely difficult to recover these from the written traditions. The last century of the Middle Ages, the period of political union, is particularly confusing, since Swedish, Norwegian, and Danish forms appear to be almost inextricably mingled. The order founded by the Swedish St. Birgitta at Vadstena Monastery spread a great number of writings in a kind of inter-Scandinavian language. The Danish administration in Copenhagen sent out documents having marked Danish characteristics to all three countries.

The writing traditions were slowly changing in response to a rapid development of local variations in speech. A strong wave of linguistic change was rolling from south to north, beginning in Jutland, spreading across Fyen and Zealand into Scania, and from here into Sweden and Norway. The wave ebbed as it moved and for the most part it never got to Iceland. It left Danish most strongly affected: all unstressed vowels fell together as schwa, the tonal distinction was replaced by glottalization, short postvocalic stops joined the spirants, and the system of cases and persons was reduced even beyond that of modern English. Swedish was more conservative, Norwegian still more so, and only Icelandic resisted almost completely this transformation of structure.

Danish was also most directly exposed to the pervasive influence from the south exerted by the speakers of Low German. In this case the influence did not enter through writing only, as did Latin, but through innumerable personal contacts on every level of society. In Holstein and southern Schleswig Low German was the folk speech, which slowly but surely pushed the Danish-speaking border northwards. The cities of Hamburg, Bremen, and Lübeck formed the powerful trading cartel known as the Hanseatic League, which early established quasi-permanent quarters in such prominent Scandinavian cities as Bergen, Copenhagen, Stockholm, and Visby. Several of the Danish monarchs in the Union Period and later were Germans, who spoke Low German at home and at court (Skautrup, Vol. 2, pp. 31–35). Great numbers of Germans immigrated to Scandinavia as tradesmen, craftsmen, and officials. The result was that all Scandinavians of any status had to learn Low German; the whole new world of bourgeois enterprise that sprang up in the late Middle Ages came to

Scandinavia by way of Low German. The inevitable result was that these languages were infused with German loans to almost the same extent that English is infused with French.

At the turn from the Middle to the Modern Age it is therefore not just facetious to speak of these countries as underdeveloped. Their populations were predominantly rural and agrarian, their industries extractive, and their commerce in the hands of foreign entrepreneurs. Their literary and religious life was largely conducted either in Latin or Low German, except in remote Iceland. Even in dominant Denmark the position of Danish was weak, though still potentially stronger than that of the other Scandinavian languages.

The Reformation

In the first two decades of the sixteenth century a sharp break occurred in the whole intellectual life of northern Europe; this quickly altered the language situation in Scandinavia. The art of printing, which reached Denmark and Sweden from Germany shortly before 1500, proved to be a tremendous factor in establishing the new religious ideas that also proceeded from that country. In 1521 the Pope excommunicated Martin Luther for heresy, but instead of exe- cuting the Pope's orders, the German princes, including the powerful Elector of Saxony, supported his adversary. They saw many advan- tages—including the possibility of gaining full control over the Church and its property—in setting up their own churches, which would not be subject to a foreign potentate. The Evangelical Church, which Lu- ther established, was to lay great stress on popular education and the use of the native tongue. Luther translated the New Testament into High German in 1522 and completed the whole Bible by 1532.

In the year of Luther's excommunication a Swedish nobleman named Gustavus Vasa succeeded in defeating the Danish troops in Sweden and having himself declared king of Sweden. He was quick to follow the example of the German princes, and with the aid of his ad- visers, the brothers Olaus and Laurentius Petri, he succeeded in establishing a Swedish Lutheran church. His advisers were able to get out a New Testament in Swedish by 1526, and eventually a complete Bible in 1541. In Denmark the royal power was paralyzed by internal dissension and revolt, until the accession of Frederick I in 1523. An official New Testament translated by Christiern Pedersen appeared in 1529, even before the organization of a Danish Lutheran church in 1536. The complete Bible followed in 1550. Although both of these versions were strongly influenced by Luther's, they were worthy representatives of their respective languages and remained central in the religious life of these countries until well into the nineteenth and twentieth centuries. Even though the complete Bibles were found in every church, they had their chief influence through printed books based on them, such as Bible stories, catechisms, sermons, and other devotional literature spread among the populace. But from our point of view the main result was to establish once and for all that there would be at least two SLs in Scandinavia: Danish and Swedish.[3]

The printing of Bibles in a relatively unified language form did not at once command complete agreement. Handwritten documents continued to be important in all administrative work, and these were often highly deviant. The printed norm was more unified, thanks to the need for orthographic consistency in books that reached a wider public and were often to be used for teaching.

Danish

The Danish norm was based on the writing tradition of Copenhagen, as modified by Chritiern Pedersen. There was great confusion in the tradition because of the extensive changes in Danish pronunciation, especially of the postvocalic consonants. Historical p t k were sometimes retained alongside various attempts to represent the new spirant or semivocalic pronunciations: b d g, bh dh gh, v w j. Pedersen usually wrote b d g, a definitely archaizing spelling which was at least clear and phonemically if not phonetically accurate for the new entities that had arisen from the confusion of stops and spirants (Skautrup, Vol. 2, pp. 180-186). Even so, the application of the rule was not historically consistent, for some words escaped their etymology and were spelled more like their current pronunciation: so møje, "exertion," compared with føde, "food" (both had ð in Old Danish), lave, "make," compared with drage, "draw" (from spirant g), bie, "wait," compared with stride, "fight" (both from ð) (Wessén 1944, p. 60).

The spellings thus partly concealed and partly revealed pronunciations and could not have corresponded to anyone's speech at the time of the normalization. Dialect speech was virtually universal and the great present-day divergences between the major Danish dialects were already present. A supralocal norm might have been developing, but it was strongly dependent on a group of people whose daily activity brought them into close contact with the written word. Denmark's first phonetician, Jacob Madsen Århus, writing in 1589, gave budding orators the same advice as had Cicero, to "learn from politicians and learned men, who have long held public office, preachers who have long practice, and sensible and respected women" (Skautrup, Vol. 2, p. 191). In discussing the rise of a spoken norm, Skautrup notes that "it is not possible on the basis of materials so far advanced to determine the exact point of origin nor to what extent this speech already was distinguished from the dialect as an independent language limited to certain higher circles" (Skautrup, ibid.). Letters written in 1523-1524 by the Danish Queen Elizabeth, who seems to have escaped the need of learning Danish orthography, show that she used a number of forms which would today stamp her as a vulgar speaker [e.g., tave (tawə), "lose," for tabe, Old Danish tapæ].

During the ensuing centuries the orthography has had a growing influence on cultivated speech, no doubt due to the spelling pronunciations encouraged in formal reading at church services, in schoolrooms, in courts, and at public ceremonies (Skautrup, Vol. 2, p. 333). In the seventeenth and eighteenth centuries a flourishing grammatical literature developed the doctrine of correctness to the same extent as in other European countries. The mid-eighteenth century saw a mild purism develop, in which some of the Romance loanwords were replaced by native formations. In this way was begun a gradual reduction of the gap between the speech of the elite and the speech of the people, which has been one of the tasks of the common public school. The spread of the standard to new layers of the population has led to a marked abandonment of local dialects by many speakers, often in favor of regional forms of the standard. At the same time the strengthening of national feeling in the nineteenth century led to the complete dominance of Danish in the public life of the nation. Danish became the language for all occasions in the domestic lives of the Danes; other modern languages taught in the schools, such as German, English, or French, were for external communication only.

        At the same time that Danish was developing into a fully ar-
ticulated standard, its domain was being restricted century by century. The new Swedish government went to work systematically to
reduce Danish power. In 1645 the island of Gotland and the province
of Halland were taken from Denmark, Härjedalen and Jämtland from
Norway. In 1658 the conquest of Scania and Blekinge followed; of the
former East Danish dialect area only Bornholm was destined to remain Danish. In 1678 King Karl I of Sweden instituted a policy of
"uniformity," which assimilated the inhabitants of the former Danish
provinces to Swedish ecclesiastical and juridical practices, including
language. (Skautrup, Vol. 2, pp. 294-296; Fabricius, 1958, p. 21).
This did not immediately affect anyone's speech (and in any case the
dialects were intermediate between Danish and Swedish), so that it
was largely a question of official written usage. Before the end of the
century, in the words of a recent Danish historian, "the Swedish government had succeeded in instilling in the Scanians the belief that
Swedish was the standard language that naturally corresponded to
their folk speech" (Fabricius, 1958, p. 297). In the Duchies of
Schleswig-Holstein between Germany and Denmark the area of Danish
was steadily encroached on by Low German. By 1864, when Prussia
took them away from Denmark, only a northern section of Schleswig
still spoke Danish; this was the area returned to Denmark by plebis-
cite in 1918. In 1814 Denmark lost Norway to Sweden, but the Norwegians succeeded in gaining home rule from the Swedes and in 1905 independence. Denmark had to grant Iceland home rule in 1918, and
Iceland declared her independence in 1944. The only linguistically
unassimilated part of Denmark that still remains (aside from the Eskimo of Greenland) are the Faroe Islands, which won home rule in 1948.

Swedish

        The development of the Swedish norm from the time of the
Reformation was in many ways parallel to that of Danish. Linguisti-
cally, as we have seen, they were very similar, except for the greater
conservatism of Swedish. As late as 1506 the Swedish Councillors of
State could write to the Danes that they were all "of one language"
(Skautrup, Vol. 2, p. 36). But in 1510 a Swedish agitator named
Heming Gadh drew up a scathing indictment of the Danes, including
some uncomplimentary remarks about their language: "In addition,

they do not trouble to speak like other people, but press their words
out as if they want to cough, and seem almost on purpose to twist their
words in the throat before they come out. . . . The German tongue
they delight in talking even if they do not know it very well, but the
language of the Goths and the Swedes they hold in contempt . . ."
(Gadh, 1871; see Skautrup, Vol. 2, p. 36). During the Swedish revolt
the phrase hvit hest i korngulf was used by the Swedish armies as a
shibboleth to detect Danes. The hastily compiled New Testament of
1526 still contains some Danish traits, but in Gustav Vasa's Bible of
1541 these have been systematically removed. As an example of the
kind of deliberate differentiation established by Swedish at this time
we may note the symbols for the three extra vowels of Scandinavian.
In Danish these were established as æ, ø, and aa, in Swedish as ä, ö,
and å—purely graphic differences stemming from various writing
traditions.

   This definitive bifurcation of Scandinavian, which some might
regret, is described as follows by a Swedish linguist, writing on the
language of the New Testament: "The mainstream [of Swedish], after
having been lost in the swamps of the Union Period, once more broke
forth into the light of day, fed by new tributaries from medieval
sources" (Lindqvist, 1928, p. 260). In less picturesque language:
the translators leaned heavily on the writing tradition of Vadstena
Monastery. Again the norm they established did not correspond precisely to anyone's speech (Wessén, 1944, p. 75). The three chief
translators were from the central Swedish area around Stockholm and
Uppsala, whereas Vadstena was southwest in East Guthnia. As in the
case of Danish, it is easy to point out features in the norm that differ
from the dialects of central Sweden such as the writing of final t and
d in forms like huset, "the house," or kastad, "thrown"; yet these
once silent consonants are now regularly pronounced. It was an archaic, etymologizing norm, even at the time of its establishment.
Lindqvist describes Laurentius Petri as Sweden's "first conscious and
consistent language reformer," noting that he adopted words not only
from older Swedish, but also from West Scandinavian and from Swedish
dialects (Lindqvist, 1928, p. 258).

   The course thus initiated in Swedish was continued in later
years, with a definite puristic trend; the church ordinance of 1575 provided that printed books be examined by the authorities before printing

"in order that we may keep our Swedish tongue correct and pure, un-
mixed with other, foreign tongues, whether they be Latin or German"
(Wessén 1944, p. 77). The seventeenth and eighteenth centuries were
rife with grammatical studies aiming to support this policy. In 1677
Professor Olof Rudbeck began lecturing in Swedish at Uppsala University, 10 years before Christian Thomasius did the same for German
at Leipzig (Wessén, ibid.; Blackall, 1959, p. 12). In 1786 King Gustav III, a great patron of the arts, established the Swedish Academy
to promote the "purity, strength, and sublimity" of the Swedish language. Not until the nineteenth century, however, did the mother
tongue become the sole instrument of national life and a regular subject of academic instruction, after its establishment in the common
public school.

As we see, the sociolinguistic situation we have sketched here
for Denmark and Sweden conforms very closely to the description of
a "national language" by the Russian scholar M. M. Guxman (Guxman,
1960, Introduction, p. 6): "a complex system of language types" including "not only a literary language with its oral and written varieties,
but also colloquial folk speech, semidialects, urban vernaculars, and
regional dialects." If I may suggest a metaphor: the national language
is a socially stratified peak rising from a broad plain of rural vernaculars crisscrossed by isoglosses. The peak loses itself in the clouds
of "correctness," but its sides are adorned by the cold aloofness of the
"best society" of Copenhagen and Stockholm, tempered by "provincial"
standards a cut below those of the capitals. The Middle Class is struggling to climb the magic mountain, while Labor is contentedly and com-
fortably talking its substandard and virtually subterranean "cockney-
like" urban vernacular.

Icelandic

At the end of the Middle Ages the Danish standard spread out
over the areas that were firmly under Danish control, specifically
Norway and her former colonies, the Faroes, Iceland, and Greenland.
In this area there was one firm projection that Danish could not absorb.
This was the hyperborean Iceland, where certain circumstances con-
spired to create resistance. In spite of its small population, Iceland
had three factors in its favor: the physical remoteness, which saved

its popular speech from participating in the extensive changes of the
continental vernaculars; an extraordinary medieval tradition of literary production, which was revered and diligently studied until it was
familiar to nearly everyone; and a type of fishing-ranching economy,
which promoted mobility and inhibited the formation of local dialects.
The resistance to Danish was supported by the language gap between
Danish and Icelandic, the two dialectal extremes of Scandinavia. Here
there was an Abstand that made a separate language inevitable, and
the Danish government recognized this by permitting and encouraging
a translation of the New Testament into Icelandic, produced in 1540 by
Oddr Gottskalkson (Helgason, 1929, 1931). The whole Bible followed
in 1584 (Bandle, 1956). This ensured the continuous use of Icelandic
in the churches, although the Danish and Danicized officials who ruled
the island used Danish in all governmental affairs down into the nineteenth century.

The orthography of Icelandic used in the Bible was largely
that of the manuscripts and reflected the changing pronunciation reasonably well (Jónsson, 1959). This meant a considerable deviation
from the earliest Icelandic spelling; but the grammar was intact. In
the Early Modern period the lexicon was heavily infused with Danish
loanwords. Not until the end of the eighteenth century was a policy
initiated of deliberate exclusion of loanwords and the return to classical Old Icelandic spelling. A pioneer was Eggert Ólafsson, who began
urging reform shortly after 1760. In 1772 the first book appeared in
which the old symbol ð was restored; in 1779 a learned society was
established to promote a reform of Icelandic. The movement won its
point through the enthusiasm of the Danish linguist Rasmus Christian
Rask, who "discovered" Icelandic and went to Iceland in 1813 to study
the language. His grammatical and orthographic writings not only established a new, classical form of Icelandic for the Icelanders themselves to use, but also made Icelandic the classic language of all Scandinavia. This was in part promoted by a confusion of Rask's to which
he clung throughout his brief life, in spite of criticism from Jakob
Grimm: he identified modern Icelandic as the common mother tongue
of all Scandinavians. The title of his grammar of Icelandic (1811) was:
Vejledning til det Islandske eller gamle Nordiske Sprog (Guide to the
Icelandic or Old Scandinavian Language). Whatever the weakness of
this position, it helped to turn the attention of patriotic grammarians
and scholars in all Scandinavia to Icelandic as the model of what a

Scandinavian tongue ought to be. Its relative purity, which was increased throughout the nineteenth and twentieth centuries by diligent
elimination of Danish and German loans, was promoted in the schools
and borne by a great wave of political opposition to Denmark. The Old
Icelandic literature inspired translations, from which ancient words
and proper names flowed into the other Scandinavian tongues in a
small, but characteristic trickle. The events of World War II, when
Iceland was cut off from Denmark by the fortunes of war and occupied
by British and American forces, completed the disjunction of Iclandic
from Danish. Although Danish continues to be taught even after Icelandic independence, its position as the obvious second language for
Icelanders is being rapidly usurped by English.

The development here sketched has given Iceland an entirely
different sociolinguistic profile from those of Denmark and Sweden.
The SL is based on a classical form of the language, and since the
country has no marked dialect differences, no traditional aristocracy,
and only a shallow urban tradition, the prestige speakers are the rural speakers, whose "unspoiled" language conforms most closely to
the standard (Benediktsson, 1961-1962). In practice the most influential speech may be that of Reykjavik, the capital; but teachers of
Icelandic firmly oppose its occasional deviations in pronunciation and
lexicon from the norm (Groenke, 1966).

Faroese

Some of the same scholars who restored Icelandic to its pris-
tine form were also actively interested in the language of the Faroe
Islands, a former Norwegian colony, which in modern times remained
with Denmark after the separation of Norway in 1814. The Faroes
consist of 17 inhabited islands midway between Iceland and Norway,
directly north of Great Britain. Contrary to Icelandic, Faroese is
deeply divided dialectally. There is no medieval writing tradition to
speak of. The earliest modern texts are medieval ballads written
down in the late eighteenth century in a phonemic orthography based
on Danish conventions. The language is less archaic than Icelandic
but more than Norwegian and has altered its phonemic structure
markedly from that of Old Norwegian (e. g. , ON long $\underline{i}$ and $\underline{y}$ > $\underline{ui}$,
lengthened $\underline{o}$ > $\underline{oa}$, $\underline{a}$ > $\underline{æa}$; postvocalic ð and $\underline{g}$ were lost and replaced

by j before i and v before u, etc.). It was not used in serious writing
until the nineteenth century; Danish was the sole language of church
and government, so that spoken Faroese has a large percentage of
Danish loanwords for all cultural vocabulary (Djupedal, 1964).

Rasmus Rask brought Faroese to the attention of the learned
world by including a short grammar of the language in his Icelandic
Grammar of 1811 (Rask, 1811, pp. 262-282). Rask described Faroese
as a dialect of Icelandic, the "Old Scandinavian language," which naturally stirred the interest of connoisseurs among the native speakers
of the language (Skårup, p. 3). Some years later he advised the editors of Færeyinga Saga (1832) on the orthography to be used in their
Faroese version of this Icelandic document. Rask did not himself
draw the logical consequences of Faroese as a dialect of Icelandic,
for his own views on spelling were phonetic rather than etymological.
This was done by others, who were caught up by the wave of Romantic
thinking in the scholarship of the day, above all the Danish writer N.
M. Petersen. In 1846 a Faroese orthography was created by V.U.
Hammershaimb along lines proposed by Petersen. This went about
as far as humanly possible in uniforming Faroese according to the
classic model of Icelandic. In effect, the orthography was a historical reconstruction based on the newly discovered methods of comparative linguistics. It was called forth by the need for a school orthography to be used in the introductory grades, for pupils who had not
yet learned to understand Danish (Djupedal, 1964, pp. 162-163). The
etymological spelling solved the problem of dialect differences by con-
cealing them in a common, nonphonetic, "starred" form (e.g., variations in the diphthongization of the vowel ew/ow are concealed by the
spelling ó, corresponding to Icelandic).

In spite of the difficulties this orthography created for Faroese children by introducing many unphonetic spellings (e.g., kvæði
for kveaji, "poem"), it has proved impregnable to all later attacks by
phonetically minded reformers. This may be due also to its conformity with the underlying system of Faroese morphology (O'Neill, 1965),
to its similarity to the spellings of the other Scandinavian languages,
and to the very air of dignity contributed by its difference from colloquial speech. Hammershaimb wrote in his Færøsk Sproglære (1854):
"The orthography of Faroese is here adapted to that of the ancient
language, which the Faroese themselves once used, wherever the

present pronunciation does not make it impossible: the true peculiarities of Faroese are carefully retained" (e.g., he did not reintroduce
ϸ, for which Faroese has either t or h). In this orthography Faroese
has gradually won its way to official recognition, in spite of sharp opposition from dissident Faroese scholars and from the Danish government. Puristic efforts to imitate Icelandic style have only partially
succeeded; but the written language has substituted many Faroese
words (or Icelandic-type creations) for Danish words which are still
used in speech. Faroese was first taught in the schools in 1912; in
1937 a Faroese New Testament appeared; in 1938 the language was
required to be taught alongside Danish, and since home rule was established in 1948, it is the main language taught. Textbooks have been
written in a number of elementary subjects; there is an extensive native literature, and in 1965 a scientific academy was established in
Tórshavn with Chr. Matras as the first resident professor of Faroese.
Today the language is easily available to foreigners through the grammar of W.B. Lockwood (1955).

Norwegian

          Closely related developments were taking place at the same
time in Norway, the motherland of Icelandic and Faroese. It will not
be possible here to give a complete statement of the complex situation
in that country; readers are referred to my Language Conflict and
Language Planning (Haugen, 1966a). The political separation of Norway from Denmark in 1814 led to widespread discussion in Norway of
the linguistic consequences which this separation ought to have. Since
the introduction of the Reformation, Norway, while retaining its name
as a partner in the united kingdom of Denmark-Norway, had in fact
been treated as a province of Denmark. All the printed literature of
the Reformation, including the Bible, was introduced into Norway in
the same form as in Denmark, and there was no longer, as in Sweden
or Iceland, a tradition of writing that could provide models for a national standard norm. As in other parts of the kingdom, the ruling
class of bourgeois and bureaucrats spoke a local version of the written standard on official occasions, a local urban or rural dialect
otherwise. By the time of Norway's independence a fairly uniform
"cultivated" speech norm had sprung up; this was the only form of
supralocal Norwegian in existence. Its characteristics distinguished
it sharply from the corresponding Danish speech norm by retaining
Norwegian pronunciation for everyday words (e.g., sag, "case," was

pronounced as <u>sak</u>, <u>tabe</u>, "lose," as <u>tape</u>; <u>ud</u>, "out," as <u>ut</u>), while
adopting spelling pronunciations of bookish words (e.g., <u>sagfører</u>,
"lawyer," <u>håbe</u>, "hope," <u>udmerket</u>, "excellent," all as spelled). The
sound system was far closer to that of Swedish than of Danish, but
the grammar was distinctively Norwegian and the lexicon strongly
Danicized. As in the other countries (except Iceland), rural speakers
were split into local dialects. The sociolinguistic profile was therefore the same as that of Denmark and Sweden, except for the fact that
the written norm was identical with Denmark's; after some three centuries of successful use, the Norwegians were persuaded (as were the
Danes in Skåne concerning Swedish) that Danish was the "standard
language that naturally corresponded to their folk speech."

It became the mission of a young self-taught linguist of rural
stock, Ivar Aasen, to prove that this was not true. In 1836, only 23
years old, he set himself the task of recovering the lost Norwegian
language from its daughter dialects. The inspiration from Icelandic,
which was thought of as the common Scandinavian mother tongue, is
clear; in 1841 he wrote a grammar of his native dialect in which he
compared it directly with Icelandic (Indrebø 1951, p. 427). He went
on to make the first field studies of Norwegian dialects, and on the
basis of these researches he created a norm which step by step de-
parted from the individual dialects and became an overarching reconstructed norm for all the dialects. He was closely familiar with developments in Icelandic and Faroese, and in his definitive grammar
of 1864 he established a norm that was less archaic than Faroese,
closer in many respects to the spoken dialects, especially in western
and midland Norway. Like the Icelanders and the Faroese he rejected
Danish, in whatever form, as a guide or even as a source of borrowing
for his new language (Haugen, 1965).

Aasen therefore rejected also the form of Danish spoken by
the upper classes in Norway. Since this was already well-established
and prestigious, however, other reformers preferred to take a more
moderate course whereby the Danish orthography should be gradually
adapted to the norms of upper-class speech. This line of "reform"
rather than "revolution" has so far proved to be the most widely acceptable. It became an absolute necessity after the official recognition of Aasen's norm in 1885 as a potential school language under the
name of Landsmål, or Nynorsk. The goal of achieving a distinctive

Norwegian language by building on cultivated speech was pursued in successive major reforms adopted in 1907 and 1917. These radically altered the appearance of Norwegian Danish, by spelling it according to the orthographic conventions of Aasen's norm while maintaining the grammar and lexicon of urban, upper-class speech. Under the name of Riksmål or Bokmål this new Norwegian norm dominates the literary life of Norway to the extent of 90 per cent of the literary production and 80 per cent of the school population. Attempts were initiated in 1917 and vigorously pursued in reforms of 1938 and 1959 to bring the two norms still closer together by homogenizing their grammars. So far these efforts have enjoyed only a limited success. Of all the norms so far discussed in Scandinavia it may seem as if the Riksmål norm of Norwegian is closest to actual speech. This is only because it has been deliberately shaped by a policy of bringing the writing into line with a speech norm felt to be more national than the Danish orthography. In practice it retains many etymological and unphonemic traits derived from its dual tradition of Danish and New Norwegian (e. g., mann, "man," rhyming with land, "land," and kan, "can," or væte, "moisture," homophonous with hvete, "wheat").

The two Norwegian languages illustrate opposite but complementary ideals in their approach to the problem of a standard norm: the folk ideal versus the élite ideal. The New Norwegian language, like Icelandic and Faroese, finds its prestigious speakers in the rural population and the principles of its normalization in a classic language. Dano-Norwegian, like Danish and Swedish, finds its prestigious speakers in the urban, upper-class population and the principles of its normalization in a traditional language. In neither case is anyone seriously trying to conform to anyone's speech; if anything, it is assumed that speech will be molded by writing, which gives writing an importance beyond its due.

Conclusion

The divergent manuscript traditions of the Middle Ages were standard languages in embryo, but were of limited influence and subject to extinction and radical alteration according to the often unstable political and religious constellations of the period. The trend toward political unification of Scandinavia under the scepter of Denmark was

beginning to have a corresponding linguistic effect at the end of the
fifteenth century. The revolt and eventual military predominance of
Sweden over Denmark upset this trend and assured the fragmentation
of Scandinavia. The invention of printing and the establishment of the
Reformation in Germany gave each of the two Scandinavian states the
technical means for setting up similar but distinct norms of writing
and subsequently spreading them through the church, the schools, and
the courts to every part of the realm controlled by each state. Eventually these were accepted as instruments of communication and symbols of identity, except where language distance or political self-as-
sertion led to their rejection (as Swedish was rejected in Finland,
which we have to disregard here; or as Danish in Scania, Schleswig,
Iceland, the Faroes, and Norway).

In each case the norms selected correspond only in the most
general sense to any particular vernacular as spoken then or later.
Latin rules were adopted to create the first writing traditions and reflect the gross features of each writer's structure. But the codified
norms of the present day are complex creations from various dialects
resulting in large part from conscious regularization by generations
of grammarians and rhetoricians. The relation of each written tradition to speech is that of providing a guide for certain types of formal
discourse, but generally the written tradition is an ideal norm which
sensible people follow only insofar as suits their personal convenience
and permits them to demonstrate a decent respect for the opinions of
their fellows.

NOTES

[1] Cf. M. M. Guxman (1960), Conclusion (tr. p. 25): "The
common national norm embodied in the literary language is never the
result of a spontaneous process of language development, but to a
certain degree the result of artificial selection and interference with
this spontaneous process." Ibid. , p. 27: "In Germany, the literary
norm of the national language is by no means a codification of the system of characteristics of the Eastern Middle German dialects, generally considered to be the basis of literary German. "
[2] I am deeply indebted to the work of Peter Skautrup, whose
monumental five-volume history discusses these problems at some
length and will be quoted frequently in the following pages.

[3] The Finnish SL, which will not be treated further here, was established in a similar way at the time of the Reformation, breaking with Swedish (Gummerus, 1941).

REFERENCES

Aasen, Ivar. 1965. Norsk Grammatik. Christiania, 1864. (Reprinted 1965, Oslo: Universitets-forlaget.)

Bandle, Oskar. 1956. Die Sprache der Guðbrandsbiblia. Bibliotheca Arnamagnæana, XVII; Copenhagen.

Benediktsson, Hreinn. 1961-1962. Icelandic Dialectology: Methods and Results. Íslenzk tunga 3, 72-113.

Blackall, Eric. 1959. The Emergence of German as a Literary Language. Cambridge: University Press.

Brun, Auguste. 1946. Parlers régionaux: France dialectale et unité française. Paris-Toulouse: Didier.

Djupedal, Reidar. 1964. Litt om framvoksteren av det færøyske skriftmålet. In Alf Hellevik and Einar Lundeby (eds.), Skriftspråk i utvikling, Oslo: Cappelen, pp. 144-186.

Fabricius, Knud. 1958. Skaanes overgang fra Danmark til Sverige. Fjerde Del. Copenhagen.

Gadh, Heming. 1871. Scriptores Rerum Svecicarum Medii Aevi, Vol. III, 1. Stockholm. 43 pp.

Groenke, Ulrich. 1966. On Standard, Substandard, and Slang in Icelandic. Scandinavian Studies, 38, 217-230.

Gummerus, Jaakko. 1941. Michael Agricola, der Reformator Finnlands. Helsinki.

Guxman, M.M. 1960. Voprosy formirovanija i razvitija nacional'nyx jazykov [Problems of the Formation and Development of National Languages], Moscow. (Here cited from preliminary translation prepared by Center for Applied Linguistics.)

Hammershaimb, V.U. 1854. Færøisk Sproglære. Annaler for nordisk Oldkyndighed, pp. 233-316.

Haugen, Einar. 1965. Construction and Reconstruction in Language Planning: Ivar Aasen's Grammar. Word, 21, 188-207. [In this volume, pp. 191-214.]

_____ 1966. Linguistics and Language Planning. In William Bright (ed.), Sociolinguistics. The Hague: Mouton, pp. 50-71. [In this volume, pp. 159-90.]

_____ 1966a. Language Conflict and Language Planning: The
Case of Modern Norwegian. Cambridge: Mass.: Harvard
University Press.
_____ 1966b. Semicommunication: The Language Gap in Scandinavia. Sociological Inquiry, 36, 280-297. [In this volume,
pp. 215-36.]
_____ 1966c. Dialect, Language, Nation. Amer. Anthrop., 68,
922-935. [In this volume, pp. 237-54.]
Helgason, Jón. 1929. Mália á Nýja testamenti Odds Gottskálkssonar,
Safn Fræðafjelagsins, VII, Copenhagen.
_____ 1931. Från Oddur Gottskálksson til Fjölnir. Tre hundra
års isländsk språkutveckling. Island: Bilder från gammal
och ny tid, Uppsala, 1931, pp. 36-50.
Indrebø, Gustav. 1951. Norsk målsoga, Per Hovda and Per Thorson
(eds.). Bergen: John Grieg.
Jónsson, Jón Aðalsteinn. 1959. Ágrip af sögu íslenzkrar stafsetningar. Íslenzk tunga, 1, 71-119.
Kloss, Heinz. 1952. Die Entwicklung neuer germanischer Kultursprachen von 1800 bis 1950. München: Pohl.
Lindqvist, Natan. 1928. Bibelsvenskans medeltida ursprung. Nysvenska Studier, 8, 165-260.
Lockwood, W. B. 1955. An Introduction to Modern Faroese. Copen-
hagen: Munksgaard.
O'Neil, Wayne. 1964. Faroese vowel morphonemics. Language, 40,
366-371.
Rask, Rasmus. 1811. Vejledning til det Islandske eller gamle Nor-
diske Sprog. Copenhagen.
Seip, Didrik Arup. 1955. Norsk språkhistorie til omkring 1370, 2
ed. Oslo: Aschehoug.
Skårup, Povl. 1964. Rasmus Rask og færøsk. Copenhagen: Munks-
gaard.
Skautrup, Peter. 1944-70. Det danske sprogs historie, 5 vols.
Copenhagen: Gyldendal.
Stewart, William A. 1962. Linguistic Typology. In F. A. Rice (ed.),
Study of the Role of Second Languages in Asia, Africa, and
Latin America (Washington, D. C.: Center for Applied Lin-
guistics), pp. 14-25.
Wessén, Elias. 1937. Vårt riksspråk, några huvudpunkter av dess
historiska uvteckling. Årsskrift för Modersmålslärarnas
förening, pp. 289-305.

_____ 1944. _De nordiska språken_. Stockholm: Filologiska Föreningen vid Stockholms Högskola.

_____. 1955. _Svensk språkhistoria. I Ljudlära och ordböjningslära_, 4th ed. Stockholm: Filologiska Föreningen vid Stockholms Högskola.

14 | Language Planning, Theory and Practice

Language Planning (LP) is a relatively new term in linguistics, but the phenomena described by it are familiar to all.[1] At many times and in many places men have proposed programs which were designed in one way or another to influence the development of language. Most of these have been concerned with the creation or regulation of written languages, ranging from matters of orthography and phonology to grammar, lexicon, and style. As I define it, the term LP includes the normative work of language academies and committees, all forms of what is commonly known as language cultivation (Ger. Sprachpflege, Dan. sprogrøgt, Swed. språkvård), and all proposals for language reform or standardization.

A reason for using the term LP is that it brings the whole enterprise of cultivation and reform of language under the point of view of social planning, an increasingly important feature of modern life. One definition of social planning is "the establishment of goals, policies, and procedures for a social or economic unit."[2] Correspondingly, LP may be defined as "the establishment of goals, policies, and procedures for a language community." From the linguist's point of view it is a part of applied linguistics, since it differs from pure linguistics in requiring the exercise of judgment concerning problems of language teaching, the central concern of applied linguistics. But it should not be overlooked that LP is also a social problem, requiring for its solution the aid of social science.

It will be the purpose of this paper to sketch a general scheme for the analysis and evaluation of various programs of LP and to apply this to one specific program. The scheme will suggest that LP always arises from someone's evaluation of a set of

sociolinguistic data which we may call the background situation. The
language planner offers a program of action, which may be analyzed
into a goal, a policy or set of policies that he believes will lead to the
goal, and specific procedures that will implement the policy. According to whether the LP is primarily a matter of form or function, we
may distinguish normalization from cultivation: normalization requires the selection and codification of form, while cultivation requires the elaboration and propagation of functions.[3] For a complete
analysis it will then be necessary to provide an evaluation of the end
result, in those cases where the program of action has actually been
carried out.

        The specific illustration I propose to analyze in this way is
the classic essay written in 1836 by Norway's linguist-reformer Ivar
Aasen (1813-1896) at the beginning of his career.[4] Although he was
only 23 years old and virtually self-taught, he was already familiar
with several languages and was aware of the main results of the new
comparative-historical school of linguistics founded by such men as
Rasmus Rask and Jacob Grimm. The essay was never printed in his
lifetime, but it served him as a program of action for a long and brilliant career during which he revolutionized the linguistic situation of
Norway. For this reason it will serve as a paradigm of a program
of LP, and I have translated it into English for the first time as an
appendix to this paper. It will obviously not be possible here to consider even this one essay adequately, let alone to evaluate other programs of LP which will be referred to in passing. The paper is intended to stimulate rather than exhaust discussion.[5]

        Aasen's essay begins with a description of the background
situation in Norway and his evaluation of this situation. His point of
departure is the political independence achieved within his generation
(1814) and the discrepancy between the political and linguistic situation. He draws the parallel: Norway had its own language when it
was politically independent in the Middle Ages; it replaced this language with Danish while it was politically dependent on Denmark; now
that it is again independent it continues to use Danish. By contrast
Sweden, which had also been politically dependent on Denmark for a
time, has its own Swedish language. While these are undeniable historical facts, they can be (and have been) evaluated differently by
other observers; while Aasen was not the only one to evaluate them

as he did, he was one of a very small minority in his day. In so
doing, he built on the premise which he enunciates: "an independent
and national language. . . is the foremost hallmark of a nation. " We
recognize in this the nationalistic thesis of LP, inspired by Romantic
thinking, especially in Germany, where it served as a slogan in the
struggle to unite all speakers of German into one political entity. It
played a major role in much of the LP in the new states of nineteenth
and twentieth century Europe, particularly where it was possible to
point back to an earlier writing tradition, what we may call the <u>dis-
possessed classic</u> (e.g. Greece, Ireland). Objectively regarded,
Old Norwegian was a writing tradition with limited functions compared to those of a modern standard language; and its failure to resist Danish encroachment suggests that it lacked the solid base among
the people that its daughter language, Old Icelandic, acquired during
the same period.

        Aasen's evaluation of the situation led to the setting up of an
"independent and national language" as a <u>goal</u> of his program of LP.
Even those who agreed with him on the desirability of such a goal
could either take the position that nothing could be done about it (the
conservative stance) or that the best policy would be to promote a
gradual separation of Norwegian from Danish through the cultivation
of native elements in the written language (the moderate stance).
Aasen's policy was based on his further evaluation of the rural dialects of Norway as the lineal descendants of the Old Norwegian literary language. In his essay, however, he emphasizes the similarity
rather than the differences of these dialects: he describes them as
"the true Norwegian folk language, which one does not get to see on
paper, nor to hear spoken except by the more humbly situated class. "
Throughout his essay he uses alternately the term "folk language"
(<u>Folkesprog</u>), "lower-class language" (<u>Almuesprog</u>), and "national
language" (<u>Nationalsprog</u>) as names for what linguists would tend to
describe as a greatly differentiated dialect area. His terms imply
an evaluation of these as constituting a unity, deriving by a set of
describable changes from Old Norwegian and still capable of being
expressed in a common written form, just as e.g. the Swedish dialects are expressed in the common written form of standard Swedish.

        Aasen's <u>policy</u> for achieving a national language was there-
fore to use the dialects as the raw material for a new Norwegian

norm (what he called <u>Hovedsproget</u>, the "main language"). We may
call this an <u>upgrading of folk language</u> (the radical stance) by the setting up of the dialects as <u>reference norms</u> for LP. Aasen's national
language should be the one "preserved and cultivated in the peasants'
cottages in our valleys and along our coasts," one that "every countryman can take part in without effort." Some of the subjective background of this evaluation is suggested by his remarks about the pain
he had suffered from observing the peasant's language ridiculed by
"well-dressed ignorance" or corrected by "a no doubt well-meant
zeal for purification." Aasen's combination of nationalism with
agrarianism is perhaps the chief characteristic of his program. However, the upgrading of folk language is found elsewhere as well, e.g.
in Štur's codification of the Slovak language or Vuk Karadžić's of
Serbian.[6] Missionaries who establish norms for writing among previously illiterate peoples are faced with the same problem. The
major difference in the situation in Norway was that the people were
not illiterate, but were already literate in Danish. Aasen's solution
therefore meant a radical break with the customary situation.

As we now turn to his <u>procedures</u>, we find that these are
less fully developed in this early essay than in his later writings, but
we get at least one paragraph devoted entirely to this theme. The
procedure of <u>selection</u> was guided by his policy of making the folk language his standard. This meant that he could not build on any one
dialect, as most LP programs have done, whether that of a social
élite, or of a particular region. "It is not my aim," he wrote, "to
promote any one of our dialects; no, none of these should be the
main language: this should be a comparison of, a basis for them all."
"Comparison" is here to be taken in the strict sense of comparative
linguistics: he was fully aware of the ideas behind the linguistic
work of Rasmus Rask and Jacob Grimm. His discussion of Swedish
shows that he conceived of the standard language as "the comparison
of the dialects of the country, the midpoint around which they turned."
He did not seem to realize that Swedish, like most of the standard
languages of early modern times, developed from the written form of
a particular region, in the case of Swedish that of the Uppland area,
and that it corresponded to the speech of an élite rather than a folk
dialect.[7] Hence he went on to create a norm for Norwegian that was
in fact a linguistic reconstruction, a form of the language such as he
conceived it would have been if Norway had never been united with

Denmark. While he does not specifically draw in the Old Norwegian language as a model in this essay, it is implicit in his reference to it as the "ancestral language." He did not wish to restore the dispossessed classic, but he did use it in guiding his own reconstruction of its modern descendant. We may therefore say that his norm was an <u>archaizing reconstruction</u>, a kind of starred form of Early Modern Norwegian.[8] The need of knowing all the dialects thoroughly before such a work could be accomplished is emphasized in his suggestion that glossaries should be collected from each major district, giving grammatical and semantic information for each. But even at this early stage he was aware that not all dialects would be considered equally, since some were influenced by the urban Danish and therefore not usable in his reconstruction: he writes that the honor of preserving the "folk language" is not due to "all districts in the same degree." His procedure of selection therefore tended to favor the dialects more remote from urban and foreign influence, which meant the fjord and mountain districts, in general the western rather than the eastern dialects. We may compare this with Dante, who favored an Italian norm that would be an amalgamation of Italian dialects, but who in practice wrote primarily Tuscan. So the West Norwegian Aasen came up with a language that clearly favored the western over the eastern dialects.

The second procedure, <u>codification</u>, was to be done by a society, wrote Aasen, "founded by men competent in languages," i.e. linguists, who should receive the glossaries, make the comparison and selection, and decide on the norm; then they should embody this in a complete Norwegian dictionary and a corresponding grammar. He was clearly thinking of some kind of academy, but as it turned out, like Samuel Johnson in England, he did the work of an academy single-handed. First he completed his survey of the dialects and wrote a comparative grammar of them which appeared in 1848, followed by a dictionary in 1850. Then he began experimenting with his codification of the national norm, presenting a volume of specimens in 1853, a definitive grammar in 1864, and a dictionary in 1873. These are classic works, models of care and precision, the pillars of the movement which he called into being by his LP. As a linguist he was probably better prepared than many of the others who engaged in similar activity in the nineteenth century; but the spirit behind it is comparable to that we find in a number of hard-working linguists from Koraís in Greece and Vuk Karadžić in Serbia to Ben Yehuda in Israel and Johannes Aavik in Estonia.

Aasen has relatively little to say in his essay about the remaining procedures of LP, those involving the cultivation of his language. He does not mention the problem of elaboration at all, by which I mean the procedures for making a primarily rural language capable of meeting the needs of a national society in a time of vast technological and literary change. For English this was accomplished in the period of the Elizabethans by the deliberate importation and imitation of Latin in the learned prose of the time.[10] For modern Icelandic and Hebrew it has been accomplished by the deliberate manufacture of myriads of terms from native materials, or a policy of vigorous purism. Aasen's procedure was determined by the policy of national self-determination propounded in this essay, where he criticizes the "foreign words" of Danish and recommends that Norwegians "search in our hiding places to find out what we ourselves possess before we go off to borrow from others." The policy that he actually put into effect in later years was one of moderate purism, directed particularly against the large body of German loanwords characteristic of Danish. He made the policy explicit in his writings and implemented it by excluding all such words from his dictionary.[11]

As for the procedure of propagating his language, he mentions this only in his last sentence: "This new language form should positively not be decreed or forced on anyone; one should encourage its use, but otherwise permit everyone to use the new or the old at his discretion." This principle of voluntary adhesion was characteristic of Aasen's own modesty and unwillingness to engage in polemics; it may be contrasted with the kind of sudden reform instituted by authoritarian governments, e.g. Kemal Atatürk in Turkey in 1924.[12] The principle remained characteristic of Aasen's movement as long as he lived; not until 1901 did his language come under official regulation. This was inevitable after its recognition for government and educational use by parliament in 1885.

Finally, we would like to make an evaluation of such a program of LP in terms of its success, or what I have called the end result. This should be measurable through a comparison of the situation before and after, but unfortunately it is extremely difficult to do

so. Some programs have obviously failed completely, e.g. attempts
to reform English spelling; others have had a very minor and limited
success, e.g. attempts to restore Irish in Ireland; some have had moderate success, e.g. the establishment of Dutch as an official language
in Belgium; while a few can be said to have succeeded fully, such as
the reestablishment of Hebrew in Israel. By comparison, Aasen's
LP falls somewhere midway on this scale: in spite of official recognition since 1885 and vigorous agitation by its followers, his Landsmål (as it was first called) or Nynorsk (as it is now officially called)
has failed to capture the lead; it is the favored language of less than
20 per cent of the people. Comparatively with the Dano-Norwegian it
has proved to be sectional, agrarian, and impractical, i.e. it is
handicapped by its western, rural, and oral origins. But its very
existence has forced the Danish written language in Norway to reshape
itself along lines that have made of it a more adequate instrument,
not only for all varieties of technical and international usage, but
also for the expression of domestic Norwegian thought and feeling.

In conclusion: it has been my purpose here to show how a
framework can be established for the description of various programs
of LP. One particular program, that proposed in 1836 and carried
through by Ivar Aasen in Norway, has been analyzed in these terms,
and others have been alluded to in passing which call for further
study in similar terms. Programs of LP have been shown to deal
primarily with written language; they arise from a background situation, which can be described and evaluated in explicit terms; out of
the evaluation of the language planners arises the conception of a
goal to be attained, of policies to be pursued for its attainment, and
of procedures to implement these policies. The procedures can be
broadly grouped under selection (of reference norms), codification
(in grammars and dictionaries), elaboration (of functions), and propagation (of the proposed norms to new users). Aasen's work was
shown to arise from a background situation of the dispossessed classic, the evaluation of the folk language as a potential reference norm
for a restoration of the classic, thereby involving an upgrading of the
folk speech into a national language, which was of the type that may
be called an archaizing reconstruction, launched full-blown in a codification based on a selection of dialect forms, proposed as a norm
capable of full elaboration and propagated by its supporters as a
voluntary replacement of the intruding Danish norm.

NOTES

This paper was presented at the International Congress of Linguists held in Bucharest, Romania, August 25-September 2, 1967.

[1] See the writer's "Linguistics and Language Planning," Sociolinguistics, ed. by William Bright (The Hague: Mouton, 1966), pp. 50-71. [In this volume, pp. 159-90.]

[2] Webster's International Dictionary of English, 3rd edition, s. v. planning.

[3] "Propagation" is here substituted for the term I have used earlier, "acceptance," as being an active rather than a passive procedure, parallel to the other three. For further discussion of this scheme see the writer's "Dialect, Language, Nation," American Anthropologist 68 (1966), pp. 922-35. [In this volume, pp. 237-54.]

[4] "Om vort Skriftsprog," in Ivar Aasen, Skrifter, 2. ed. (Oslo: Gyldendal, 1926), pp. 47-50; first printed in Syn og Segn, 1909, p. 1ff.

[5] For a fuller discussion of the work of Aasen see the writer's "Construction and Reconstruction in Language Planning: Ivar Aasen's Grammar," Word, 21 (1965), pp. 188-207. [In this volume, pp. 191-214.] For an account of the movement initiated by Aasen's work and the present status of the language problem in Norway see the writer's Language Conflict and Language Planning: The Case of Modern Norwegian (Cambridge, Massachusetts: Harvard University Press, 1966).

[6] On Štur see L. Auty, "The Evolution of Literary Slovak," Transactions, The Philological Society, London, 1953, pp. 143-60; on Karadžić see A. Gallis, "Vuk Karadžić, Jugoslavias Ivar Aasen," Det Norske Videnskapsakademi i Oslo, Årbok 1949, pp. 20-21 (also in Vukov Zbornik, Beograd, vol. 1, 1964, pp. 97-105).

[7] On Swedish see E. Wessén, "Vårt riksspråk: Några huvudpunkter av dess historiska utveckling," in Modersmålslärarnas förenings årsskrift, 1937, pp. 289-305.

[8] In his later writings the importance of Old Norwegian is emphasized, e.g. "Dannelsen og Norskheden" (1858), Skrifter, 2. ed., pp. 78-79.

[9] On Koraïs see V. Rotolo, Koraïs e la questione della lingua in Grecia (Palermo, 1965); on Ben Yehuda see Robert St. John, Tongue of the Prophets: The Life Story of Eliezer Ben Yehuda (New York: Doubleday, 1952); on Johannes Aavik see his article "Der

Entwicklungsgang der estnischen Schriftsprache," Förhandlingar, Språkvetenskapliga Sällskapet i Uppsala, 1946-48, pp. 93-111, also V. Tauli, "Om språkvårdsproblemet, " in same publication, pp. 113-31; J. Aavik, "Language Reform," in Aspects of Estonian Culture (London, 1961), p. 175ff.

[10] R. F. Jones, The Triumph of the English Language (Stanford, Cal.: Stanford University Press, 1953).

[11] Cf. "Om Sprogsagen" 1858, Skrifter, 2. ed., esp. pp. 99-108.

[12] U. Heyd, Language Reform in Modern Turkey (Jerusalem: The Israel Oriental Society, 1954).

APPENDIX
IVAR AASEN: CONCERNING OUR WRITTEN LANGUAGE (1836)

1

Now that our native land has again become what it once was, namely free and independent, it must be urgent for us to use an independent and national language, inasmuch as this is the foremost hallmark of a nation. As long as Norway was regarded as a Danish province and the offices of the nation to a great extent were filled by Danes, and even those Norwegians who enjoyed a scholarly education were trained in Denmark and in Danish, and consequently Danish or Copenhagen speech and writing at length became dominant among us, it was natural that the nationality of our language had to be lost. That period of dependence is past, and we ought now to show the world that in this presumably not unimportant matter we also desire to be independent.

Our sister country Sweden has in this respect been more fortunate. It now has a language such as one would expect on that side of the mountains; for it resembles so beautifully the true Norwegian folk language, which one does not get to see on paper, nor to hear spoken except by the more humbly situated class. If we should have to sin in one of two respects, it would be more excusable to lean toward Swedish than Danish. This is confirmed by the location of

the countries and the similarity of the folk languages. Such an incli-
nation would not be un-national, nor any amalgamation (to use the
currently accepted terms); it would be the natural likeness of two
growths from the same seed. We do not need ever to go outside our
borders for a language; we should search in our hiding places to find
out what we ourselves possess before we go off to borrow from others.
Just as little as it would honor a free man to beg from others what he
himself has a supply of, just so little does it honor us that we would
rather collect foreign words than employ those that are commonly
known and used in our country districts.

2

Since now each one thinks best of that which he is accustomed
to from childhood, and since all who write in our generation in a way
are bound to the Copenhagen manner, and perhaps for the most part
accustomed from their youth to despise our folk language, it is to be
expected that such a reform will be regarded with little favor by most
people. At the same time there are some—as has been seen in our
public press and other writings—who seriously wish to have our language formed in such a way that one could more rightfully call it Norwegian. The less educated part of the people, however slavishly it
submits to existing conditions, must for a long time have looked forward in silence to such a change. No doubt a great many misunderstandings and improper purifications would to a great extent be
avoided. It has always pained me bitterly when I heard our folk language scorned or ridiculed, whether by well-dressed ignorance, or
by a no doubt well-meant zeal for purification. Must we then, I
thought, renounce this precious treasure from the past, which our
ancestors through all their trials have faithfully preserved and be-
queathed to us as a sacred heritage? Shall the possession of it, however just, still be denied us now that national freedom again lives
among our mountains?

3

While time and circumstances, as previously stated, made
the Copenhagen dialect dominant among us, our national language was
nevertheless preserved and cultivated in the peasants' cottages in our
valleys and along our coasts; even if this is not true of all districts

in the same degree. That time has had its effect on the folk language as well is natural; but when one considers how widely the population of our country is scattered, for how long a time the language was not cultivated in writing, as well as other previously mentioned circumstances——then one must regard it as something great that this national possession can still be handed down to us in such good condition. If Norway through these centuries had asserted its political independence, then our main language would also have been that of the people; it would have been the comparison of the dialects of the country, the midpoint around which they turned. But we allowed ourselves, with an astonishing patience, for so long a time to be unjustly ruled by others; therefore we lost our fortune and our honor; therefore we lost our mother tongue. To regain this is not yet impossible for us; our national honor demands it, and the happily altered position of our country entitles us to it. The peasant has the honor of being the savior of the language; therefore one should listen to his speech.

4

It will be objected that a language reformation is something that should not be undertaken at once, but should be submitted to time and to the effect of the century. But this I regard as having less validity in a state which good fortune has suddenly made free and independent, and whose true folk language, although for so long unseen on paper, still exists. Nor do I think that one can sustain the opinion that the new language would be confusing to beginners or that at first it would be difficult for all to understand; or that foreigners would thereby find a new stone in their path. It would of course have to be so contrived that all natives could understand it; for all merely provincial words and turns of phrase should be avoided as far as possible. It would furthermore not be so different from the two other Nordic languages that anyone who knew one of these would have much trouble understanding this one. ——Besides, that "reformation of the century" which is referred to above would be an everlasting building up and tearing down, since the language, lacking a definite base, would constantly waver from one to the other, so that one would not know what one should go by. And in addition I fear that the truly national at length would yield to the foreign, that indeed it would be the folk language and not the written language that would be reformed.

That we through the reform or adjustment here proposed would get a main language that is much too vulgar and plebeian is an objection based solely on prejudice and habit. We wish for ourselves just such a folk language as every countryman can participate in without effort; our constitution entitles us to this wish. And why should we be so anxious about these so-called vulgarisms? They are not that; they are Norwegianisms. Let us set aside our prejudices and not be ashamed to use the proper tongue of our country.

5

Proposal. It is not my aim by this to promote any one of our dialects; no, none of these should be the main language: this should be a comparison of, a basis for them all. In order to accomplish this, word collections should be made for each of the major provinces of the country, with grammatical information and precise word definitions. To compose these, men should be encouraged who not only believe they know but who really do know the folk language. These collections should be submitted to a society, established by men competent in language, who would undertake comparisons and make selections, and after the main language was established, this society should prepare a complete Norwegian dictionary, with a corresponding grammar. This new language form should positively not be decreed or forced on anyone; one should encourage its use, but otherwise permit everyone to use the new or the old at his own discretion.

15 | Linguistics and Dialinguistics

One of the problems that has concerned some of us for a
number of years is to ask what contribution linguists could make to
the study of bilingualism. In the rapid growth of linguistics that we
see taking place before our eyes, there is a danger that the kind of
problems which bilinguals face may be neglected. The topic of bilingualism has interested psychologists and educators a good deal more
than it has linguists, and much of the literature on the subject is
written by non-linguists. This is surprising in view of the fact that
linguists are (or ought to be) bilingual by definition, and one would
expect them to take an interest in their own problems.

The situation has been acutely pointed up in a free-swinging
article by Joshua A. Fishman, who accuses linguists of not being
'truly impartial to the language of bilinguals' (Fishman 1968a: 29).
We are told that linguistic research on bilingualism 'has but two
basic notions to it, the first being that of two "pure" languages and
the second, that of "interference" between them.' The concept of
'languages in contact' is characterized by Fishman as 'the interaction
of two entities that normally exist in a pure and unsullied state and
that have been brought into unnatural contact with each other.' 'The
underlying model of pure, monolithic langue leads the linguist to
assume that the interaction or fusion of two such is "interference",
that is, deleterious, harmful, noxious.' The linguist's ferreting out
of interference is described as being like that of 'a housewife looking
for smears of wet paint. . .what structures of language X have rub-
bed off on language Y and vice versa?' As a result, we are told,
linguists have 'frequently failed to familiarize themselves with the
communities and speakers from which they have obtained their cor-
puses of speech' and have overlooked the fact that 'in many ways bilinguals are people like other people' (Fishman 1968a: 29-30).

At first sight one is inclined to take this salvo rather lightly, as a piece of science fiction, since it does not correspond to any conceptions harbored by those of us who have carried on research in bilingualism over the past generation. Happily, Fishman does not footnote his charges, so that no one needs to feel hurt. If Joshua's trumpets are going to bring the walls of Jericho down, one would be happy not to be living in that particular city.

Among the linguists who have dealt seriously with bilingualism in America, Uriel Weinreich certainly is preeminent. He introduced the terms that are the particular targets of Fishman's critique, namely 'interference' and 'languages in contact' (Weinreich 1953). As I read Weinreich's book, these terms are entirely neutral and dispassionate designations of important aspects of bilingual behavior. He defined languages as being in contact 'if they are used alternately by the same persons.' Interference phenomena were 'those instances of deviation from the norms of either language which occur in the speech of bilinguals as a result of their familiarity with more than one language' (Weinreich 1953: 1). I find no reference to these norms as being 'pure' or to interference as being 'noxious'. Instead, Weinreich notes that to the bilingual a 'partial identification' of the two systems is 'a reduction of his linguistic burden'. He discusses the possibility of systemic merger, but for most bilinguals he prefers to speak of 'two coexistent systems' (Weinreich 1953: 8). In long-established bilingual communities, however, he recognizes that 'there is hardly any limit to interference' (Weinreich 1953: 81), so that some speakers might be said to have 'only one language with two modes of expression' (Weinreich 1953: 9). As for familiarity with bilingual communities, one could hardly overlook the fact that Weinreich lived in New York and did field work in Switzerland.

As one who from time to time has written on this subject, perhaps I may be so bold as to quote a sentence or two from my own writings. More than thirty years ago, in my first article in Language, I wrote: 'When the speakers of [Norwegian] were transplanted to American soil. . .a more or less gradual transformation of their speech became inevitable. . . [This process is] generally referred to under the inaccurate metaphor of "borrowing", and the result is called a "mixed language". . . These terms obscure the fact that what has really taken place is a shift in structure. . .correlated to a

shift in cultural and social form.' (Haugen 1938: 113). In a 1950
article published in Language I demonstrated that 'the process of
learning changes the learner's view of the language' (Haugen 1950:
216). In my Norwegian Language in America I documented the rise
of new linguistic norms in bilingual communities; I called them
'bilingual norms' or 'bilingual dialects' (Haugen 1953: 60). (I was
therefore somewhat surprised to read in an article by Ma and Hera-
simchuk [in Fishman 1968b: 644] that linguists had not noticed that
'speakers generate their own bilingual norms of correctness'.) In
the same work I inveighed against the views of educated native speakers who rejected the emigrant's language as either 'comical or offensive' (Haugen 1953: 57). The book was based on memories of participation in bilingual communities since childhood and active field
work over a period of years. As for admitting that 'bilinguals are
people,' I can only say that I am one myself.

The point of these quotations has merely been to demonstrate
that Fishman's charges can hardly be based on the work of linguists
who have actually concerned themselves with bilingualism. Knowing
his writings and his outlook, I suspect that he would exonerate us and
other linguists who have worked firsthand with these problems and
say that we were not writing as linguists, but as sociolinguists.

The charge is therefore more properly directed at the linguists proper, those who are generally recognized as being in the
mainstream of American linguistics. In their writings we find precious little either about bilingualism or any other kind of linguistic
variability. If we peek in the standard textbook of American struc-
turalism, H. A. Gleason's Introduction to Descriptive Linguistics
(1955, revised 1961), we find that only one of its twenty-eight chapters deals with what he calls 'variation in speech'. Under this head-
ing he throws together borrowing, dialectology, levels of speech,
etc. These are all marginal to his definition of descriptive linguistics, which is concerned only with 'minimal contrastive elements and
their combinations', i.e. the synchronically defined structure of a
single idiolect. If we turn hopefully to the linguists of the New Grammar, who speak freely of 'creativity' in language, there is little
change on this point. On the very first page of Chomsky's Aspects
we read that linguistic theory is 'concerned primarily with an ideal
speaker-listener, in a completely homogeneous speech-community'

(Chomsky 1965: 3). Since the bilingual by definition lives in a non-
homogeneous speech community and usually (if not always) falls short
of being an ideal speaker, there is little encouragement to bilingual
study in this pronouncement.

        Any scholar is of course entitled to exclude from his re-
search strategy any set of data he chooses if this enables him to make
more powerful generalizations. Sooner or later, however, the excluded data will rise up to haunt him. The appeal to the speaker's
native intuition for judgments on grammaticality has shown that each
speaker has his own distinct competence, and that this can vary with
time and place. Gleason recognized the limitations of his approach
and suggested that it might be a valid objective to make 'an empirical
description of the range and significance of variation' and to make
'generalizations about linguistic variation as a characteristic feature
of language'. He even suggested that such generalizations might
become 'the basis for a second type of linguistic science', but found
that 'we lack a general term for this discipline as a whole' (Gleason
1961: 392).

        In the meanwhile, 'sociolinguistics' has offered itself as a
candidate for such a term. William Bright declared linguistic diversity to be the essential criterion of the field in his introduction to the
UCLA symposium on sociolinguistics (Bright 1966: 11). From the
hard-core linguist's point of view, however, the prefix socio- compro-
mises the term by identifying variation with its social correlates,
which he feels are not his primary business. In 1956 I proposed
'dialinguistics' as a possible name for the kind of interlingual confrontation that is now often known as 'contrastive' or 'differential'
linguistics (Haugen 1956: 41). I was impressed by the number of linguistic terms in this area that begin with the Greek prefix dia-, all
of which suggest variation: 'diachronic' linguistics studies variations
in time, 'dialectology' variations in space. Weinreich proposed 'dia-
system' for the compound system of bilinguals. In 1954, at a Georgetown lecture, I suggested the use of 'diaphones' and 'diamorphs' to
identify interlingually defined phonemic and morphemic units. Recently Dingwall (1964) has used the term 'diaglossic' for a similar
operation; the step is short to 'diaglossics' or 'diaglottology'. The
disjecta membra are present to constitute a field of dialinguistics,
if only a coherent theory and terminology could be developed.

Within such a theory seen from an entirely linguistic point of view, the concept of the 'nonunique' or 'variable' structure would seem to be central. Perhaps the very word 'structure' is unfortunate as suggesting a rigidity which is not characteristic of human behavior. We would certainly have to examine once more whether Meillet's famous dictum of the coherence of language systems is really true. If a language is really un système où tout se tient, how does it happen that bilinguals find it so easy to accept novel elements into their systems ?

There are other well-known linguistic dogmas that require reexamination in the light of the data furnished us by bilingual speakers. One of them is the distinction between langue and parole, now reformulated into English by Chomsky as 'competence' and 'performance'. Mackey began his description of bilingualism (1962: 51) by assigning bilingualism to the domain of parole, as a characteristic of the individual rather than of the group. But every time a bilingual draws upon the resources of his other language, he is by ever so little altering the nature of his competence in both. Every performance alters one's competence by the increment of what one has learned or unlearned during the performance. Our linguistic competences are changing from moment to moment throughout our lives, and there is no set of data which reveals this more clearly than the life cycle of bilinguals.

What I have called a 'bilingual dialect' in the bilingual speech community may prove to be either stable (as in India) or unstable (as in the United States). This is a matter for empirical examination in each given instance. The main thing is that bilinguals exhibit in principle a succession of variable competences, which may be infinite in number, since they represent points on a continuum from one language to another. The concept of the variable competence is one that needs to be developed in order to account not only for the interferences of bilinguals, but for all kinds of idiolectal, dialectal, social, and historical variation. Only in this way can we get away from the stultifying logico-mathematical formalism and devise models that reflect more accurately what speakers actually do.

It is not my intention here to outline a full-scale theory of bilingualism, only to suggest a few lines of inquiry, some of which are well represented in the literature, and others less so. The

characteristic features of bilingual behavior include the complementary processes of learning and unlearning one's two codes, and one's
success in switching from one to the other. While a first language is
learned step by step as the child matures, a second language has to
establish its structure under constant reference to the first. If we
recognize that every item and every rule that is established in the
second language adds to the competence of the speaker, which grows
and expands with each successful performance, we will accept the
concept of variable competence. On the way from monolingualism to
bilingualism the learner passes through stages that may be called
(with Nemser 1969) 'learner's systems', some of which can be studied in children and an entirely different set in adolescents or adults.
Generative linguists speak glibly of 'adding' or 'deleting' rules, as if
one could just write it into the learner's system. But each item and
each rule in a second language is somehow related to those of the
first, and each one is the response to an opportunity and a need for
learning.

The gradual 'build-up' of competence in the second language
may be matched by a gradual 'unlearning' of the first language. An
extreme example of this occurs in aphasics, which as Roman Jakobson showed many years ago (1941) proceeds in the inverse order to
the learning. A mild form of it is observed in immigrants who lose
fluency in their native language after some years in a new linguistic
environment. To some extent the first language is dismantled—by
the forgetting of words, complex sentence structures, subtleties of
meaning. The same person may be building up one language and
partly tearing down another; or better still, he is rebuilding his first
language to suit the occupancy of a new personality. The German
language can here provide us with a handy set of tags: if we call the
building-up a language an Aufbau and the aphasic dismantling an
Abbau, the bilingual's restructuring can be called an Umbau. This is
the goal of all the studies of bilingual interference: in what way has
a language been rebuilt or umgebaut because of the coexistence with
another language in the minds of bilingual speakers?

This conception of the symbiosis of languages and the ever
varying competences of individual speakers and speech communities
is as far as possible from the rigid conception of monolithic systems
for which linguists were castigated, and not without reason, by

Joshua Fishman. Linguists have an opportunity to study the infinite variability of language more clearly and easily among bilinguals than among monolinguals. I would be glad to scuttle the word 'interference' if it is felt to imply a condemnation. It would have been nice if someone had started calling the same phenomenon 'enrichment', for it can easily be argued that the bilingual who reaches into his other language for an expression is in fact enriching his effective range of communication, for he is using a word or a form that feels right to his interlocutors. However, the term 'enrichment' is as loaded as 'interference', and if we want a really neutral word, we will have to accept some such term as 'transfer', originally launched by Zellig Harris. Only in normative grammar does it make sense to speak of 'interference'. for then the speaker is violating a rule laid down by fiat and not by custom. But that is another problem entirely.

It is my conviction that linguistics can profit by becoming dialinguistic, and that the problems of bilinguals can receive a linguistic solution if linguists are willing to settle for a variable rather than a static competence.

REFERENCES

Bright, William, ed. 1966. Sociolinguistics: Proceedings of the UCLA Sociolinguistics Conference, 1964. The Hague: Mouton.

Chomsky, Noam. 1965. Aspects of the theory of syntax. Cambridge, Massachusetts: The M.I.T. Press.

Dingwall, William Orr. 1964. Diaglossic grammar. Ph.D. dissertation, Georgetown University. Washington, D.C.

Fishman, Joshua A. 1968a. Sociolinguistic perspective on the study of bilingualism. Linguistics 39.21–49.

———— et al. 1968b. Bilingualism in the barrio. Final report, U.S. Department of Health, Education and Welfare. New York: Yeshiva University.

———— 1968c. Readings in the sociology of language. The Hague: Mouton.

Gleason, Henry A. 1955 (rev. ed. 1961). An introduction to descriptive linguistics. New York: Holt, Rinehart and Winston.

Haugen, Einar. 1938. Phonological shifting in American Norwegian.
Language 14.112-120.
_____ 1950. The analysis of linguistic borrowing. Language
26. 210-231. [In this volume, pp. 79-109.]
_____ 1953. The Norwegian language in America: a study in
bilingual behavior. Philadelphia: University of Pennsylvania Press (reprinted 1969, Indiana University Press).
_____ 1954. Problems of bilingual description. Georgetown
University Monograph Series on Languages and Linguistics,
No. 7, 9-19.
_____ 1956. Bilingualism in the Americas: a bibliography and
research guide. University, Alabama (Publications of the
American Dialect Society, No. 26).
Jakobson, Roman. 1941. Kindersprache, Aphasie und allgemeine
Lautgesetze. Uppsala. (Språkvetenskapliga Sällskapets i
Uppsala Förhandlingar 1940-1942).
Mackey, William F. 1962. The description of bilingualism. Cana-
dian Journal of Linguistics 7.51-85. (Reprinted in Fishman
1968c, 554-584).
Nemser, William. 1969. Approximative systems of foreign language
learners. Yugoslav Serbo-Croatian-English Contrastive
Project, 3-12. Zagreb, 1969.
Weinreich, Uriel. 1953. Languages in contact. Findings and Prob-
lems. (Publications of the Linguistic Circle of New York,
1). New York.

16 | The Stigmata of Bilingualism

I. The Ambiguities of Bilingualism

There is a strange kind of lopsidedness in the literature on bilingualism. Perhaps I can put my finger on the problem by saying that I have been a bilingual as far back as I can remember, but it was not until I began reading the literature on the subject that I realized what this meant. Without knowing it, I had been exposed to untold dangers of retardation, intellectual impoverishment, schizophrenia, anomie, and alienation, most of which I had apparently escaped, if only by a hair's breadth. If my parents knew about these dangers, they firmly dismissed them and made me bilingual willy-nilly. They took the position that I would learn all the English I needed from my playmates and my teachers, and that only by learning and using Norwegian in the home could I maintain a fruitful contact with them and their friends and their culture. In the literature I found little mention of this aspect. What I found was a long parade of intelligence tests proving bilinguals to be intellectually and scholastically handicapped. When I came to read about the trilingual Luxembourgers, I learned that they were considered untrustworthy, presumably by the French and Germans whose languages they spoke without becoming either loyal Frenchmen or loyal Germans. My own happy experience with bilingualism, which enabled me to play roles in two worlds rather than one, was apparently not duplicated by most of those whom the researchers had studied.

The reason for this discrepancy has only become clear to me after I realized that in speaking of bilingualism, many people are quite simply not talking about the same thing as I. Linguists like

Uriel Weinreich, Werner Leopold, William Mackey, and myself,
who have been concerned with bilingualism over the years, have
offered definitions that were based on the literal meaning of the word
and its relation to the learning of two languages. Having defined our
universe in terms of second language learning, we found bilingualism
in every country and on every level of society, from the aborigines
of New Guinea to Joseph Conrad and Albert Schweitzer. But those
children in our Southwest or in the ghettoes of New York who have
enjoyed the tender concern of educational, psychological, and political authorities have one feature in common that is not mentioned in
any academic definition of bilingualism. This is the fact that for
many people "bilingual" is a euphemism for "linguistically handicapped. " It is a nice way of referring to children whose parents
have handicapped them in the race for success by teaching them their
mother tongue, which happens not to be the dominant language in the
country they now inhabit. The term has enjoyed a semantic development not unlike that of "minority group," a term one would not normally apply to the English aristocracy or to American millionaires.
Even the Bilingual Education Program, financed by our Congress
since 1965, suggests by its wording that it grew out of concern with
the children's inadequate English and not out of tenderness toward
their native language. Its first goal is "to develop greater competence in English," and the limitation of its benefits to "families with
incomes below 3,000 dollars" shows clearly enough that it is mostly
a kind of poor relief and thereby confirms the association of "bilingualism" in the popular mind with poverty and alienation.

        This view is of course not limited to the United States. Bi-
lingualism is a term that evokes mixed reactions nearly everywhere.
On the one hand, some people (especially academics) will say: "How
wonderful to be bilingual!" On the other they warn parents, "Don't
make your child bilingual!" In a recent article Mackey points out the
necessities that impel speakers in small countries to learn second
languages and says, "In many countries to be educated means to be
bilingual. " (Mackey 1967: 18). Unfortunately, the converse is also
true: in many countries to be bilingual means to be uneducated. If
we look around at the countries where bilingualism has risen to the
status of a national problem—say Belgium, Canada, Finland, Ireland,
Wales, Yugoslavia—it has usually been due to the refusal of a dominated social group to submit to the imposition of the language of a

dominant group. The power relationships of victor over vanquished, of native over immigrant, of upper class over lower class: these have bred bilingualism as it is commonly understood. The fact that it is unilaterally imposed by a dominant group is a major source of the pejorative connotations where these exist. It is part of what keeps underprivileged groups underprivileged, and it is taken up for general discussion only when it forms part of a syndrome of segregation. Our neighbor Canada offers a charming example of the ambiguities of the situation. The English-speaking Canadians are heartily in favor of bilingualism, so long as it means that the French will learn English; the French, however, think of it as requiring that all the English learn French. But in the meanwhile the French are doing what they can to ensure that Quebec at least will remain all French —and no more bilingual than is absolutely necessary.

II. Necessity is the Mother of Bilingualism

Fortunately, there are other kinds of bilingualism without this stigma. In many countries it is part of the privilege of the upper classes to be bilingual. In the Middle Ages all men of learning were bilingual; the great reformer Martin Luther spoke in a mixture of Latin and German which has been fascinatingly preserved for us in the records of his table talk (Stolt 1969). The aristocracy and royalty of Europe were normally bilingual: in Russia and Romania they spoke French, in Hungary Latin, etc. There are bilingualisms of a humbler sort which have not raised any serious problems. Wherever neighbors have lived peacefully together, a rough and ready bilingualism has arisen as part of daily intercourse. And, of course, second languages have been taught for ritual purposes, fulfilling a special function in the lives of even very simple tribes.

If we try to find a common feature in all of these and many other "bilingual" situations, we can turn to the definition offered by Uriel Weinreich in his well-known Languages in Contact: Bilingualism is "the practice of alternately using two languages" (or more, as he points out in a footnote) (Weinreich 1953: 1). There is no need, however, for a bilingual to use both his languages: it is enough that he know them. I would therefore change the definition to "knowledge of two languages." This brings it within the field of linguistics, since (as we have been learning recently) it is the task of linguistics to explicate the speakers' knowledge of their language. We may even take a step further and say that a bilingual has dual linguistic competence, the potential of performing in two distinct languages. The crucial point is not the number two, since one or both of the competences may and usually will fall short of full native competence. The bilingual may have only one and a half competence; it is still more than one, and we shall have to admit him to the company of bilinguals. The ideal bilingual is of course two native speakers rolled inside one skin; but he is about as likely to occur in real life as Chomsky's "ideal speaker-listener in a completely homogeneous speech-community" (Chomsky 1965: 3).

It is only because bilinguals fall short of being ideal bilinguals that they offer anything of interest for either sociolinguistic or linguistic research. The proper study of bilingualism is the interrelationship between the two languages of the bilingual, both on the level of competence and performance, if these can be distinguished. Before I analyze this relationship, however, I shall offer a few sociolinguistic thoughts on the best ways of distinguishing various kinds of bilingualisms. The clear difference between learning a first and a second language is that the first is a universal human acquisition, while the second may meet resistance from the first and is not in the same way universal. The only reason for learning a second language is that the first does not suffice for the speaker's communicative needs.

Most of the learning situations fall into one of three typical kinds: supplementary, complementary, and replacive.

(a) Supplementary: the second language is learned as a supplement to the first language, for certain occasional needs, as what the Germans would call a Hilfssprache. Say one travels briefly to a foreign country; or one is anxious to read a foreign writer. Such needs are individual and sporadic, even when they are built into the school system.

(b) Complementary: the second language fulfills a complementary function with the first in the life of the speaker. This could include a dialect speaker who learns to read and write the standard,

or a Yiddish speaker who learns Hebrew for his religious activities,
or a Belgian who speaks Flemish at home and French at his place of
business. Such situations tend to remain stable over a long period.

(c) Replacive: the second language gradually comes to fulfill all the communicative needs of the speaker so that he fails to use
the first language at all and does not pass it on to his descendants.
This is the situation of many immigrant and subject populations; in a
fully bilingual group one of the languages is superfluous.

Any given social situation can have elements of all three;
and a community may have individuals who are in various situations.
The three situations may even follow one another chronologically by
the gradual change of the generations. The monolingual speaker of A
may pass through the supplementary use of B (Ab), the complementary
(AB), and the replacive (aB), coming out at the end as a monolingual
B.

Before we leave the sociolinguistic aspects, let me point out
that most speakers in most societies are more concerned with communicating than with the medium in which they communicate. Such
concepts as language loyalty and language purity are instilled by
teaching and are not inevitable accompaniments of language use.
They are factors to be reckoned with when they do exist, but most
untutored speakers are untouched by them. This is one reason for
the many language shifts and for the impact that bilingualism has had
on the history and structure of languages. Power demands compli-
ance, and often gets it even if it means rejection of the mother tongue; but this says nothing about how long it can take or what cultural
losses it may entail. As so often in human life: to those that have
shall be given. To most real bilinguals the learning of a second language is a necessity, and the problem for the educator and social
planner is to make the process preserve human dignity rather than
destroy it.

III. Linguists Squint at Bilingualism

In my years of following the growth of linguistics in America
since it was a gleam in Bloomfield's eye, I have been impressed by

the cleavage between what I would like to call the Procrusteans and
the Heracleans. The Procrusteans take delight in devising models
and theories. If a bit of data sticks out here and there, they are not
averse to lopping it off in the name of elegance. Men like Saussure
in France and Hjelmslev in Denmark were eminent Procrusteans,
whose rigid dichotomies made for neat classifications. Bloomfield's
behaviorism was such an approach, which compelled him and his followers to exclude data to fit their theories. The corrective furnished
by Chomsky's generative approach is in danger of becoming another
bed of Procrustes. What used to be called patterns is now called
rules, and anything that cannot readily be formalized as a rule is
trivial and uninteresting. Who are the Heracleans? They are the
followers of Heracles, who had no theory other than that monsters
should be liquidated when they appear and that Augean stables should
be cleaned when the stench becomes unbearable. They can even
gather the manure and make it yield a fertile crop, by putting the data
into piles until some kind of pattern emerges. Otto Jespersen in
Denmark and Edward Sapir were such thinkers, whose insights were
brilliant and who were willing to do the hard work necessary to justify
them. Uriel Weinreich was this kind of thinker in American linguistics.

Bilingualism has not fared well in the textbooks of linguistics
in this country over the past thirty years. There is not one single
general textbook of linguistics since Bloomfield that has taken adequate account of the topic. Even he had no special rubric on it, but
treated it under several headings, especially "borrowing," which is
only one of the interesting aspects of bilingualism. Gleason's Introduction to Descriptive Linguistics just brushes the topic in one of his
twenty-eight chapters. However, with his usual acumen he suggests
that it might be a valid objective to make "an empirical description
of the range and significance of variation. . . as a characteristic
feature of language." This might even become "the basis for a
second type of linguistic science," for which we lack a name. Actually, in 1953 Weinreich offered the term differential description and
and in 1954 I proposed bilingual description (parallel to a bilingual
dictionary), or alternatively dialinguistics (1954). Even without a
generally accepted name, the field has flourished, as I learned to my
somewhat bemused regret after I recently undertook to survey the
output of the last decade and a half for the tenth volume of Current
Trends in Linguistics.

One reason for the neglect of bilingualism and allied fields
is that historical linguistics has fallen into disfavor generally. But
it is an error to confine the topic to the diachronic axis, for bilinguals
have two simultaneous competences and are functioning in a synchronic context. The reason is probably deeper: it is that most theoretical linguists have felt unequal to coping with linguistic diversity and
variability. The structural phonemicists were anxious to reduce the
multiplicity of phonetic variation to the smallest possible number of
units, the phonemes. This was easy enough for positional variants,
which came to be called "allophones"; but other kinds of variants
were simply lumped as "free variation" and left out of account. Now
William Labov has picked up the challenge and proved conclusively
that some kinds of linguistic variation can be statistically linked to
variations of social class and situation: for New Yorkers the more
formal the situation, the more post-vocalic r's they use and the lower
they make their o's. To most of us this makes excellent sense, since
the notion of an absolute either-or was never very congenial. However, this is not an approach that can easily be fitted into either a
structural or a generative approach to language, though efforts are
being made. It certainly is not a part of the now orthodox theory,
which is built on the concept of a homogeneous society.

All this is preliminary to my suggestion that the emphasis on
linguistic uniformity may have passed the point of fruitfulness. It
was axiomatic to the structuralists as it seems to be to the generati-
vists that any given language formed a system. Meillet's famous
dictum has been the model for all such thinking: "Une langue est un
système où tout se tient." No one would deny the value of this epi-
gram, if only as a memorable and challenging formulation which
cries out for falsification. It is clear enough that the necessities of
communication require a basic network of distinctive structures in a
language. But their realization is only a shade less arbitrary than
the words for 'horse' or 'apple' or 'tree.' What relationship can one
find, for example, between the fact that English has the interdental
fricatives /θ/ and /ð/; a set of suffixed morphemes in / -s, -z,
-iz/ ; that these can signal either plural of nouns or third person
singular present of verbs; that English has a past tense; that English replaces finite verbs in questions and deletions with the pro-verb
do; that English has no word for French langue, but does have one
for home, etc. We know from the history of English that it was more

or less accidental that just these forms became fixed as a co-occur-
rent set of entities in standard English. We know from dialectology
that other forms of English and Germanic exist in which some or all
of these features may be absent. But the full confirmation of the
arbitrariness of this system can be found in the variable and intermediate systems of bilinguals.

IV. The Competence of Bilinguals

The key to the bilingual's competence lies in the necessity
for alternating his codes, a process usually referred to as switching.
Switching occurs in response to some kind of triggering, a term
introduced by Michael Clyne (1967). The most obvious kind of trigger
is the entry into the conversation of a new addressee, who does not
understand language A or to whom it would not be appropriate to
speak it. Often, also, a new topic may trigger a switch, if the
speaker or his listener is more comfortable in speaking about this
topic in language B. Certain domains of life (Fishman's term) demand one language rather than another, either because they are more
appropriate or better known. Finally, internal needs of the speaker
himself may trigger the switch: we shall call this expressive switching. For a variety of reasons which we cannot always identify, the
speaker shifts back and forth from language to language. In some
cases it is stylistic, if one language has a special tone of humor or
appeal that the other lacks. With some speakers the switches seem
to be almost completely random, when they are speaking to other
bilinguals.

Now experience with bilinguals shows that they differ greatly
in the precision with which they can switch from code to code. Some
speakers take pride in staying within one language at a time and making a clean switch, while others tend to overlap the languages and
produce what has been called "ragged" switching (Hasselmo 1961).
We need not describe further the character of such switching, only
point out that clean switching requires a clear code marking of each
rule and each lexeme that is stored in the speaker's memory. Such
code marking may be called tagging. If I may comprise lexemes and
rules under the term items, one can say that an effective bilingual
must have a tag on every item and that he must see to it that the tags

do not fall off! For within his brain the tags are all that keep his two
codes apart. When he reaches into his store of items for the formulation of a new sentence, the tags block him from coming out with the
wrong items.

      In other words, there is no such thing as two separate stor-
age tanks for the languages: in switching the bilingual activates a
feature which keeps the items of language B inactive while he is
speaking language A. It has been suggested, e.g. by DeCamp, that
such a switching feature is part of the base rules "whose presence
triggers all the necessary changes which the subsequent components
of the grammar must make in any derivation marked with that feature." (1968: 4) However, it seems to me that the essential characteristic of the feature marking is that it is negative. Each Item
learned is marked by the situation of learning: but for the monolingual this feature is redundant. The speaker does not mark the items
as [+A] until he begins to learn B, which must then be marked as
[-A]. At first we can say that there develop two polar oppositions in
which [+A, -B] contrasts with [-A, +B]. Tagging is established at
the time of learning and is reinforced by use.

      There are many problems in tagging, however. All human
languages have some overlap, which is greater the closer they are.
In terms of tagging, this means that there are items which are [+A,
+B]. These interlingual identities form what has been called sandwich words (Clyne), or in the terminology of the Japanese haiku
poets, we may call them pillow words. Having lost the blocking
effect, they tend to disorient the speaker and make him lose his linguistic bearings. They will rise into the speaker's consciousness
even when they ought to be blocked, and having used them, he will be
strengthened in his error by the reinforcement of having used them
in a new situation. The negative feature will gradually be weakened
and the area of overlap between the codes will be enlarged. Every
act of performance will alter his competence by ever so little.

      Let me give you an example from my own experience of such
loss of marking. There are two common Norwegian words plugg and
svamp, which are ultimately cognate with English plug and swamp. I
choose these among thousands of examples because they have a highly
characteristic phonological form. They feel thoroughly native in each
language, and their meanings are well known even if they are of rela-

tively low or medium frequency. I have more than once been blocked
by the word plugg because of the overlap in meaning in English plug.
In both languages the reference is to "an object used to stop a hole or
a gap, " but I would be hard put to it to find an object which both languages would agree in so designating. The most common application
in English today, an electric plug, is known in Norwegian as kontakt,
which offers further problems of recall since it also means the same
as English contact. Most of the objects known as plugg in Norwegian
would be called peg in English, and so it goes. As for the word
svamp, a bilingual rather intimately known to me one said: "I find it
hard to remember that Norwegian svamp does not mean a swamp. "
In this case there is no actual overlap at all, since there is no object
that could be identified by this word in both languages. However, the
meanings have in common a purely abstract sense of "a moist, porous
object": in English a "marsh", in Norwegian a "sponge".

        It belongs to the story that while the two bilinguals referred
to were struggling to keep them apart, the community of speakers in
the rural sections of the Middle West did not even bother to try. The
swamps they had to drain on their farms were called svamp, not myr,
and the plugs they put in their houses were called plugg, and not kontakt. But more than that: while the American Norwegian speaks of
sparkplugs as sparkplugg, in Norway the spark plug is known as a
tennplugg, in which the first element is Norwegian, the second a
clear case of borrowing from English.

        These examples show with sufficient clarity what some of
the bilingual's problems are. If the parts of a language were really
a rigid, inflexible system, in which every item somehow presupposed
every other, such freedom of transfer would be impossible. There
is nothing in the structure of Norwegian or any other language to stop
speakers from introducing new meanings of familiar words in imitation of similar words in other languages. Nor is there anything to
stop a speaker from replacing familiar words like myr, of feminine
gender, with svamp, of masculine gender, or to make new words like
sparkplugg or tennplugg. In these cases there is a clear diaphonic
equivalence of $_E/w > v/_N$ or $_N/\upsilon > \ni/_E$ and a diamorphic equivalence of swamp/ svamp and plugg/ plug such that the words lose
their tags and become a part of both structures. The [−N] and [−E]
have been turned into [+N, +E] and the storage problem of the bilingual has been correspondingly reduced.

V. Intermediate Structures and Variable Competence

The examples I have given so far have been lexical, and some may object that the lexicon is not part of the language. This point of view I do not share, since my experience with language has been that without lexicon I have nothing to communicate. There is a kind of looking-glass linguistics, which quotes Alice in Wonderland to prove that grammar is more important than lexicon. It is extremely popular in introductions to linguistics to quote Jabberwocky to show that a sentence can be grammatical without conveying any meaning. As Humpty Dumpty explained to Alice, whatever meaning Lewis Carroll's nonsense conveys is due to the similarity of the content words to well-known English terms: slithy means 'lithe' and 'slimy.' A sentence consisting of all content words will usually convey some meaning, while one consisting of all form words will convey none. The only purpose of the form words is to establish more precise relationships between the content words. The form words, too, have to be tagged, and they can be transferred into the zone of overlap, until it becomes impossible for the bilingual to distinguish them with confidence.

In the world of the bilingual anything is possible, from virtually complete separation of the two codes to their virtual coalescence. The reasons for this are clearly rooted in the possibilities for variable competence in the human brain.

The deeper reasons for this are seen in the process we ordinarily refer to as language learning. The many recent studies of first language learning have demonstrated how a child builds up its knowledge by a combination of memorization and creativity, in which he generalizes from inadequate evidence and is corrected by his environment until he learns the limits of his rules, i.e. the constraints of his language. In learning a second language he is at every point both guided and misguided by his first. To the extent that the two processes go on side by side, they show mutual influence: each code may be different because of the existence of the other.

There is an enormous variety of second language learners. I shall concentrate on three typical ones with which you are all familiar: the child, the pupil, and the adult.

(1) The child learner may acquire language B simultaneously
with A, as did Ronjat's son and Leopold's daughter in the classic studies by their fathers (Ronjat 1913; Leopold 1939-49). These studies
show that at first the children try to fuse the two into one, and only
after a time does it dawn upon them that daddy and mummy speak differently and that their systems must be kept apart. The struggles of
the learners to accomplish this end and their eventual success in doing
so offers us many striking instances of intermediate language structures. Similar developments occur when children are transported into
a new linguistic milieu at a later age: while they are building up language B, their language A may suffer considerable weakening and dilu-
tion. A body of data was furnished me by a Norwegian mother [Åse
Gruda Skard] whose children (aged 4 and 7) lived in Washington, D. C.
for a time. While they shifted easily back and forth between the languages, there were numerous examples of overlapping. These often
involved a considerable adjustment to the system of the host language.
There were loanwords in their English like screeve 'write' (for N
skrive) and stain 'stone' (for N stein) and there were loanshifts like
wash up for 'washing dishes', I'm angry on you instead of at you,
pack up instead of unpack, etc. The sentence "We buried and buried"
was meant to be "we kept carrying," but telescoped Norwegian bære
with English carry. Their Norwegian showed a much more serious
shift, being supported only by home conversation. "I can beat you"
came out as Jeg kan bite deg, which literally would mean "I can bite
you." A verb like lage 'make' got its meaning extended by being
inserted into a word-for-word Norwegian translation, e. g. Tass laget
meg skrike 'Tass made me cry', for the standard Tass fikk meg til
å skrike. There appeared to be few if any limitations on the extent
of mutual interpenetration. In time such children would either forget
one of the two languages or develop both to maturity, or else leave
one in its childhood form with inadequate vocabulary while the other
developed to maturity.

(2) The school learner is under the severe handicap of having no speech community behind him. As has been said by someone,
neither he nor his teacher has anything to say to each other. The
pupil will learn exactly as much as the school is willing to force upon
him and not all of that. While he is pre-adolescent, he can still
learn a great deal if the school sees to it that language B is used not
just as a subject, but as a medium of instruction in some or all of

the classes. An ongoing experiment in Montreal, under the supervision of Wallace Lambert, has shown that children from English-
speaking homes can get their early grades in French without damage
to their English and with the bonus of achievement in French. However, where the home language is dominated rather than dominant,
the school with its sudden enforcement of the dominant language may
cause a trauma which can be a serious setback to the pupils. This is
the situation of most immigrant minorities in the United States, above
all those whose visibility makes them liable to social exclusion and
segregation.

     The school situation that most of us are familiar with is that
in which the adolescent meets language B at a time when he is so far
advanced in A that B can rarely become anything but a supplementary
language, if that. It is usually only a subject, not a medium, and
therefore doomed to be learned largely through the first language.
This is what Weinreich called a "subordinate bilingual," whose meanings are mediated through another language, i. e. if he wants the word
for 'book' in another language, he can do so only by way of the English word. This, too, is a kind of bilingualism, in which all that is
stored is a set of synonyms: next to the word 'book' is a string of
equivalents such as Buch or libra or livre or kniga, each of which can be
triggered by the English word. In this situation many experiences
are reported of erroneous triggering: it is as if one drew words out
of a bag by lot. While one is speaking a weak German, the French or
Italian word comes out instead.

     These systems may seem painfully inadequate, especially to
foreign language teachers; but they exist, and they are worthy of
study. Student bilingualism, with its often pidginlike structures, is
an achievement of its own, which should be studied for other purposes
than that of assigning the students their appropriate merit badges.
Adolescence is a difficult period in more ways than one; the crossing
of the puberty threshold comes close to ending the learners' possibility for acquiring a native phonology, whether this be due to neurolo-
gical hardening, as Penfield (1959) maintains, or to character formation and the establishment of personality.

     (3) The adult learner is characteristically an immigrant,
who has arrived in a new linguistic ambience for reasons of employ-

ment, at an age when he neither has the advantages of the child learner nor the handicaps of the adolescent. His primary badge of identity is his accent, which few succeed in losing after puberty. It is even questionable whether he should, for the result may be that he is expected to behave like a native in all respects. A Greta Garbo or a Charles Boyer would not have been the same without their exotic accents. There is of course nothing to prevent an adult from becoming fully fluent and grammatically accurate in his new language. But there is a high degree of probability that whole areas of experience will remain closed to him: his infancy and his childhood were lived in another language, so that all the nursery rhymes and the endearing terms of motherhood will be missing. Poetry in the new language may seem colder and less appealing, while work and thought may develop new structures within him. Meanwhile, what happens to his language A? This will depend on the extent to which he uses it. He is less likely than the child to forget entirely, but without practice it can easily recede into the past. I have known adult immigrants who claimed to have forgotten their native tongue in two or three years' time, and whose halting attempts to use it showed extensive interference from English. I have also known people who have retained it to the end of their lives, a half century or more, with virtually no diminution.

The usual thing in American immigrant history has of course been that immigrants sought out friends and kinsmen and settled near them, either in rural or urban enclaves. Here the immigrant's shock was cushioned, allowing postponement of his functioning in English while the native language continued to serve some or even all needs. Here there was even the possibility of stabilizing the two languages in a balance of complementarity, language A being used for home, neighborhood, and church, language B for work, trade, and politics. In this situation, which has been the special object of my own researches, we now have a fairly clear picture of the normal curve of development. Language B is learned by those members of the group who have to deal with the outer world. It is spoken as well as need requires, usually with an accent. Language A is gradually restricted to the inner world, losing large parts of its vocabulary, which are then replaced by items from language B wherever this reflects more accurately and effectively the cultural realities of the new environment. For no matter how attached the immigrant remains to his language, he cannot rebuild in a previously established culture anything like a replica of the world he left. Even the French Canadians are not living in the world of France, however French they may think of themselves as being.

The linguistic result is a spectrum of intermediate structures, a set of variable competences which are keyed into the various groups and domains of the immigrant community. Bilingual norms arise which are accomodations between the two languages, reducing the effort needed to switch from language to language. When the Swedish naturalist Pehr Kalm visited his countrymen in Delaware in 1750, a century after their settlement there, he declared that their Swedish was already so mixed with English terms that it had become a new tongue. Nearly two centuries later a Norwegian immigrant to western Wisconsin recalled his consternation on arriving in a community where everyone spoke his native dialect of Suldal: "There they were, talking genuine Suldal, and they all talked alike. But whether they talked Suldal or they talked French made no difference at all to me, for I did not understand a word. They were chattering about 'baren' and 'fila' and 'sheden' and 'malkeshantie', 'vinnmøllo' and 'pompo' and all those words. I couldn't understand a single thing they were talking about, even though I undersood about ninety percent of all the words they used. I couldn't understand it because all the names were half or wholly English. They talked about 'mekar' (makes) and 'fiksar' (fixes) and so forth. . . But when I went to church, the preacher preached so fine, you see, just as they did in Norway, and I understood every word." (Haugen 1953: 59). A series of doctoral dissertations on immigrant communities in America have confirmed the existence of bilingual norms, and also of deviances from them in response to variable speech situations.

We have now looked briefly at these three selected types and observed how in each case the bilingual accommodates his two languages to one another. He keeps them apart only to the extent that the communities demand it, and he uses the one to enrich the other. Wherever there is a stable situation, the two languages arrive at an accommodation in which both of them can express roughly the same distinctions, often by a word-for-word equivalence that leaves only the bare skeletons of the languages untouched. The ultimate example of this development is the pidgin and creole speech of disadvantaged learners. But wherever the situation is in flux, the learner is build-

ing one or both languages at the same time. The general profile is
one that we can describe as either a learning or an unlearning. If
we call the build-up of a language an <u>Aufbau</u>, we can call the restructuring that takes place in bilingual situations an <u>Umbau</u>. While language B is being built up, it is not unusual that language A is being
dismantled and replaced with parts from B. I have hinted at some of
the possibilities: we have children's systems, school learners' systems, and adults' systems, each of them somehow intermediate
between the standard systems postulated for ideal monolingual speakers.

In studying these we need to get away from the notion of
'interference' as somehow noxious and harmful to the languages.
The bilingual finds that in communicating he is aided by the overlap
between languages and he gets his message across by whatever devices are available to him at the moment of speaking.

VI. The Fruits of Bilingualism

What is the value of studying what I have here called intermediate systems and variable competence? As I see it, there are
aspects which should be of pedagogical, historical, and theoretical
interest.

(1) Pedagogical. It is necessary for the teacher of language
to realize that even his students' mistakes may offer evidence of
their learning. The mistakes in language B may be due to features
of language A, but they may also be due to the formation of new rules
on which the teacher need only build further. One of our major problems is precisely that we are usually teaching standard, i.e. arbitrarily fixed languages, so that a premium is set on the elimination
of intermediate systems. Yet these systems are indeed a bridge over
which most learners must go to reach the other language, and sometimes they succeed quite happily without actually ever getting off the
bridge. Perhaps we don't need to labor so hard to eliminate all
traces of their bridgework.

(2) Historical. In diachronic linguistics the study of intermediate and variable systems has long been of central concern. What
is often called substratum influence can be identified quite simply as

the result of adult bilingualism: a whole population subjected to the need of learning the language of their conquerors. Its opposite, the superstratum influence, as in the case of French on English, results from the resistance of a dominated population to language shift while admitting elements that make a new, bilingual dialect of the old language: consider the change from Old English to Middle English. While linguistic divergence results from isolation, convergence results from contact, and the study of bilingual systems is the key to convergence.

(3) Theoretical. The fact that intermediate systems exist should be a matter of concern to all theorists of language. There are varieties of English that do not have /θ/ and /ð/, spoken by adult bilinguals who substitute either /t/ and /d/ or /s/ and /z/. There are bilingual systems of English which lack an alternation between /s/ and /z/, so that the allomorphs of the s-morpheme are not distinguished. There are creolized varieties of English that have no copula or pro-verb and some that do not distinguish a present and a past tense. Granted that none of these are "standard," the fact remains that they are mutually intelligible with English. But the main point is that "English" is not a monolithic structure, with only one possible form at every node. Throughout its grammar there are available choices, and any tags that are attached to these must enable the speakers to make the right switches when the triggering factor is present. Natural languages can be realistically described only if we recognize that their grammars and lexica are not rigid, but flexible, not fixed, but variable. What I have called "intermediate" is therefore not necessarily "intermediate"; it is a real part of human communication, and is intermediate only when considered in relation to some arbitrary standard. The standard is itself only an intermediate system which has been temporarily frozen by social or academic fiat.

NOTE

This paper was presented as a lecture at Brown University in 1970.

REFERENCES

Chomsky, Noam. 1965. Aspects of the theory of syntax. Cambridge, Mass.: M. I. T. Press.

324 The Ecology of Language

Clyne, Michael G. 1967. Transference and triggering. The Hague: Martinus Nijhoff.

DeCamp, David. 1968. Toward a generative analysis of a post-creole speech continuum. Conference on Pidginization and Creolization of Languages, Jamaica. (To appear).

Fishman, Joshua A. 1966. Language loyalty in the United States: the maintenance and perpetuation of non-English mother tongues by American ethnic and religious groups. The Hague: Mouton and Co.

Gleason, H. A., Jr. 1961. An Introduction to Descriptive Linguistics. Revised ed. New York: Holt, Rinehart and Winston.

Hasselmo, Nils. 1961. American Swedish: a study in bilingualism. Diss., Harvard.

Haugen, Einar. 1953. The Norwegian Language in America: a study in bilingual behavior. 2 vols. Philadelphia. University of Pennsylvania Press. [Second printing, revised, 1969, 1 vol. Bloomington, Ind.: Indiana University Press.]

_____ 1954. Review of Weinreich 1953. Languages in Contact. Language 30. 380-388.

_____ (to appear). Bilingualism, language contact, and immigrant languages in the United States. A Research Report 1956-1970. Current Trends in Linguistics, ed. T. Sebeok, vol. 10.

Leopold, Werner F. 1939-1949. Speech development of a bilingual child. 4 vols. Evanston, Ill.: Northwestern University.

Mackey, W. F. 1967. Bilingualism as a world problem. E. R. Adair Memorial Lectures, Harvest House, Canada. [Also in French: Le bilinguisme: phénomène mondial].

Penfield, Wilder and Lamar Roberts. 1959. Speech and brain mechanisms. Princeton: Princeton University Press. [Chapter on "The Learning of Languages" reprinted in Michel 1967, 192-214].

Ronjat, Jules. 1913. Le développement du langage observé chez un enfant bilingue. Paris: H. Champion.

Stolt, Birgit. 1969. Luther sprach "mixtim vernacula lingua." Zeitschrift für deutsche Philologie 88. 432-435.

Weinreich, Uriel. 1953. Languages in contact: findings and problems. New York. (Publications of the Linguistic Circle of New York, No. 1) [Reprinted 1963, The Hague].

17 | The Ecology of Language

Most language descriptions are prefaced by a brief and perfunctory statement concerning the number and location of its speakers and something of their history. Rarely does such a description really tell the reader what he ought to know about the social status and function of the language in question. Linguists have generally been too eager to get on with the phonology, grammar, and lexicon to pay more than superficial attention to what I would like to call the "ecology of language." I believe we could profit from paying special attention to this aspect, which has been explored in some depth in recent years by linguists working in cooperation with anthropologists, sociologists, political scientists, and psychologists. Most linguists have been willing to leave the field to the non-linguistic social scientists, but I believe that there is a strong linguistic component in language ecology.

Language ecology may be defined as the study of interactions between any given language and its environment. The definition of environment might lead one's thoughts first of all to the referential world to which language provides an index. However, this is the environment not of the language but of its lexicon and grammar. The true environment of a language is the society that uses it as one of its codes. Language exists only in the minds of its users, and it only functions in relating these users to one another and to nature, i.e. their social and natural environment. Part of its ecology is therefore psychological: its interaction with other languages in the minds of bi- and multilingual speakers. Another part of its ecology is sociological: its interaction with the society in which it functions as a medium of communication. The ecology of a language is determined primarily by the people who learn it, use it, and transmit it to others.

In writings of the nineteenth century it was common to speak
of the "life of languages," because the biological model came easily
to a generation that had newly discovered evolution. Languages were
born and died, like living organisms. They had their life spans, they
grew and changed like men and animals, they had their little ills
which could be cured by appropriate remedies prescribed by good
grammarians. New species evolved in the course of their "progress,"
often as a result of competition which ensured the survival of the fit-
test. Others looked on language change as a degeneration from the
perfection of a classical paradise, which in an imperfect world could
only be partially restored by eternal vigilance on the part of the
guardians of good taste. I need hardly document the titles in which
such metaphors are contained; they are familiar to all of us.

Today the biological model is not popular among linguists.
It was clearly a metaphor only, which brought out certain analogues
between languages and biological organisms, but could not be pushed
too far. Any conclusions drawn about language from this model were
patently false: a language does not breathe; it has no life of its own
apart from those who use it; and it has none of the tangible qualities
of such organisms.

Other metaphors have replaced the biological one, generally
in response to the strong constructive aspect of our industrial civilization. Language is called a "tool" or an "instrument of communication," by which it is compared to a hammer or a wheelbarrow or a
computer, each of which serves as a means to achieve a human goal
that might be difficult or impossible to achieve without it. But unlike
these it has usually not been deliberately constructed. It cannot be
taken apart and put together again, or tinkered with to improve its
efficiency: to overlook this is to fall into the trap of calling for
greater "efficiency" in language. Even the term "structure" as used
in linguistic description is misleading, since it builds on the notion of
language as an organized entity in which (as Meillet put it) every part
depends on every other. It should be, but is not always clear that
when we speak of the "structure" of French, we are speaking of something quite different from, say, the structure of the Eiffel Tower.

Even if we reject the biological, the instrumental, or the
structural metaphors, we recognize the heuristic value of such

fictions. Languages do have <u>life</u>, <u>purpose</u>, and <u>form</u>, each of which
can be studied and anlayzed as soon as we strip them of their meta-
phorical or mystical content and look upon them as aspects of human
behavior. We recognize that behavior is always dual: it is outward
action, performance, but it is also inward potential, competence,
which we infer from the performance and in turn use to explain the
performance. There is consequently no reason to ask whether language is an <u>érgon</u>, a product, or an <u>enérgeia</u>, an activity. It is both:
we study it in performance, but the generalizations we draw from the
performance constitute the competence. It appears as action, like
all behavior, but it exists in the mind as a potential, which can be
treated as a thing, a thing that implies the possibility of action.

In this paper I propose to treat the "life" of language in the
spirit which I take to be that of the science of ecology. The term
grew up as the name for a branch of biology and may be defined as
"that branch of biology that embraces the interrelations between
plants and animals and their complete environments" (Part 1966).
Sociologists have extended the meaning of the term to the interrelations between human societies and their environments, e.g. in A. H.
Hawley, <u>Human Ecology</u> (1950). Language ecology would be a natural
extension of this kind of study and has long been pursued under such
names as psycholinguistics, ethnolinguistics, linguistic anthropology,
sociolinguistics, and the sociology of language. Linguists have been
concerned with it in their work on language change and variability,
on language contact and bilingualism, and on standardization. In the
United States recent work has been associated above all with the
names of Uriel Weinreich, Charles A. Ferguson, William A. Stewart,
William Labov, John Gumperz, Joshua Fishman, Dell Hymes, Joan
Rubin, and Edgar Polomé, to mention only a few.

The only previous use of "ecology" in relation to languages,
which was unknown to me when I first prepared this paper, is that
made by the Voegelins and Noel W. Schutz, Jr. in a paper entitled
"The Language Situation in Arizona as Part of the Southwest Culture
Area" (1967). The long-time concern of Carl Voegelin with problems
of this kind is well-known. Being in a position astraddle the fields of
anthropology and linguistics, it was natural for him to initiate the use
of the term in dealing with the complex interrelationships of the languages of the American Southwest. He restricts the term to bilingual

or trilingual societies (p. 405), but in a later paper (Voegelin and Voegelin 1964, p. 2; actually written after the 1967 paper) the Voegelins speak of an "intra-language" as well as an "inter-language" ecology. They suggest that "in linguistic ecology, one begins not with a particular language but with a particular area, not with selective attention to a few languages but with comprehensive attention to all the languages in the area." While this is true, the choice of region can be fairly arbitrary, as in the case of the American Southwest; one can equally well speak of the ecology of a particular language or dialect, seeing the problem from the point of view of its users.

The importance of having competent linguists working on topics of this kind is evident when we turn to the now fifty-year old tradition of research in human ecology. It is rather shocking to find that most writers in this field failed to consider language as part of this environment. Pioneers in the field like Park, Burgess, McKenzie, and Hawley concentrated on the American metropolis with its phenomenal spatial growth. In the spirit of Darwin they studied the "struggle for existence" in this environment, and only later realized that a person's membership in an ethnic group (with its own language) might be a factor in his ecological behavior (Hollingshead 1947). A classical study in this new spirit was Everett C. Hughes' French Canada in Transition (1943); similar studies of ethnic groups in the United States brought out the importance of shared values in determining spatial distribution (Theodorson 1961). Very few, however, made it clear that the possession of a common language might be one of the shared values in question. Since the rise of a sociolinguistic school in the 1960's the role of language cannot be as totally neglected as before. In 1964-65, Charles Ferguson brought together in the Social Science Research Council's Committee on Sociolinguistics sociologists like Everett Hughes and linguists like the present writer. There we were confronted with a younger generation of scholars from various disciplines like Susan Ervin-Tripp, Joshua Fishman, Dell Hymes and John Gumperz, to mention only a few. This proved to be a meeting of like-minded people who had previously been working in disparate areas.

The name of the field is of little importance, but it seems to me that the term "ecology of language" covers a broad range of

interests within which linguists can cooperate significantly with all
kinds of social scientists towards an understanding of the interaction
of languages and their users. One may even venture to suggest that
ecology is not just the name of a descriptive science, but in its application has become the banner of a movement for environmental sani-
tation. The term could include also in its application to language
some interest in the general concern among laymen over the cultivation and preservation of language. Ecology suggests a dynamic rather
than a static science, something beyond the descriptive that one might
call predictive and even therapeutic. What will be, or should be, for
example, the role of "small" languages; and how can they or any
other language be made "better," "richer," and more "fruitful" for
mankind?

We cannot here enter upon all the possible aspects of the
ecological problems of language. We shall have to take for granted
certain familiar principles of the learning and use of languages: that
a child internalizes whatever language variety or varieties it is functionally exposed to in the first years of its life; that the competence
it acquires is different from that of every other child; that it has a
greater passive than active competence, being able to receive and
interpret signals which it would not normally be able to reproduce;
that maturation leads to certain restrictions on the adult's ability or
willingness to learn new languages; and that societies are so organized as to impose other, more or less arbitrary restrictions on the
actual learning of language, by the reduction of contact from a theoretical infinity to a practical minimum.

Among the factors that recur in many parts of the world and
are probably universal are the partially independent factors of status
and intimacy. We here use status to mean association with power
and influence in the social group. While status may be ordered on
one or several scales, in dealing with two varieties we may speak of
one as having [+ status], the other as [- status]. This marks the
fact that the plus status variety (H) is used by the government, in the
schools, by persons of high social and economic rank, or by city-
dwellers, while the minus status variety (L) is not used by one or all
of these groups. Intimacy is used here in the sense of being associated with solidarity, shared values, friendship, love, in short the contacts established through common family and group life. Certain

forms of address and behavior are appropriate between interlocutors
having high intimacy which would be resented or misunderstood between strangers. Again we are dealing with a continuum, which would
be segmented differently in different cultures, but in most cases it is
not difficult to locate languages varieties along a scale of [+ intimacy]
and [- intimacy].

As shown by Brown and Gilman (1960) and Brown and Ford
(1961) the use of pronouns of address in European languages and of
last names in American English are describable in terms of these
two factors. While Rubin (1968a) found that she could not use the
same two dimensions in ordering the use of Guaraní and Spanish in
Paraguay, she did find that these factors were strongly present in
the situations she investigated. Her detailed questionnaire concerning such situations brought out the importance of a series of choices
made by potential interlocutors; these were (1) location (rural:
Guaraní, urban: both); (2) formality (formal: Spanish, informa-
lity: both); (3) intimacy (intimate: Guaraní, non-intimate: both);
From this series one must, however, extract a factor to which she
refers, which is fundamental in language choice: expectation (or
knowledge) of the interlocutor's linguistic potential. Her question 21
asked which language one would speak to "a woman in a long skirt
smoking a big black cigar." It is not surprising that 39 of 40 answered Guaraní, since only a rural woman would appear in this situation
and rural speakers are by definition speakers of Guaraní. The factor
of location must therefore be discounted as being non-bilingual in the
case of rural Paraguayan: he speaks Guaraní primarily because it
is the only language in which he feels at ease or even capable of communicating at all.

The remaining factors clearly fall into the dimensions of
status and intimacy: Spanish is [+ status], while Guaraní is [+ inti-
mate], and for many speakers these are mutually exclusive. Para-
guayans, we are told, use Guaraní abroad to emphasize their solidarity, even if they might use Spanish at home (Rubin 1968b: 523).
Abroad, the status relation among them is suspended, and solidarity
grows in a hostile environment. Even at home, we learn that growing intimacy in courtship leads to the use of Guaraní for saying
"something which is sweeter" and in non-serious situations as well,
because "jokes are more humorous" in Guaraní.

There is no reason to see anything unique in the Paraguayan situation, except insofar as every situation is historically unique. I have myself observed at first hand the identical factors at work among Norwegian immigrants in America and have reported on them in detail (Haugen 1953). The same scale of status relationships applies to English among Norwegians in America as well as to Spanish among the Guaraní. The initial consideration is of course communicative potential: there is no use speaking English to a monolingual Norwegian or vice versa. But even within the bilingual group there is a clear differentiation between topics, occasions, and persons which lead to the status use of English and those in which intimacy leads to the use of Norwegian. Stewart (1962) has reported a similar set of attitudes among the creole languages in the Caribbean, which force a choice of either standard or creole according to the dimensions of status (which he calls "public-formal") and intimacy ("private-informal"). Among his examples of the former are "official governmental activities, legal procedures, academic and other formal educational activities, public speaking, the programmed part of radio and television broadcasts, and ceremonies of introduction between strangers (1962: 39). The last is an example of [− intimacy], while all the rest are examples of [+ status], as these are determined by the power structure of the countries involved.

There is in this respect no difference between the standard-creole relationships of the Caribbean and the standard-dialect relationships of Europe. Moreover, the many types of diglossia and bilingualism induced by the conquest of one language group by another or the immigration of one group into the territory dominated by another are of the same nature. What does differ is the degree of language distance between the dominant and the dominated varieties, what one may call their autonomy. In some cases, e. g. in Jamaica, there may be a continuous scale, while in others, e. g. in Haiti, there may be a clear break, even where the varieties are related. The cleavage is even greater where the languages are unrelated, as with Breton or Basque against French. The extremity of [+ status] is the case in which a population (or a small segment of the population) imposes on itself a language used almost exclusively in written form and transmitted only through the school system, either for reasons of religious and cultural unity and continuity, or for purposes of wider scientific and international communication. This second

language may be the standard of another country (as when the Flemish
accept Dutch or the Swiss accept German); it may be a unifying religious language (Biblical Hebrew for the Jews or Classical Arabic for
the Arabs); or it may be simply an archaic version of one's own language, adopted for reasons of cultural continuity, i. e. communication
with the past (Katharevousa in Greece).

From the point of view of the language learner, these situations represent varying burdens of second language learning. If we
assume that his infancy is blessed with a single vernacular used for
all purposes, he may either grow up in a society which permits him
merely to add range and depth to his vernacular as he matures; or
he may grow up in a society which asks him to continue learning new
grammars and lexica or even to unlearn almost completely the one he
learned first. Whatever vernacular he learned first, if he continues
to use it, is likely to remain the language of intimacy. With minor
additions in the form of a writing system and an expanded vocabulary,
it may also become a status language which he can use in all possible
life situations, with minor variations to express degrees of status or degrees of intimacy. In most European countries this would
only be true for children born in upper-class families, where the
spoken form of the standard is established as a vernacular. It is
generally true for middle and upper-class Americans, born into educated families of white, Anglo-Saxon background. As things now
stand, it is not true in most of the countries of the world, where
children face a status ladder that increasingly removes them from
their language of intimacy.

Various interesting attempts have been made to establish a
universal scheme of ecological classification of languages. Ferguson
(1959) characterized the situation he called diglossia as having a high
(H) and a low (L) variety of the same language. His examples of L
were Swiss German, Dhimotiki Greek, Spoken Arabic, and Haitian
Creole. These were a rather mixed bag, because Swiss German is a
prideful symbol of Swiss nationality, and Dhimotiki is the literary
medium of radical Greek writers, while Spoken Arabic and Haitian
Creole appear to be looked upon with disdain by most of their users.
However, they all illustrate the situation of inverse correlation between status and intimacy, already discussed. The special claim
made, that no one speaks the H languages in daily, informal life, even

among cultivated families, neglects the fact that models are available elsewhere for both German and French, well-known to the educated classes. In any case, the general relation of H to L, with overlapping due to the fact that status and intimacy are not direct contrasts (status differences can exist among intimates, and intimacy differences among status bearers), is not only characteristic of all standard-dialect relations, but also of vernacular-classic relations (e.g. Yiddish vs. Hebrew, as pointed out by Fishman 1967). H then becomes a shorthand expression for high status/ low intimacy varieties in contrast with L for low status/ high intimacy varieties.

Ferguson (1962) has also characterized the state of the languages themselves in terms of two parameters, writing and standardization. Writing is given three index numbers (W^0 W^1 W^2) for "normally not written," "normally written," and "used in physical science." "Normal" use includes the production of letters, newspapers, and original books. Standardization is similarly given three index numbers (St^0 St^1 St^2) for "no important standardization," "conflicting standards," and "ideal standardization," the last being "a single, widely accepted norm which is felt to be appropriate with only minor modifications" (Ferguson 1962: 10). Most of the world's languages fall into the categories W^0 and St^0; in fact, we may regard this as the "normal" state of a language. Writing and standardization are imposed by governments, schools, and churches, inter alia, and very few people speak "according to the book." Even though the countrymen of Dalecarlia, Jutland, Bavaria, or Sicily understand the respective standards of their countries, they do not often speak them except as status, non-intimate languages, if at all.

Another useful attempt to classify the possible situations of a language is that of William Stewart (1968). He assigns four attributes to a language: (1) standardization; (2) autonomy; (3) historicity; (4) vitality. Each of these is then taken as an either-or quality (plus/minus) and seven types are distinguished: Standard (plus 1-4), Classical (plus 1-3), Artificial (plus 1-2), Vernacular (plus 2-4), Dialect (plus 3-4), Creole (plus 4), Pidgin (all minus). The classification is useful for some purposes, such as making a compact sociolinguistic profile of a given region, particularly when supplemented with specifications for functions (of which Stewart lists ten) and degrees of use (in terms of percentage of the national population).

The real problem is that the four attributes are not independent of one another: <u>autonomy</u> (as German vs. Dutch) is dependent on separate <u>standardizations</u>. Vernaculars are distinguished from dialects by having <u>autonomy</u> and both are distinguished from creoles by having <u>historicity</u>. Since all three types function as first languages in their communities and lack the prestige that comes from standardization, it is hard to see just what synchronic importance the differences have. Classical and artificial languages are distinguished from standard ones by lacking <u>vitality</u> (i. e. native speakers); but most standards also have few native speakers, while classical languages like Hebrew have become vital in Israel and an artificial language like New Norwegian now claims both <u>historicity</u> and <u>vitality</u>.

Another weakness of this classification is its exclusion of linguistic overlap among speakers. It is of less interest to know that ten percent of the speakers in a country use a language than to know whether they also use other languages and under which circumstances. It is important also to know whether their bilingualism is stable or transitional, i. e. what the trend in language learning is within the group of speakers. A typical profile of a speech community (A) in contact with another (B) is that A, if it is dominated by B, may change from monolingual A to bilingual Ab (A dominant, B subordinate), AB (A and B equal), aB (A subordinate, B dominant), and finally to monolingual B. These three types of bilingualism may be described as <u>supplementary</u> (Ab: in which B is only an occasional <u>Hilfssprache</u> for specific pruposes), <u>complementary</u> (AB: in which the two alternate according to important functions in the speakers' lives), and <u>replacive</u> (aB: in which A has become only a language used with older people while B fulfills all the important functions). Another set of terms might be <u>inceptive</u>, <u>functional</u>, and <u>residual</u>, when these three types are seen as historically ordered in a transitional bilingualism. But of course each one of them can also be stable, if there is no incentive or possibility for change of group membership through learning language B.

The analysis of ecology requires not only that one describe the social and psychological situation of each language, but also the effect of this situation on the language itself. As a starter it will be necessary to indicate the languages from which influence presently flows, as reflected in the <u>importations</u> and <u>substitutions</u> now being

created in each. This is usually obvious enough, since current
creations are often the subject of discussion and even controversy.
A fuller account would require some description of the composition
of the total vocabulary from this point of view. For English, for
example, it involves recognition of the existence of at least two structural layers, the Germanic and the non-Germanic, mostly Mediterranean (French, Latin, Greek, Italian). Historically this means that
at certain periods in the life of each language, influential men have
learned certain languages and have enriched (or in the opinion of
some, corrupted) their languages by modeling their expression on
that of certain teacher languages. Similarly, Finnish and Hungarian
have been "Indo-Europeanized" by borrowing from their West European neighbors.

The whole notion of borrowing, however, is open to grave
objection, and we may say that the so-called "cultural" loans are
only islands in a sea of interrelationships among languages. The
concept of a language as a rigid, monolithic sturcture is false, even
if it has proved to be a useful fiction in the development of linguistics.
It is the kind of simplification that is necessary at a certain stage of
a science, but which can now be replaced by more sophisticated
models. We are all familiar with certain specific situations of linguistic symbiosis, in which language systems are stretched almost
out of recognition. One is that which is known as a "foreign accent":
in effect this means that one can speak a language with an entirely
foreign sound system. A study of "Marathi English" by Ashok Kelkar
(1957) has shown that speakers of Marathi have their own well-established dialect of English, using the Marathi sound system which may
even make it difficult for native English speakers to understand. We
may call such a dialect a "substratum" or "contactual" dialect. Then
there is what may be called "learner's dialect," in which language
learners struggle their way from one language into another, replacing
not only the sound system, but also the grammar with novel creations
unforeseen by native speakers. In stable bilingual communities there
is a further accommodation between symbiotic languages, such that
they cease to reflect distinct cultural worlds: their sentences
approach a word-for-word translatability, which is rare among
really autonomous languages. I have observed this process in immigrant American communities first hand (Haugen 1956: 65). The
result was an immigrant language in which nearly every concept was

American, so that either a loanword or a semantic loanshift had
aligned the modes of expression under the pattern of the dominant
language. Gumperz (1967) has made similar observations from India,
in areas where informal standards of Indo-Aryan and Dravidian languages have lived in centuries of symbiosis.

The key to this development is the possibility of switching
or alternation among languages. Psychologists have been deeply
interested in the problem of how languages are stored, whether as
separate entities or as a single store of concepts to which words are
attached. It does not appear that either of these possibilities is
entirely true to the facts. Rather one can say that each item stored
is somehow tagged as belonging to one or the other language and is
called up by a common switching device that blocks out the items not
so tagged. However, the similarity between items in different languages leads to confusion: the tags fall off, and the items become
available in both languages. This reduces the speaker's effort in
switching, and in time it leads to the homogenization of the two languages. Such a reduction of difference goes on all the time between
mutually comprehensible languages and dialects. But it also goes on
between mutually unintelligible languages wherever there are bilingual
speakers who are required to alternate between them. Their systems
quickly become intermediate systems (or as Nemser, 1969, has called them, approximative systems) between the "pure" forms of their
languages, the latter being those that are maintained either by monolingual populations or by rigid regulation. However, even the pure
systems are intermediate between the past and the future of their own
language and intermediate between their neighbors on all sides. They
just happened to get frozen for a time, either by governmental or by
literary fiat.

For any given "language," then, we should want to have
answers to the following ecological questions: (1) What is its classification in relation to other languages? This answer would be given
by historical and descriptive linguists; (2) Who are its users? This
is a question of linguistic demography, locating its users with respect to locale, class, religion or any other relevant grouping;
(3) What are its domains of use? This is a question of sociolinguistics, discovering whether its use is unrestricted or limited in specific ways; (4) What concurrent languages are employed by its users?
We may call this a problem of dialinguistics, to identify the degree

of bilingualism present and the degree of overlap among the languages;
(5) What <u>internal varieties</u> does the language show? This is the task
of a <u>dialectology</u> that will recognize not only regional, but also social
and contactual dialects; (6) What is the nature of its <u>written tradi-
tions</u>? This is the province of <u>philology</u>, the study of written texts
and their relationship to speech; (7) To what degree has its written
form been <u>standardized</u>, i.e. unified and codified? This is the province of prescriptive linguistics, the traditional grammarians and
lexicographers; (8) What kind of <u>institutional support</u> has it won,
either in government, education, or private organizations, either to
regulate its form or propagate it? We may call this study <u>glotto-
politics;</u> (9) What are the <u>attitudes</u> of its users towards the language,
in terms of intimacy and status, leading to personal identification?
We may call this the field of <u>ethnolinguistics;</u> (10) Finally we may
wish to sum up its status in a <u>typology</u> of <u>ecological</u> classification,
which will tell us something about where the language stands and
where it is going in comparison with the other languages of the world.

NOTE

This paper was presented at a Conference Toward the Description of
the Languages of the World (August, 1970), under the direction of
John Lotz.

REFERENCES

Brown, Roger and Albert Gilman. 1960. The pronouns of power and
    solidarity. Style in Language, ed. by Thomas A. Sebeok,
    253-276. New York: The Technology Press.
Brown, Roger and Marguerite Ford. 1961. Address in American
    English. Journal of Abnormal and Social Psychology 62. 375-
    385.
Ferguson, Charles A. 1959. Diglossia. Word 15. 325-340.
_____ 1962. The language factor in national development. In
    Rice 1962, 8-14.
Fishman, Joshua. 1967. Bilingualism with and without diglossia;
    diglossia with and without bilingualism. The Journal of
    Social Issues 23. 29-38.

_____ ed. 1968. Readings in the sociology of language. The
        Hague: Mouton.
Gumperz, John J. 1967. On the linguistic markers of bilingual
        communication. The Journal of Social Issues 23.48-57.
Haugen, Einar. 1953. The Norwegian Language in America: A
        study in bilingual behavior. 2 vols. Philadelphia: Univ.
        of Pennsylvania Press (Reprinted 1969, Bloomington, Ind.:
        Indiana Univ. Press).
Haugen, Einar. 1956. Bilingualism in the Americas: a bibliography
        and research guide. Publications of the American Dialect
        Society, No. 26. (Reprinted 1964, 1968).
Hawley, Amos H. 1950. Human ecology: a theory of community
        structure. New York: The Ronald Press Co.
Hollingshead, A. B. 1947. A reexamination of ecological theory.
        Sociology and social research 31.194-204. (Reprinted in
        Theodorson 1961, 108-114).
Hughes, Everett C. 1963. French Canada in transition. Chicago:
        University of Chicago Press.
Kelkar, Ashok R. 1957. "Marathi English": a study in foreign
        accent. Word 13.268-282.
Nemser, William. 1969. Approximative systems of foreign language
        learners. The Yugoslav Serbo-Croatian-English Contrastive
        Project, Studies B. 1. Zagreb: Institute of Linguistics.
Park, Orlando. 1966. Animal ecology. Encyclopedia Britannica
        7.912-923.
Rice, Frank A., ed. 1962. Study of the role of second languages in
        Asia, Africa, and Latin America. Washington: Center for
        Applied Linguistics.
Rubin, Joan. 1968a. National bilingualism in Paraguay. The Hague:
        Mouton.
_____. 1968b. Bilingual usage in Paraguay. In Fishman 1968,
        512-530.
Stewart, William A. 1962. Creole languages in the Caribbean. In
        Rice 1962, 34-53.
_____ 1968. A sociolinguistic typology for describing national
        multilingualism. In Fishman 1968, 531-545.
Theodorson, George A., ed. 1961. Studies in Human Ecology. New
        York: Harper and Row.

Voegelin, C. F. and F. M., and Noel W. Schutz, Jr. 1967. The language situation in Arizona as part of the Southwest Culture Area. Studies in Southwestern Ethnolinguistics, ed. by Dell H. Hymes and William E. Bittle, 403-451. The Hague: Mouton.

Voegelin, C. F. and F. M. 1964. Languages of the World: Native America Fascicle One. Anthropological Linguistics 6.6. 2-45 (Contemporary language situations in the New World).

18 | Author's Postscript

The invitation to participate in the series edited by Professor Dil on Language Science and National Development was a welcome opportunity for me to consider whether my writings did in fact contain anything of interest for this topic. After some puzzlement and scrutiny I found that two of the major problems I had considered from time to time might be appropriate for inclusion: immigrant bilingualism and language normalization. These are contrary facets of the same problem, in that the former represents a dislocation of language and the latter a restoration of language.

Both aspects have been present in my experience and thinking from childhood, and much of my writing is simply an attempt to clarify and explicate the existential problems I have faced. Bilingualism as dislocation faced me in two ways: as an inheritance from my parents, who maintained the use of Norwegian in a home surrounded by speakers of English; and as a personal experience when I was transported to Norway, and plunged as an eight-year-old into a preindustrial rural community speaking a dialect only remotely similar to standard Norwegian. Language normalization as a restoration of linguistic equilibrium faced me both in English and Norwegian, as I learned to read books and to converse with people who read books. In English the midwestern-midland base had to be elaborated by a superstructure of literary English that led into the labyrinth of artistic and intellectual usage. In Norwegian the local dialect had to be replaced by active command of a Dano-Norwegian norm that performed the same function for Norway as the English literary norm for the English-speaking world, and by passive command of a New-Norwegian norm of uncertain status but great fascination.

In selecting essays that would bear on these topics I have been mindful of the fact that these should not be too technically linguistic. Some of my readers might prefer the more purely linguistic essays I have published, in which case I refer them to my Studies (The Hague: Mouton, 1971). For this collection I have selected those papers that are generally readable by educated laymen as well as social scientists. On looking them over I see that they fall into two chronological periods, corresponding roughly to the topics named above.

The first period runs from 1938 to 1953, which includes my years of active field work and writing on the language of the Norwegian-American immigrant. The present essays and others from the same period were largely preparation for the writing of my Norwegian Language in America, which appeared in 1953; I have included one chapter from that book ("The Confusion of Tongues"). The first essay is a popular account of the findings, in which I presented a general interpretation of borrowing as an adjustment to the host culture which permitted the retention of the immigrant language. This view of linguistic influence as a factor in the stability and continuity of an immigrant group contradicts the puristic fears and prejudices of many guardians of language. I concluded that the linguistic dislocation so often reprimanded and ridiculed by critics was a natural and even a healthy response to cultural dislocation. The alternative was a strenuous form of bilingualism, which required more "linguistic backbone" than most people could muster or even afford. I emphasized what later students of bilingualism have developed further, that any pair of languages functioning within the same cultural framework inevitably approach one another.

In the other articles from this period I have taken up specific problems within the cadre. In the second I proposed a plan of research covering all the Scandinavian languages in America; in the third and fourth I broadened my researches from the phenomena observed among Norwegian immigrants to their parallels elsewhere and to the general analysis of borrowing. I suggested a novel formulation of the classic distinction between "loanwords" and other kinds of loans, calling the latter "loanshifts" to include loan translations as well as semantic loans, since both represented a shift in position of the native material under outside influence. The distinction

corresponds essentially to the two possible ways in which a developing
language can most easily respond to the demands placed upon it by the
needs of becoming a language of culture. But this consideration leads
us into the second group of essays.

The second period runs from 1961 to the present, and represented a return to problems raised in my dissertation of thirty years
before. The stimulus came from an invitation to participate in a symposium on Urbanization and Standard Language organized by Paul Garvin at the 1958 meetings of the American Anthropological Association
in Washington, D. C. This was the first time I used the word "language planning" in public, a topic which continued to occupy me for a
number of years. As suggested above, the immediate data on which
I could work were Norwegian, where controversy over the national
language was more than a century old. While the language planners
in that country saw their task as one of healing a national wound and
bringing the written and spoken languages of the people together, the
effect proved to be more divisive than unifying. Again I found, on
looking into the parallels in other countries, that there were many
striking similarities, not only with situations of conflict, but also
with the development of the great standard languages, such as French
and English. I found that one could see the users of the standard or
national language as a speech community on a higher level, but in
principle similar to any face-to-face speech community with a unified
dialect.

While one result of my researches was a book on the Norwegian language controversy under the title of Language Conflict and
Language Planning (1966), the other result was that I found myself in
the midst of an awakening interest in problems of language development. The inbreeding of American linguistics as a purely structural
and grammatical discipline was being attenuated by the creation of
the Center for Applied Linguistics under the leadership of Charles A.
Ferguson (1959). By the time of the UCLA Conference on Sociolinguistics in the spring of 1964 a whole new atmosphere had been created,
one in which anthropologists, sociologists, and dissident linguists
like myself could feel entirely at home. The name of the discipline,
if such it is, might be new, but the idea was old, and like M. Jourdain
who discovered he had been speaking prose all his life, I discovered
that I had been a sociolinguist all my life. But even so, the emphasis

is on the root of the word, the linguist. Without a solid background
in linguistic analysis and observation there can be no good sociolinguistics.

In presenting these essays together, I am aware of a certain
repetitiousness, perhaps even some self-contradictions. On some of
them I have second thoughts. For example, my essay on language
planning in Norway was written somewhat too much under the impression that the fusion of the two standards of Norway was inevitable. In
the sixties the positions have hardened, and my belief that the two
were only "stylistic norms" has been shaken by the intransigence of
the combatants. Norway offers a classic example of Ferguson's
"bimodal standardization," in which it is impossible to say with
assurance whether we are dealing with two dialects or two languages.
At present I am inclined to think of them as two languages.

The last essay, which has given its name to the collection,
was written as my contribution to the Conference on the Description
of the Languages of the World organized by John Lotz. It is a call
for better and more sophisticated data collection concerning the life
environments of language, and is therefore appropriately named "The
Ecology of Language." It is unfortunate that the word "ecology" has
become so popular as to weaken the serious content with which it is
concerned. I cannot claim to deal with all of sociolinguistics; but
both aspects of it which are represented in this volume are ecological.
Bilingualism is one response to the linguistic environment of social
dislocation and discontinuity. Language planning is another, since it
comes into being only when language becomes a problem to its users,
when dismemberment of a speech community has to be overcome and
communication established between all of its parts.

Bibliography of
Einar Haugen's Works

Compiled by Anwar S. Dil

List of Abbreviations:

AA	American Anthropologist
Am Scand R	American Scandinavian Review
Am Sp	American Speech
An L	Anthropological Linguistics
IJAL	International Journal of American Linguistics
JAF	Journal of American Folklore
JEGP	Journal of English and German Philology
Lg	Language
LL	Language Learning
Mod lang J	Modern Language Journal
M Phil	Modern Philology
MSLL	Georgetown University Monograph Series on Languages and Linguistics
NASR	Norwegian-American Studies and Records
PMLA	Publications of the Modern Language Association of America
Scand St	Scandinavian Studies
Scand St N	Scandinavian Studies and Notes
SIL	Studies in Linguistics

1930   Strindberg the regenerated. JEGP 29.257-70.

1931 a. Norwegians at the Indian forts on the Missouri river during the seventies. NASR 6.89-121.

b. The origin and early history of the New Norse Movement in Norway. Ph.D. dissertation, University of Illinois. (Unpublished)

1932   Ivar Aasen as a writer of Dano-Norwegian. Scand St N 12.53-59.

1933 a. The linguistic development of Ivar Aasen's New Norse. PMLA 48.558-97.

b. O. E. Rølvaag: Norwegian American. NASR 7.53-73.

c. Review of History of Norwegian Literature, by T. Jorgenson. M Phil 31.205-9.

1934 a. Beginning Norwegian: a grammar and reader. First edition. Minneapolis: Burgess. (Mimeographed)

b. (With H. Larson). Bjørnson and America—a critical review. Scand St N 13.1-12.

c. Ibsen in America: a forgotten performance and an unpublished letter. JEGP 33.396-420.

d. Ibsen i Amerika. En ukjent førsteopførelse og et Ibsenbrev. Edda 35.553-59.

1935   Review of National Romanticism in Norway, by O. J. Falnes. JEGP 34.147-50.

1936 a. Tale holdt ved Vosselaget June 20, 1936. Vossingen 32. 12-18.

b. Review of Four Icelandic Sagas, tr. by G. Jones. M Phil 33.317-18.

c. Review of Was man in Runen ritze, by W. Krause. Monatshefte für Deutschen Unterricht 28.278-79.

1937 a. Beginning Norwegian: a grammar and reader. Second edition. New York: F. S. Crofts.

b. A critique and a bibliography of the writings of Rasmus B. Anderson. Wisconsin Magazine of History 20. 255-69.

c. Modernizing the Norwegian Bible. Mere Lys 24. 88-96.

d. Review of Norwegische Konversations-Grammatik, by M. Sandvei, and Beginning Swedish, by W. G. Johnson. Scand St N 14. 110-12.

e. On translating Peer Gynt. Scand St N 14. 187-98.

f. Review of Old Norse Poems, by L. M. Hollander. Monatshefte für Deutschen Unterricht 29. 178-79.

g. Review of Norwegian Emigrant Songs and Ballads, tr. and ed. by T. Blegen. Minnesota History 18. 198-201.

1938 a. Studies in Norwegian literature during 1936. Scand St N 15. 12-25.

b. Norwegian emigrant songs and ballads. JAF 51. 69-75.

c. Phonological shifting in American Norwegian. Lg 14. 112-20.

d. Georg Brandes and his American translators. JEGP 37. 462-87.

e. Language and immigration. NASR 10. 1-43.

f. Notes on "voiced t" in American English. Dialect Notes 6. 627-34.

g. Review of Livsminner, by K. Knudsen. Scand St N 15. 91-93.

1939 a. Om en samlet fremstilling av norsk-amerikansk sprogutvikling (= Avhandlinger utgitt av det Norske Videnskaps-Akademi i Oslo II. Historisk-filosofisk Klasse, 1938, No. 3) (Oslo). 10 pp.

b. Norsk i Amerika. Oslo: J. W. Cappelens Forlag.

c. Et norsk ordregister under utarbeidelse. Maal og minne
    1-6.

d. Review of O. E. Rølvaag: A Biography, by T. Jorgenson
    and N. Solum. Am Scand R 27. 280.

1940 a. Reading Norwegian. New York: F. S. Crofts.

b. Norway and the war. Address. Capital Times, Madison,
    Wisconsin, May 17. [Reprinted by the American-
    Scandinavian Foundation, New York, 1940.]

1941 a. Knut Hamsun and the Nazis. Books Abroad 15. 17-22.

b. On the consonant pattern of Modern Icelandic. Acta
    Linguistica 2. 98-107.

c. Voyages to Vinland: the first American saga. Bibliophilic
    edition. Chicago: Holiday Press.

d. Intonation patterns in American Norwegian. Lg 17. 40-48.

e. Review of Six Scandinavian Novelists, by A. Gustafson.
    The Saturday Review, January 18.

f. Review of A Book of Danish Ballads, by A. Olrik, tr. by
    E. M. Smith-Dampier. Monatshefte für Deutschen Unter-
    richt 33. 237.

1942 a. Voyages to Vinland: the first American saga. New York:
    Knopf.

b. Norwegian word studies. Volume 1: The vocabularies of
    Sigrid Undset and Ivar Aasen. Volume 2: The vocabular-
    ies of the Old Norse Sagas and of Hendrik Wergeland.
    Madison, Wisconsin: University of Wisconsin Press.

c. Problems of linguistic research among Scandinavian immigrants in America. <u>Bulletin</u> (American Council of Learned Societies) 34. 35-57.

d. (With W. F. Twaddell). Facts and phonemics. <u>Lg</u> 18. 228-37.

e. On the stressed vowel systems of Norwegian. <u>Scandinavian Studies Presented to George T. Flom by Colleagues and Friends</u> (= <u>Illinois Studies in Language and Literature</u>, 29), 66-78.

f. Analysis of a sound group: <u>sl</u> and <u>tl</u> in Norwegian. <u>PMLA</u> 57. 879-907.

g. Review of <u>Norway: Neutral and Invaded</u>, by H. Koht. <u>Annals of the American Academy of Political and Social Science</u> 220. 227-28.

h. Review of <u>Sunnfjordlaget i Amerika gjennem tredive Aar 1912-1942</u>. <u>Wisconsin Magazine of History</u> 25. 482-83.

1943 a. Ibsen in the mill race. <u>Scand St</u> 8. 313-16.

b. Myten om Vinland. <u>Nordmannsforbundet</u> 36. 67-69.

c. Da Alexander Kielland tenkte seg til Amerika. <u>Nordmannsforbundets Julehefte</u> 38-42. [Reprinted in <u>Edda</u> 66. 403-409 (1966).]

d. Translation of "You must not sleep, " by A. Øverland. <u>Am Scand R</u> 31. 5-7.

e. Review of <u>Scandinavian Studies Presented to George T. Flom by Colleagues and Friends</u>. <u>Germanic Review</u> 18. 304-5.

f. Review of <u>Anthology of Norwegian Lyrics</u>, by C. W. Stork. <u>JEGP</u> 42. 288-91.

1944 a. Spoken Norwegian: basic course. Madison, Wisconsin: U.S. Armed Forces Institute. [= War Department Education Manual 532.]

b. Norske timer for amerikanske soldater. Nordmannsforbundet 37. 37-40.

1945 a. Scandinavian for war and peace. Modern Language Notes 60. 26-29.

b. G. I. talk in Iceland. American Speech 20. 228-29.

c. Review of The Voice of Norway, by H. Koht and S. Skard. JEGP 44. 107-8.

d. Review of The Scandinavian Countries, by B. Hovde. American Historical Review 50. 795-97.

1946 a. Et norsk hedersskrift i Amerika. Maal og minne 91-96.

b. Thomas Wolfes siste bok. Samtiden 55. 641-45.

c. Amerikansk universitetsliv i dag. Nordisk tidskrift 22. 230-43.

d. Pastor Dietrichson of Old Koshkonong. Wisconsin Magazine of History 29. 301-18.

1947 a. Spoken Norwegian. New York: Henry Holt.

b. Nordmenn og svensker i Amerika. Nordisk tidskrift 23. 330-37.

c. Swedes and Norwegians in the United States. Norsk geografisk tidsskrift 11. 189-98.

d. Articles on Aasen, Bojer, Bull, Elster, Heiberg, Hoel, Janson, Kielland, Kinck, Obstfelder, Vogt, Wildenvey, Øverland. Columbia Dictionary of Modern European Literature, ed. by H. Smith. New York: Columbia University Press.

e. A Norwegian calendar stick in Wisconsin. Wisconsin
    Magazine of History 31.145-67.

f. Review of The Place-Names of Dane County, Wisconsin,
    by F. G. Cassidy. Wisconsin Magazine of History 31.
    209-11.

g. Review of The Morphology of the Dialect of Aurland, by
    G. T. Flom. Lg 23.166-70.

h. Review of Me-Vi, by P. Tylden. JEGP 46.431-34.

i. Review of Studier över slutartikeln i starka feminer, by
    I. Modeer. Lg 23.445-48.

j. Review of Det danske sprogs historie, Vol. 1, by P. Skau-
    trup. Lg 23.448-53.

k. Review of R-bøygning, by O. Beito. Word 3.144-47.

1948 a. Norwegian dialect studies since 1930. JEGP 47.68-79.

b. Litt om åndslivet i det norske Amerika. Vinduet 2.333-43.

c. En ætling av Romerike forteller om livet i Wisconsin.
    Norsk-amerikanske språkprøver. Romerike, Studier og
    Samlinger 39-49.

d. Mere om r-bortfall i sørøstlandsk. Maal og minne 117-22.

e. Translation of Winged Letter, by A. Vaa. Am Scand R
    36.122.

1949 a. Sigmund Skard og Amerika. Verdens gang, Oslo, Febru-
    ary 25.

b. A note on diachronic sound charts. SIL 7.63-66.

c. Phoneme or prosodeme? Lg 25.278-82.

d. A Norwegian-American pioneer ballad. <u>NASR</u> 15.1-19.

e. Norges litterære profil i den engelsktalende verden.
<u>Vinduet</u> 3.473-79.

f. The unstressed vowels of Old Icelandic. <u>Norsk tidsskrift</u>
<u>for sprogvidenskap</u> 15.384-88.

g. A note on the Romany "language". <u>Norsk tidsskrift for</u>
<u>sprogvidenskap</u> 15.388-91.

h. Phonemics: a technique for making alphabets. <u>Am Sp</u> 24.
54-57. [Review of <u>Phonemics</u>, by K. L. Pike.]

i. Review of <u>Svensk språkhistoria</u>, and <u>De nordiska språken</u>,
by E. Wessén. <u>Lg</u> 25.62-63.

j. Review of <u>English Loan-Words in Modern Norwegian</u>, by
A. Stene. <u>Lg</u> 25.63-68.

k. Review of <u>A Short History of the Swedish Language</u>, by G.
Bergman. <u>Lg</u> 25.307-8.

1950 a. <u>First grammatical treatise: the earliest Germanic phonol-</u>
<u>ogy, an edition, translation, and commentary.</u> <u>Lg</u> 26:4,
Supplement. <u>Language Monograph</u> 25.

b. Terminological notes: an objection. <u>SIL</u> 8.1.

c. The analysis of linguistic borrowing. <u>Lg</u> 26.210-31.
[Reprinted in: <u>Approaches to English Historical Linguis-</u>
<u>tics</u>, ed. by R. Lass (New York: Holt, Rinehart and Win-
ston, 1969), 58-81; <u>Readings for the History of the English</u>
<u>Language</u>, ed. by C. T. Scott and J. L. Erickson (Boston:
Allyn and Bacon, 1968), 319-44; <u>English Linguistics: An</u>
<u>Introductory Reader</u>, ed. by H. Hungerford, J. Robinson,
and J. Sledd (New York: Scott, Foresman, 1970), 429-
456.]

d.   Problems of bilingualism. <u>Lingua</u> 2. 271-90.

e.   Wisconsin pioneers in Scandinavian studies. <u>Wisconsin</u>
      <u>Magazine of History</u> 34. 28-39.

f.   Review of <u>Portuguese-American Speech</u>, by L. Pap. <u>Lg</u>
      26. 436-39.

1951 a.   The Swedish attorney in Waupaca County. <u>The Swedish</u>
            <u>Pioneer Historical Quarterly</u> 1. 39-43.

      b.   <u>A study of the Norweigan University entrance examination</u>
            <u>or "Artium" degree with notes on the University of Wis-</u>
            <u>consin policy for foreign students.</u>   Third revised edition.
            [Reprinted by Kirke- og Undervisnings-departementet,
            Oslo.]

      c.   Directions in modern linguistics. <u>Lg</u> 27. 211-22. [Re-
            printed in <u>Readings in Linguistics</u>, ed. by M. Joos (Wash-
            ington, D. C. : American Council of Learned Societies,
            1957), 357-63.]

      d.   From army camp to classroom. <u>Scand St</u> 23. 138-51.

      e.   The background of "Iron Curtain" and "Moola". <u>Am Sp</u>
            26. 203-4, 305.

      f.   Review of <u>Seven One-Act Plays</u>, by L. Holberg, tr. by
            H. Alexander. <u>JEGP</u> 50. 426-27.

1952 a.   The struggle over Norwegian. <u>NASR</u> 17. 1-35.

      b.   Perspektiver i norsk målføreforskning. <u>Dagbladet</u>, Oslo,
            May 26.

      c.   The impact of English on American-Norwegian letter
            writing. <u>Studies in Honor of Albert Morey Sturtevant</u>
            (Lawrence, Kansas: University of Kansas Press), 76-102.

      d.   (With M. Joos). Tone and intonation in East Norwegian.
            <u>Acta Philologica Scandinavica</u> 22. 41-64.

e. Lyspunkt i språkstriden. Arbeiderbladet, Oslo, November 26. [Review of Nuggets of Norse, by Ph. Boardman.]

f. Review of A Study of Six Plays by Ibsen, by B. W. Downs. JEGP 51.290-92.

g. Review of Die mittelhochdeutsche Lehnprägung nach altfranzösischem Vorbild, by E. Öhmann. Lg 28.397-401.

1953 a. The Norwegian language in America: a study in bilingual behavior. Vol. I: The bilingual community. Vol. II: The American dialects of Norwegian. Philadelphia: University of Pennsylvania Press. 695 pp.

b. Henrik Ibsen, Peer Gynt: a glossary and commentary for American students. Madison, Wisconsin: Department of Scandinavian, University of Wisconsin. (Mimeographed)

c. Snorri Sturluson and Norway. Am Scand R 41.119-27.

d. Til Halvdan Kohts 80-årsdag. Nordisk tidende, Brooklyn, N.Y., July 9.

e. On resolving the close apposition. Am Sp 28.165-70.

f. Nordiske språkproblemer—en opinionsundersøkelse. Nordisk tidskrift 29.225-49.

g. Review of Speech Development of a Bilingual Child, and Bibliography of Child Language, by W. F. Leopold. JEGP 52.392-97.

h. Review of Gammelnorsk homiliebok etter AM 619 QV, by T. Knudsen. Scand St 25.151-54.

i. Review of Vokalismen i Iddenmålet, by R. Myhre. Lg 29. 544-47.

1954 a. Some pleasures and problems of bilingual research. IJAL 20.116-22.

b.   Norwegian migration to America. NASR 18.1-22.

c.   Ibsen's mill race once again. Scand St 26.115-17.

d.   Tvetoppet vokal i Oppdalsmålet. Maal og minne 66-78.

e.   Problems of bilingual description. MSLL 7.9-19.

f.   Comments. MSLL 7.50, 51-53, 80-81, 95, 96, 137-38.

g.   Review of Norsk målsoga, by G. Indrebø. JEGP 53.94-96.

h.   Review of Prolegomena to a Theory of Language, by L.
     Hjelmslev, tr. by F. J. Whitefield. IJAL 20.247-51.

i.   Review of Languages in Contact, by U. Weinreich. Lg 30.
     380-88.

1955 a.   Problems [Elements] of bilingual description. General
          Linguistics 1.1-9.

b.   The living Ibsen. Quarterly Journal of Speech 41.19-26.

c.   Norway and America: the ties that bind. Wisconsin Maga-
     zine of History 38.139-44.

d.   Linguists and the wartime program of language teaching.
     Mod lang J 39.243-45.

e.   Tonelagsanalyse. Maal og minne 70-80.

f.   Review of Agder og Amerika, by T. Aamland and I. Sem-
     mingsen. Wisconsin Magazine of History 38.120-21.

g.   Review of Njáls Saga, tr. by C. F. Bayerschmidt and
     L. M. Hollander. Monatshefte für Deutschen Unterricht
     47.245-46.

h.   Review of Norsk folkemål, ed. by B. Birkeland and R.
     Djupedal. Lg 31.139-41.

i. Review of <u>Fjoldemålets lydsystem</u>, by A. Bjerrum; <u>Houl-bjergmålet</u>, by E. Jensen; <u>Synchronisk beskrivelse af Aabenraa bymaal</u>, by K. Olsen; <u>Brøndummålet</u>, by I. Ejskjær. <u>Lg</u> 31.141-47.

1956 a. <u>Bilingualism in the Americas: a bibliography and research guide</u>. University, Alabama: University of Alabama Press. [= Publication of the American Dialect Society, 26.] [Second printing, 1964.]

b. Translation of <u>A History of Norwegian Literature</u>, by H. Beyer. New York: New York University Press.

c. Norske bøker i norsk-amerikanske hyller. <u>Kulturopti-misme og folkeopplysning: Festskrift til Arne Kildal på 70-års dagen, 10 desember 1955</u>, ed. by I. Lyche <u>et al</u>. (Oslo: Aschehoug), 55-63.

d. Inntrykk fra Ibsenuken. <u>Arbeiderbladet</u>, Oslo, June 11.

e. Syllabification in Kutenai. <u>IJAL</u> 22.196-201.

f. The syllable in linguistic description. <u>For Roman Jakob-son</u>, ed. by M. Halle <u>et al</u>. (The Hague: Mouton), 213-21.

g. Letters from Iceland. <u>Capital Times</u>, Madison, Wiscon-sin, March 2-April 19.

h. Thalia in Reykjavík. <u>Am Scand R</u> 44.335-40.

i. Ibsen in America. <u>Edda</u> 56.270-88.

j. Review of <u>Njál's Saga</u>, tr. by C. F. Bayerschmidt and L. M. Hollander. <u>Speculum</u> 30.459-60.

k. Review of <u>Henrik Ibsen, Peer Gynt</u>, tr. by H. M. Finney. <u>Am Scand R</u> 44.284.

l. Review of <u>Lehnbildungen und Lehnbedeutungen im Alteng-lischen</u>, by H. Gneuss. <u>Lg</u> 32.761-66.

1957 a.   Beginning Norwegian: a grammar and reader. Third
          revised edition. New York: Appleton-Century-Crofts.

     b.   The first international conference on Scandinavian studies.
          Scand St 29. 19-23.

     c.   The phoneme in bilingual description. LL 7. 17-23. [Re-
          printed in: The English Language Teachers' Magazine 7.
          123-28 (1958); Teaching English as a Second Language,
          ed. by H. B. Allen (New York: McGraw-Hill, 1965),
          120-25.]

     d.   Landið mitt og landið ykkar. Eimreiðin 63. 210-20.

     e.   The semantics of Icelandic orientation. Word 13. 447-59.
          [Reprinted in Cognitive Anthropology, ed. by S. Tyler
          (New York: Holt, Rinehart and Winston, 1969), 330-42.]

     f.   Talt og skrevet i Amerika. De tok et Norge med seg, ed.
          by J. Hambro (Oslo: Dreyers Forlag), 224-41.

     g.   Review of The Age of the Sturlungs, by E. Ó. Sveinsson,
          tr. by J. S. Hannesson. JEGP 56. 462-64.

     h.   Review of The Cultural Heritage of the Swedish Immigrant:
          Selected References, by O. F. Ander. Wisconsin Maga-
          zine of History 40. 301-2.

     i.   Review of The Saga of the Jomsvikings, tr. by L. M.
          Hollander. Monatshefte für Deutschen Unterricht 49. 284.

     j.   Review of L'emprunt linguistique, by L. Deroy. Lg 33.
          587-89.

1958 a.   Tungumálakennslu i Bandaríkjunum beint inn á nýjar
          brautir. Skírnir 131. 21-39.

     b.   The phonemics of Modern Icelandic. Lg 34. 55-88.

c.   Nordiske studier i Amerika. Proceedings of the First
     International Conference on Scandinavian Studies, Cam-
     bridge, England, July 2-7, 1956. [Cambridge, England],
     9-20. (Mimeographed)

d.   Language contact. Proceedings of the Eighth International
     Congress of Linguists, ed. by E. Siversten (Oslo: Oslo
     University Press), 771-85.

e.   Review of An Introduction to Old Norse, by E. V. Gordon.
     Second edition revised by A. R. Taylor. Scand St 30.98-
     102.

f.   Review of Papers in Linguistics 1934-1951, by J. R. Firth.
     Lg 34.498-502.

g.   Review of Om utvecklingen av gammalt a framför u i nordi-
     ska språk: tilljaämning och omljud, by H. Markström.
     SIL 13.83-87.

1959 a.   New paths in American language teaching. English Lan-
          guage Education Council Publications 3.11-23. [Reprinted
          in Applied Linguistics and the Teaching of English, ed. by
          T. Yambe (Tokyo: The English Language Education Coun-
          cil, 1970), 133-47.]

b.   Planning for a standard language in modern Norway. An L
     1:3.8-21.

c.   Review of The Scandinavian Element in French and Norman,
     by R. P. de Gorog. Lg 35.695-99.

1960 a.   From idiolect to language. MSLL 12.57-64.

b.   Comments. MSLL 12.45, 52.

c.   Vilhelm Mobergs amerikasvenska "sammelsurium av orim-
     ligheter". Svenska Dagbladet, Stockholm, May 11.

d.   Mobergs amerikasvenska—en replik. <u>Svenska Dagbladet</u>, Stockholm, June 3.

e.   Andrew Petersons språk. <u>Svenska Dagbladet</u>, Stockholm, December 2.

f.   Goals and methods in foreign language teaching. <u>English Language Education Council Publications</u> 4. 5-17. [Reprinted in: <u>English Language Teachers' Magazine</u> 2. 74-82; <u>Applied Linguistics and the Teaching of English</u>, ed. by T. Yambe (Tokyo: The English Language Education Council, 1970), 148-62.

g.   Japanese phonemics: some alternative solutions. <u>English Language Education Council Publications</u> 4. 30-44. [Reprinted in <u>Nadbitka z prac filologieznych</u> t 18 cz., 1. 29-42 (1963).]

h.   The problems of bilingualism. <u>The Bulletin of the Institute for Research in Language Teaching</u> (Tokyo), 244. 6-21.

i.   Bjørnson opdager Amerika. <u>Edda</u> 60. 169-84.

j.   Rettskrivningsstrid i det moderne Japan. <u>Arbeiderbladet</u>, Oslo, April 6-8.

k.   Review of <u>Nya vägar inom språkforskningen: en orientering i modern lingvistik</u>, by B. Malmberg. <u>Lg</u> 36. 524-27.

l.   Review of <u>The Phonemic Analysis of English Loan-Words in Croatian</u>, by R. Filipović. <u>Lg</u> 36. 548-51.

m.   Review of <u>Norsk Målsoga</u>, by G. Indrebø. <u>Maal og minne</u> 71-77.

1961 a.   The bilingual individual. <u>Psycholinguistics: A Book of Readings</u>, ed. by S. Saporta (New York: Holt, Rinehart and Winston), 395-407.

b.   The Scandinavian languages, and supplement on teaching aids. Report of the Conference on Neglected Languages, Appendix 12, 174-86. [= Work Paper for the Conference on Neglected Languages.]

c.   Language planning in modern Norway. Scand St 33. 68-81. [Reprinted in Readings in the Sociology of Language, ed. by J. A. Fishman (The Hague: Mouton, 1968), 673-87.]

1962 a.   Laxness and the Americans. Afmæliskveðjur heiman og handan. Til Halldórs Kiljans Laxness sextugs (Reykjavík: Helgafell), 44-47.

b.   J. R. Reiersen's "indiscretions". Norwegian-American Studies 21. 269-77.

c.   On diagramming vowel systems. Proceedings of the Fourth International Congress of Phonetic Sciences, Helsinki, 1961, ed. by A. Sovijärvi and P. Aalto (The Hague: Mouton), 648-54.

d.   Norway's language problem. The Norseman 3. 17-19.

e.   Schizoglossia and the linguistic norm. MSLL 15. 63-73.

f.   Comments. MSLL 15. 40-41, 42, 60, 83, 176.

1963 a.   Pitch accent and tonemic juncture in Scandinavian. Monatshefte für Deutschen Unterricht 55. 157-61.

b.   Introduction to Giants in the Earth, by O. E. Rølvaag (New York: Harper and Row), ix-xxvi.

c.   Notes on a dictionary: John Brynildsen's Norsk-engelsk Ordbok. Scand St 35. 295-306.

d.   Review of The Icelandic Saga, by P. Hallberg, tr. by P. Schach. Western Humanities Review 17. 283-84.

e.   Review of Problems in Lexicography, ed. by F. Householder and S. Saporta. AA 65. 752-55.

1964 a.   (With K. Chapman). <u>Spoken Norwegian</u>. Revised edition.
            New York: Holt, Rinehart and Winston.

      b.   Introductory and concluding remarks. <u>Proceedings of the
            Ninth International Congress of Linguists</u>, Cambridge,
            Massachusetts, 1962, ed. by H. Lunt (The Hague: Mouton),
            4-7.

      c.   Translation of <u>Driving Forces in History</u>, by H. Koht.
            Cambridge, Massachusetts: Harvard University Press.

      d.   Review of <u>Foreign Language Units of Kansas I</u>, by J. N.
            Carman. <u>Am Sp</u> 39.54-56.

      e.   Review of <u>Universals of Language</u>, ed. by J. H. Green-
            berg. <u>Lg</u> 40.260-69.

      f.   Review of <u>Pastors and Immigrants</u>, by N. Tavuchis. <u>AA</u>
            66.1233-34.

1965 a.   <u>Norwegian-English dictionary: a pronouncing and trans-
            lating dictionary of Modern Norwegian, with a historical
            and grammatical introduction</u>. Oslo: Universitetsforlaget;
            Madison, Wisconsin: University of Wisconsin Press.
            [Second printing, 1967.]

      b.   Amerika, Ísland og Leifur Eiríksson. <u>Lesbók Morgun-
            blaðsins</u>, Reykjavík, October 24.

      c.   Bilingualism as a goal of foreign language teaching. <u>Con-
            ference on Teaching English to Speakers of Other Lan-
            guages</u>, ed. by V. F. Allen (Champaign, Illinois: National
            Council of Teachers of English), 83-87.

      d.   Construction and reconstruction in language planning: Ivar
            Aasen's grammar. <u>Word</u> 21.188-207.

1966 a. Language conflict and language planning: the case of Modern Norwegian. Cambridge, Massachusetts: Harvard University Press. xvi, 393 p. [Norwegian translation by D. Gundersen: Riksspråk og folkemål: Norsk språkpolitikk i det 20. århundre. Oslo: Universitetsforlaget, 1969.]

b. Om ikke å ta standpunkt i sprogstriden. Aftenposten, Oslo, May 10.

c. Linguistics and language planning. Sociolinguistics, ed. by W. Bright (The Hague: Mouton), 50-71.

d. Semicommunication: the language gap in Scandinavia. Sociological Inquiry 36.280-97.

e. Dialect, language, nation. AA 68.922-35.

f. Comments. Sociolinguistics, ed. by W. Bright (The Hague: Mouton), 20-21, 26, 42-43, 47, 158-59, 160, 164-65, 209-10, 257-58, 318, 319.

g. The sources of the Vinland map. Arctic 19.287-95.

h. National and international languages. Voice of America Forum Series, 10. [Reprinted in Linguistics Today, ed. by A. A. Hill (New York: Basic Books, 1969), 103-13.]

i. Alf Axelssøn Sommerfelt. Lg 42.612-14.

j. What is the oral approach? Teaching English: A Collection of Readings, ed. by G. E. Wishon and T. J. O'Hare (Cairo: American University in Cairo Press), 1-12.

k. Bilingualism and bidialectalism. Social Dialects and Language Learning, ed. by R. W. Shuy (Champaign, Illinois: National Council of Teachers of English), 124-26.

l. Translation and adaptation of Introduction to O. E. Rølvaag, Peder Victorious, by G. H. Gvåle (New York: Harper and Row), vii-xix.

m. Review of <u>The Vinland Map and the Tartar Relation</u>, by
    R. A. Skelton, T. E. Marston, and G. D. Painter. <u>Spec-
    ulum</u> 41.770-74.

n. Review of <u>Phonotactic Structures in Swedish</u>, by B. Sigurd.
    <u>Scandinavica</u> 5.145-46. [≠ <u>Lg</u> 43.803-9.]

o. Review of <u>Introduction to the Scandinavian Languages</u>, by
    M. O'C. Walshe. <u>Scandinavica</u> 5.147-48.

p. Review of <u>Det danske sprogs udforskning i det 20. århun-
    drede</u>. <u>Scand St</u> 38.347-49.

q. Introduction. <u>Language Loyalty in the United States</u>, by
    Joshua A. Fishman <u>et al</u>. (The Hague: Mouton), 9-11.

1967 a. <u>The Norwegians in America: a students' guide to localized
         history</u>. New York: Teachers College Press, Columbia
         University.

b. The prosodic system of Norwegian. <u>Scand St</u> 39.47-51.

c. The mythical structure of the ancient Scandinavians: some
    thoughts on reading Dumézil. <u>To Honor Roman Jakobson</u>
    (The Hague: Mouton), 855-68. [Reprinted in <u>Introduction
    to Structuralism</u>, ed. by Michael Lane (New York: Basic
    Books), 170-83.]

d. On the rules of Norwegian tonality. <u>Lg</u> 43.185-202.

e. General introduction, Introduction to and translation of
    <u>The Wish</u>, Introduction to <u>The Golden Gate</u>, Introduction
    to and translation of <u>Atoms and Madams</u>. <u>Fire and Ice:
    Three Icelandic Plays</u> (Madison, Wisconsin: University of
    Wisconsin Press), 3-88, 171-264.

f. Review of <u>Early Icelandic Script</u>, by H. Benediktsson.
    <u>Speculum</u> 42.513-15.

1968 a. Isoglosses within a dialect. Verhandlungen des zweiten internationalen Dialektologenkongresses, Marburg/Lahn, 5.-10. September 1965, ed. by L. E. Schmitt. Zeitschrift für Mundartforschung, N. F. 332-41.

b. The Scandinavian languages as cultural artifacts. Language Problems of Developing Nations, ed. by J. A. Fishman et al. (New York: Wiley), 267-84.

c. On the pronunciation of Old Norse. Nordica et Anglica, Studies in Honor of Stefán Einarsson, ed. by A. H. Orrick (The Hague: Mouton), 72-82.

d. Two views of Old Norse pronunciation: IP or RP? A discussion. Medieval Scandinavia 1.138-73.

e. Review of J. C. Svabo's Dictionarium Færoense, I: Ordbogen, by C. Matras. Scand St 40.159-63.

f. Review of Svensk-engelsk fackordbok för näringsliv, förvaltning, undervisning, och forskning, by I. E. Gullberg. Lg 43.561-64.

1969 a. The Norwegian language in America: a study in bilingual behavior. Vol. I: The bilingual community. Vol. II: The American dialects of Norwegian. Second printing, in one volume. Bloomington, Indiana: Indiana University Press.

b. On the parsimony of the younger futhark. Festschrift für Konstantin Reichardt, ed. by C. Gellinek (Bern and Munich: Francke), 51-58.

c. On translating from the Scandinavian. Old Norse Literature and Mythology: A Symposium, ed. by E. Polomé (Austin, Texas: University of Texas Press), 3-18.

d. Language planning, theory and practice. Actes du Xe Congrès International des Linguistes, Bucarest, 1967, I, ed. by A. Graur (Bucharest: Editions de L'Académie de la République Socialiste de Roumanie), 701-11.

e.   Review of The Kensington Rune Stone: New Light on an Old Riddle, by T. C. Blegen. Minnesota History 41.237-39.

f.   Review of Introduction to a Theory of Language Planning, by V. Tauli. Lg 45.939-49.

g.   Phonemic indeterminacy and Scandinavian umlaut. Folia Linguistica 3.107-19.

1970 a.   Linguistics and dialinguistics. MSLL 23.1-12.

b.   Comments. MSLL 23.40-41, 223-24, 226, 309-10.

c.   Thor Helgeson, schoolmaster and raconteur. . Norwegian-American Studies 24.3-28.

d.   On the meaning of bilingual competence. Studies in General and Oriental Linguistics, ed. by R. Jakobson and S. Kawamoto (Tokyo: TEC Corporation for Language and Educational Research), 221-29.

e.   The language history of Scandinavia: a profile of problems. The Nordic Languages and General Linguistics, ed. by H. Benediktsson (Reykjavík: Vísindafélag Íslendinga), 41-86.

f.   Translation of We Murderers, A Play in Three Acts, by G. Kamban (Madison, Wisconsin: University of Wisconsin Press). 74 pp.

1971 a.   The ecology of language. The Linguistic Reporter, Supplement 25, 19-26.

b.   Bishop Eric and the Vinland Map. Proceedings of the Vinland Map Conference, ed. by W. Washburn (Chicago: University of Chicago Press), 137-44.

c.   (With T. L. Markey). The Scandinavian languages: fifty years of linguistic research. Current Trends in Linguistics, Vol. 9, ed. by T. A. Sebeok (The Hague: Mouton), in press.

d. Instrumentalism in language planning. Can Language Be
    Planned? Sociolinguistic Theory and Practice for Devel-
    oping Nations, ed. by J. Rubin and B. H. Jernudd (Hono-
    lulu: East-West Center Press), in press.

e. (With A. E. Santaniello). Translation of Life of Ibsen, by
    H. Koht. Revised edition. New York: Benjamin Blom.
    507 pp.

f. Norsk i Amerika: studier og status. Språk i Norden 1971
    (Norsk språknemnd, Skrifter 8), 111-23.

g. The stigmata of bilingualism. In this volume, pp. 308-25.
    [To appear in Travaux de la Cercle linguistique de Prague,
    Vol. 5, ed. by J. Vachek.]

h. Review of Språk i Norden 1970 (Norsk språknemnd, Skrif-
    ter 7). Scand St 43. 290-92.

i. Bilingualism, language contact, and immigrant languages
    in the United States: a research report 1956-1970. Cur-
    rent Trends in Linguistics, Vol. 10, ed. by T. A. Sebeok
    (The Hague: Mouton), in press.

j. Some issues in sociolinguistics. Cours d'été et colloques
    scientifiques, Sinaia, 1971 (University of Bucharest).
    48 pp. (Mimeographed)

k. The perfect tense in English and Scandinavian: a problem
    of contrastive linguistics. Canadian Journal of Linguistics,
    in press.

l. Translation and edition of The Gods of the Germanic Peo-
    ples, by G. Dumézil. Los Angeles: University of Califor-
    nia Press, in press.

m. The Scandinavian languages. Encyclopaedia Britannica,
    in press.

n. Author's postscript. In this volume, pp. 340-43.

o. First grammatical treatise: the earliest Germanic phonol-
    ogy, an edition, translation, and commentary. Second
    revised edition. (Classics in Linguistics Series). London:
    Longmans, in press.

p. Einar Haugen on the ecology of language. Perspectives in
    Linguistic Education: Conversations with Language Schol-
    ars, by Anwar S. Dil (Abbottabad, West Pakistan: Linguis-
    tic Research Group of Pakistan), in press.

Haugen, Einar   1906–
          The ecology of language:
essays by Einar Haugen.   Selected and Introduced
by Anwar S. Dil. Stanford, California:
Stanford University Press [1972]
          xvi, 368 p. 24cm.
(Language science and national development series,
Linguistic Research Group of Pakistan)
          Includes bibliography.

I. Dil, Anwar S., 1928–   ed.
II. (Series) III. Linguistic Research Group of Pakistan